GEORG LUKÁCS AND THOMAS MANN

A Study in the Sociology of Literature

JUDITH MARCUS

The University of Massachusetts Press
Amherst, 1987

Library of Congress Cataloging-in-Publication Data

Marcus, Judith,   date.
  Georg Lukács and Thomas Mann.   20.⁵⁰

    Translation of: Thomas Mann und Georg Lukács.
    Bibliography: p.
    Includes index.
      1. Mann, Thomas, 1875–1955—Influence. 2. Lukács, György, 1885–1971—Influence. 3. Mann,
Thomas, 1875–1955—Friends and associates. 4. Lukács, György, 1885–1971—Friends and associates.
    I. Title. PT2625. A44Z7462713   1987   833'.912   86–1261
    ISBN 0–87023–486–2

56720

CONTENTS

PREFACE

In 1925, Walter Benjamin informed his friend Gershom Scholem that he had just finished reading two extraordinary and exciting books. Singled out as the best products of the time, they were Thomas Mann's novel *The Magic Mountain* and Georg Lukács's *History and Class Consciousness*. To the best of my knowledge this was the first time that a perceptive reader established a connection of sorts between the works of two towering figures of twentieth-century European cultural life. It was not to be the last. For a number of reasons, however, among which figured prominently the political and social upheavals on the continent that eventually landed Mann in sunny California and Lukács in Stalin's Moscow, it took almost four decades for anybody to take a closer look at the possibility of a certain connection between the two men and their work. In the meantime, there grew up an immense literature around Mann and Lukács. Since Mann died in 1955 and Lukács in 1971, it is all the more surprising that no serious attempt has been made to examine the now proven relationship between the author and "his" critic. And it is outright astonishing that no major undertaking exists to write the life of either. (The notable exception is Richard Winston's excellent biographical fragment, *Thomas Mann: The Making of an Artist, 1875-1955*, regrettably incomplete because of Winston's untimely death.) To undertake either task obviously means to enrich and supplement the other.

Even though a number of critics and scholars have paid attention to the relation between these two men, they have seldom gone beyond the "fact" that Lukács's physique and/or revolutionary career inspired Thomas Mann's portrait of Leo Naphta, the Jewish–Jesuit–Communist protagonist of *The Magic Mountain*. (To this suggestion Lukács responded with his good-humored, "So what if I lent him my nose? He gave so much to me—I am happy I could do that little for him in return!") This is not to imply that the focus on that *one* aspect would need justification: even if we could only prove beyond doubt that Lukács served as the model for one of the most interesting, strangest and most complex figures in Thomas Mann's œuvre, this alone would be worth a separate study. I myself felt the fascinating ambivalence emanating from this fictional character and devoted my first paper on Thomas Mann to its analysis; moreover, my previous acquaintance with Lukács's work (and person) made me weary of accepting *in toto* the (mostly Marxist) interpretation of those—among them, Hans Mayer and Lukács himself—who saw in the character the prototype of the fascist intellectual. In due time, the subject matter so engaged my attention that it turned into a dissertation (1976), written in German, and a book, published in Germany in 1982. I should note that my initial plan met with considerable scepticism, based on the assumption that Mann and Lukács had precious little in common, and thus that no case could be made for interaction, influence, or congruence—in short, for a meaningful author–critic relationship. Those scholars who knew better—among them Wilhelm Emrich and Herbert Lehnert—were enthusiastically supportive.

The aim of this study is to clarify and gain deeper insight into the intricate process of literary interaction between Thomas Mann, the creative artist, and Georg Lukács, the philosopher and literary critic. To this end, it is necessary to examine *all* aspects of their relationship although it goes without saying that not all aspects can be treated exhaustively. I can also state without sounding immodest that most of the material presented in my dissertation—and now in this book—was new, mostly based on previously undiscovered, untranslated and/or unpublished materials located either in the Thomas Mann Archiv of Zurich or at the Georg Lukács Archiv of the Hungarian Academy of Sciences in Budapest. Most of the more recent studies devoted to the subject of the Mann–Lukács connection have in one way or another used some of the material or conclusions presented in my research reports, starting with my short article in *Die Weltwoche* (Zurich) in 1971.

The fact that the focus on some selected problems of such a relationship helps to establish the validity and fruitfulness of the interpretive method called "sociology of literature" was one reason behind my decision to explore this specific author–critic relationship. In addition, the examination of the interaction of two men who are representative polar opposites in a common time involves both literary and ideological issues; they, in turn, help to highlight some central characteristics of the modern novel and the artistic properties of Thomas Mann's work, on the one hand, and to illuminate part of the inner history of an epoch, on the other. In order to accomplish this, the relationship has to be examined against the political, social, cultural and intellectual background of early twentieth-century Central Europe.

ACKNOWLEDGMENTS

A considerable part of the research and writing leading to this book was supported by the American Association of University Women in the form of a Dissertation Fellowship which enabled me to spend a year at the Thomas-Mann-Archiv in Zurich followed by a shorter research stay at the Georg-Lukács-Archiv in Budapest. It is my pleasure to give special thanks to Professor Ferenc Jánossy, stepson of Lukács and executor of his literary estate, for his kindness in assisting me at every stage of the work and for his granting me the copyrights to several of Lukács's early writings, the translations of which are to be found in the Appendix.

My greatest intellectual debt is to Wilhelm Emrich, Professor Emeritus of German at the Free University, Berlin, who intensified and focused my thinking on the modern novel and its social context. I owe much to Georg Lukács, Professor of Philosophy and Aesthetics at Budapest University when I started my studies there. He was a great teacher who made things sound simpler than they really were: "while he spoke, he was right."

I am especially grateful to Herbert Lehnert whose conviction of the importance of my inquiry into this particular literary relationship was crucial to its beginning. My special thanks go to those scholars and colleagues who kindly gave their time and advice, offered invaluable suggestions and/or supplied data, and, above all, whose writings on the subject were inspirational: Professors Ehrhard Bahr, Frank Benseler, Franco Ferrarotti, Iring Fetscher, Gajo Petrović, Hans Vaget, Harry Zohn, and the late Peter C. Ludz.

I am indebted to those scholars, critics, and friends who helped in more ways than I could publicly thank them for. I am grateful to Professor Lee Congdon, Jeanette Hudson, Edith Kurzweil, Joseph B. Maier, Robert Lilienfeld, and Laurent Stern in the United States, to Michael Löwy in Paris, and to László Sziklai, Ferenc Tőkei, and Erzsébet Vezér in Hungary. I am also indebted to the late Tibor Gergely, Arnold Hauser, and Katia Mann for sharing of their past experiences, reminiscences, and facts.

Thanks are due to Marianne Fischer-Eich, former archivist of the Thomas-Mann-Archiv, for her willing and extremely able assistance whenever needed; special thanks are due to my good friend, Hope McAloon, for always being there when needed and for her technical assistance.

It is my pleasure to express my gratitude to my editors, Richard Martin of the University of Massachusetts Press, Amherst, and György Balázs of Corvina Kiadó,

Budapest. I was lucky to have found in them fellow scholars and sympathetic readers without whom this book would not be.

My deepest gratitude goes to my husband, Zoltán Tar, for his generous help and intellectual guidance from the very inception of this study. His readiness to help in whatever form was necessary was a crucial factor in the successful completion of my project. When needed, he was a teacher, critic, or research assistant; at other times, he was a provider, adviser, or simply a friend to lean on—but always: a believer.

New York, August 1986

JUDITH MARCUS

INTRODUCTION

"Rigor must be achieved empirically, through a substantive acquaintance with the relevant texts," writes Harry Levin, "and with the exact relations between imaginative fiction and the socio-cultural facts—not by the imposition of vague absolutes from on high or the importation of categorical sanctions from the east."[1] This definition of a correct stratagem for the sociological approach to literature was addressed to Lucien Goldmann and was meant as a corrective for Goldmann's interpretation of Malraux's work in 1963. By substituting an imaginative re-creation of perception, feelings, attitudes, and thoughts for "imaginative fiction," the stratagem recommends itself for an investigation of the relationship between the great twentieth-century German novelist Thomas Mann and the Hungarian Marxist philosopher and literary critic Georg Lukács. (The irony of the matter is that Lukács was made responsible by scholars for most of the import of "categorical sanctions from the east.")

A substantial degree of incompatibility has to be assumed between these two men—one a thoroughly bourgeois man and artist, and the other just as thoroughly a communist philosopher—whose representativeness as "polar opposites in a common time" is recognized by all. Common sense would suggest sharp distinctions that are biographically grounded and should summarily be outlined. For obvious reasons, I will have more to say about Lukács's life and work and his literary connections, including his lifelong preoccupation with Mann's work, than about Mann.

Thomas Mann (1875–1955), one of the greatest European novelists of the twentieth century, is also considered to have been the most representative of German writers and as such, in the words of Georg Lukács, symbolized "all that is best in the German bourgeoisie." Through his work, Mann succeeded in giving a complete picture of the *bürgerliche* life and its predicament in a certain stage of development. Although the emerging picture was of a critical nature, he treated the spiritual and moral problems of the *Bürger* as his own, stressing the significance of his social and cultural inheritance. His philosophical foundations were in Nietzsche, Schopenhauer, and Wagner—as was the case for a large segment of the German intelligentsia of his time. This is not the sole reason for his being called a thoroughly German writer and a very conservative one. Nor is the fact that he passionately pleaded for the just cause of Wilhelminian Germany's going to war in 1914 (especially in his early work, *Reflections of a Non-Political Man*) for imperialistic and expansionist purposes. After all, many liberal Germans, Max Weber and Georg Simmel among them, were equally enthusiastic if only for a time.[2] Nor was it the young Mann's slightly anti-Semitic inclinations, clearly traceable in his early writings and private utterances. It is partly because among the German writers of his generation few have been as conscious of tradition and have stressed so insistently their relations to tradition. "I am a man of the nineteenth century," Mann said on many occasions, thinking more likely of Goethe and the Romantic School (especially of Novalis) than of the industrializing Germany. But again: there was also in Thomas Mann an almost Faustian urge to experiment, to explore; as Henry Hatfield put it: "The cautious bourgeois is an explorer, as bourgeois often are."[3] Mann also possessed the conscious thoroughness of the bourgeois (he did "research" for his artistic task at hand in the strict meaning of the word), a trait attributed to the Germans in general. For him, only the thorough was truly interesting, as he remarked in the introduction to *The Magic Mountain*.[4]

Finally, and more important, a consistency runs through Mann's literary career. Students of Mann's artistry often emphasize the break in his life work; it is pointed out time and again that although he confined himself almost exclusively to ingenious variations on the theme of the artist in his early writings, there was later a move away to novels of ideas on a grand scale. An argument for such a case can be made if we put on the scale works like the novelette *Tonio Kröger,* or *Death in Venice,* the story "Tristan"—or even the novel *Buddenbrooks,* in which the solid bourgeois degenerates into an artistic one—and then weigh them against the series of grand novels of ideas starting with *The Magic Mountain*. However, there appears a continuity to the discerning eye: these variations on the artistic theme are played out against the sociopolitical, cultural, or intellectual background of their times. Whether we think again of *Buddenbrooks,* written at the turn of the century, of the short story, "Mario and the Magician," placed in Mussolini's Italy, or of *Doctor Faustus,* written in the 1940s and depicting Germany's slide into Nazism, the need for "much full-blooded reality" was always there, supplied in part by "concrete observation."[5] On the other hand, the artistic variation is played out as late as the *Joseph* tetralogy, *Doctor Faustus,* and *Felix Krull, The Confidence Man,* as the other aspect of that consistency. Last but not least, there was the very element of the German *bürgerliche* artistry, the transferring of "the ethical characteristics of the burgherly way of life: order, sequence, rest, 'diligence'....in the sense....of faithful workmanship—to the exercise of art," in Mann's apt summation. This "primacy of ethics over *esthetics,*" says Mann, was the main characteristic of his work first recognized by Lukács.[6]

At the opposite pole was Georg Lukács (1885–1971), born in Budapest as György Bernat Löwinger into an assimilated, wealthy Jewish family. (His father was a self-made millionaire banker, who changed his name to Lukács in 1891 and became ennobled in 1901; after this, the "von" was attached to the name.) Lukács received his education, including his two doctoral degrees, in Hungary; thus he seems to be situated in an entirely different social, cultural, and intellectual context from that of Mann. But Lukács not only grew up bilingual (his Viennese mother, Adele Wertheimer, never quite mastered the Hungarian language); he also received a cosmopolitan education. At the age of eighty-six, Lukács still fondly recalled his *Gymnasium* graduation present from his father: a trip to Norway to visit the ailing Ibsen, the admired artist of his childhood.

Lukács chose German at an early age as a medium for his public discourse and often for his private one. He pursued his postdoctoral studies in Germany in the same Wilhelminian era that was the background for Mann's early works, including *The Magic Mountain*. He came under the influence first of Wilhelm Dilthey and Georg Simmel and then, more important, of the neo-Kantian Emil Lask and the sociologist Max Weber, both in Heidelberg. This meant a change in general orientation from pure aestheticism to philosophy and social science, followed by a change in philosophical orientation from Kant to Hegel and, finally, to Marx. But the definitive change in Lukács's life and intellectual career came with his change in political orientation, his embracing of Marxism and Communism, moving, as George Steiner put it, "into the Marxist promise of social justice or rather, into the Marxist promise of method."[7] Lukács thus became less and less compatible with everything Thomas Mann stood for. Just as Mann's solid anchorage in German cultural tradition and "high bourgeois values" is stressed in the critical literature, so is Lukács's essential "homelessness," the fact that "exile was his natural habitat" in several respects. Admittedly, this is not so clear-cut an issue, and the following insightful and concise statement of Steiner's explains why:

> Yet, in another sense, Lukács was deep-rooted. He was curtly dismissive in reference to his own Judaism, but a Jew to the tip of his fingers. Unhoused, peregrine, he is one of the tragic constellations (Ernst Bloch, Walter Benjamin, Adorno, Herbert Marcuse) of Jewish abstractionists, possessed by a Messianic rage for logic, for systematic order in the social condition of man. Lukács's Marxism is, in essence, a refusal of the world's incoherence. ... Like other Jewish self-exiles whose radicalism out of Central Europe has so incisively marked the century, Lukács is an heir in immanence to the transcendence of Spinoza.[8]

The characterization is interesting and also important in the sense that, as will be shown, Thomas Mann's perception of Lukács partly corresponds to the portrait drawn by Steiner.

At any rate, Lukács has been called by European—and more recently by American—critics and scholars of widely differing persuasions in turn "the finest Marxist since Marx," the man whose "influence upon Western thought has been considerable," and "probably the only Communist philosopher and literary critic in East Europe who still has the power to interest and to teach many readers in the West."[9] He achieved almost instant fame with the 1911 publication of his book *Die Seele und die Formen* (Soul and Form); one of its essays, "The Foundering of Form Against

Life," has been credited with bringing back into prominence the philosophical notions and the tragic life of Søren Kierkegaard, thus promoting a Kierkegaard renaissance. Shortly after, during his Heidelberg sojourn (1912–17), Lukács came into close personal and intellectual contact with leading scholars and intellectuals of the time, among them Max and Alfred Weber, Emil Lask, Martin Buber, and Ernst Bloch. One of their contemporaries, the sociologist Paul Honigsheim, reported many decades later on the close relationship between Max Weber and Lukács and quoted Weber as having said after a Sunday afternoon discussion, "Whenever I have spoken with Lukács, I have to think about it for days."[10] Less known—and largely still undocumented—is the stature and role of Lukács among his peers in his native Budapest. Here the so-called Sunday Circle, which was founded by Béla Balázs (the first theoretician of the cinema) and his friends in 1915 and which attracted Hungary's young intellectual elite, regarded Lukács as *the* philosopher of their generation. Arnold Hauser, the renowned art historian, was one of the members who later spoke of Lukács as his intellectual mentor; he expressed the sentiment of his one-time peers and friends such as Karl Mannheim, Frederick Antal, Charles de Tolnay, and René Spitz when he stated unequivocally shortly before his death: "Lukács was from the very beginning, their acknowledged leader,…their teacher,…and more or less, all of them were under his influence."[11]

After the publication of *History and Class Consciousness* in 1923, the sphere of Lukács's influence widened considerably; since then, it has been impossible to ignore Lukács in discussions on the pros and cons of Marxian thought. Generations of philosophers and social scientists, from Walter Benjamin, Ernst Bloch, and the Frankfurt theorists (especially Theodor W. Adorno and Herbert Marcuse) to Jean Paul Sartre, Lucien Goldmann, and Jürgen Habermas, have read, discussed, interpreted, critiqued, or learned from Lukács.

It was literature above all, however, that retained its conspicuous presence throughout Lukács's career—a preoccupation that started in his early youth and remained an accompaniment to the end. His commitment to literary art had manifested itself in diverse ways, such as methodological treatises, aesthetic fragments, and the late, Marxist *Aesthetics*; it resulted in volumes of literary criticism, a monograph on the historical novel, and his typology of the novel, *Die Theorie des Romans,* which remains to this day "possibly the most penetrating essay that ever addressed itself to that elusive subject," in Harry Levin's opinion;[12] even more significant, it brought forth the still untranslated *Entwicklungsgeschichte des modernen Dramas* (The History of the Development of Modern Drama), published in Hungarian in 1911 (the German language edition first appeared in 1981). Lukács even tried his hand at "creative writing"; as told in his autobiographical fragment of 1971, *Gelebtes Denken* (Lived Thought), he first entertained the idea at the age of fifteen that he might himself "become a writer," and wrote plays in the manner of Hauptmann and Ibsen. "Thank

God," he said, "that all trace of them has now disappeared."[13] Not quite: there is a "confessional" writing extant in the form of a "letter and a dialogue," entitled "Von der Armut am Geiste" (On Poverty of Spirit), written and published in German in 1912. Moreover, two early pieces resurfaced in the 1970s and have since been published in Hungary. The first is a dialogue between "friends," entitled "Das Gericht" (Judgment), written in 1913 in a somewhat Kafkaesque manner. The other is a stylized fairy tale, "The Legend of King Midas" (1908), about loneliness, longing and the impossibility of living an ordinary life of happiness. One has to concur in Lukács's own estimation of his literary limits, however, which made him adopt the "secret criterion" for judging literary works: "Literature began where I felt that something had been written which I could not emulate."[14] In sum, to look into the question of Lukács's literary connections, that is, to explore his influence on contemporary literary activities, to inquire about the nature and extent of interaction between Lukács and his work and the literary practice of his time, is not only legitimate but is also a basic component of the complex Lukács picture.

There are at least passing references mainly to two important literary connections in almost all critical works on Lukács: The first is the mention of the role that Thomas Mann played in "rescuing" Lukács from the consequences of his political actions and/or beliefs, once in 1919 when Mann protested Lukács's extradition to the semi-fascist Horthy regime in Hungary, and the second time in 1929 when Mann wrote his now famous "Letter to the Chancellor of Austria, Dr. Ignaz Seipel," protesting the plans for Lukács's deportation from Austria, the place of his exile. The second connection with far-reaching consequences concerns the so-called Expressionism Debate which pitted Lukács against Anna Seghers, Bertolt Brecht and his one-time friend, Ernst Bloch.[15] The reference to the relationship between Lukács and Stefan George, the German poet, belongs in the realm of myth and is based solely on the fact that both Lukács and a member of the so-called Stefan George *Kreis,* the literary historian Friedrich Gundolf, were invited guests at the house of Max Weber in Heidelberg. (The survival of this myth illustrates how an erroneous statement can be reproduced and even enlarged upon by authors who do not take the trouble to check on their sources and facts.) The close personal and intellectual friendship that *really* existed between Lukács and Paul Ernst, a German neoclassical playwright and writer, and a very mediocre artist to boot, remained virtually unknown until the German-language publication in 1974 of their long-lasting correspondence, *Paul Ernst und Georg Lukács: Dokumente einer Freundschaft* (Documents of a Friendship).

It remained a thoroughly sad and inexplicable fact for Lukács himself that no such documentation of a friendship between him and Thomas Mann could ever be realized. The opportunity for a *direct dialogue* carried out in a correspondence that would include debates, discussions, and exchange of ideas or opinions was there in that Lukács had approached Mann repeatedly only to be met by silence. While

Lukács believed firmly that at one time there existed a "spiritual closeness" between them, he also came to the realization that any such symbiosis had to be broken when they took up "opposite positions vis-à-vis the imperialist First World War," followed by Lukács's being drawn to Marxism and ultimately joining the Communist Party.[16] Contrary to critical opinions, Lukács was well aware of Mann's reservations about him and thought that "in Thomas Mann's eyes, I am not sure what the Hungarian word is, I was something of an uncanny figure." Moreover, there was "no doubt" in his mind that he "was the model for Naphta."[17] Lukács only protested when the identification was carried too far to suit him, and he found it both annoying and comical that some critics attempted to interpret his life work in the light of Naphta's philosophical notions and political standpoint—and not the other way around. He was equally wary of asides and "literary gossip" (a term used by Karl Kerényi).[18] As far as Thomas Mann and his possible borrowing of Lukács's physical and intellectual features for his fictional character are concerned, Lukács had the following to say: "I am very liberal in such matters. *A good writer can be allowed almost anything!*"[19] This statement provides partial answer to all the speculations about the reasons for Lukács's "blind devotion" to Mann and his work. It was further enhanced by a rare showing of ironic wit on the part of Lukács—a trait not usually attributed to him: "Thomas Mann took an extremely diplomatic view of [his] relationship with me," said Lukács; answering the question of what form Mann's diplomacy took, he summed it all up with, "He would never say anything good about me without immediately qualifying it."[20]

Yet it was not empty flattery but a deeply felt and genuine homage when Lukács stated that one can only treat the artistry of Mann "with the deepest reverence and rapturous love *[mit ergriffener Achtung und hingerissener Liebe]*".[21] And Mann himself spoke of Lukács's insights and perceptions in respectful tone and gave him credit for his essayistic skills and interpretive talents. Indeed, he called Lukács "the most important literary critic of today." This literary connection seemed to me an intriguing one full of question marks and ambiguities, and because the story of Mann's distant respect and Lukács's "unrequited love" has never been told, I felt it worth exploring.

The present study cannot lay claim to being an exhaustive monograph on the subject but—without sounding immodest—I trust it offers a significant contribution toward it. It is to be hoped that the material presented here—most of it made available for the first time in English—will prove to be a useful source and will stimulate further exploration and interpretation. Up to now, only one aspect of the Lukács-Mann interconnection has received any attention—the Naphta connection. This was largely due to an unawareness of certain other connections and/or the unavailability of source material. For this reason, the secondary literature was not extensively drawn upon; in some cases mention is made of some critical studies only to call attention to inaccuracies or needed factural corrections. The study is based almost entirely on primary material: the creative work of Thomas Mann and the essayistic work of both Mann and Georg Lukács. In addition, I have consulted the published and unpublished correspondence of both Lukács and Mann as well as relevant historical, sociological, and political treatises, documentations, memoirs of contemporaries, and newspapers and journals of the period involved. Last but significantly, I sifted through the material deposited in the Thomas Mann Archiv in Zurich, and the Georg Lukács Archiv in Budapest. Without access to these archival materials, the book could not have been written in its present form.

Moreover, I did not hesitate to employ methods that were considered fruitful such as that of oral history. Important and of inestimable help to this study were the conversations and interviews which I had the good fortune to be granted. Many helpful facts, hints, anecdotes, and clues as to relationships as well as attitudes and reactions toward events came my way through talks with, for example, Georg Lukács; Katia Mann, the writer's widow; Arnold Hauser, the art historian; Tibor Gergely, the Hungarian painter, illustrator, and one-time member of the Sunday Circle; Dr. Hans Staudinger, former high-ranking official of the Weimar Republic and then Dean of the New School for Social Research; Ernst Bloch, the German-Jewish philosopher and one-time close friend of Lukács; Karl August Wittfogel, at one time friend and Party associate of Lukács; and, finally, the son and confidant of Lukács, Professor Ferenc Jánossy of Budapest, who is the sole executor of Lukács's literary estate (contrary to claims by others) and who generously granted me permission to use archival material and to copyright several hitherto untranslated and unpublished writings.

Along with the research came the realization of why my topic must have presented enormous obstacles to almost any student of Lukács or Mann. Any such project has as its prerequisite not only the investigation of two very productive writers but also an exploration of voluminous archival material, and, finally, thorough knowledge of both German and Hungarian. At the end, however, my research activities yielded proof of the existence of *weltanschauliche* agreements and of reciprocal literary and personal relationships. It can now be documented that the spiritual closeness Lukács referred to was indeed present—at least in the early period of their encounter.

Part One of the book deals with the genesis and development of their literary relationship in some detail. This is not a critical but an objective examination of the main works of the young Lukács and Mann, intended to show the degree of spiritual and intellectual affinity between the two that lasted until World War I. According to Lukács's own statement, his youthful production was greatly influenced by the early works of Mann, especially by *Tonio Kröger*. Consequently, the problems discussed and the conclusions reached in Lukács's *Soul and Form* and in Mann's fragmentary work, "Intellect and Art," as well as in his short novel, *Death in Venice*, show marked similarities. It is demonstrated that some of Lukács's musings on

Socrates, the concept of love and decadence, and the possibilities of the modern artist inspired Mann's conception of the fate of his hero Gustav von Aschenbach. I venture to say that without the special sensibility displayed in Lukács's essays of that time, Mann's *Death in Venice* would be a vastly different work. Part One also describes the unsolved mystery of Lukács's life, that is, Mann's personal distance from Georg Lukács the man.

Part Two is devoted entirely to an analysis of *The Magic Mountain,* that is, of its fictional character, Leo Naphta, the second and more important teacher of the novel's hero, Hans Castorp. In the course of the discussion of Lukács's "contribution" to this highly irregular figure—irregular as a Jew, as a Jesuit, and as a Communist—I trace the importance of the Jewish intellectual as an ideal type throughout Thomas Mann's œuvre. In this connection I claim that it was *not* the Marxist Lukács who inspired Mann in his portrayal, but rather that the radicalism, rigidity, dogmatism and asceticism of the young Lukács helped to shape the totalitarian personality of Leo Naphta. As Mann himself pointed out to Pierre-Paul Sagave:

Neither in the nineteen-twenties or ever did I read anything by Lukács dealing with matters of political nature. I only read his literary criticism. *History and Class Consciousness* was and is unknown to me. And as to Karl [*sic*] Schmitt: I have only heard about him. ...It is, however, understandable to think that I had studied all these things while working on *The Magic Mountain*.[22]

This only serves to illustrate my original thesis about the young Lukács being at least in part the inspiration for the intellectual personality of Leo Naphta. Thomas Mann's evaluation of Lukács's intellectual physiognomy was based on the early writings of Lukács, that is, on his pre-Marxist thought. During my interview with Lukács, I presented him with this hypothesis and elicited the following response:

Look, I am convinced that you are correct in this matter. I won't dispute it at all. But then, the question presents itself whether, and to what extent, Thomas Mann had noticed that there were things—and one should not forget that even *the young* Lukács of *Soul and Form* was much farther from the bourgeois view than Mann ever imagined—in which I already stepped over the limits of bourgeois propriety. This alone is and remains the problem [to be solved].[23]

The problem that presented itself to and was thus formulated by Lukács is the content of this book. I believe that the section dealing with *The Magic Mountain* will make it clear to the reader that after reading *Soul and Form* it indeed dawned on Thomas Mann in just what way the young essayist, Georg von Lukács, had overstepped the limits.

PART ONE:
THE AUTHOR AND HIS CRITIC

Chapter 1.
SPIRITUAL CLOSENESS:
INTERACTION, INFLUENCE, AND CONGRUENCE

Any examination of the interrelationship between artist and critic must presuppose their mutual influences: the impact of art on the critic and the impact of insightful criticism on the artist. It presupposes further the affinity of each for the other's statement. For the artist, it involves a changed self-awareness as an artist, a new awareness of both his/her original intentions and the effects of the artistic product; indeed, the artist may even be inclined to heed some critical suggestions, and in subsequent work may show signs of those suggestions. On the critic's part, we assume that the contemplated work of art had so aroused the critic's intellect, spirit, and feelings that the enraptured mind had given birth to an inspired and deeply insightful interpretation, a kind of poetic retelling of the work which enriches the understanding and even aspires to an artistic value of its own. The history of German literary criticism shows many examples. One of the best known is Friedrich Schlegel's "poetic" interpretation of Goethe's *Wilhelm Meister*. Admittedly, this notion amounts to a "poetizing" of that literary activity that is more prosaically called "interpretive reading." But this very notion was precisely what the young essayist Georg von Lukács had in mind when he wrote, "There is a ... science of the arts; but there is also an entirely different kind of expression of the human temperament, which usually takes the form of writing about the arts."[1]

For this reason, Lukács calls it a mistake—shared by most people, to be sure—to believe that the writings of the critic "are produced only to explain books and pictures, to facilitate their understanding."[2] Instead of discussing books or pictures as "inessential and pretty ornaments of real life," in reality he speaks about the "ultimate problems of life" and reveals his own "innermost substance."[3] To hold such a view of the critic's vocation means not only to adhere to the idea of uncompromising critical integrity, of absolute truth; it also implies an unsparing critical attitude toward everybody and everything concerned—not to mention the necessity of an affinity between the chosen subject of critical activity and the critic, whose evaluation is the act of sitting in judgment (to paraphrase Ibsen) not only of the work of art, but of himself.

To begin with, a close relationship exists between the artist and "his" critic in at least one sense, explains Lukács in his essay "Platonism, Poetry and Form." He speaks here of the *two main types* of all those who live in art, and defines them as "the Poet" and "the Platonist," using the term first employed by Rudolf Kassner, the Austrian essayist. Although the two main types, the *creative artist* and the *critic*, are "opposite poles," at the same time they complement each other; what characterizes and distinguishes them as true or "really typical" representatives of two opposites is that

the poet always speaks about himself, no matter what he sings; the Platonist never dares to think aloud about himself; he can experience his own life only through the works of others, and by understanding others he comes closer to his own self.[4]

The chosen poet, through whose understanding Lukács the Platonist came closer to his own self, was above all Thomas Mann. No doubt Lukács had given some serious thought to the reasons for the existence of a so-called "elective affinity" (Wahlverwandtschaft) between himself and the German writer. He came to the conclusion that "every Platonist speaks his most significant words when he speaks about the poet. Perhaps there is a mystic law which decides which poet shall be allotted to each critic, so that he may then speak about him in this special way."[5]

This statement may well serve as the motto for the presentation of the relationship between the critic Lukács and the artist Thomas Mann.

Almost forty years later, the Marxist Lukács had no use for such lofty phrases as "mystic law." Rather, he spoke in terms of determining factors and described the reasons that compelled him to chose Mann as his "allotted poet":

I was still at the gymnasium when his writings made their first and decisive impact on me. The Tonio Kröger problem ... was a major influence in determining the main lines of my own youthful production. It was not so much the direct connection ... that [was] decisive, but rather the whole atmosphere in which problems were raised and solutions sought.[6]

The Tonio Kröger problem Lukács was alluding to was that of the isolation of modern art and the modern artist, in general, and the problem of the artist's existence as manifested in the irreconcilable conflict between "form" and "life" in particular. Not only in Mann's novella, but in the perception of many contemporaries, the alienation of the artist from a "normal," everyday life was inevitable, indeed, necessary; the voluntary exclusion from the "banality" of bourgeois life for the sake of the preservation of artistic integrity was a moral imperative. Lukács had devoted one of his best essays to Mann the artist as a "burgher gone astray," whose early literary works were about the "search for the burgher [die Suche nach dem Bürger]". That is, they depicted a search for a world in which it was still possible to be an honest artist and a burgher at the same time. Such a world has become a dream, a remembrance of a glorious past, a vision of a Goethean world, if you will. The same yearning underlies much of the essayistic enterprise of the young Lukács. Indeed, some of Lukács's most insightful critics perceived the common denominator in the seemingly radically different stages of his life and thought to be his search for solutions to the problems of a world unhinged. The problematic state of a "literature at the end of a cultural period" (in Mann's words) was a preoccupation shared by Lukács and Mann, as repeated references make clear. Their mutual concern gave rise to reflections on the seriousness of the situation at the beginning of the twentieth century, starting in 1909 for Mann and in 1908 for Lukács.

Lukács had published the result of his musings on the state of the world, of the art of literature, and of his mind in 1911 in the essay collection *Die Seele und die Formen* (Soul and Form). Mann's probing into the relations between the artist and the cultural climate of his time and his own inner debate about his artistic aims and methods were to have been the content of a large-scale essay with the provisional title "Geist und Kunst" (Intellect and Art). Mann's characteristic way of approaching problems by the posing of antitheses such as *Dichter* (poet) versus *Schriftsteller* (writer), or art versus criticism, could not at this time cope with the complexity of the issues involved, and so led to the abandonment of this overly ambitious project. In due time, the aborted effort was listed among Gustav von Aschenbach's accomplishments in *Death in Venice*. Parts of Mann's notes were also published in 1913 under the title, *Der Künstler und der Literat* (The Artist and the Literati). Mann's introductory note explains the reasons for not being able to carry out the project:

I once dreamed of writing a large-scale treatise on intellect and art, criticism and sensuous, plastic art, insight and beauty, reason and the daemonic. The subject matter gradually went beyond all limits and the essayistic discipline of the author proved inadequate to the task.[7]

It is not difficult to see that many of these concepts thus set against each other enriched two subsequent works, *Death in Venice* and the controversial essay *Reflections of a Non-Political Man*. Lukács the Platonist, on the other hand, possessed the essayistic discipline to outline the general situation and his own while ostensibly offering analyses of literary forms in his book *Soul and Form*. He was of the opinion that the "modern essay has lost that backdrop of life" which alone can give its practitioner strength.[8] Thomas Mann had thought along the same line in relation to modern art.

It is striking that the statement of problems not only was quite similar but coincided in time; this problematic situation deserves a more detailed analysis than can be undertaken here. A brief discussion of certain aspects of the similarity in their formulations should prove instructive, because it is indicative of existing analogies. One should keep in mind the common basis of their statement of the problem, namely, their grave concern about the possibilities (*Möglichkeiten*) of literary art in a problematic world.[9] It cannot be determined precisely to what extent *Soul and Form* contributed to Mann's thought process.[10] What can be said safely is that Lukács and Mann were wrestling with the same or similar problems in the same time period, and that they often arrived at similar conclusions. We can find the interplay of ideas as well as that "intellectual symbiosis" (*geistige Symbiose*) Lukács was referring to.[11]

According to Hans Wysling, Mann's planned project intended to focus on five groups of problems.[12] One line of argument referred to Mann's objection to the then fashionable distinction between *Dichter* (poet) and *Schriftsteller* (a mere writer) or—as another variation on the same theme—between *Kritiker* (critical intellectual) and *Plastiker* (sensual, plastic artist). Obviously, Mann himself felt the need for clarification of these and similar antithetical concepts, due to the interlacing of the concepts of *Geist* (spirit, intellect) and *Kunst* (art) in his novella *Tonio Kröger*. At a very early stage in his deliberations, Mann jotted down the following (Note 13): "*Intellectuality of the typical modern artist...*"; this was clearly a reference to the problems discussed in the so-called *Kunstgespräch* (discussion on art) between Tonio Kröger and Lisaveta Ivanovna, artist and confidante.[13] Since Nietzsche first raised the issue, we are instructed by Note 40, we know that "it is indeed possible to fancy that *Lyrik* and *Kritik* go well together, are related or even identical." That is, it is no longer possible to maintain that the creative writer *(Dichter, Lyriker)* is superior to the critical, analytical writer *(Schriftsteller)*.[14] It assumes the character of self-justification when Mann remarks (Note 47), "In Germany, there is altogether too much fuss made about the *Dichter* as against the mere *Schriftsteller*."[15] He also calls attention to past periods and literary movements in which the borderline became blurred between the analytical-critical writer and the "unconsciously creating poet" *(naiv gestaltender Dichter)*. Mann identifies German Romanticism as such a period, and begins his reflections by pairing "*Romantik* and criticism, i.e., the literary approach," represented mainly by Friedrich Schlegel (Note 42). He then goes on:

In Romanticism generally, *intellect,* irony is the main thing. Romanticism is deeply literary. Tieck. Wackenroder, a standard work of Romanticism, wholly analytical and literary. It is the same with "Lucinde" [a novel by Friedrich Schlegel]. On the whole, the Romantics are not strong on "plastic" effects: philosophical. Their naiveté is a calculated one. "What knowledge they display of the nature of poetry, of language and culture!... (Gundolf)."[16]

In 1925, shortly after the publication of *The Magic Mountain,* Mann once more tried to summarize his thoughts on the matter. First, he noted with a certain degree of satisfaction that the once fashionable, sharp, and above all arbitrary distinction between *Dichter* and *Schriftsteller* was beginning to fade. Mann wrote:

We have as antecedents first the Romantics, then Nietzsche for the extreme fluidity of the distinction between poet and writer, or between art and criticism, until we reached the point where today it amounts to aesthetic pedantry and would, indeed, be quite old-fashioned to insist on it. If I am allowed to talk about my own case, I have in the past composed more than one essay that I would not for a minute hesitate to include in a collection of my stories; I can just as well imagine that it would work the other way around. Contemporary observers of the literary scene speak of the "critical moment in the modern novel" and by that they not only have the German novel in mind but the European novel in general. .... Thus, the phenomenon is characteristic of our times.[17]

In October 1910, during his Florence sojourn, Georg Lukács had finished writing an essay which was to introduce the forthcoming collection *Soul and Form*. The introductory essay, entitled "On the Nature and Form of the Essay," was intended partly to spell out and justify the volume's "unifying idea." More important, Lukács had addressed himself to the very same complex of problems Thomas Mann was preoccupied with at that moment—although from the vantage point of the critic, the "Platonist." Lukács's reflections on the critique, the essay, as a possible "work of art, a genre," had one main purpose; he asked, "To what extent do the standpoint of such a work [the essay] and the form given to this standpoint lift it out of the sphere of science and place it at the side of the arts, yet without blurring the frontiers of either?"[18] Just as Mann looked back at the Romantic School as a point of reference, Lukács too saw in the fusion of artistic and critical moments a "familiar truth ... that was already known to the German Romantics, a truth whose ultimate meaning the Greeks and Romans felt, quite unconsciously, to be self-evident: that criticism is an art and not a science."[19] Indeed, Lukács argues along with Friedrich Schlegel (as Mann did), reminding us that the "older Schlegel" called the essays he was speaking of "intellectual poems." Unaware of Mann's preoccupations and conclusions, Lukács fully agrees with the statement on the "identity of *Lyrik* and *Kritik*". Of course, Lukács reminds us that "poets" and "critics" are "opposite poles" in regard to their temperament, life-problems, and style of expression. Lukács, like Mann, approaches the problem by posing antitheses, and he too defines the "plastic artist"—though using a different term—as the "true type of poet" who has "no thoughts," that is, who is "never problematic." But the problem is that the really typical poet thus described becomes rarer and rarer. Consequently, "Expression and the way to a goal, *verse and prose become a life-problem only when the two contrasting types combine within a single man*—which must inevitably happen in the course of history."[20] Lukács's view of the problematic state of modern art and of the modern artist can undoubtedly be traced back to what he called his "Tonio Kröger experience."

Just what was this experience? As mentioned before, both in the notes to the essay project and in *Tonio Kröger,* Thomas Mann calls attention to the "intellectuality of the modern artist." In the novella, Mann formulated his thoughts on the nature of the artistic enterprise through his fictional character Lisaveta Ivanovna. Lukács echoes Lisaveta's "defense" of the artist's calling as he circumscribes the critic's mission. Lisaveta berates Tonio Kröger for his faintheartedness and speaks of the "purifying and healthy influence of literature," of the "redeeming power of the word," of literary art as the "noblest manifestation of the human mind," and of the poet as the "most highly developed of human beings," in fact, as a "saint."[21] The nature *and* social function of the artistic enterprise still figures prominently in the notes to the essay project. Hans Wysling points out that one of the five themes to be discussed was the distinction between the *true* artist—in this case the critical–analytical writer— and the artist–charlatan (and demagogue, like Wagner); the former has an important mission, as Mann sees it, just as literature and its critical discernment are considered absolutely "necessary in [a] country" such as Germany, where "there is no psychology,... no deeper knowledge, no sensitivity, no bite to analysis—where there is a lack of critical passion.[22] Keeping in mind his mission, which includes "criticism of morals" and "criticism of life," the artist has to exhibit purity, integrity, dignity, and ascetic severity. Parts of the project that had been published in 1913 *(Der Künstler und der Literat)* still contain Mann's thoughts on the type of writer who lives and creates "consciously and in a fully responsible way" because that is what "the times demand." (Mann always had a well-developed sense of what should be the "order of the day.") Although the polemical tone and the view of the artist's function remain much the same, the published version has a remarkably altered vocabulary and terminology. There is no hard evidence for any direct borrowing, but it seems to me significant that Lukács's *Soul and Form* came out in the meantime (1911) and was carefully read and annotated marginally by Mann. In the 1913 version, Mann defines the writer as a human being who is "decent to an absurd degree" and also "honest to a degree of sainthood—indeed, who is both a man of acute insight and a judge and as such closely related to the prophets of the Old Testament." For him, art means to "dissect and to designate precisely." He is "by birth the supreme judge...who has the talent to ruthlessly unmask the truth behind things" and has been "chosen to do it."[23] In addition to being honest and decent, he is also a "radical"; "radicalism for him is synonymous with purity, generosity and depth. He abhors half-heartedness...and any hint of compromise." The writer and the poet experience things very differently in that the "writer expresses himself through his experience; he is experiencing through his expression and he experiences in order to give form to it."[24]

These and similar thoughts had been tossed around in the notes but never before had they acquired such sharpness of formulation and such a semireligious tone. Thus, it is interesting to see what Lukács had to say about the complex relationship of experience and expression. "There are experiences," he writes, "which cannot be expressed by any other gesture and which yet long for expression. ..." What he meant by that was the "intellectuality, conceptuality as sensed experience [*sentimentales Erlebnis*], as immediate reality, as spontaneous principle of existence. ..."[25] Intellectuality as *sensed experience* is the counterpart to Mann's statemen that one is "experiencing through expression [*erlebt, indem man ausdrückt*]." Lukács elaborates on this point:

Form is the [critic's] great experience, form—as immediate reality—is the image-element, the really living content of his writings. This form which springs from a symbolic contemplation of life-symbols, acquires a life of its own through the power of that experience.[26]

Concerning the moralistic aspect of Mann's characterization, almost all the criteria he listed are present in the Lukácsian discussion. Contrary to what people say about the poet not being "obliged to tell the truth about his subject matter," Lukács insists that *both* the critic and the artist are "impelled towards an inner truthfulness."[27] He acknowledges that both the artist's and the critic's existence and craft have in modern times become "problematic." Thus, both the artist and critic have to look for "redemptive" measures, which, in Lukács's words, "can only come from accentuating the problems to the maximum degree, from going radically to its [sic] roots."[28] For Lukács's way of thinking, the moment one becomes conscious of the fact that "salvation is necessary," it also becomes "possible and real." Lukács's ethical approach to matters aesthetic reaches its heights in a somewhat exalted declaration that in all possibility was highly suggestive to Mann who—with an ironic twist— dressed *his* statement in the Old Testament garb:

> The critic has been sent into the world in order to bring to light [the] *a priori* primacy [of the idea of the work of art] over great and small, to proclaim it, to judge every phenomenon...; it is a soul-value, world-moving and life-forming force in itself... the atmosphere of the idea is enough to judge and [to] condemn. ... The essayist is delivered from the relative, the inessential, by the force of judgment of the idea he has glimpsed; but *who gives him the right to judge?*... The criteria of the essayist's judgment are indeed created within him, but it is not he who awakens them to life and action: the one who whispers them into his ear is the great value-definer of aesthetics, the one who is always about to arrive, the one who is never quite yet there, the only *one who has been called to judge.* The essayist is John the Baptist *who goes out to preach in the wilderness about another who is still to come,* whose shoelace he is not worthy to untie.[29]

As a consequence, the essay itself is the "judgment, but the essential, the value-determining thing about it is not the verdict... but the process of judging."[30] There is a meeting of minds here, in that both Lukács and Mann allude to Ibsen's dictum that "writing is putting on trial your innermost self." About the same time, Mann jotted down the following lines (Note 110): "Criticism that is not confessional in character is worthless. The really deep and passionate critique is poetry in the sense of Ibsen: putting one's own self on trial."[31] As far as the "psychologization" (Mann's term) of the writer's task is concerned, Mann used the term "dissect" *(zergliedern)* in his published fragment, no doubt influenced by Lukács's description of the critic, the Platonist, as a "dissector of souls" *(Seelenzergliederer)* and "not a creator of men."[32] A summary statement can be made that Thomas Mann's characterization of the critically perceptive writer is what Lukács calls a "problematic human being," whose form-giving activity is the crystallization of diverse and divergent forces within him. Thus both Mann and Lukács perceive the modern writer as "the artist in whose created form poet and Platonist become equal."[33]

One final parallel in the ways in which both men posited problems can be indicated in their discussion of the ethical dimension of the modern writer-critic's calling.

Thomas Mann regarded his critical-essayistic preoccupations as the "order of the day" and as his own way of attacking the "entrenched and dominant cultural features" of his age. This struggle against one's own time and its dominant features originates in the "will for the knowledge of one's self" and may, indeed, "promote knowledge of one's own time and the overcoming of its limitations."[34]

Lukács's zeal for truth and self-knowledge equaled Mann's and was also due to "the problematic of the situation," which made efforts for salvation necessary. Thus Lukács comes to the conclusion that the essayist has to become conscious of his own self, "must find himself and build something of his own out of himself."[35] In other words, Lukács too demands overcoming through critical insight. Whether or not becoming conscious of one's own self (Selbstbesinnung), that is, knowledge of one's own self (Selbsterkenntnis), would bring salvation is left undecided. The point is, according to Lukács, to raise the possibility of finding a road upon which to travel.[36] Along with Thomas Mann, Lukács too was practicing Kulturkritik, all the while discussing the calling of the writer and/or the critic.

H. J. Maitre's observation that a survey of Thomas Mann's essayistic work "reveals an overabundance of treatises of the work and personalities of great figures," of cultural history, applies also to Lukács's early essays.[37] The essays of Soul and Form are devoted to such figures as Søren Kierkegaard, Novalis, Theodor Storm, Lawrence Sterne, Richard Beer-Hofmann, Stefan George, Rudolf Kassner and Paul Ernst. Of these essays, the one on Storm, entitled "Bürgerlichkeit und l'art pour l'art" (The Bourgeois Way of Life and Art for Art's Sake) especially caught Mann's attention: his many underlinings and marginal notes attest to a studious reading of the piece. Bearing the mark of Lukács's "Tonio Kröger experience," that essay discusses the "problematic of the bourgeois artist." Mann had marked Lukács's discourse on the yearnings of today's "sophisticated" and "unsatisfied" man, his "hysterical nostalgia" for a world gone; this is a longing

for the great, holy simplicity, the natural, holy perfection to be born out of the birthpangs of an ever-growing awareness, to be *forced* into life *by the ultimate, gasping energy of a sick nervous system.* The bourgeois way of life, which consists of cutting down the conduct of one's life to a strictly and narrowly bourgeois measure, is simply a way of coming closer to such perfection. It is a form of *asceticism, a renunciation of all brilliance in life* so that all the brilliance, all the *splendour may be transferred...into the work of art.*[38]

Lukács's description may have fed itself on the "Tonio Kröger problematik" but it underwent a sharpening of perception and expression. In this new form, the depiction of the artistry of the bourgeois writer as well as its sources comes closer to that of Gustav von Aschenbach than that of Tonio Kröger. The artist depicted here is a "heightened *gesteigert* and hardened Tonio."[39] At the very beginning of *Death in Venice,* we are told that Gustav von Aschenbach was overburdened with the tasks "imposed upon him... to be an amateur *[Liebhaber]* of the outer world." Lukács expressed this thought as the "renouncing of all brilliance in life"; again, Aschenbach too learned "very early in his youth" to limit his life interests and repress any "feeling" of being "content with easy gains and blithe half-perfection." The life and working habits of Aschenbach could have come from the following passage in Lukács's essay, which, by the way, was heavily underlined by Mann:

> Life exists for work, and work for an artist is always an uncertain thing. Some-times, as a result of hysterical effort, his sense of life can be raised to an almost ecstatic intensity, but this ascent to the heights has to be paid for by terrible nervous and psychic depressions later. Work is the purpose and meaning of life.[40]

Thomas Mann had at a later point referred back to this Lukácsian essay, though *not* in connection with *Death in Venice*. Talking about the "nature of the burgher," about "burgherly nature and art, about burgherly artist nature," Mann calls on Lukács as the chief witness for his defense of the "Germanic figure of the burgherly artist" as a "complete and legitimate form of life." Mann writes:

> There is a beautiful, profound book by the young Hungarian essayist, Georg von Lukács, entitled *Soul and Form*. In it there is a study on Theodor Storm that is, at the same time, an investigation of the relationship of "burgherly nature and *l'art pour l'art*"—an investigation that to me, when I read it years ago, imme-diately seemed to be the best that had ever been said on this paradoxical subject, and that I feel I have a special right to cite, since the author was perhaps thinking of me—and at one place expressly mentioned me. Doubtless we have special claim to the knowledge to which we ourselves have contributed by our existence, and when we accept it as our own, we are somewhat in the position of a father who smilingly lets himself be taught by his learned son.[41]

Mann has high praise for Lukács's insight into *the* kind of "genuine, burgherly, artistic genius" whose essence is the "mortifying denial of life in favor of the work" and which is, basically, the kind of artist that has been created in the figure of Gustav von Aschenbach. Furthermore, Mann regards as particularly significant the Luká-csian statement about the "burgherly calling as a life form," which means "first of all the *primacy of ethics*" (emphasis added). He recognized right away that Lukács was thinking not only of Theodor Storm but also—possibly, mainly—of Thomas Mann; accordingly, he underlines this passage in his copy of *Soul and Form*. Years later, Mann remarked in reference to Lukács's treatise on the "burgherly artist": "This is brilliant—exceedingly beautiful and true! But may I be allowed not only to praise it but also recognize myself in it?"[42] This primacy of ethics of which Lukács speaks, Mann asks, "Does it not signify the predominance of ethics over *aesthetics*. And is this predominance not present even without a burgherly vocation...?" He answers his own question in the following way:

> An artist is burgherly when he transfers the ethical characteristics of the burgherly

way of life: order, sequence, rest, 'diligence'—not in the sense of industriousness, but of faithful workmanship—to the exercise of art.[43]

In the final analysis, Thomas Mann goes beyond his first attempt at defining artistry—or better, his own artistry—in the essay project. He gains his new perception with the help of "his" critic Georg Lukács and concludes, "Life is not the means for the achievement of an aesthetic ideal of perfection; on the contrary, the work is an ethical symbol of life."[44]

During the reading of Lukács's essay, Thomas Mann realized that, first, the author had undergone the same inner experience as he; second, that the young Hungarian essayist Georg von Lukács had discovered and correctly depicted the specifically German element in Mann's "life-form," that is, that Mann represents the "Germanic figure of the burgherly artist."[45] Thus arose the paradoxical situation that "this spiritual closeness... had ceased to exist when Mann wrote [these] lines," as Lukács remarked.[46] It is even more paradoxical that the Hungarian–Jewish Georg Lukács, whose one-time statements served Mann so well in his defense of a very German kind of artistry, should have also served very well as a model for the figure of Leo Naphta, a fictitious character who was designed to be a symbol for the quintessentially "other," the "stranger".

Be that as it may, Mann proudly cites Lukács and the fact that Lukács "expressly mentioned" him in a passage on Storm's "personal ability" to "bring together a thousand opposing tendencies" in his epic work; in this, Storm is compared to a "quiet goldsmith." But what Storm still was not able to depict was the "atmosphere of decay which engulfs his world." It was only "strong and conscious enough to become monumental once more... [in] the case of Thomas Mann's *Buddenbrooks.*"[47] What Lukács says so well, explains Mann, is the possibility that *Tonio Kröger* is "*Immensee* [a novella by Storm] transformed into a modern problematic work, a synthesis of intellectualism and mood, of Nietzsche and Storm." It is in this sense that "in *Buddenbrooks,* late awareness (which has nothing to do with rank) made possible the monumentalization of that mood of decay that permeates Storm's burgherly world."[48] As late as the 1940s, while working on *The Story of a Novel: The Genesis of "Doctor Faustus",* Mann recalls the Lukácsian words and notes: "If earlier works of mine had assumed a monumental character... they had done so unexpectedly and unintentionally."[49]

Thomas Mann had left unmentioned—probably *not* unintentionally—another essay from the same volume by Lukács, entitled "Sehnsucht und Form: Charles-Louis Philippe" (Longing and Form), even though it is of great importance in the context of the Lukács–Mann relationship, as direct evidence for the presence of a *geistige Symbiose* (intellectual–spiritual affinity). Well before its inclusion in the collection, the essay had been printed in a somewhat shortened form in the February 1911 issue of *Die Neue Rundschau,* the house journal of S. Fischer Verlag, Mann's German publisher. Mann, a subscriber and avid reader of the magazine, read the essay before starting work on *Death in Venice* in the fall of 1911. The essay in question contains the following themes and their connectedness: Eros, Socrates, the Platonic dialogues, Longing, Beauty, Transcendence, and the problematic situation of the modern artist. It is generously spiked with quotations from Plato's dialogues in the translation of Rudolf Kassner. Even a superficial glance makes it evident to the perceptive reader that the above themes are of central significance to Mann's story. Rigorous textual analysis would, no doubt, find even more correspondence between this most neo-Platonic of Lukács's essays and the novella that is discussed here.[50]

The most important among the work notes to *Death in Venice*, however, is Note 4 (followed by Note 6, clearly a case of misnumbering by Mann). The note's title reads: *"Beziehungen von Kap. II zu, V"* (Connections between Chapters Two and Five). Since the central issue to be treated in the novella is sketched here, and thus the note is of structural significance, the full text is given both in German and in English:

Vorfahren, dienstlich tapfer
Ruhmliebe und *Befähigung* zum Ruhm
Durchhalten. Zucht. Kirchendienst. Unter der
Spannung grosser Werke. Das Trotzdem.

Aufstieg von der Problematik zur Würde. Und nun!
Der Konflikt ist: Von der Würde aus, von der
Erkenntnisfeindschaft u[nd] zweiten Unbefangenheit,
aus anti–analytischem Zustande gerät er in *diese*
Leidenschaft. Die Form ist die Sünde. Die Oberfläche
ist der Abgrund. Wie sehr wird dem würdig gewordenen
Künstler die Kunst noch einmal zum Problem! Eros
ist für den Künstler der Führer zum Intellektuellen,
zur geistigen Schönheit, der Weg zum Höchsten geht
für ihn durch die Sinne. Aber das ist ein
gefährlich lieblicher Weg, ein Irr- und Sündenweg,
obgleich es einen anderen nicht gibt.

"Den Dichtern wird ein solcher Aufschwung immer
versagt bleiben. Ihr Aufschwung ist immer die
Tragödie ... Im Leben (und der Künstler ist
der Mann des Lebens) muss die Sehnsucht *Liebe*
bleiben: es ist ihr Glück und ihre Tragödie."

Einsicht, dass der Künstler nicht würdig sein
kann, dass er notwendig in die Irre geht, Bohemien,
Zigeuner, Libertiner, liederlich, Abenteurer des
Gefühls bleibt.
Die Haltung seines Stiles erscheint ihm als Lüge,
und Narrentum, Orden, Ehren, Adel höchst lächerlich.
Die Würde rettet allein der Tod (die 'Tragödie,'
das 'Meer')—Rat, Ausweg und Zuflucht aller höheren
Liebe.

Der Ruhm des Künstlers eine Farce, das Massenzutrauen
zu ihm nur Dummheit, Erziehung durch
(continued on Note 6):
die Kunst, ein gewagtes, zu verbietendes Unternehmen.
Ironie, dass die Knaben ihn lesen. Ironie der
Offizialität, der Nobilitierung. ...

Zuletzt: Zustand der Verweichlichung, Entnervung,
Demoralisation.[51]

Forbearers, honest officials; bent on fame and *qualifications*
for it. Endurance. Discipline. Clerical service. Under the
strains of great works. Defiance.

Ascent from the problematic state to that of dignity. And then!
The conflict: from the state of "dignity," from hostility to
insight and second innocence, due to an anti-analytical
inclination he gets involved in *this* passion. Form is the sin.
The surface is the abyss. How deeply art again becomes problematic
for the artist who had attained dignity! Eros is the guide
for the artist toward things intellectual, spiritual beauty;
for him, the path to the pinnacle goes by way of the senses.
But this is a dangerously delightful path, a wrong way and a
sinful way, although there is no other.

"But it will always be denied to ... poets to soar as high
as this. ... Their soaring is always tragic. ... In life
(and the artist is a man of life) longing has to remain *love:*
that is its happiness and its tragedy."

Realization that the artist *can never* attain dignity, that he
necessarily goes astray, remains a bohemian, gipsy, libertine,
an adventurer of emotions.

The discipline of his style appears to him as a lie and folly;
medallions, honors, nobility, as highly ludicrous. Dignity is
rescued only by death (this is the 'tragedy,' the 'sea') —
as a solution, a way out and refuge of all elevated love.
The fame of the artist is a farce; the trust of the masses is
sheer idiocy; education *via* art is a risky undertaking, to be
prohibited, the irony that the boys are reading him, the
irony of his official standing, of his being granted nobility....
At the very end: state of decadence, enervation, demoralization.

As has been shown, Mann took up and elaborated upon the Lukácsian notion in
his development of the idea about the inevitable fate of the artist who succumbs to
Eros; being the conscientious craftsman that he was, Mann placed the borrowed text
between quotation marks. In the passages leading up to the cited lines, Lukács discusses
Socrates's conception of love whose "object is to procreate and bring forth in
beauty." Socrates, the philosopher, forced his life "towards this high point," although
he must have realized "the ultimate hopelessness of all longings." The words of
Socrates, the teacher and prophet of longing, had seduced Athens's youth "to love,
but then he led them towards virtue, beauty and life."[52] It is in this sense that a
"great love has something ascetic about it." Socrates himself transferred his longing
into a philosophy "whose peak was eternally unattainable, the highest goal of all
human longing: intellectual contemplation"; instead of being a god of love, Eros
becomes a "cosmic principle." Socrates, the man, "disappeared behind his philosophy." Lukács concludes with a warning:

But it will always be denied to men and poets to soar as high as this. The object of
their longing has its own gravity and its own self-demanding life. Their soaring is
always tragic, and in tragedy hero and destiny must become form. But, in tragedy,
only hero and destiny can do this, and hero and destiny they must remain. In life,
longing has to remain love: that is its happiness and its tragedy.[53]

The fact that the Lukácsian notion evolved into a central idea of the novella has
wider implications and is certainly more significant than finding a critic's ideas and/or
statements echoed in a subsequent creative work. It is also in harmony with Mann's
acknowledgment in his autobiographical writing, *Sketch of My Life,* that he owes
much to happenstance: "Nothing is invented in *Death in Venice.* The 'pilgrim'...
the gray-haired rake,... Tadzio... the cholera,... all that and anything else you
like, they were all there. I had to arrange them... as elements of composition."[54]

Another element that came in handy was the central theme outlined in Note 4, supplied by the Lukács essay. In his treatise on *Death in Venice,* Wolfgang F. Michael asked the question: "Did Thomas Mann in fact have Plato in mind while working on his novella, or is this merely a case of interpretive hindsight, reading a personality into a complex web of the work? It would be interesting to include in the speculation Platon, ... or even Stefan George."[55]

In tracing the source of a decisive intellectual stimulus to Lukács's essay, Michael's question has at least in part been answered.

The impression left behind by this essay reaches beyond its impact in the novella. It aroused Mann's interest in a French writer, Charles-Louis Philippe, little known and even less read in Germany, to whose work Lukács's essay is devoted. As late as 1917, Mann still remembered Lukács's treatise on Philippe: In a letter to Philipp Witkop, he speaks of his recent illness and notes that "illness is a form of existence that has its own attraction and benefits and always reminds me of the very appropriate words of Ch. L. Philippe: *'les maladies sont les voyages des pauvres.'* I am given to quoting this quite often."[56] The often quoted line comes straight out of the essay of Lukács, who sprinkled his treatise with French quotations from Philippe's works. I should like to note that in this essay Lukács supplied the story outlines of several novels by Philippe. Interestingly, some of the situations and problems described by Lukács have their parallel in Mann's late novel *Doctor Faustus,* which, according to Mann, he conceived as early as 1901 and had begun collecting material for in 1905. One of the Philippe works mentioned by Lukács is the novel *Marie Donadieu,* in which two friends struggle over a woman, just as in the case of Marie Godeau in Mann's *Faustus.* One of the friends wins the woman over through "fine and clever monologues," says Lukács; Rudolf Schwerdtfeger in *Doctor Faustus* uses his "clever talk" to win the heart of Marie. Furthermore, Lukács summarized another Philippe novel, entitled *Bubu de Montparnasse,* the story of which takes place against the backdrop of the disease syphilis. Lukács writes, "The relationship between the student and the little whore—a relationship which is convincingly beautiful and pure—begins when he catches syphilis from her. The disease brings them together."[57] Similarly, the incident in the brothel was the "deathly unchaining" of everything to come in *Doctor Faustus.* It is true, as Gunilla Bergsten masterfully argues, that "Mann's idea of linking artistic genius with syphilis was suggested by the case of Nietzsche," and the novel in addition "contains many of Nietzsche's favorite thoughts and concepts."[58] Coincidence or not, the description of the second and fateful encounter between Adrian Leverkühn, the student, and the little "wench", the prostitute, shows in at least one respect a remarkable similarity: in *Doctor Faustus* too, the ultimate union between the student and the whore was accomplished by the transmission of the disease, through the "embrace, in which the one staked his salvation, the other found it." The "beautiful and pure" relationship of the Philippe novel has its counterpart in Mann's describing the encounter as "purifying" and "sublimating" or "magical."[59] This startling characterization of the fateful encounter cannot be connected to the "Nietzsche—*Erlebnis*" of Mann. It does not seem too farfetched to assume that Mann's well-known tendency to "collect" and to use by way of his "montage–technique" (Bergsten) every available bit of information, text, and/or person was indeed at work. And Mann retained his preoccupation with Philippe for a long time. He remarked in a letter of 1920, "Lately, I have read a lot of Ch. L. Philippe and have fun with playing him off against [Romain] Rolland. ..."[60] The quote he used three years earlier ("les maladies sont les voyages des pauvres") was also from the novel *Bubu de Montparnasse*. These instances of borrowing (if it was that) do not have the importance of other findings on the Lukács–Mann interconnection; they merely serve as hints and clues for the nature of Mann's literary techniques.

In response to my query as to whether Lukács was immediately aware of the role his essay played in the conception of *Death in Venice,* he said:

> No, quite honestly, I did not notice it. This was so masterfully integrated— hidden—in the text that the thought never even entered my mind. The realiz- ation that there was a connection between my early work and Thomas Mann, came much, much later. Still, for me this discovery is an extraordinarily inter- esting and exciting thing.[61]

Lukács must have perceived the connection between his early writings and Mann's work after the publication of *The Magic Mountain* in 1924. It must have dawned on him then—and this supposition is going to be convincingly argued in the second part of my study, in the discussion of the personality of Leo Naphta—that Thomas Mann had drawn the Naphta figure more on the basis of Lukács's early works than on that of the political writings of his Marxist period. The personal encounter between him and Thomas Mann in 1922 was certainly stimulating and informative for Mann, and its significance should not be belittled. However, that meeting and "Lukács's propounding his theories" to Mann would not have been sufficient to establish the personality traits and line of argumentation that truly make the connec- tion between the fictional character and the real Lukács.

Beyond the Lukács–Naphta constellation and in addition to this specific biographi- cal echo, it might prove interesting to explore a further connection between the early work of Lukács and Mann's novel. I am inclined to believe that Lukács's second major book in German, *Die Theorie des Romans* (1920), was also fruitful. As Lukács points out in the 1962 preface to his reissued study, in spite of his misgiving about this early work, he had succeeded "in principle" in uncovering "interesting correlations." He then supplies one, "the most characteristic example: the analysis of the role of time in *L'Education sentimentale.*" "We have here," declares Lukács not without a trace of self-satisfaction,

an unambiguous formulation of the *new function of time in the novel,* based on the

Bergsonian concept of 'durée.' This is the more striking as Proust did not become known in Germany until after 1920, Joyce's *Ulysses* not until 1922, and Thomas Mann's *The Magic Mountain* was not published until 1924.[62]

Lukács adds, regarding his *Theory of the Novel*, that "its success (Thomas Mann and Max Weber were among those who read it with approval) was not purely accidental."[63] (It is also not accidental, in my opinion, that Lukács mentions Mann repeatedly in this connection.) To my knowledge, Lukács was the first to observe that "time can become constitutive" in the modern novel, "whose very matter is seeking and failing to find the essence *[dessen Stoff das Suchen-Müssen und das Nicht-Finden-Können des Wesens ausmacht]*." Only in the modern novel is "time posited together with the form."[64] "Thus it is," says Lukács, "that time becomes the carrier of the sublime epic poetry of the novel." The experiences of time which "give rise to action and stem from action" are "the experience of hope and memory; experiences of time which are victories over time: a synoptic vision of time as solidified unity *ante rem* and its synoptic comprehension *post rem*."[65] Lukács thinks that such experiences of time form the base of Flaubert's *L'Education sentimentale;* he makes the lack of such a positive view of time responsible for the failure of the other major novels of disillusionment. Flaubert's novel is held up as an exception and model because of how it handles the experience of time; it is thought to be exemplary "in the representation of the passage of time and in the relation of time to the artistic centre–point of the entire work."[66]

In my discussion of *The Magic Mountain*, I will use the designation *Zeitroman* (historical novel); it is meant in the historical sense, just as Thomas Mann evaluated his novel as a work which "sought to represent the inner significance of an epoch." The author pointed out, however, that the novel is a *Zeitroman* in a double sense in that time is one of its themes: "time, dealt with not only as part of the hero's experience, but also in and through itself."[67] The similarity of the conception and "function" of time is suggestive and lets us assume that Lukács's highly theoretical, abstract formulations turned Mann's attention toward the possibilities of making time related "to the artistic centre–point" of his work. In his novel, Mann had tried his hand precisely at that artistic device that Lukács called the "highest duty" of the modern novelist: to obtain through the experience of time and the "representation of the passage of time" the "most profound and authentic means of accomplishing the totality required by the novel form."[68]

Thomas Mann had the same idea in mind, although he expressed it differently when he came to discuss "the mystery of the time element" in his book. "The book itself is the substance of that which it relates," writes Mann about *The Magic Mountain*, because

> it depicts the hermetic enchantment of its young hero within the timeless, and thus seeks to abrogate time itself *[aufheben]* by means of [giving]...complete

presentness at any given moment to the entire world of ideas that it comprises. It tries, in other words, to establish a magical *nunc stans*. ...[69]

Thus we find in Mann's *magische Formel* a variation of the Lukácsian expositions of the "synoptic vision of time *[Leben als geronnene Einheit]*," the experience of time as "remembrance" and "hope" which at the same time abrogates time *(Überwindung der Zeit)*.

It becomes evident from the demonstrated interaction and influence and the examination of the texts that the problems and issues explored by Lukács in his early works, especially in the essay collection *Soul and Form,* correspond with Mann's inner struggles and probings into the nature of his artistic enterprise and that of his time; more important, they coincided relative to both problems and time just when Mann was gestating the idea of a new work out of which crystallized *Death in Venice*. Yet the existence of an intimate spiritual closeness *(intime geistige Nähe)* could not persuade Mann to establish friendly personal relations with Lukács, and the personal distance remained unbridged forever.

Chapter 2.
RESPECT AND DISTANCE:
THE STORY OF THE PERSONAL RELATIONSHIP

Georg Lukács observed somewhat ruefully in the foreword to the fifth edition of his essay collection *Thomas Mann* that, by presenting to the reading public his "interpretive appropriation" *(auslegende Aneignung)* of Mann's work, he himself had become "the object of literary history." He had been cast in this, for him, unusual role by permitting the publication of the sum total of his critical preoccupation with Mann's work, starting with a review of *Royal Highness* in 1909 and concluding with an obituary in August 1955—a critical preoccupation spanning almost fifty years of his intellectual career.[1] The essays, assorted reviews, and scattered comments may at first seem unconnected, but in their entirety they are a testimonial to the development of Lukács's own critical positions vis-à-vis individual works and the life work of Thomas Mann. Moreover, notes Lukács, even the small-scale, more or less journalistic, often polemic utterances served an important function—the "propagation of the works of Thomas Mann." Lukács's mediating role was not limited to introducing and taking up the lance for Mann's work in Hungary, where even today he is considered the greatest novelist of the twentieth century. It reached far beyond, as Hans Vaget perceptively remarks: "Lukács achieved almost single-handedly the seemingly impossible: a very favorable reception of [Mann's] novels and stories in the Socialist world. Even in the non-socialist part of the world, is it not the authority of Georg Lukács which still lends a considerable weight to Mann's reputation?"[2] Indeed, numerous reviews and comments from the 1930s, during Lukács's exile in the Soviet Union, have been devoted to the propagation of Mann's works, to his acceptance as the "best representative" of bourgeois humanism, and to the "respectability" of Mann's "critical realism." It was no small achievement that in 1936, in Stalin's Russia, Lukács published the review essay "Thomas Mann über das literarische Erbe" (Thomas Mann of Literary Heritage), in which he proclaimed Mann's "critical method" and historical judgment to be extremely fruitful for the "exploration of tradition." At the same time, Thomas Mann was accorded the honor of being one of "the most important representatives of the anti-fascist front."[3] Lukács wanted to make it clear that the reason for his unerring approval and endorsement of Mann's artistic enterprise went beyond matters of personal literary taste. It was "subjectively and objectively" justified by the fact that "the writer Mann was striving to express" the dialectic of art and of the bourgeoisie, to state "a key problem of dying bourgeois culture as a whole," which could be seen in Mann's works as much as in Lukács's critical analysis of them. He believed that his critical reflections touched "the nub both of Thomas Mann's own work and of the cultural crisis" of that time.[4] He summed up the significance of their literary encounter:

It may seem an immodest claim but I happen to believe that my critical relationship to Thomas Mann, and my interpretive appropriation of his life-work never was and is not my private affair [*Privatangelegenheit*]. Rather, it is at least a symptomatic element of the literary culture of our time.[5]

The question of Lukács's relationship to Mann in general, and the issues of how far it was a "private affair" in particular, came up during my last interview with Lukács, just four weeks before his death. The main purpose of my visit was to present Lukács with the copy of Thomas Mann's hand-written working notes for his story *Death in Venice*. Lukács was seemingly moved by this posthumous "recognition" on the part of Mann. "This is an extraordinarily interesting and exciting document for me," he said, "a great present, so to speak." He then went on:

I have to admit that my relationship to Thomas Mann, was so to speak, the only dark spot in my life. By "dark spot" I do not mean something negative. What I mean is that there is an unexplained element in our relationship. And because for me personally, the matter is of the greatest importance and of utmost interest, it is only understandable that I wish to see this unexplained moment turn into a clear one.[6]

In light of this "confession," Isaac Deutscher's definition of the Lukács–Mann relationship as an "intellectual love-affair" on Lukács's part seems to be justified.[7] Although it is possible to explore the puzzling aspects of this relationship other than by focusing "on the frustrating and melancholy aspects of [Lukács's] love," as Vaget does, his point is well made that the

biographical aspect of their relationship highlights... an important and still topical conflict of recent intellectual history—a failure of communication between the two most important attempts made in this century to revive the heritage of classical German humanism.[8]

Thomas Mann is largely responsible for this failure of communication. He was well aware of Lukács's mediating role of many decades; he also knew of Lukács's lifelong critical preoccupation with his work. Indeed, Mann had appreciated and often referred to the correctness and insightfulness of many Lukácsian reflections and reviews. We find numerous references in his diaries, letters, and in his own essayistic work to that effect. As to the personal relationship in the form of a fruitful and continued dialogue, it was thwarted by Mann's unresponsive attitude. Lukács himself summarized the manner and nature of their relationship in an unpublished 1961 letter to Mann's daughter, Erika:

It was brought to my attention by my friend Ernst Fischer that you are interested in any letters I may have in my possession written by Thomas Mann. It goes without saying that I would with pleasure cooperate. However, the yield will be very slight, on account of the manner and nature of my relationship to Thomas Mann. Throughout his life, we met only twice, the first time in the early 1920s, in Vienna, and the second and last time in Weimar in 1955; on that occasion, as you know, there was no opportunity for extensive discussion. Accordingly, my relationship to Thomas Mann is represented by my essays and his relationship to me in his occasional remarks.

Even the very slight material I had in my possession became the victim of the times. I can recall, for example, that Thomas Mann wrote a very interesting letter to me reflecting on my review of his *Royal Highness,* shortly before the First World War. As with all of my papers, it got lost in the chaotic aftermath of the failed Hungarian Soviet Republic. Things were not much different during the years of emigration. I still remember an exchange of letters concerning some problems of pressing importance at that time, but that too was lost during my being hunted *[Gejagtsein]* from one country to another.

This being so, I have only one letter in my possession from Thomas Mann, addressed to my wife. Thomas Mann had asked one of his Hungarian translators to convey his best regards to me. Since I was about to go on a trip, it was my wife who wrote to him a note of thanks and received his answer.[9]

It should be noted that while Lukács remembered correctly the exchange of letters regarding his review of Mann's *Royal Highness,* he was mistaken in placing it before World War I. His letter, which was saved by Mann and is deposited at the Thomas Mann Archiv, is dated February 18, 1918. In it Lukács wrote:

Our mutual friend, Dr. Franz Baumgarten, has mentioned to me that you have expressed interest in my old (1909) essay on your *Royal Highness.* Since I do not plan a German language publication of my old Hungarian essays at any time in the near future, I do not possess a translation of any of them which I would consider stylistically adequate.

The enclosed translation was prepared at my request by a lady friend who is also an admirer of your work. The translator aimed only at communicating the content of the essay; it was not at all done with the intention of publication and does not pretend to be stylistically perfect, which does not have to be pointed out to you.

I am extremely glad to have been able to do this small favor for you.[10]

We can only assume that upon receiving the translated review essay, Mann wrote the "very interesting letter" Lukács referred to.

The second exchange of letters concerning "problems of pressing importance at that time" was not only interesting but also had a certain politically explosive power, as Lukács explained to me during our discussion. The nature of that correspondence certainly did not help to improve the already strained relationship between the two men. Lukács approached Mann on behalf of Zoltán Szántó, a member of the Central

Committee of the illegal Hungarian Communist Party, who was to go on trial in Budapest for his illegal political activities. Since a trial almost certainly meant the death sentence, Lukács asked Thomas Mann to intervene in the form of a "private" telegram to Admiral Horthy, Regent of Hungary. Mann's answer was unsatisfactory: he spoke of the "role of the writer" being something different from intervention in the "political arena." Lukács was incensed. He sent a letter to Thomas Mann stating, "You are a high-minded liar [vornehmer Lügner]" who "visits Warsaw, the country of a Pilsudski, gives a talk there on humanitarianism, and then shies away from any action in the service of it." After a few days, Lukács received a telegram from Mann stating, "I have sent a cable to Admiral Horthy." Lukács then destroyed both his letter and Mann's reply on orders from the Communist Party.[11]

Throughout his long life, from the very beginning of his literary career, Lukács had wrestled with the puzzling question of Mann's unresponsiveness to his many overtures and appeals for an intellectual dialogue. In this connection, Lukács made reference to what he called the "Fall Bertram" (the Bertram case). Ernst Bertram, a young German essayist and literary scholar residing in Munich, had sent an essay of his and a letter of homage to the "honored writer," Thomas Mann. Out of this gesture developed a close spiritual, intellectual, and later personal relationship—and a thick volume of correspondence.[12] Lukács obviously asked himself about this many times and also put the question to me: "What was the reason that such a relationship never developed between us even after I made the first steps?" The question obviously was a painful one for Lukács—and highly justified. It is important to know in this connection that Thomas Mann left behind a vast correspondence; he had been extremely conscientious in answering even the most trivial letters; in this he went beyond the call of duty. Moreover, there were several cases when the deep affection and respect of younger men for the older writer struck a responsive chord, and resulted in frequent exchanges of letters and ideas, such as in the cases of Paul Amann and Karl Kerényi.[13] Why, asked Lukács, was such a response never forthcoming specifically in his case? We may call this question the "Gretchen–Frage" of Lukács's life, for the answer cannot be found even by the most diligent scrutiny of the available material, personal or literary, left behind by Mann.[14] He alone could have provided his personal motivation. While I tried to give a more or less satisfactory answer to Lukács by calling attention to the "radicality" and "dogmatism" of his early thought and writings, which may in part explain Mann's unease and aloofness, the problem warrants a more detailed examination. As Vaget correctly observes, there are several reasons for exploring this author–critic relationship, and the biographical aspect is just as important as any other.[15]

Without considering their fraternal bond, the relationship between Thomas Mann and his brother Heinrich goes a long way, in my opinion, toward highlighting some of the hidden reasons for Lukács's frustrating "love affair." Both in the critical literature and in Thomas Mann's own utterances, much is made of the emotional closeness and of the mutuality of the brothers' youthful experiences before World War I, of their total estrangement during the war due to *"weltanschauliche* conflicts," and, finally, to the renewal of friendly relations of sorts grounded in respectful distance and tolerance toward "otherness." A definition of the brothers' relationship as *repräsentative Gegensätzlichkeit* (representative contrariness) should be applicable to that between Thomas Mann and Lukács. Similarly, Hermann J. Weigand's description of the "complex web of connections" between the brothers Mann, which was characterized by an "astonishing degree of parallelity of problems and motives" regardless of the "marked differences in temperament," thus creating "a certain degree of complementarity," is a fair approximation of the complex Lukács–Mann relationship.[16]

In his letters to his brother, Thomas Mann often comments on the problematic nature of their relationship, and mention is made of their differences as well as those things they shared. Mann's musings on his brother's "shortcomings" and "virtues" provide a valuable picture of the kind of personality that either "frightened" him or "offended" his sensibilities. A close look at Mann's shopping list of offensive traits may prove helpful in that it could provide a partial explanation for his aloofness toward Lukács. What Thomas Mann has to say about his brother's tendency toward "absolute" and "extreme" positions is of utmost interest; the accusatory tones are at times mixed with those of envy: "You seem finally to have found yourself," he writes in 1905, "and seem to know nothing anymore of such doubts and defeats [as I do]. We both seem to possess the fatal tendency—maybe because we are neurasthenics—toward extremism."[17] Thomas Mann, who liked to describe himself as a man of the *sowohl-als auch* (one as well as the other), a "man of the middle," was obviously determined not to give in to *his* fatal tendency. On the opposite pole, Lukács was a man of the "either–or," a man of the "extreme." The *schöngeistige* (aesthetic) Lukács formulated this best in one of his youthful essays (on Kierkegaard), which was thinly disguised confessional writing. "The only essential difference between one life and another is the question whether a life is absolute or merely relative;…whether the life–problems…arise in the form of an either–or, or whether 'as well as' is the proper formula."[18] In Thomas Mann's fictional world, the "extreme" position was assigned to some key characters, among them to that of Leo Naphta in *The Magic Mountain*. But more about this later.

In 1910, Thomas Mann was embroiled in a controversy about the forthcoming publication of his *Judennovelle* (Jewish story), entitled *Wälsungenblut* (The Blood of the Walsungs) in the *Neue Rundschau* because even the *Rundschau* editors were unhappy with certain Yiddish expressions, and too many friends seemed to recognize in the incestous twins of the story Mann's wife Katia and her twin brother Klaus. Mann turned to his brother for advice and support, and Heinrich encouraged the publication with the words: "the world be damned." The story was subsequently withdrawn from publication, and its author tried to explain to his brother the compelling reasons by stating that "in human and societal terms" he was not "a free agent any more." ..."Since then, I cannot get rid of a feeling of unfreedom,...and you no doubt will call me a cowardly burgher. It is easy for you to talk—*you are absolute*."[19] To be sure, Lukács would never have characterized Mann as a "cowardly burgher," but he did call him an *echter Bürger* (genuine burgher), and the notion certainly includes the idea of readiness to compromise. Lukács, on the other hand, "had it easy": he was absolute.

Even on the occasions when Thomas Mann found high praise for Heinrich's literary accomplishment, he did not let his brother forget that there were certain unwholesome traits he disliked immensely. When Heinrich's novel *Zwischen den Rassen* (Between the Races) was published in the spring of 1907, Thomas wrote to him on June 7, 1907: "*Zwischen den Rassen* is... my favorite among your works. Why?" He gives the following answer:

> Never have you shown such involvement, and despite all the discipline behind its beauty, this book has something gentle, human, devoted... But *the real grounds* for its unusual effect on me lie deeper, I think. It lies in the fact that [there is] ...no tendentiousness,...or derision, no trumpery and no contempt, no taking sides in spiritual, moral or aesthetic matters. ...[20]

Mann's critical judgment contains certain undesirable characteristics that found their way into his fictional world, in the description of some of his characters. At least in part, they characterize Lukács as well.

Lukács was well aware of all or some of the causal factors of the chasm between him and Mann, but he never let this knowledge impinge on his respect, admiration — indeed, his love of the life work of Mann. He finally let Mann know how he felt about him and his work in a letter of March 29, 1949: "I cannot describe the delight and satisfaction which your letter gave me," writes Lukács in answering Mann's letter to his wife. Then he goes on to confess:

> Throughout my entire literary activities I held on to the maxim regarding the writers I dealt with: "And if I love you what is it to you?" I strove to consider each writer—even the living and one dear to me—as a historical phenomenon, and I tried to explore his possible contribution to his own time and to future times through the content and power of form [*Formgebung*] in his work. In order to be able to do this, I had in principle to be inconsiderate of the effect of my critique on its "object." Precisely for this reason, it fills me with joy and gives me great satisfaction in human and personal terms that a writer like yourself finds himself correctly perceived and comprehended in my interpretation.[21]

Lukács thus used the opportunity supplied by an indirect communication to make a final appeal for direct contact. We have every reason to believe that this "letter of

43

homage" to a writer he respected and who was dear to him was not answered. The speculation that, by quoting Philine's famous line, Lukács may have in fact "invited Mann's refusal" cannot be verified.[22] What contraindicates the otherwise well-argued contention is the existence of other letters confirming not only Lukács's "yearning for a sustained intellectual intercourse with Mann," but also the fact that he made repeated efforts to reach that goal.[23] The one-sided correspondence is a story with both a *Vorgeschichte* and a *Nachgeschichte* (prehistory and posthistory). It all started with a letter of Mann to a Dr. Kerpely of Budapest, in which Mann devotes considerable space to "his critic," Georg Lukács:

> It caused me great surprise and delight to receive the news that Professor Georg Lukács has published a book on my work, and that this study is also on its way to me. It has been for a long time a great satisfaction to me that this extraordinary mind and prominent critic has time and again occupied himself with my life work. I assume that the book in question is made up of the essays devoted to my work from diverse points of view; among them, I consider the most significant the essay he wrote on the occasion of my seventieth birthday, entitled "Auf der Suche nach dem Bürger" [In Search of Bourgeois Man], which was published in the *I. L. [Internationale Literatur]*. Had I been in the possession of his address, I would have written him long ago in order to express my gratitude. May I ask you to convey to him my best wishes and warmest regards, and to tell him that I have retained the pleasant memory of our only personal meeting; I certainly wish there would be a chance for a second one.[24]

Dr. Kerpely obliged, forwarding not only Mann's greeting but also a copy of the letter itself. It was up to Gertrud Lukács to send an answer:

> My husband, Georg Lukács, has just left for a well-deserved vacation after a very strenuous trip to Paris, and this is why I am writing instead. He has received a copy of your letter to Dr. Kerpely and was very happy to learn that you have received the article he wrote for your 70th birthday and that you liked it. ... He would have been very interested to learn whether or not the letter accompanying the article reached you also? His book, *Thomas Mann*, is in fact not a collection of his diverse studies on your work but consists of two articles only: one of them is indeed the article you mentioned, entitled "Auf der Suche nach dem Bürger." The second study is a thorough analysis of your *Faustus* novel, which affected him deeply ....[25]

Gertrud Lukács's letter elicited a warm response from Mann. His answer of February 23, 1949, clearly indicates Mann's awareness of Lukács's mediating role. "Many thanks for your letter of the 12th of this month," wrote Mann. He went on:

> In the meantime I have read the first part of your husband's large-scale study of my *Faustus* that appeared in the *Aufbau* of Berlin with great pleasure and outright admiration. I look forward to its sequel with eagerness. It is indeed good

news that the book by Georg Lukács—which is already on my desk in the Hungarian language—will finally reach the western zones of Germany where they still have much to learn, in my belief.

I regret to have to tell you that the letter you mentioned having been sent by your husband never reached me. I wish he had a copy of it so that I may one day read it.[26]

Mann concluded his letter by expressing "highest esteem" for Lukács. Whether he ever received Lukács's letter, or a copy of it, remains open. What we know for certain is that Lukács made repeated attempts to initiate a critic–author exchange—to no avail. Even after admitting that Lukács had "profound" things to say about his work, and in the knowledge of the upcoming publication of a book devoted to him, Mann let the opportunity pass by to express his appreciation of Lukács's critical attention and promotion of his work by simply writing a few lines to Lukács himself. Mann's motives are difficult to guess; within a month, however, he felt compelled to respond to Lukács's latest reading of his work—by writing again to Gertrud Lukács. "Let me inform you," writes Mann, "that the *Aufbau* with the second part of your husband's study has reached me safely. I read this magnificent treatise from beginning to end with rapt interest; I was moved and also proud that my novel was able to inspire the most eminent critic of our time to write one of his best studies to date."[27] Mann's endorsement of Lukács the critic was not meant to be empty flattery; this is evident from a follow-up note sent to Bodo Uhse, editor-in-chief of *Aufbau*, in which Mann expresses his thanks to the journal for "publishing this impressive and thoughtful analysis by the Hungarian critic." He adds, "I am very proud that my work would inspire such a profound study by undoubtedly the most important literary critic of our time."[28] Shortly after, Mann must have received Lukács's letter containing his "declaration of love" with Philine's words. In light of these exchanges it should not surprise us that the question of Mann's reluctance to establish a corresponding—not to mention a personal—relationship was a vexing one for Lukács. He assumed that Mann may have harbored a feeling of unease *(Unheimlichkeitsgefühl)* toward him. The question that interested him even more, was whether this feeling had already existed in Lukács's "pre-Marxist period" (that is, pre-1918), and if so, why? My discussion of Mann's perception of Lukács, based on his early works, goes a long way to provide an answer. Further documentary evidence suggests, however, that Mann himself was well aware of the impropriety of his behavior. We sense his discomfort at not having contacted Lukács in the letter to Dr. Kerpely; another, earlier, letter to Hans Mayer, a noted German–Jewish literary critic, shows the writer quite ill at ease:

What I am most happy about is that [in your planned collection of essays on Goethe] I am in the company of a Georg Lukács. I am quite familiar with his Goethe studies and am ready to consider him to be the greatest living literary critic—on the account alone that he means so well toward me. His treatise in *Internationale Literatur,* entitled "Auf der Suche nach dem Bürger," eclipsed all other contributions that had been written on the occasion of my seventieth birthday; but then, he had on many occasions in the past extremely clever things to say about my work. *It is a shame that I have never thanked him for it.* I should at least send him now the *Faustus* book. How is one supposed to address him?[29] To be sure, Thomas Mann never made up for past omissions, not even after Lukács's "letter of homage" to him. This constitutes an unusual display of discourtesy on Mann's part. His discomfort in the face of "addressing" a critic living in communist Hungary is obvious, but cannot wholly explain his neglect of duty. What makes the problem even more puzzling is the fact that Lukács did not let the matter rest at that. According to a copy of his letter of June 29, 1949, he made a last attempt to elicit a response from Mann. "I have read with great pleasure and immense satisfaction," states Lukács, "your comments on my literary criticism in your book *Die Entstehung des Doktor Faustus.* It is especially gratifying to me that my perception of certain connections between your early works and later phase seems entirely plausible to you." Lukács hastens, however, to defend his silence—called "side-stepping" by Mann—on the *Joseph* novels, and remarks, "Since you have read my *Faustus* essay in the meantime, you must know by now that your hypothesis was incorrect in that the manner of composition *[Gestaltungsform]* of the *Joseph* novels did not impair my evaluating it within the framework of your life work." Lukács also felt prompted to enlighten the author that his "side-stepping" the treatment of the *Joseph* novels had nothing to do with being *linientreu* (toeing the Party line). Rather, the reasons were "quite simple and prosaic": Lukács did not have the complete set of the *Joseph* saga at his disposal at that time, due to the war situation and its aftermath in the Soviet Union. Thomas Mann must have accepted Lukács's argument that he could not "in good conscience" discuss such an important work without having read it as a whole. The concluding sentence of the letter, however, must have infuriated Thomas Mann: "You see, this is just another, albeit minor, example of how prejudicial notions about our 'totalitarianism' turn out to be just that—groundless prejudices."[30] As in the 1920s, Lukács severely reprimanded the admired writer, who was not known to accept such treatment easily; Lukács's last letter was destined to be ignored. If Lukács was insensitive to some of the real causes of the chasm between him and Thomas Mann, as Vaget suggests, the righteous tone employed in this letter is a case in point. It is well documented that even in the case of brotherly relations between Thomas Mann and Heinrich Mann, even a hint of reprimand or instruction *(Belehrung)* was not tolerated by Thomas. To be first called a *vornehmer Lügner* and then accused of being prejudicial could not contribute to the establishment of a fruitful personal relationship.

Thus it happened, as Lukács stated in his letter to Erika Mann, that Mann's "occasional remarks" remain the only visible expressions of his relationship to Lukács. The occasional remarks Lukács referred to were the often quoted "Letter to the Chancellor of Austria, Dr. Ignaz Seipel," in which Thomas Mann interceded for Lukács, the communist intellectual, whom he once met personally, and who once "spent a whole hour... propounding his theories" to him. "While he was talking he was right," wrote Mann, even "if the impression he left was an almost hair-raising abstractness...."[31] This was not the first intervention of Mann on behalf of Lukács. In 1919, he had raised his voice against the extradition of Lukács by Austria to Horthy's Hungary. The "young Lukács" received honorable mention in Mann's *Reflections of a Non-Political Man* (1918), and his name can be found in numerous diary entries and in letters to others (e.g., to T. W. Adorno); the "old Lukács" received Mann's homage through a congratulatory piece, "Georg Lukács," written for his seventieth birthday (April 13, 1955) by the eighty-year-old author, who died a few months later. Mann praised Lukács's *Sinn für Tradition und Kontinuität* as the trait he was most in empathy with.[32] Mann had devoted more than a page to Lukács in his *Story of a Novel: The Genesis of Doctor Faustus* (1949); his opinions and evaluations of Lukács's critical activities deserve to be quoted at length as they add up to a handy summation of Mann's perception of Lukács. "This Communist," writes Mann,

> who is deeply concerned with the "bourgeois heritage," and who can write fascinatingly and intelligently about Raabe, Keller, or Fontane, had earlier—in his series of essays on German literature in the age of imperialism—discussed me with intelligence and respect. In doing so he had maintained the capacity, indispensable in a critic, to distinguish between opinion and being (or action sprung from being), and to take only the latter... at face value. ... He sets me incontrovertibly side by side with my brother, and says: "Heinrich Mann's *Der Untertan* and Thomas Mann's *Der Tod in Venedig* can both be regarded as great forerunners of that trend toward signaling the dangers of a barbarous underworld existing within modern German civilization as its necessary complement."[33]

Mann finds this statement "so very good," first because, it lays bare "prophetically" the relationship between his early (1911) work and *Doctor Faustus* and second because "the concept of signaling is of the foremost importance in all literature and all study of literature." The writer and philosopher are in Mann's opinion, seismographs, reporting instruments, mediums of sensitivity. Mann concludes with both praise and scorn:

> [His] birthday essay, *The Search for the Bourgeois,* was a sociologic [sic] and psychological portrayal of my life and work grander in scale and manner than anything I have ever yet received, and hence arousing me to honest gratitude—among other things because the critic did not regard my work only in a historical light, but also related it to Germany's future. *It is strange,* however, that

in all such appreciations, no matter how benevolent, *by this particular school of criticism,* the *Joseph* novel is *consistently omitted or side-stepped.* That seems to spring from conformity to a faith, from *totalitarian* teachings. It is a pity.[34]

The positive evaluation of his literary critical career was "deeply gratifying" for Lukács just as Mann's reference to "totalitarian teachings" aroused his ire and brought in his reprimand. That Mann's appreciative words were not meant to be merely public gestures of politeness is proven by his very private comments. Mann's diary entry, for example, from Tuesday, June 2, 1936, includes the following sentence: "There was an extremely interesting article by Georg *von* Lukács (!) in the *Internationale Literatur* of Moscow on the topic of 'Thomas Mann on the Literary Heritage'." Another entry calls Lukács's article on Nietzsche as Fascist "significant," albeit a bit too "scholastic–Marxist."[35] These and similar utterances were not meant for public consumption but are still almost identical in their positive tone. Thomas Mann the author undoubtedly held Georg Lukács the critic in high esteem. But how did he perceive Lukács the man?

Regardless of his reluctance to establish a meaningful, direct personal contact, Mann referred on occasions to Lukács as a person in positive terms. He respected certain characteristics of Lukács, as his aforementioned letter to Dr. Seipel shows. In this letter, Lukács's conduct in his Vienna exile (1919–29) is characterized by Mann as not that of "small and indolent" spirits; he points out that Lukács is a "theoretical man through and through" and that his type of intellectuality is alien to Mann's own. However, he cannot but have "respect and moral admiration" for Lukács's "strong, ascetic and proud mind." Mann then admits that he was as much put off by Lukács's "hair-raising abstractness" as by his "ascetic nature" concerning both the "sensual and spiritual sphere."[36] A feeling of "otherness" must have existed in Mann's perception from the very beginning, that is, from the time when Mann became acquainted with Lukács's first work in German, *Soul and Form,* published in 1911. Even though there are numerous references to Lukács which point to steady and ongoing preoccupation with his work, scant reference is made to Lukács as a person. As Lukács himself said, things were very different in the Bertram case. Like himself, Ernst Bertram made an approach to Thomas Mann and the encounter blossomed into a longlasting close personal and intellectual relationship. A close reading of the Mann–Bertram correspondence reveals the basis for this closeness— a basis that did not exist in Lukács's case.

After the exchange of a few letters with Bertram, Mann came to realize that they were of the "same disposition" and were "of one mind" about most things. The extent of their closeness is shown by Mann's remark that Bertram's writing "stirred him so deeply" that he was close to tears. Not only did Mann feel "completely and finally understood" but indeed thought that his and Bertram's writings "complement each other." In due time, Bertram was invited into his house (1913) and even became the godfather of Mann's favorite daughter, Elisabeth. During World War I, when there was total estrangement between Heinrich and Thomas Mann, the latter wrote to Bertram: "I have so much to tell you! Please, come to visit us in Munich: an exchange with you would give me so much pleasure. I have almost nobody else!"[37] Mann also told Bertram that his brother is "of no use"; as a consequence, Bertram was chosen to be his "spiritual brother." While Mann publicly stated that Lukács's *intellektuelle Natur* was alien to him, he entrusted to his diary his feelings about Bertram's: "In the evening, read with emotion and a feeling of being completely 'at home' in Bertram's book to which I am attached as *it is so akin to my own*."[38] To be sure, events in 1933 and after brought along gradual estrangement between the "spiritual brothers": in 1933, Bertram was already listed among the "intellectuals who... see Hitler as the 'savior'. ..."[39] The contact with Bertram was not yet broken in 1935, as Mann's diary illustrates: "Katia's brother Peter gave a belated account of Bertram's visit, and the unbelievable tactlessness with which he went on about 'Germany's greatness,' and how everyone, even though they might disagree about details, must work together. His was once a sensitive mind!"[40] In light of Bertram's embracing the Nazi regime and its ideas, Mann remarks the same year, "I spent the morning after breakfast writing a long letter to Bertram in a friendly and ironic vein."[41]

Is it any wonder that Lukács was vexed by such preferential treatment? During my visit, he took the Mann–Bertram correspondence from the bookshelf and asked the by now rhetorical question: "Why did he never extend to me this kind of courtesy?" The only possible answer to Lukács's question has to be sought in the fact that for Thomas Mann, the very proper German bourgeois writer, Lukács represented an alien social, national, and personal sphere in which he could not feel at home. There is a passage in Mann's letter to Paul Amann, the Jewish–German philologist and cultural historian, which, in my opinion, may provide us with some clues. Referring to Franz Ferdinand Baumgarten's book on Conrad Ferdinand Meyer, Mann writes:

I am glad that you have read the Baumgarten. It is certainly a fine book. I would call your slight resistance to the revelation of secrets and to psychological indiscretions strikingly *conservative* [Mann's emphasis] (for what is more democratic than psychology?). *But when you consider that B. is a Budapest Jew* (very rich, incidentally, and also an invalid; he has to have a nurse constantly at his side and walks with a cane, a monocle in his eye)—*then you must agree that it has come off reasonably well.*[42]

This in a letter in which Mann praises Baumgarten's perceptive remarks about C. F. Meyer as a *"bourgeois manqué* and an artist with a guilty conscience," whose prejudices as a bourgeois "spoiled for him the freedom of the artist, and the temptations of his artistic blood weighted upon his bourgeois conscience." He, of course, recognized immediately that, like Lukács, Baumgarten was deeply influenced by his *Tonio Kröger*. Mann's remarks are instructive for several reasons. First of all, we see the artist's sharp observational and descriptive qualities at work, and also his tendency to use individual characteristics in the construction of representative types. We also learn what he thought about psychology and, finally, we have the remark about Baumgarten being a "Budapest Jew" who can be trusted to have a sense of indiscretion, eccentricity and sharpness because he comes from an alien sphere.

The fact that the early, pre-Marxist Lukács happened to be a man of "either–or," of the "extreme," who came from the non-German world and who in addition became a revolutionary, had to have an alienating effect on Thomas Mann and had to produce a chasm between him and Lukács.[43] To be sure, Lukács became for Mann a "revolutionary in the sense of maintaining tradition," and insofar as he was a safekeeper of traditional values, he earned Mann's respect and esteem. Both of them were intent upon preserving the great achievements of high bourgeois culture and transposing them into the new, postbourgeois era. Thomas Mann proudly declared himself to be "a man of the nineteenth century" and Lukács wrote in "praise of the nineteenth century."[44] This alone would account for the mutual respect which they retained even during the time of the deepest chasm caused by immediate political realities and actions. Thus the relationship between the two men can be summed up in two words: respect and distance.

PART TWO:
THE MAGIC MOUNTAIN AS A *"ZEITROMAN"* AND A NOVEL OF ITS TIME

Chapter 3.

SOURCES AND NARRATIVE TECHNIQUES IN MANN'S WORK:
THE FIGURE OF LEO NAPHTA AND *GENIALE WIRKLICHKEIT*

On May 10, 1939, Thomas Mann lectured on *The Magic Mountain* at Princeton University. The author sought to enlighten his American student audience about the genesis and conception of this admittedly "very German book." He characterized his 1924 novel as a "document of the European state of mind and spiritual *(geistige)* problematic in the first quarter of the twentieth century."[1] The fact that the documentation was proffered within the framework of the "charmed circle of isolation and invalidism" did not in any way detract from the validity or potency of the problems. On the contrary! The setting itself, the tuberculosis sanatorium at Davos, was seen by Mann as nothing but a symbol of certain social arrangements of the period:

> These institutions represent—or rather represented—a typical pre–war phenomenon They were only possible in a capitalist economy that was still more or less intact. Today, they have largely disappeared. *The Magic Mountain* became the swan–song of that form of existence.[2]

Thus, when Thomas Mann defined his novel as a *Zeitroman,* he meant it partly in a historical sense: the novel tried to capture the psychic temper, the "inner significance of an epoch."[3] But it is by no means contradictory to classify it as a *Bildungsroman* (novel of education and self–development) in the best German tradition; it is that also. Does not the book, after all, record the development of a "simple–minded young man," Hans Castorp, who has to undergo a heightening process *(Steigerung)* which enables him to have those sensual, moral and intellectual adventures he could not even dream of in his former everyday existence?

For all that, it should be kept in mind that the narrative takes place well before that epoch when a "certain crisis shattered its way through life and consciousness and left a deep chasm behind."[4] The "heightening process" our fictional hero goes through becomes a means of relating the author's own development; thus the novel itself is the artistic distillation of all the physical, spiritual, intellectual, and moral experiences that the author had in common with his nation and that "he had betimes to let ripen within him."[5] The artistic maturation process took twelve long years, from 1912 to 1924; everything Mann read, wrote, and struggled with during this time incalculably enriched the content of the work at hand; it also accounts for the "extreme pastness" *(hochgradige Verflossenheit)* of the narrative.[6]

No attempt will be made here to give an all-encompassing analysis of the novel as a *Zeitroman*. Probably more than any other work of Thomas Mann, *The Magic*

Mountain has been thoroughly subjected to evaluations in almost all its aspects and has stimulated some of the best critical essays and studies of the Thomas Mann literature, including one study on the "making and sources of the novel."[7] Mann was quite emphatic about one thing, namely, that "ten years earlier the book could not have been written nor would it have found readers" for the simple reason that "while the subject matter was not by its nature suitable for the masses," the problems it dealt with were burning questions for the bulk of "the educated classes." The prevailing crisis atmosphere had generated the feeling of distress which in turn enhanced the receptivity of the reading public. The author and his nation having shared the same problems and experiences made it inevitable that "the German reader [would] recognize himself in the simple-minded hero... of the novel."[8] But what was that period of general distress like—a period out of which grew a sizable literature that spoke of the crisis, decay, and decline of Germany and even of the West? One need only recall a few of the "typical" products of that special, high-tension atmosphere to perceive the vastness and diversity of reactions to the crisis situation. We have, for example, the artistic, creative, response in Mann's *The Magic Mountain* (1924); the cultural-critical and morphological treatise in Oswald Spengler's *The Decline of the West* (the first part published in 1918; the second, in 1922); the philosophical assessment of Ernst Bloch in his *The Spirit of Utopia* (1918); and at a later point, the treatment of the problematic situation from a perspective of the sociology of knowledge in Karl Mannheim's *Ideology and Utopia* (1929). These responses had their French and Spanish counterparts in Julien Benda's *The Treason of the Intellectuals* (1927) and José Ortega y Gasset's *Revolt of the Masses* (1930). Nor must we forget Georg Lukács's *History and Class Consciousness* (1924), which undoubtedly belongs to the most significant and influential products of the time, although it is a manifestation of a different kind of response that entailed a radically different solution. Louis Wirth (of the Chicago school of sociology) has come up with one of the best summaries of the prevailing sentiment of that period in his preface to the English language edition of Mannheim's work. Wirth calls that sentiment "the product of chaos and unsettlement," and he writes:

> It is doubtful whether such a book as this could have been written in any other period, for the issues with which it deals, fundamental as they are, could only be raised in a society and in an epoch marked by profound social and intellectual upheaval...[and] at a time when... people are not merely ill at ease, but are questioning the bases of social existence, the validity of their truths, and the tenability of their norms... *[Ideology and Utopia]* proffers no simple solution to the difficulties we face, but it does formulate the leading problems.[9]

No doubt, this summation of the *Zeitgeist* could just as well have prefaced Thomas Mann's novel; it is surely not by accident that Mann used almost identical words when pointing out the topicality *(Aktualität)* of his work. The nature of experiences shared are underscored by the titles Mann had given to the subchapters depicting the *Zeitgeist*: "Vom Gottesstaat und von übler Erlösung," "Der grosse Stumpfsinn," and "Die grosse Gereiztheit" (not quite accurately rendered by Mann's English translator as "Of the City of God and Deliverance by Evil"), "The Great God Dumps" and *Hysterica Passio*.

This epoch of social and spiritual upheaval marked the end of a long path that the German bourgeoisie and intelligentsia had covered since 1848, a path that in Thomas Mann's words, "led from the revolution to disillusionment, to pessimism and a resigned, power-protected inwardness *[machtgeschützte Innerlichkeit]*."[10] Taking Mann's reflections as a starting point, Lukács in his essay on Thomas Mann painted a panoramic view of Central European history culminating in the crisis situation of the post–World War I years, the period of the Weimar Republic; in Lukács's opinion, Mann most aptly described the problematic state of affairs both in his fiction and in his essayistic output. When the protecting power, the Wilhelminian empire, was frustrated in its first attempt at world conquest and finally collapsed, the German bourgeoisie was left to start anew with a "double ideological baggage": first the "front–line experience" and second, the hope that everything might be tried once again, with "improved methods, to bring off what eluded" it the first time. And Lukács saw the reason why the Weimar Republic attracted more enemies and opportunistic tolerance than real friends and partisanship in the fact that "German democracy after 1918 was not something that had been striven for and fought for, but the—unwelcome as it appeared—gift of an adverse destiny."[11] About the same time Lukács was advancing his ideas on German destiny in his Moscow exile, Thomas Mann in *his* exile in California was recalling the impressions and discussions in German intellectual circles of the post–World War I period relating to Germany's immediate and future possibilities, all of which were subsequently incorporated into *Doctor Faustus*:

> It is probably superfluous to state that not for a moment did they recognize the form of government which we got as a result of defeat, the freedom that fell in our laps, in a word the democratic republic, as anything to be taken seriously as the legitimized frame of the new situation. With one accord they treated it as ephemeral, as meaningless from the start, yes, as a bad joke to be dismissed with a shrug.[12]

While the two men were worlds apart geographically and ideologically, they came to an almost identical conclusion in their assessment of the historical situation—and of the German psychic temper.

In Lukács's opinion, there were painfully few Germans who tried to link up their newly experienced democracy with German history. Thomas Mann, because of his search for such a connection, was the "only bourgeois writer of this period for whom democracy became a matter of *Weltanschauung*, and a problem of German

Weltanschauung in particular." Therein lies also the reason for Mann's isolated position during the Weimar democracy; his complete and wholehearted break with German imperialism is mirrored in the artistic record of the time, in *The Magic Mountain*. Mann describes in fictional terms his own personal struggle *for* democracy and *against* decadence, Lukács asserts. War is waged on the pages of the novel "over the soul of the average German bourgeois," and the symbolic duels became the main theme of the book. As a result of his fearless struggle with the "bewildering pros and cons" of the *true* German tradition, Mann finally emerges as the educator of his country. He is the "educator *sui generis*," declares Lukács, because he eschews imparting to his pupils a "lesson from the outside"; Mann is an "educator in the Platonic sense of *anamnesis*: the pupil himself should discover the new idea within him, and bring it to life."[13] Accordingly, the inner search of the author and the intellectual duels of his novel are designed to make the average bourgeois think, to make him partake in his own *Steigerung*, that is, to help him undergo a transubstantiation. The instigators of the symbolic duels are "teachers" themselves and from very different schools of thought indeed: they represent possibilities inherent in these duels that are of the "intellectual–human, emotional–political, and moral–philosophical" kind.[14] Thomas Mann's own comments seem to confirm this Lukácsian interpretation of his work: in the same way that "realism" serves as a "vehicle for intellectual and ideal elements," the author notes, the characters are merely means to educational ends. "In effect, they are nothing but exponents, representatives, emissaries from worlds, principalities, domains of the spirit."[15]

Keeping in mind both the importance of "real material" (actual events, people, environment, and ideas) for the author and the symbolic role he assigns to his characters, the following analysis will focus on one *central* figure of the novel in an attempt to expose all of its *geistige* (spiritual–intellectual) components. In doing so, one important problem of Mann's creative process comes to the fore: the problem of *Anlehnung* (borrowing, appropriation, a reliance on factual information). The question arises: Where do the elements that taken together constitute the biography, the physique, the character, and the intellectual makeup of a fictional character come from?

Given the nature of Thomas Mann's artistry, it is certainly not a matter of idle curiosity to ask the question: Where did the author get his material? What were his sources and the influences? As is well known, Mann had to defend his compositional principles in the face of sharp criticism, indeed, against personal attacks, after the publication of his first novel, *Buddenbrooks* (1901). Among other things, he was accused of having shamelessly exploited and tactlessly exposed "foibles, large and small" (as one contemporary newspaper put it) of many of the burghers of his hometown, Lübeck, including members of his immediate family, in his artistic endeavor to re-create the particular reality of that place and time. He was said to have gone "too far" even for a "naturalist" in his quest for verisimilitude. In the essay "Bilse und Ich" (Bilse and I), Mann put up a vigorous defense.[16] For starters reference is made to such "authorities" as Goethe, Shakespeare, and Turgenev, who had borrowed widely and used living models for *Werther, Falstaff* and *Fathers and Sons*. Thomas Mann takes up the cause of artistic freedom in using "real material" and contends that it is not the material itself that is important but what the artist makes *of* it, through the "act of transcendence"; the process of transcendence alone decides whether the appropriation was justified or not—and constitutes art or not. Mann concedes, though, that "the artist may—in the heat of the creative process—become guilty of reckless exploitation [of real people]." Such a poetic ruthlessness is mitigated, however, by the author's "subjective absorption" into the character, by his "becoming one with his model" in a spiritual sense.[17] Eager to explain and to give clues to his literary technique, Mann elaborates on the technical aspects of the artistic process, which he calles *Aneignung und Kolportage* (appropriation and dissemination):

> The artist has the daemonic urge "to observe" in a flash and to perceive with painful wickedness every single detail which he deems *characteristic* in a literary sense, or meaningful *in a typical way* and which may open up vistas for him, marking the *racial, social and psychological characteristics*—and all this ultimately will become fruitful for the "work" at hand.[18]

Mann's admonition to his critics and readers necessarily follows: what was originally observed, that is, "reality," is only a "means to the exposition of an idea, an experience." He is quite emphatic about one thing: "The material" is nothing, the *Beseelung* (bestowing of a soul) is everything. "The precipitous difference between the two is what forever separates the world of reality from the realm of art."[19] As long as we do not lose sight of this differentiation, we do not have to apologize for trying to search for sources and "models" of a central figure. The main task should remain the illumination of the complexity of the *geistige* content of the work, and/or to shed light on a significant principle of creation of a work of art, and not to contribute to "literary gossip."[20] Accordingly, it is my intention to examine closely one of the central figures of the novel, the figure of Leo Naphta, and establish once and for all whether we are confronted here with a case of simple *Abbildung* (copy, portrayal) of one or several living persons or with a much more complex situation.

As is generally known, Thomas Mann had spent three weeks at a sanatorium at Davos in the summer of 1912 visiting his wife who had a mild case of tuberculosis. The impressions he gathered from the very special milieu of the place and his experiences there, all the details from the life of patients and personnel, contributed to the realistic background of the story he set out to tell. The results of that short stay were that he began the plans for his next work before he even had time "to recover from the mental exertions" that resulted from his completing *Death in Venice*. We have been told by the author himself, and by his wife, friends, and interpreters, that the many letters Katia Mann sent were full of details of the daily life of the sanatorium. As they were lost during World War II, we have no way to reconstruct their value as source material, but they surely supplied many of the realistic touches of the novel. Be that as it may, as early as July 24, 1913, Thomas Mann in a letter to Ernst Bertram outlined the main ideas of the planned book that was originally intended to be a "humorous pendant" or "satyr-play" to accompany the tragic story of *Death in Venice*. "This novel of mine," wrote Mann, "already takes shape, in the form of a satyrical counterpart to the D. i. V. piece."[21] The outbreak of World War I contributed to the novel in the form of additional details, problems, and an additional dimension. In this respect, Mann's letter of 1915 to Paul Amann (an Austrian literary critic) proves highly important in that the author speaks of a different, somewhat enlarged conception, and already suggests the antithetical character of the final version. Mann writes:

> Before the war I had begun a longish story... with pedagogical and political overtones, in which a young man comes up against the most seductive of powers, death, and runs the gauntlet, in a comic–gruesome manner, of the *intellectual polarities* of Humanism and Romanticism, progress and reaction, health and disease; but not so much that he may be forced to decide, as for the sake of orientation and general enlightenment. The spirit of the whole is humoristically nihilistic, and the bias leans rather toward the side of sympathy with death. *The Magic Mountain* is its name. ... For conclusion, for resolution—I see no other possibility but the outbreak of the war. As a storyteller *one cannot ignore* this *reality*, and I believe I have some right to it, since the premonition of it has been in all my conceptions. Look at *Death in Venice*! Good or bad—but is there a book that could stand in its place as more *pertinent to the times*?[22]

The comments' significance lies in its pointing toward the "pedagogical-political" overtones and its recording of the author's own development. In 1915, bias toward "sympathy with death" is still evident. This position has much to do with the ongoing struggle between Germany and the Western world, as Mann sees it. Indeed, the above cited letter to Amann not only explains what he means by linking up Romanticism and "sympathy with death" but also gives one of the best illustrations of the "great confusion" that reigns in Mann's thinking at that time: "The curious aspect of the matter is," confessess Mann, "that we all at bottom believe in the war, regard it as a judgment of God, and are prepared to accept its verdict beyond appeal." This is the case, in Mann's belief, because "all historic justice, all real modernity, future, certainty of victory, lie with Germany." He then goes on to claim—with a curious twist—that the "Western powers strike [one] today as... old, in fact old-fashioned." In that they represent "achieved imperialistic and cultural goals," they "seem aristocratic." Thus "a good deal of sympathy for the West which flourishes among us, allegedly for democratic elements, is in truth sympathy for the aristocratic, sympathy with old, noble, vanishing worlds: is Romanticism, 'sympathy with death'."[23] Similarly, Mann's letters to Bertram, the archconservative aesthete and professor of literature, speak affirmatively of the ongoing "Great War" because it will inevitably bring forth "great accomplishments." Just as passionately, the letters assail that "miserable bunch" of "humanitarian literary intellectuals" (Heinrich Mann, among them) who dare to speak of the struggle in malicious tones, and keep uttering such pompous phrases as "human freedom, peace, *pfui Teufel, noch mal* [the Devil may take them]!"[24] These outbursts of Mann, at times both passionate and unintentionally comical, were undoubtedly just one of the manifestations of that time of *grosse Gereiztheit* (great agitation; as *Hysterica Passio,* it became one of the sub-chapters of the novel) which finally compelled the author to stop working on his fiction and engage in the composition of the large-scale essayistic *Auseinandersetzung* with the issues which in due time became *Reflections of a Non–Political Man* (1918). This very work, considered by Mann to be a prelude, a sort of "preparation for the work of art" itself, had made it possible for him to finalize the conception of the novel by allowing him to "unburden" himself of a quantity of peripheral material; in short, it accomplished the "analytical–political" spade work.[25] What the author was able to unburden himself of included the kind of problems that he had at heart *(innig am Herzen lagen)* and also the problems of European conflicts and polarization. Together with Mann's "painful introspection," these problems or their presentation amounts to a panoramic view of the epoch in *The Magic Mountain.* Again it was Amann who received word of the progress the author made in the altering and expanding of the original concept of the novel. In his letter of March 25, 1917, Mann notes that "the young man" (Hans Castorp) is placed "between a Latin oratorical advocate of 'labor and progress'... and a despairingly witty reactionary—in Davos..."[26] In the chapter "On Virtue" of his *Reflections,* Mann gives a more detailed account of the growing complexity of the story, without hiding his opinion that "virtue" and "democracy" are nothing but "treason against tradition" *(Verrat am Kreuze)*:

> Before the war I had begun to write a little novel, a type of pedagogical story, in which a young person, landed in a morally dangerous locale, found himself between two equally quaint educators, between an Italian literary man, humanist, rhetorician and man of progress, and a somewhat disreputable mystic, reactionary, and advocate of anti-reason—he had the choice, the good youngster, between the powers of virtue and of seduction, between duty and service to life and the fascination of decay, for which he was not unreceptive; and the turn of phrase, "sympathy with death" was a thematic constituent of the composition.[27]

As the above cited passage demonstrates, first of all, that from almost the very beginning, the two educators as exponents of "experiences and ideas" were part and parcel of the conception. Without intending to analyze *Reflections* extensively, the point has to be made that the humanist rhetorician, the progressive intellectual, one of the formative components of the Settembrini figure, had, at that time, very negative connotations for Thomas Mann. But what should we make of the antagonist, characterized as the somewhat disreputable figure of the mystic, the reactionary? Just as the first "educator" stands for "virtue" and "service to life," the second symbolizes the powers of seduction and the "fascination of decay." This latter tendency is related to the concept of the "sympathy with death"—certainly "not a phrase of virtue and progress." Rather, it is the formula of all Romanticism and the "final word of romanticism."[28] Nothing can stop him, states Mann unequivocally, from seeing the *same intellectual force in romanticism* and *nationalism,* namely, the dominant force of the nineteenth century."[29] And as Mann himself pointed out time and again, his intellectual roots lay in the nineteenth century.[30]

Yet it is important to keep in mind that the views and ideas of the figures of *The Magic Mountain*—or, for that matter, of any of the fictional characters in Mann's oeuvre—are not identical with those of the author. Thomas Mann was, as is well known, too much a master of ironical *Aufhebung* and a formulator of the *sowohl-als auch* (not only–but also) positions to allow us to make straight equations between fictional statements and his own personal positions. Even in his essayistic work, Mann held on to the maxim that there are two sides to every thought. (Only in a very few exceptional cases such as his essay project *Geist und Kunst,* did Mann assume hasty and rigid positions—to his later chagrin.) As Hans Mayer observed correctly in his book on Mann's life and work, the author merely let his figures convey the range and nature of his own life experiences. In this way, the figures of the novel become the "elements of his own development."[31] Among the determining life experiences Mayer lists are the "Russian experience" *(Russland-Erlebnis),* the Hanseatic world, the Romantic, death–wish tendencies, the relationship to democracy, traces of the feud between the brothers, and, finally, the revolutionary events in Munich in 1919. Mayer categorically states that a substantial part of the spirit that "dominates *Reflections of a Non-Political Man* has subsequently gone into the figure of the dubious educator [Naphta]. It is thus not quite incorrect to say that the spiritual sum total of the author's youthful experiences speak to us through this figure."[32] Mayer's concluding remark that we can detect precious "little sympathy toward this character" by its creator seems, however, to contradict the preceding assertions. Almost as an afterthought, Mayer writes, "Maybe, just maybe, certain disagreeable personal encounters, acquaintances, have left their imprint on this character."[33]

Arthur Eloesser, who in 1925 published the first and only authorized biography of Thomas Mann, was also the first to discuss possible "living models" for the diverse figures of *The Magic Mountain*. According to Eloesser, Mann had not only made himself available for long sessions at his home but had also answered "with admirable straightforwardness" the questions put up to him in connection with his work. It speaks for the credibility of Eloesser's book that after having read it, Mann commented on it favorably and never objected to any of its statements, as was his wont in cases of disagreement. Mann told Eloesser that he had encountered both "Settembrini" and "Mme. Chauchat" at Davos; an Italian literatus was identified as the model for Settembrini and was, in Mann's words, a "charming braggart."[34]

Finally and due to the "originality of reality *[geniale Wirklichkeit]*, Mann was supplied with the "symbolic physiognomy" of Leo Naphta. He received it

> in the person of *a little, ugly Jew,* a *raving theoretician* of steely logic who, *on one occasion, defended* each and every form of *absolutism* and anti–individualism, beginning with the counter–reformation and Jesuitism up to the Communist revolution and Leninism, presented to him [Mann] in a dangerously ingenious combination.[35]

It is significant that Eloesser speaks of a "once only encounter" between Thomas Mann and the "living model" who imparted some decisive impressions to the author. Considering Eloesser's authoritative source, it is downright puzzling that the critical literature refers almost exclusively to Pierre-Paul Sagave's pioneering efforts in tracing the model(s) for the character of Naphta and completely ignores Eloesser's path-breaking work. Eloesser can be credited with first calling attention to one of the most important compositional principles of Thomas Mann, to the problem of *Anlehnung* (borrowing); he was also the first to point out that Naphta represents at least in part the romantic conception of *Kultur* that Mann advocated in *Reflections* as the positive antidote against the sickness of *Zivilisation*. But, Eloesser reminds us, the concept of *Kultur* has been placed in the company of such dubious matters as "oracle, slavery, human sacrifice, the Inquisition, black magic," and other assorted phenomena.[36] Such a loaded and nebulous concept of *Kultur* may indeed be linked up with the concept of *terror* and could envision "a classless Empire of God under Pope Gregory just as nicely as under Lenin."[37] Eloesser asserts—as Hans Mayer later did—that the spiritual essence of the Naphta figure bears the traces of the author's former viewpoints, which have been overridden in the meantime.[38]

Eloesser's critical sensitivity was praised by Mann. Nothing illustrates that fact better than his observations, first, that Leo Naphta, this "debauchee of absolutism" *(Wollüstige des Absolutismus),* symbolizes a yearning that was ready to welcome a (world) catastrophe if only it would "redeem mankind of its radical scepticism";[39] and second, that the future will surely tell "how much prophesy there is in Thomas Mann's great European novel."[40]

For all that, it was not the Naphta figure (and its model) that ignited the first heated discussion immediately after the novel was published; rather, the controversy swirled around the figure of Mynheer Peeperkorn, the most enigmatic of *The Magic*

Mountain characters. Nevertheless, the case as such is related to our discussion because certain aspects of the Naphta-Lukács controversy were a replay of this earlier one, and also because it allows a glimpse of Mann's narrative technique at work. Following the publication of the novel, Herbert Eulenberg asked the author to what extent Gerhart Hauptmann had served as the model for the character of Mynheer Peeperkorn. Horrified by the thought of a public spectacle, Mann immediately wrote to Eulenberg, imploring him not to make any such suggestion, not to "rub the public's nose in it," and thus "create a scandal." Mann warned that in case of such publicity

I should have to defend myself indignantly against the charge of having portrayed Gerhart Hauptmann in the character of the Dutchman. I did nothing of the kind! But in saying this I certainly want to tell the truth. At the time the character became a pressing matter for me, in the fall of last year, in Bozen, I was under the impress of the great writer's powerful and touching personality. This experience gave a certain stamp to the characterization of Peeperkorn, to some of his outward features. I cannot and would not deny it. ... [Peeperkorn is]... *a product of imagination involuntarily and half consciously colored by a powerful real experience.*[41]

Thomas Mann stated emphatically that "the idea and the essential features of the character, as a contrasting figure,... was of course established long before I met Hauptmann." The author begged Eulenberg in vain: the scandal broke and Mann was compelled to send a letter of explanation to Hauptmann, asking his forgiveness. Mann made his appeal as one artist to another:

I have sinned against you, I was in need, was led into temptation and yielded to it. The need was artistic: *I was seeking a character* vital to my novel long since provided for in its scheme, but *whom I did not see, did not hear, did not hold.*[42]

It has been three decades since the question was asked again about another "powerful real experience" that lent some decisive features to the figure of Leo Naphta. Maurice Colleville, a French scholar, reviewed two Lukács books in the September 1950 issue of *Etudes germaniques* and made this surprising remark: "M. Lukács,... on essure qu'il a fourni à Thomas Mann l'original de Naphta du 'Zauberberg'...."[43] Colleville may have been acquainted with the 1934 dissertation of his colleague Pierre–Paul Sagave, who discussed the possibility of living models for the figure of Naphta; it is almost certain that Sagave read Eloesser's book, the only Thomas Mann biography, and that his interest was kindled by Eloesser's allusions to certain "real experiences" of Mann, with their far-reaching consequences for his fiction. In 1934, Sagave approached the author himself and asked for confirmation of possible models for his fictional characters. Mann responded:

The figures of both Settembrini and Naphta are as good as a product of imagination; the reality of life had only minor hints [*Anhaltspunkte*] to offer. I have never encountered a communist Jesuit, but that such a combination is both possible and plausible seems to be borne out by the intellectually extremely well-rounded view of life [Weltbild] of Herr Naphta. The human characters of both "emissaries"—for whom, as I said, some vaguely suggestive models had indeed crossed my path—follow from their respective dispositions which were of the cheerful-humane kind in the first case, and of the ascetic-violent kind in the other case. Or to put it better: [character and disposition] were in harmony and well-suited to each other, fictionally speaking.[44]

Upon completion of his dissertation, Sagave sent it to Thomas Mann, who remarked good-humoredly that had he read everything Sagave attributed to him, the dialogues and intellectual duels between Settembrini and Naphta would have yielded to even more cumbersome excesses.[45] Almost twenty years later, preparing his work for publication, Sagave again approached Mann for a "final clarification" concerning the Naphta-Lukács constellation. Sagave was particularly intent on finding out to what degree the political theoretical works of Lukács and Carl Schmitt had left their stamp on Naphta's line of argumentation. Thomas Mann replied:

I have to answer both of your questions in the negative. Neither in the 1920s nor ever did I read any of the political writings of Lukács; I only read his literary criticism. *History and Class Consciousness* is unknown to me. And as to Karl [sic] Schmitt, I have only heard about him.

It is understandable to think that I had studied all these things while working on *The Magic Mountain.* There are things in it, such as the nature of freemasonry and the education of a Jesuit, which *had* been studied. But most of it I got from what was around me. So many things were in the air then—and all of those problems were already once thoroughly discussed in my *Reflections of a Non-Political Man,* as a kind of preparation for the novel.

I beg you not to bring up Lukács's name in connection with *The Magic Mountain* and Naphta. He had only high praise for the novel, and it obviously never occurred to him that he could be regarded as the model for Naphta. I don't want anybody to put such an idea into his head. Imagination and reality are as dissimilar as can be, and quite apart from the differences in origin and biographical details, the real Lukács had nothing to do with the mixture of Communism and Jesuitism which is my invention and which, intellectually speaking, is quite a good one.[46]

Just as in the case of Gerhart Hauptmann and in almost identical words, the author implored the scholar not to make public his "findings" and name a "living model." And in this case too, the author's request was not honored. Sagave's book, which came out in 1954, contains the following assertion: "S'il est nécessaire d'insister sur les similitudes entre Lukács et Naphta—le physique, l'art de la discussion et peut-être aussi certaine tendence au déviationnisme." Sagave claimed he had obtained a picture of Lukács in the 1920s which helped him to "establish certain similarities" between Lukács and Naphta's physiognomy in addition to their manner of argumentation:

Il est aisé d'en vérifier l'exactitude en comparant l'aspect physique de Lukács, d'après une photographie prise vers 1920, au "signalement" que Thomas Mann donne de Naphta et qu'il résume dans le qualificatif "acéré," épithète servant à désigner le nez, la bouche, les verres de lunettes et enfin la manière de raisonner de celui-ci.[47]

In his short essay, "Der Schneider Lukacek" (Lukacek the Tailor), Henry Hatfield repeats Sagave's "findings" and emphasizes the theme of "cutting sharpness"; Hatfield concludes that one can grasp the essence of the novel much better if one is aware of the Lukács components in Naphta.[48]

About the same time, Karl Kerényi, the eminent Hungarian classicist and mythologist, published an article, "Thomas Mann und der Marxist," which was later expanded and included in his collection of essays *Tessiner Schreibtisch* (At my Desk in Tessin). Kerényi makes no bones about having been encouraged to explore another "literary gossip" from Klaus Pringsheim's (Katia Mann's twin brother) publication of "family gossip" relating to a short story by Mann, "The Blood of the Walsungs."[49] In what turned out to be a rather polemical piece, Kerényi retraces Sagave's research and then gives vent to his immense personal dislike of Lukács. He upbraids the grand bourgeoisie of Budapest for its boundless admiration of Thomas Mann in particular and for German literature in general—an admiration that was "most ardently displayed by the son" of this Jewish bourgeoisie, Georg Lukács.[50] In Kerényi's opinion, Lukács's admiration for Mann was not motivated by artistic considerations: it had "other reasons," namely, the "fateful propensity" of the Budapest (Jewish) bourgeoisie for "everything German, in sharp contrast with the Francophile inclinations of the Hungarian poets and writers."[51]

The widely held notion that the question of the Lukács–Naphta connection has finally been settled for good was based on Thomas Mann's letter of December 24, 1947, to Max Rychner, a Swiss literary critic, in which Mann commented:

Lukács, who is so well disposed to me (and who obviously did not recognize himself in Naphta), may have written the best article on the occassion of my seventieth birthday, published in the *Internationale Literature;* but true to the party line he left my *Joseph* unmentioned.[52]

This sentence contains the implicit statement that Lukács could rightfully have recognized himself in Naphta. But let us first examine the assumption that Lukács remained well disposed toward the writer because he failed to "recognize himself in Naphta." Being interested in the correctness of Mann's assumption, I put the question to Lukács outright in my conversation with him. He said:

Look, I don't have the slightest doubt—and indeed, never have had—that the Naphta-figure "borrowed" certain features of mine—and not even outward ones. I must say, though, that Thomas Mann went about this business in a particularly gentle and cautious manner: he emphasized in Naphta's outer appearance the very things that were in direct opposition to my appearance. What I mean is that not even my greatest enemy would dare to say that I was an elegantly attired man. I should say that in this case Thomas Mann committed a kind of "falsification."[53]

In the light of Lukács's statement and attitude, one must agree with Ehrhard Bahr's assessment: "It is a tribute to Georg Lukács's artistic insight and humanity that he did not feel insulted by the obvious similarities. Not all of Thomas Mann's models were able to muster such magnamity."[54]

While Lukács was willing and able to display this degree of forbearance toward the author, he was less tolerant toward interpreters and scholars who viewed the connections as a "literary scandal," as gossip, or as a sensationalizing of the case—not to speak of those who instead of examining the probity of the Lukács components in Naphta started to interpret Lukács's life work as a reflection of Naphta's views. In a letter to Hans Mayer, Lukács angrily declared: "You do, indeed, perform a useful service in playing down the Naphta angle. It starts to become a farce when [critics and interpreters] undertake to interpret my work from the vantage point of Naphta."[55]

This survey of the literature dealing with the question of the Naphta-Lukács connection leads to the conclusion that none of these treatises succeeded in pinpointing the Lukács components in Mann's fictional character—or even attempted to go beyond mere summary statements and assumptions. The analysis of the features—biographical, physical and intellectual—which Lukács may have lent to the figure was still outstanding. To find a satisfactory answer, one has to go beyond conjecture and beyond the purely philological, to the utilization of source material. As Saueressig pointed out in his study of the sources of *The Magic Mountain,* we do not have an extensive collection of source material at our disposal as is the case with *Doctor Faustus.*[56] Much, if not most, of the documentation of readings, personal experiences, notes, and so forth were left behind in Germany in 1933 and were lost. Mann's enormous correspondence is still the best extant source; however, a substantial part of it remains either unpublished or untranslated. The author's personal library in the Thomas Mann Archive in Zurich yields numerous clues, as did my conversations with Lukács, Katia Mann, and others.

It seemed to me advisable to ascertain first other possible sources of influence, because once the sources were established for the characteristics of Naphta, which could not—and *did not*—originate in the "Lukács-experience" of Mann, our investigation could more easily be narrowed down to those specific features that *did* come from Lukács.

To begin with, one prominent characteristic of Thomas Mann's life work should be mentioned: that the figures, types, motives and relations in Mann's fictional world represent a "multitude of possibilities" *(Vielfalt der Möglichkeiten)*. As Max Rychner noted, they all keep appearing and reappearing in ever different and expanded variations, fulfilling their functions and disappearing (at least temporarily) in the "giddy, rotating progression of the story."[57] After decades of gestation, an inconsequential element of a story may evolve into an important motive of the next one. The same is true with regard to the figures. One main character may have grown out of a mere sketch of a preceding one, and almost "all of the figures [of diverse stories and novels] relate to others."[58] The adaptation of this artistic method is not accidental in the case of a writer who creates "organically," as Thomas Mann does.[59] The artistic phenomenon can best be characterized by the term *ideal-typical presentation*—to use a social scientific concept. It has been noted that the main characters of *The Magic Mountain* turned out to be exceptionally well drawn and marvelously apt because "they made visible in an ideal-typical way the essence of whole movements, directions and ideologies" of the period.[60] The application of Max Weber's conceptual tool is not unwarranted in this case. In his *Wissenschaftslehre,* Weber addressed himself to the problem of the possible standards governing judgments and the question of the validity of value judgments *(Werturteile)* that underlie the utterances of scholars and critics, writers and policy-makers alike. Weber's social scientific approach to the problem becomes relevant in that his conceptual construct is, in the final analysis, comparable to what we call the "poetic prototype." Weber speaks of a conceptual pattern evolving "into a cosmos, which is conceived as an internally consistent system"; this construct is substantially a *utopia*. This utopian construct is "arrived at by the analytical accentuation *(Gedankensteigerung)* of certain elements of reality."[61] Utopia can be many things: a historical or artistic period as well as the analytical construction of a personality. The relationship of the construct to reality, says Weber,

> consists solely in the fact that where... relationships of the type referred to by the abstract construct are discovered or suspected to exist in reality to some extent, we can make the *characteristic* features of this relationship pragmatically *clear* and *understandable* by reference to an *ideal type.* ... It is not a *description* of reality but it aims to give unambiguous means of expression to such a description.[62]

Weber elaborates about the method that makes it possible to arrive at an ideal type:

> An ideal type is formed by the one-sided *accentuation [Steigerung]* of one or more points of view and by the synthesis of a great many diffuse, discrete, more or less present and occasionally absent *concrete individual* phenomena...into a unified *analytical* construct *(Gedankenbild)*. In its conceptual purity, this mental construct cannot be found empirically anywhere in reality. It is a *utopia*.[63]

We have no grounds for believing that Mann had been acquainted with Weber's article. And it is even more surprising to see the main ideas of a social scientific paper undergo a "poetic transformation" in Mann's hands. In this connection, I wish to take issue with those critics and scholars who dismiss the author's own essayistic exculpations or self-interpretations from consideration.[64] There are numerous passages in Mann's essays that can shed light upon the process of composition, and we ignore them at our peril. In his large-scale essay *Reflections of a Non–Political Man*, Mann comes to speak of his (constructivistic) attempt at a "comedy in novel form that is called *Royal Highness*." The author's comments on his artistic intentions and compositional method amount to an unconscious reformulation and application of the Weberian train of thought:

> Suddenly here is a book—not at all the result of "becoming," "growth," far removed from all luxuriance and exuberance, *a thoroughly formed book,* attuned to measure and proportion, *rational,* lucid, *dominated by an idea, an intellectual formula* that is reflected everywhere, repeatedly called to mind, made as alive as possible, that seeks by a hundred details to *create the illusion of life* and that still never reaches life's original... fullness.[65]

Royal Highness is dominated by the idea of an "austere happiness," a *utopia* which had to be arrived at by an "analytical accentuation" of many details. As to the synthesis, it is personified in the figure of Klaus Heinrich; a different possibility (of synthesis) and direction manifests itself in the character and philosophy of Dr. Raoul Überbein. (More about this in Chapter Six.) In a letter to Hugo von Hofmannsthal, Mann described his intentions and method: "I cannot, it seems to me, elevate the novel better than by *making it a construction to bear ideas.*"[66]

What Thomas Mann had to say about his second novel is even more valid for his third, *The Magic Mountain*. To be sure, the formulation of a synthesis, or utopia, proved to be impossible. But of the possibilities, or directions, was made "visible in an ideal–typical way" in the figure of Leo Naphta. It may not be too farfetched to state that Naphta represents the pinnacle in the ideal–typical presentation of a fictional character: the extreme features of his life story and the cutting sharpness of his physical attributes herald the fully developed pungency of the personality and intellectuality of Naphta.[67]

As will be shown, the figure of Naphta did not surface from a void. Nor did it disappear without a trace in Mann's oeuvre. Starting from the assumption that Naphta has his precursors as well as his descendants, it should be of primary interest to establish the kinship for a simple but compelling reason: a survey of common or related features of diverse characters will enable us to pinpoint the specific *fictional prototype* that answers for a particular idea—the idea of the *Sonderfälle des Lebens* (cases of exceptionality) which is elaborated upon in *Royal Highness*.[68] If we examine Mann's oeuvre with this particular aspect in mind, we should be in a position not only to sort out the Lukács components in Naphta but also to see more clearly why and in what way the person of Lukács supplied Mann with the badly needed "symbolic physiognomy."[69]

Thus it is well to approach the problem of the Naphta Lukács connection with some things in mind: first, that Mann needed the "originality of reality" in order to give form to his ideas, that is, in order to give shape to a character that was provided for in the narrative scheme but that he had yet "to see, to hear and to hold"; and second, that in the case of Naphta, Mann encountered the genius of reality, the living model, in the person of Georg Lukács. This is not to say, however, that Lukács *is* Naphta or vice versa; what is meant is that as in the case of the Gerhart Hauptmann–Mynheer Peeperkorn constellation, a "product of imagination [was] involuntarily and half-consciously colored by a powerful real experience."[70]

Although Thomas Mann had repeatedly been a guest at the home of Lukács's parents, he met the son, Georg Lukács, in person for the first time in January 1922. The opportunity presented itself during Mann's three-week lecture tour, which took him "to the East" (as he put it) and on which he read his great essay *Goethe and Tolstoy* in Prague and Budapest. While at the latter city, he stayed "as a houseguest of the well-known patron of arts, *Hofrat* Josef von Lukács," a German-language Budapest daily reported.[71] He left Budapest and arrived in Vienna on January 17 and delivered the same lecture there in the evening. He was back in Munich on January 21, 1922, as his letter to André Gide attests.[72] Thus, their personal encounter must have taken place between January 18 and 20. As Lukács told me, Thomas Mann initiated the meeting:

It was simply this: before Mann came to Vienna, he visited my father in Budapest, and in this connection he wanted to talk to me. It so happened that we had a lively conversation in his hotel room, which lasted for about one and a half to two hours. As to the impression that our meeting left on Thomas Mann, all anybody needs is to read the letter he wrote to Dr. Seipel, the then Chancellor of Austria. As he said in that letter, "As long as he was talking he was right," and "He propounded his theories to me," and so forth. It is all there really.... [See Appendix.]

Concerning the topic of their conversation, Lukács said:

In the main, we discussed the problematic situation of art, the mission and function of art, especially of the literary art, in that period. About the historico-philosophical particularities of that talk, I cannot say much anymore—understandably. But there is no doubt in my mind that that was the sole topic of our conversation. As to the political role that I had played during the events in Hungary in 1919—we did not really go into that. ... We discussed mainly what the function of literature or art should be in our world at that time.[73]

Lukács conceded that he held an extremely pessimistic view about the situation of art, which was to be expected; after all, he said, "We should not forget that we are talking about the early 1920s, shortly after the collapse of the Soviet Republic [in Hungary].[74] Therefore, I could not but be a pessimist concerning the possibilities of art. I did not give art a real chance." In order to fully comprehend what Lukács meant by this statement, it is necessary to know that whenever Lukács was alluding to the possibilities for art (especially during and after World War I), he was not only, or even primarily, thinking in aesthetic terms but in ethical ones. Thus, he alluded here to the chances of principled action in an "amoral time"—a time to which he applied Fichte's dictum by calling it "the age of absolute sinfulness."[75] As he recalled in his preface to the reissue of his *Theory of the Novel* (1963), Lukács had already considered in his pre-Marxist period "the problems of... form" as the "mirror image of a world gone out of joint," and art as a symptom "of the fact that reality no longer constitutes a favourable soil for art."[76] These recollections of Lukács culminated in the statement that his typology of the novel was a "subversive work," grounded in his romantic anticapitalism and based on a "highly naive and totally unfounded utopianism."[77] Such feelings were obviously no longer present when Lukács met Thomas Mann in a mood of "extreme pessimism." If not directly, then, at least in this sense the topic of politics—or better, the political role as one's conduct in life—should have entered their discussion. For this reason—and also in order to find out whether the view that Thomas Mann was totally unsympathetic toward the character of Naphta is correct—I pressed Lukács on the issue of political discussion and asked whether Mann voiced any negative sentiments. Lukács said:

Look, it was precisely about the political aspect of our conversation that we came to a sort of understanding. I should say, the political aspect turned out to be the positive aspect of the conversation. All I can say today with some certainty is that Thomas Mann was on my side in this matter. How could I remember the details of our discussion after almost fifty years? As you know, so much depends on the accentuation, on the subtle coloring of the words .... But the positive must have outweighed the negative in order to leave that general impression on me.[78]

Be that as it may, not long after this meeting, Thomas Mann wrote in a letter to Ernst Bertram, dated June 2, 1922:

Leo Naphta, a partly Jewish Jesuit *has surfaced,* and is constantly engaged in sharp disputations with Herr Settembrini; and one of these days it will inevitably lead to an intellectual duel.[79]

Is this a coincidence? I don't think so. It is probably nearer to the truth to suggest that Lukács's personality had provided a powerful stimulus. Eloesser's remark about a "one-time encounter" that put its stamp on the Naphta figure and supplied the "symbolic physiognomy" underscores this assumption. It is my conviction that the Naphta figure took shape after the author encountered Lukács; that is, after Thomas Mann finally "saw, heard and held" the character.

Chapter 4.
LEO NAPHTA—JEW, JESUIT, COMMUNIST:
ORIGINS AND LIFE STORY

While defending his poetic technique of relying on living models for his fictional heroes, Thomas Mann also called attention to the artistic process of transformation that is meant to disguise as well as transcend real experience. In the case of the figure of Naphta, "Description and reality were as dissimilar as could be," especially in relation to "differences of origin and biographical details" of the fictional figure and the "real Lukács."[1] Mann's dialectical irony transposed the character from Lukács's "Jewish upper-middle class milieu in Budapest into the world of eastern European Jewish orthodoxy."[2] Indeed, Lukács's roots and background appear far removed from Naphta's. Even Sagave, who was intent on finding as many parallels as possible between Lukács and Naphta, had to admit that there was "rien de plus dissemblable que les origines de Naphta, fils d'un sacrificateur de Galicie, et celles de Lukács, fils de la grand bourgeoisie...."[3] These disclaimers to the contrary, points of agreement do exist: both Naphta and Lukács are of Jewish origin, underwent conversion to Christianity, had an intellectual—albeit not strictly academic—career, and "came in from the East."

Naphta's life story is told in the sub-chapter entitled "Operationes Spirituales," long after we have become thoroughly acquainted with his physical traits as well as his intellectual makeup and manner of argumentation. Thus, Naphta's origin and development fill out the picture and provide the basis and explanation for everything that has already been told about him. Within the narrative structure, it appears entirely logical that Naphta's life story is told after the figure fulfills its narrative function and disappears from the center stage.

"Leo Naphta came from a little place near the Galician–Volhynian border. His father, of whom he spoke with respect, ... had been the village *schochet,* or slaughterer," begins Naphta's biography.[4] The father, Elie Naphta, who is described as a "starry eyed," critical, "brooding and refining spirit," was above all an "outsider" even within his own religious community. He was surrounded by an aura of "uncanny piety" that evoked respect and fear—and proved his undoing. He died a horrible death following the "unexplained" death of two gentile boys: he was found "nailed crucifix-wise on the door of his burning home" (441). His tubercular wife and five children—including Leo, or Leib, as he was still called—flee the country in terror and settle in a small town of the Vorarlberg; she becomes a factory worker and the family lives in abject poverty. Leo stands out among his brothers and sisters, whom he despises as he did his mother. Delicate and blessed with enormous mental gifts,

Leo has "lofty ambitions and an ardent yearning" for the "more refined side of life." His extraordinary intelligence and diligence so impress a learned rabbi that he is taken on as a private pupil. From him Leo learns Hebrew, the classics, mathematics and logic. Early, Leo displays a great degree of "irritability, captiousness, scepticism and [a penchant for] cutting dialectics." He devours Hegel and Marx, makes the acquaintance of a politician's son, and soon applies "his passion for logic to the field of social criticism." The boy's turn of sophistry and insatiable intellect lead to interminable *disputationes* with his patron, and as a result, to his dismissal. Just when he is coming of age and thus "turned loose," Leo's mother dies; at sixteen, completely alone, and facing an uncertain future, he leaves his brothers and sisters to their fate "with the callousness of a born aristocrat" (444).

Following an accidental meeting with a Jesuit, who is on the staff of the *pensionnat* of the Society of Jesus and who fully appreciates Leo's "keen and tortured intellect" and the "caustic elegance" of his thinking, Leo is invited to enter the school (443). The milieu has great appeal for him, with "its discipline and elegance, its quiet and good cheer, its well-being, its intellectual atmosphere and the precision of its... regimen" (444). Leo Naphta finally feels "at home" and secure. *"Like many gifted people of his race,"* we are told, *"Naphta was by instinct both aristocrat and revolutionary"* (443, emphasis added). As he expresses his desire to study theology and to become a full member of the Society, Leo is admitted to the *noviciate*. However, his health suffers, but not from the environment—rather, "from within." The disease he has inherited—tuberculosis—makes his stay in the college in the flatlands impossible; Leo is sent to the mountains for an extended cure at the expense of the Society. When he is introduced in the story, he is in his sixth year there; his life is "colored by some activity as Latin master in the Davos gymnasium" (445–447.) Thus, "Brother Naphta" never reaches his goal, full priesthood, and his existence remains marginal.

Introduced to Hans Castorp by Settembrini, Leo Naphta succeeds Settembrini as a "second educator" of the young man. The learning process grows out of the extensive and long-winded intellectual contest between Settembrini and Naphta. An exceptionally acrimonious and embittered debate culminates in a real duel; after Settembrini—true to form—refused to fire a shot, a desperate Naphta ends his own life by blowing his brains out.

What are the main characteristics of this strange life story? Like Mme. Chauchat, Naphta comes from the eastern region of Europe; unlike her, he is a perpetual outsider within the hemisphere and its national entities. He is a Jew and exposed constantly to the threat of physical annihilation—as his father's fate demonstrated. No stranger to hunger and deprivation, he is well aware of the value of self-reliance. His extraordinary intelligence and perseverance help him overcome these impediments. Naphta's repression of his roots and traditions (including family and religion) is motivated by his craving for "higher forms of existence." The path of full assimilation is not to lead to the desired goal, however, for reasons that lie beyond Naphta's power. He never reaches the stage of full ordination, the sign and symbol of full membership in the chosen community, because of his illness. But the disease— handed down to him from his mother—constitutes his only ancestral inheritance. It is well to remember that the disease is of symbolic significance in the novel; it is a precondition, the basis and vehicle for the experiences to come in *The Magic Mountain*. Naphta's origins condemn him to life as an outsider; his disease makes for an "exceptional existence." Even in his capacity as "educator," Naphta forever remains an outsider: first, his college career within the Society comes to naught; second, he is loosely attached to an educational institution that in itself is marginal—a gymnasium for tubercular boys; and finally, he is to become a very special kind of "private tutor" to Hans Castorp. Naphta's suicide appears an inevitable and suitable end to a doomed life experiment, and it "fits" Naphta's character. We may recall what Hans Castorp says to Joachim after their very first meeting with Naphta: "Do you think he would have the courage, *'de se perdre ou même de se laisser dépérir'*?" (386). Indeed, Naphta has the courage of his convictions.

And what of the elements of the biography? In every respect, Naphta is a much more complex type than Settembrini. Naphta the thinker represents many facets of modern currents of thought as well as some entrenched views of a bygone era. Consequently, his biography is a blend of elements which in Mann's fictional world have long been the necessary ingredients of the life story of an outsider or "exceptional case," only to be resurrected in parts, rearranged, and further enhanced and enriched by newly acquired knowledge and experiences of the author. Thus, once we have succeeded in establishing how the details of Naphta's life relate to other works (and life stories) and then determined the contributions from other source material, we will be in a better position to estimate the extent and nature of Lukács's contribution, that is, to see more clearly how the biographical details of the "real Lukács" enriched and filled out this fictional biography.

There are several principal points in the Naphta biography that were conceived as significant traits because they are, as Mann noted, "typical," or "meaningful in a typical way" by denoting "social," "racial," and other characteristics which may "open up perspectives" for the author.

We first encounter the Jewish outsider type in embryonic form in one of Mann's earliest stories, "Der Wille zum Glück" (Will to Happiness), written in 1896 and even now not translated into English. Although the artistic merits of this story are few, it is an interesting and valuable piece in that it offers many clues to the nature of Mann's more mature works. In quick succession, the following narrative devices are employed: the use of autobiographical details, from South American ancestry to Hanseatic heritage (see *Buddenbrooks, Tonio Kröger* and *Doctor Faustus*); the motive of "exceptionality" and the love of a native son for the exotic "other" because he is an "opposite and foil" *(Tonio Kröger);* the tentative use of "montage technique" by the verbatim inclusion of a line from Heine's poem "Underworld" (a technique fully developed in *Doctor Faustus*); disease as a symbol of otherness; and, finally, the introduction of the figure of the quintessentially other in the person of Baron Stein, who was unquestionably of "Semitic origin" and belonged to the *Geldadel.* To be sure, the figure of Baron Stein is crudely drawn; the "racially typical" features amount to a few biographical snippets and the merest sketch of physical appearance. Baron Stein is a newcomer to Munich who has made his fortune at the Vienna Bourse; nothing more is revealed about him. His wife is simply "a little ugly Jewess" who wears "large diamonds in her ears" (a description quoted verbatim in *Buddenbrooks*). A more detailed and sophisticated description of the type is to be found in "The Blood of the Walsungs," the object of heated controversy.[5] There Baron Stein reappears as the enormously wealthy Herr Aarenhold, who makes no bones about where he came from: "He had been a worm, a louse if you like. ... [He] had been born in a remote village somewhere in the East. ..." Proud of the fact that he "did it" entirely on his own, he now feels "like an enchanted prince" who fully enjoys life's amenities. He talks a lot about his origins and achievement, knowing well that his children, the second generation, despise him "for his origins, for the blood which flowed in his veins and through him in theirs; for the way he earned his money." Aarenhold makes it clear that it was his capacity to realize his situation so fully that "had become the ground of that persistent, painful, never-satisfied striving which had made him great."[6] In this early work the striving is directed almost exclusively toward the material aspect of the "higher existence," but there are traces of the coming "decadence" (first mentioned by Baron Stein and later so magnificently formulated in *Buddenbrooks*): Aarenhold is given to "acquiring old books, first editions, in many languages, costly and crumbling trifles, with which he spends much time in his library."[7] In sum, Herr Aarenhold's origins go back to the world of the *shtetl,* and, as far as he is concerned, the world is welcome to know. For all that, in the story he represents the assimilated bourgeois who now belongs—at least in his own consciousness. The artistic realization of the outsider theme is more accomplished and yields many more details in Mann's next work, *Royal Highness* (1906). As the author himself noted, the novel is "an advanced step"; it is a remarkable expansion of the idea of the isolated, lonely, but elevated existence of all those Mann calls "special cases," "different," or "exceptional existences."[8] The novel has often been called a rather lightweight, straightforward tale, and a letdown after *Buddenbrooks*. Some critics read the story as a reformulation of the *Tonio Kröger* problem, albeit with a prince as hero instead of an artist. A closer look at the novel reveals that the outsider theme is played out at several levels and in different configurations. While at one level it "analyzes the life led by royalty as a formal existence" and an isolated one, the novel also plays with that favorite theme of Mann: the variety of "special cases."[9]

At one and the same time, the prince is both a special case and an outsider within the royal family due to a "birth defect"—meant in this case literally. To further complicate matters, we have two characters in the novel who exemplify something close to the prototype of the outsider, the stranger, and as such may be regarded as preliminary studies for the character of Naphta. (In fact, the author stated unequivocally that this novel was "an essay in preparation for the dialectical orchestration of *The Magic Mountain*"; without it, that mature novel could not have been written.)[10] To be sure, one of the characters, Dr. Raoul Überbein, the "younger assistant teacher with a doctor's degree," is not explicitly Jewish but otherwise possesses the prerequisites of the outsider status. "It was said that his origin was obscure," we are told, also, "he had no father" and "he had once been starved."[11] Dr. Überbein displays the "superiority of a man who had knocked about the world," and takes pride in the fact— like Herr Aarenhold—that "although he had been left alone in the world," he had distinguished himself and even obtained a college education.[12] That his "very birth [was] a misfortune" and that he was "as poor as a sparrow" were "good qualifications," Überbein himself says, because they "brought with them a never ending imperious call to be up and doing"; such circumstances exist to strengthen one's "moral fibre."[13] His career is not a regular establishment career; he is called upon to be the "private tutor" to the young prince. As the result of a "professional duel," Dr. Überbein comes to a "miserable end": he is found one day "with a bullet through his heart."[14]

Dr. Überbein has only one friend in his whole life, with *"the unsympathetic name of Dr. Sammet."*[15] Sammet is also an outsider, and with him Überbein shares certain characteristics. Dr. Sammet, a doctor of medicine, is "in a similar position and like him *ill-fated by birth in so far as he was a Jew.*" Consequently, they had much to say about such things as "fate and duty."[16] Dr. Sammet also distinguishes himself by obtaining his education through sheer perseverence. When asked by the Grand Duke whether "he had ever found his origin to stand in his way," Dr. Sammet's short discourse sums up the meaning of exceptionality:

No principle of equalization, if I may be allowed to remark, will ever prevent the incidence in the life of the community of exceptional and abnormal men who are distinguished from the burghers by their nobleness or infamy. It is the duty of the individual not to concern himself as to the precise nature of the distinction between him and the common herd, but to see what is *essential in that distinction* and to recognize *that it imposes on him an exceptional obligation* towards society. *A man is at an advantage, not at a disadvantage,* compared with the regular and therefore complacent majority, *if he has one motive more* than they *to extraordinary exertions.*[17]

This summary is a good indication of the function ascribed to the outsiders in Mann's oeuvre; and Dr. Sammet's role, to provide explanation and solace to the royal family in their hour of distress, is a case in point. What Mr. Aarenhold, Dr. Sammet, and

Dr. Überbein have in common is the perception of their "misfortunate birth" as a motive for extraordinary achievements.

In light of what has been said about the elements of an outsider's biography in all of its repetitions and variations, it becomes evident that Leo Naphta and his fictional forerunners have the following basic features in common: *places and circumstances of birth* ("obscure," somewhere in the East, or Galicia); *childhood and family life* ("no father," starving, extreme poverty, family bonds not known or obliterated, self-reliance and perseverance, negative situations turned into "positive qualifications" for life); *education and development* (great mental gifts coupled with diligence, scant formal education helped by "patronage" or "seminary" connections, self-improvement emphasized, "aestheticization," also called "decadence" within one generation); *racial classification* (mostly Jewish, with the exception of Dr. Überbein, who is "of unknown origin"); *social classification* ("special case," "outsider," professional status mainly as symbolic "educator," "tutor," "wise man," or mentor; Aarenhold and Baron Stein are borderline cases: formerly businessmen, now leading a "decadent" or "aesthetic existence"); and *later fate* (either unspecified, or suicide). These shared biographical details are by no means the only points of contact among these figures; other shared features will be discussed *in extenso* at a later point. But the common threads of these life stories suggest the presence of a prototype (within the fictional world) that Mann had conceived of very early in his literary career and that had a very definitive function in his fiction, even in his earliest stories. The prototype serves as a symbol and an elaboration of the "special cases" of life; as such it appears in ever changing variations, acquiring new dimensions.

As Mann himself reminded us, "the theme of the artist as isolated and 'different'" or as a special case predominated in his thinking and early works. It is our contention that the second most important special case is that of the "intellectual mentor" or "educator," more often than not identical with the type of the Jewish intellectual. Leo Naphta is the culmination in the development of this prototype in Mann's fictional world; after all, his personality and intellectual makeup were produced by what Mann called the "unbridled arbitrariness of combinatory imagination."

Naphta's portrayal by no means exhausted the possibilities inherent in the prototype. Because the author's perceptions, personal experiences, and awareness of contemporary dilemmas *(Zeitprobleme)* constituted the underlying reality of *Royal Highness* and other works *(The Magic Mountain, Doctor Faustus)*, the prototype of the educator or Jewish intellectual could easily find a place and function in diverse narrative patterns.

In the late work, *Doctor Faustus* for example, the educator or intellectual mentor appears in several configurations and has retained its important role, even if we don't consider the actual narrator—and closest friend of the hero—in the story. He is "Serenus Zeitblom, Ph. D.," an "ex–teacher" who has been "unable to agree fully with our Führer and his paladins"; hence his resignation from the teaching staff. As to his place in the social structure, he admits that his "position of aloofness vis–à–vis the authorities of his Fatherland" has "isolated" him.[18] Though in a round-about way, Serenus Zeitblom's isolation can be traced back to a youthful experience, his encounter with "the rabbi of the place, Dr. Carlebach by name [who] used to visit in our home." Zeitblom elaborates:

> I have retained the impression... that the little long-bearded, cap–wearing Tal-mudist far surpassed his colleague of another faith in learning and religious pen-etration. It may be the results of this youthful experience, but also because of the keen-scented receptivity of Jewish circles [for the arts]; but I have never, precisely in the Jewish problem and the way it has been dealt with, been able to agree... with our Führer. ...[19]

More relevant to our discussion are the two outsiders—and marginal educators—Pri-vatdocent Eberhard Schleppfuss and the "disreputable" Dr. Chaim Breisacher.

Eberhard Schleppfuss enters the scene just as Adrian Leverkühn and Serenus Zeit-blom take leave from their "liberal" teacher at Halle, who had shown himself as a buffoon—like Settembrini the "windbag". Zeitblom reports, "But I must devote a few words to another figure *[noch einer]*" because "the equivocal nature of this man intrigued me, so that I remember him better than all the rest."[20] (The German text is more suggestive: Naphta is introduced as *noch jemand* and Schleppfuss as *noch einer*.) The biographical details echo those of Naphta to some degree: Schleppfuss is a Privatdocent who for a short time lectured "at Halle among the *venia legendi* and then disappeared from the scene."[21] His origins remain "obscure," as did Dr. Über-bein's. Like Naphta, he was a student and is now a teacher of *theology;* his material is not only highly "exclusive" but draws only students with intellectual and "revolutio-nary" aspirations. That Schleppfuss is given to wearing a "sort of soft hat...rather like a Jesuit's," is obviously an allusion to the earlier figure.[22]

The other character, Dr. Chaim Breisacher, is placed within a group of scholars and artists (the Kridwiss circle) who are very thinly disguised real people from pre-Nazi Munich. Breisacher's life and career are also kept in "obscurity." We are told only that he is a "polyhistor" and of Jewish descent. Breisacher, in fact, amounts to a caricature of Naphta and other forerunners of the type; neither his mental gifts nor his personality command respect. He is not the outsider in a positive or even neutral sense. Just the opposite. Breisacher is a private scholar and a "racial and in-tellectual type in high, one might almost say reckless development and of fascinating ugliness." In the circle he plays the role of a "fermentous alien body *[fermentöser Fremdkörper]*."[23] Zeitblom, who professes his "friendliness toward Jewish people," calls Breisacher one of the most "annoying specimens" of that race. While he respects the Jewish spirit and its receptivity for ideas, Zeitblom perceives Breisacher as repre-senting that trend in which the "avantgarde coincides with the reactionary"; this is the "new world of anti-humanity."[24] Breisacher is *not* simply the prototype of the outsider, the Jewish intellectual, but the symbol for a certain kind of possible development already inherent in the conception of the Naphta figure: the "conservative revolutionary," or the "fascist Jew."[25] It should be noted that the figure of Breisacher is more closely related to a living person than was the case with Naphta: Breisacher is based on the Jewish scholar Oskar Goldberg, who published his controversial book, *Die Wirklichkeit der Hebräer* (The True World of the Hebrews), in 1925. Goldberg himself advanced the claim that he and his book inspired the figure of Naphta and some of his argumentation. The claim is characteristic of the man: his book was published in 1925, while *The Magic Mountain* came out in 1924.[26] Moreover, Thomas Mann's diary reveals that Goldberg and Breisacher are as good as *identical*.[27]

Even if the details of Lukács's life have not determined the particularly appropriate fate of Naphta, it does not mean that Lukács or any other real persons had nothing to offer this fictional biography. Shortly before meeting Lukács, Thomas Mann reflected in an 1921 article on his encounters with Jews:

> In my childhood I was on friendly terms with a boy called Fehér, who was of *Hungarian* origin and was *the epitome of the type* with all of its characteristics fully present and *well-developed to an ugliness*—with a flat nose and the premature trace of a moustache. His *father had a small tailor's shop* somewhere in the vicinity of the harbor. ...[28]

It might have been an interplay of these dredged-up memories, complete with the sharp features of "the type" and the "tailor's shop" and refreshed by the impression of a personal encounter with Lukács, another Hungarian Jew, that induced Mann's playful suggestion of a Lukács–Naphta connection by situating his fictional character in the house of Lukacek, the tailor. Mann remarked in his article that he "had never entered the house of the Jewish tailor" due to "the reserve of the young master of the house *[Herrensöhnchen]* and to social prejudice."[29] Was it Mann's well-developed sense of irony and pleasure in hide-and-seek at work when he let his young hero, Hans Castorp, enter the house of Lukacek, the tailor, so as to make up for past omissions?

The same article mentions "another Jewish schoolmate" whom Mann "used to play with in the schoolyard: he was *the son of a slaughterer*, ... so slight and bony that his lips provided the only fullness in his appearance. ..."[30] The author's autobiographical musings coincide with his intense working on *The Magic Mountain* and have undoubtedly left their mark on the colorful and highly dramatized life story of Leo Naphta.

Ferdinand Lion, a contemporary and friend of Thomas Mann, was right in suggesting that we consider the author's firsthand experience with revolutionary events and personalities as a possible influence. In the spring of 1919, Lion says, Mann could observe the (Russian) Jewish-agitator-and-revolutionary type in action right there in Munich.[31] He must have had in mind Eugen Leviné, who had come to Germany from Russia, studied at several universities (for example, at Heidelberg, where he had met Max Weber), and become the leader of the short-lived Soviet Republic in Bavaria. Leviné's determination, great mental gifts, asceticism, and fanaticism were the talk of the town. Mann, who often refers to his own "eager absorption" of events and thought, no doubt let these experiences enter the creative process. This assumption is reinforced by the surprising timing of his taking up work again on *The Magic Mountain* after a long hiatus. Mann notes in his diary on April 9, 1919, "After breakfast...unpacked the manuscript of [the novel] and took a first look at the material again. I spent some time with what has been written, which *I shall probably rewrite completely for objective and subjective reasons.*"[32] The events suggested to Mann a "new ending," as his entry of April 17 shows: "The conflict between reaction... and humanistic rationalism is by now entirely historical, pre-war. The synthesis appears to lie in the (communist) future."[33] The synthesis was not to be: the novel ends at the outbreak of the Great War.

It is of course nearly impossible to establish fully the readings which Mann may have utilized as sources. His own library contains many books with underlinings and notes in the margin which enable us to reconstruct their influence on other aspects of the Naphta characterization (especially Nietzsche, Spengler, Brandes and Lukács's early works). I was unable to find any such documentation of source for the biography of Naphta. There is only one work which in all probability Mann read and used, although it is not among the books that have been preserved. It is Ernst Bloch's *Thomas Münzer als Theologe der Revolution,* published in 1921. In the chapter "Life," Bloch describes Münzer's origins and youth as follows:

From the very beginning, his situation was an extremely bleak one: the mournful young man grew up in total abandonment. He was born... the son of poor people. ... He lost his father at a very early age; his mother was roughed up and had to flee the town. The victim of a horrible act of mass rage, his father died by hanging. Thus it came that the boy learned of the bitterness of shame and injustice at a very early age.[34]

There are many obvious features in common with Naphta's biography: bleak beginnings, fatherless childhood, poverty, abandonment, mother's flight, and last but not least the "horrible act" resulting in the father's hanging (in Naphta's case "crucifix–wise") and the mother's subsequent flight from town. The parallel of these vivid details of very unlikely childhood experiences suggests a case of borrowing.

There are other similarities concerning the development of Münzer and Naphta: we are told, for example, that Münzer was determined to overcome these impediments by means of "extraordinary accomplishments": he was moved by the "liveliest intellectual passion" and was extremely well-read; we hear that his "mind was sharp," and never "lukewarm," and that in his youth his ascetic tendencies were already obvious.[35] Bloch also described Münzer's innate contrariness, which crystallized in his stand against the Lutheran "establishment." As a result, Münzer was positioned outside all confessional hierarchies and power blocks. Having fought Luther and the pope alike, he became an "outsider" and "one who never quite belongs," both as a religious revivalist and as an ideologue. It will be shown later what other aspects of Münzer's personality may have contributed to the construct of Naphta's character.

As has been noted in the critical literature, the distance between the real Lukács and the fictional figure "is especially marked in the description of Leo Naphta's origin."[36] The full text of Lukács's curriculum vitae illustrates this most aptly. Dr. Georg von Lukács, then residing in Heidelberg, had forwarded to the faculty of philosophy of Heidelberg University his request to "grant him the *venia legendi* in philosophy on the basis of the enclosed supportive material" on May 25, 1918. That material depicts his career until 1918:

I was born in Budapest on April 13, 1885, son of József von Lukács, *Hofrat* of the Hung.[arian] Cr.[own], Director of the Hungarian General Credit Bank; I am a Hungarian citizen of Lutheran confession. At the completion of my secondary education at the Lutheran Gymnasium of Budapest, I received my maturity certificate [*Reifezeugnis*] in June 1902. I then embarked on a study of law and national economy at the University of Budapest and received a doctorate in law from the University of Kolozsvár in October 1906. Already during my aforementioned studies, literature and art history as well as philosophy moved to the center of my interests. Thus, after briefly serving with the Royal Hungarian Ministry of Commerce, I decided to devote myself exclusively to the study of these areas and attended the universities of Budapest and Berlin. While none of the professors at Budapest University exerted any measurable influence on my development, I was inspired by and benefited in a decisive way from the lectures of Professors Dilthey and Simmel. The influence of Dilthey consisted mainly in the awakening of my interest for cultural–historical interconnections; I am greatly indebted to Simmel for demonstrating to me the possibility of a sociological approach to cultural objectifications. At the same time, I had benefited greatly from the diverse methodological works of Max Weber. In November 1909, the University of Budapest conferred on me a doctoral degree in philosophy.

The beginnings of my literary activities preceded this latter phase of my studies. Some of my essays, collected in my book, *Die Seele und die Formen,* are the product of an earlier period, as is the first version of my *Entwicklungsgeschichte des modernen Dramas,* written in Hungarian, that had received the prize of the Kisfaludy Society of Budapest in February 1908. The completely revised work was subsequently published by the Kisfaludy Society in 1912. Negotiations about a German-language edition—in Alfred Weber's "Sociology of Culture Series"—were interrupted by the outbreak of the war. So far, only Chapter Two (which together with Chapter One comprised my doctoral dissertation at Budapest University) appeared in print, in the *Archiv für Sozialwissenschaft und Sozialpolitik*, in the Spring of 1914.

Following my doctoral exams, my interest increasingly turned toward purely philosophical problems albeit without abandoning my awareness of particular problems of literature and the arts. In the fall of 1909 I moved to Berlin and lived there until the spring of 1911, a stay interrupted only by an occasional trip to Italy. During that time my philosophical studies had focused on classical German philosophy, on Kant, Fichte, Schelling, and Hegel. The ever clearer comprehension of the concept of value *[Geltungsgedanke]* has soon led me to modern German philosophy, above all to Windelband, Rickert and Lask. In addition, the methodological stimulus of Husserl's writings had a great impact on me. From Berlin I moved to Florence only to leave after one year in order to settle in Heidelberg permanently. My decision to move was motivated by my desire to meet and have personal contact with the men whose writings had so greatly influenced my development. I have developed an especially close relationship with Emil Lask and have published a lengthy article in the *Kunststudien* in his memory. In the first years, my sojourn in Heidelberg was interrupted by trips to Holland and to Rome and more recently by my military service. I married Miss Helena Grabenko, daughter of Andrej Michailowitsch Grabenko, *semstvo* secretary of Cherson district, in Heidelberg in the spring of 1914.

This period saw the first draft and then the almost completed writing of a systematic philosophy of art. I have also written several works on ethics and on the theory of science *[Wissenschaftslehre]*, most of which are yet to be published.

My published works are as follows:

1. *Die Seele und die Formen* (Soul and Form). Essays. Berlin, 1911. The volume contains the essay "Metaphysics of Tragedy," which had also been published in *Logos* 2, 1911.

2. *Entwicklungsgeschichte des modernen Dramas* (History of the Development of Modern Drama). Publication of the Kisfaludy Society, Budapest, 1912. German language publication of Chapter Two, "Zur Soziologie des modernen Dramas" (Sociology of Modern Drama) in *Archiv für Sozialwissenschaft und Sozialpolitik* 1914.

3. *Methodologie der Literaturgeschichte [sic]* (Methodology of the History of Literature). 1910. In Hungarian.

4. Reviews of substance in *Archiv für Sozialwissenschaft und Sozialpolitik* on methodological problems in the social sciences.

5. Small–scale works relating to problems of form in literature, published in diverse journals.

6. *Die Theorie des Romans* (Theory of the Novel). Published in *Zeitschrift für Aesthetik und Allgemeine Kunstwissenschaft* 11, nos 3–4 (1916). This work represents the introductory chapter of a large-scale work.

7. "Die Subjekt–Objekt Beziehung in der Aesthetik" *[sic]* (The Subject–Object Relation in Aesthetics.) In *Logos* 7, no 1. (1917–18). The article constitutes one chapter of my otherwise unpublished *Philosophy of Art*.

8. "Emil Lask: Ein Nachruf" Obituary. In *Kunststudien* 22, no. 4 (1918).[37]

The tale of Naphta's life and Lukács's account of a privileged existence have precious little in common—and Mann was well aware of that. In his 1929 letter to the Austrian Chancellor, Mann spoke of Lukács's "life story, his wealthy bourgeois origins," and the fact that had he not chosen the career of a revolutionary, he "could have led the life of a young master of the house *[Herrensöhnchen]*". To be sure, Lukács was of "Semitic origin" and "came from the East"—but this is not an exclusive link, as the discussion of Naphta's forerunners has shown. On the other hand, Naphta's origins and development are a true composite, and Lukács's life and family circumstances apparently contributed a few details. At any rate, these details embellished a construct already in place. Among them are the description of Naphta's father and the boy's special relationship to him. "His father, of whom he spoke with respect" was at the onset of the story too remote to admit openly to such filial feelings. We also learn that the father had "blue eyes, which the son described as sending out gleams like stars, [and] held in their depth a wealth of... fervor" (440). At the risk of sounding speculative, I venture to say that Mann's intimate knowledge of the Lukács household and family relationships therein played an underground role in Naphta's life story.

As is known, Georg Lukács visited Thomas Mann at his Vienna hotel at Mann's request. Prior to this meeting (in January 1922), Mann was the house guest of Josef von Lukács at his Budapest villa and there learned of the father's unhappiness with his son's political involvement and subsequent fate. Just as he had appealed to Max Weber and Paul Ernst before, the distraught father now asked Mann to do what he could to turn his son away from this entanglement; at the same time, Mann was to inform Georg Lukács about certain financial arrangements his father made for him. Thus, Mann took upon himself the role of mediator. The following year Mann was again a guest of the Lukács household and obviously discussed with Lukács *père* the son's fate as well as his meeting with him. Mann's impression is described in a letter written to Dezső Kosztolányi, a Hungarian poet. In it, Mann advises the poet to ask "the good, old, wise man, Herr von Lukács," for help.[38] The same impression is conveyed in Mann's famous letter to Dr. Seipel:

In the past I had often been a guest in his father's house, and I can't help thinking—while I am writing this letter to you—of the proud and blissful smile on the face of the recently deceased old gentleman when he heard one speak with respect of the great intellectual powers of his son. [See Appendix.]

Thomas Mann's sly irony turned the relationship around in the novel and had the son speak "with respect" of the great gifts of the father. In the same letter, Mann depicts Lukács's refugee existence in words which echo Naphta's situation and state of mind when facing the bleak future: "He has been living here…in abject poverty, devoting himself entirely to his intellectual pursuits. …"

The relationship between Lukács and his father is today a well-documented one: the exchange of letters shows a marked degree of understanding, tolerance, and respect for each other's intellectual gifts. Not even Lukács's revolutionary career would change that. On the other hand, the sketchy treatment of Leo Naphta's relationship to his mother is as striking as it is negative. We are told that Leo's utterances and intellectual development "made the failing mother draw her head down crookedly between her shoulders and look at him with both wasted hands flung out" (442). The mother is completely overwhelmed intellectually and frightened out of her wits when confronted with Leo's unconventional attitudes and thought. In this respect, the relationship of the real Lukács to his mother, characterized by unmitigated alienation, corresponds to an amazing degree with the fictional one. Lukács's notes to his autobiographical sketch *Gelebtes Denken* (Record of a Life), refer to the father as a "very decent, respectable man," but add, *"I was completely estranged from my family, or at least from a part of it."*[39] His mother was a "shrewd woman who soon saw what was happening. She fell seriously ill and died of breast cancer. Under pressure from other members of the family [!] I wrote her a letter. When she received it she said, 'I must be very ill for Dr. Georg to write me a letter.' "[40] Already as a very young boy, Lukács admittedly waged a "guerilla war against the mother." According to contemporaries, her conventional outlook and mediocrity dominated the household. In one of the interviews given in Hungary, Lukács was asked to give the reasons that led him to abandon his class. Pressed for more details, he said that if there were such a thing as a "psychological reason," it would be found in his "extremely poor" relationship with his mother. For him, she symbolized all the negativity and excesses of the haute bourgeoisie. So, even before he found the ideological underpinnings for his contempt of the class he was born into, there existed an instinctive rejection due to the nature and ways of his mother.[41] Not much better was his relationship to his brother and sister; he found his brother simply contemptible. In the memoirs of one of his childhood friends, we find similar sentiments: the mother was rather disliked and the brother held in contempt by Lukács's like-minded friends.[42] In this respect, a parallel situation exists in the family relations of the real Lukács and the fictional figure. Thomas Mann's well-informed view of the Lukács family thus appears to have colored his depiction of the fictional one.

In conclusion, let us emphasize that Thomas Mann was not a mere realist intent on grasping and describing the life, appearance, or ideas of a certain person as a unique phenomenon. He was interested in finding out what was "characteristic" of an idea or situation and what was "typical" about men. One of the tasks he set himself was to discover a characteristic feature, because in its capacity as a sign—indeed, as a prophetic omen of the times, it helped him to perceive certain connections. Following in the footsteps of Nietzsche, whose anthropo-psychological analysis and interpretation was grounded in biological considerations, Mann sought out those factors that were intrinsic to this or that person, that would be considered as necessary and characteristic appendages of that *type,* that is, factors that were not "accidental." For Thomas Mann, certain types had to exhibit specific physical appearances, have specific biographies, and so forth. His long essay "Goethe and Tolstoy" provides the best summation:

> It seemed to me *not accidental* that Schiller and Dostoevsky *were sick men* and did not, like Goethe and Tolstoy, arrive at a reverend length of days. Rather I was inclined to regard their poor *health as fundamental to their character.* Quite as *symbolic* is the further *external fact,* that the two great realists and creative artists were of upper station, *born to* a privileged *social status,* whereas the heroes and *saints of the idea,* Schiller and Dostoevsky...were *children of modest people* and *spent all their days in pinched... undignified circumstances.*[43]

The author calls this biographical fact "symbolic" because "it testifies to the Christianity of the spirit, whose kingdom, as the Scriptures say, is not of this world—in personalities as little as in the realm of the ideal and the artistic. ... Therein lies their 'realism'."[44]

Such were the artistic premises upon which rests Mann's explanation to his critics that a novel such as *The Magic Mountain* had to have in it a Naphta, who was represented in his own way; the character, moreover, had to have biographical foundations similar to those of "heroes and saints of the idea." The biography, being a composite, could well accommodate elements of Lukács's life—and most likely did. Mann's expositions on this aspect of his artistry recall Dilthey's postulate that the understanding of any individual existence lies possibly only within the systems of life *(Lebenszusammenhänge).*

Chapter 5.
PHYSIOGNOMY OF LEO NAPHTA

Ever since Sagave gave "proof" of a "striking" similarity in the outer appear-ances of Lukács and Leo Naphta, the physical aspect of Thomas Mann's "borrow-ing" received undue attention at the cost of other possible parallels, such as intellectual makeup or personality. Subsequent scholarship merely restated—often verbatim—Sagave's "findings" and let the matter rest at that.[1] Neither the validity nor the soundness of Sagave's assertions were submitted to critical scrutiny.[2] His statement that the "sharpness" of Naphta's appearance and further facial details, such as the "hooked nose," the mouth, and the "bevelled lenses of his glasses," were modeled after Lukács was accepted uncritically. Lukács, on the contrary, regarded the physical aspect as the least significant and characteristic aspect of the borrowing, and believed, in fact, that the author had as good as "falsified" Naphta's outer appearance—by which Lukács meant Naphta's elegant attire—in order "to make the matter less obvious." Who is right?

The reader meets Leo Naphta in the sub-chapter entitled "A New–Comer" (*noch jemand*) whose appearance is described as follows:

The stranger...was small and thin, clean-shaven, and of such piercing, one might almost say *corrosive ugliness* as fairly to astonish the cousins. *Everything about him* was sharp: the *hooked nose* dominating his face, the narrow, *pursed mouth,* the thick, bevelled lenses of his glasses in their light frame, behind which were a pair of pale-grey eyes—even the silence, he preserved, which suggested that when he broke it, his speech would be incisive and logical. According to custom he was bareheaded and overcoatless—and moreover *very well dressed,* in a dark–blue flannel suit with white stripes. Its quiet but modish cut was at once noted by the cousins. ... The worldly and superior quality of *the ugly stranger's tailoring* made him stand nearer to the cousins than to Settembrini. ...

...Though blond-haired—his hair was a metallic, colourless ash-blond, and he wore it smoothed back from a lofty brow straight over his whole head—[he] also showed *the dead-white complexion of the brunette races.* ... Naphta's *[hands] and his feet as well, were small and delicate,* as befitted his build.[3]

The picture Sagave used for his claim was *supposed* to show Lukács in his Vienna exile in 1920. The photo was first reproduced in a German-language anthology for Lukács's seventieth birthday; Fritz J. Raddatz subsequently included it in his Lukács monograph, in the chapter entitled "Naphta in Exile," and identified the picture as "Georg Lukács. Vienna. 1920."[4] Before discussing any similarity between the picture and the fictional portrait, let me point out that all the above identifications are *incorrect* in that the photo in question was taken in approximately 1937 and not in 1920. It is an enlargement of one part of a group picture taken on an excursion in a forest near Moscow: beside Lukács, the group includes his wife Gertrud; the German Expressionist poet (and later minister of culture of East Germany) Johannes R. Becher with his wife; and Olga Halpern, wife of a Hungarian Communist writer, Andor Gábor.[5] So much for the pictorial evidence. It is, however, true that there is a manifest change in Lukács's facial details and demeanor compared to earlier pictures of him. With or more often without glasses, adorned with a bushy, Nietzschean moustache and soft, full lips in a rounded face, we have before us in the pictures of the 1910s a youthful, haute bourgeois Georg von Lukács, whom many of his contemporaries described as having "romantic looks"; indeed, some of them compared his looks and demeanor to that of Novalis, the German Romantic poet.[6]

All the available photos from the 1920s, on the other hand, may with some imagination show something of a likeness between Lukács's facial details and Naphta's features. Here as there, we have the "thin face," "clean-shaven," the "hair smoothed back" from the peaked forehead, and the "glasses in their light frame."[7] Raddatz's monograph also contains a reproduction of an identification card, issued by German authorities, at Mannheim in 1925, for a certain "Dr. Georg von Lukács, born April 13, 1885 in Budapest (Hungary), Hungarian citizen, presently living at Kepplerstrasse 28, Heidelberg; Occupation: Independent scholar." The physical description is as follows:

Figure:	medium
Face:	oval
Hair:	brown
Eyes:	gray
Mouth:	regular
Nose:	regular

Special features: none[8]

From this description, only the color of the eyes (gray) matches the fictional portrait. On the basis of my personal acquaintance with Lukács, I could neither deny nor confirm corresponding physical traits. Lukács was undeniably "small and thin," and his hands and feet proportionally "small and delicate," but I see nothing particular in the fact; his eyes were more brightly blue than pale gray. And he was truly not well dressed. His peers and contemporaries emphasized his "aristocratic bearing" and elegant attire, but as he was wont to say, he left this "aesthetic period" (meaning: bourgeois) behind in 1919 and never again cared much about his appearance.[9] All in all, it is nearly impossible to imagine that the refugee Lukács of 1922, whose poverty Thomas Mann so eloquently described in his letter to the Austrian chancellor, could have worn a "dark–blue flannel suit with white stripes."

As to Lukács's reaction to the "problem" of physical parallels with Naphta, it is best indicated in a 1960 interview. When asked by Günther Specovius, a journalist from Hamburg, whether he felt any resentment at being "caricatured" by Mann, Lukács replied calmly:

Why should I bear a grudge against him because he may have borrowed my nose or my mouth for his Naphta character? I owe him so much! It is as if a friend had come to me and asked: "I have forgotten to bring my cigar-case, could I have one of your cigars?" This is how I have lent my features to Thomas Mann.[10]

Ehrhard Bahr's exclamation that very few people would have been as magnanimous as Lukács is thus wholly justified. But as will be shown, Lukács's own statement about his having lent other than merely facial traits to the figure of Naphta is more to the point.

To be sure, there exist certain connections with regard to the physiognomy of Lukács and Naphta. Nevertheless, they are insufficient for establishing an unequivocal identification for reasons that have previously been discussed: the synthetic character of Mann's artistry is also present in the case of Naphta's physiognomy, that is, the creative process of repetition, synthesis, elevation and perfection of previous constructs is operative here too. Just as in the case of the life story of a certain *type* (that of the "exceptional case," the outsider), we encountered the variations of a basic concept, the physiognomy of Naphta must turn out to be a composite—and cannot be regarded as a solitary and unique construct. It is not by accident that Joachim remarks after having met Naphta that "nobody but Jews" have such "puny figures" and such a "big Jewish nose" (385). Even a cursory examination of Mann's work attests that all of his characters of "Semitic origins" are endowed with certain "typical" or "characteristic" features—physical or otherwise. Accordingly, Naphta's physiognomy is a composite of elements that have been visible in some form or another in other works of Mann, and also in his accounts of his personal perceptions. This artistic tendency to fix "racially typical features" because of their symbolic function has been shown to be at work in the earliest stories, and in the large-scale works up to the late novel *Doctor Faustus*. The first important work in which the symbolic significance of external factors was dominant was the novel *Buddenbrooks*. The members of the Hagenström family are true to type (and were conceived as the family "Cohn" according to Mann's notes to the novel): the daughter Julchen is small and lively, with "large, staring black eyes"; the mother has "thick, heavy hair" and both mother and daughter have "large diamonds in their ears."[11] One of the brothers, Moritz, has a "weak chest" but "finished school brilliantly"—significantly, he has the "reputation of a connoisseur" and is a patron of the arts. The other brother, Hermann, a successful businessman, "wore a full, short reddish–blond beard, and he had his mother's nose, which came down quite flat on the upper lip."[12]

In the next novel, *Royal Highness,* the description of external features is more differentiated and reaches a higher, more symbolic level. Dr. Sammet, the Jewish physician,

> wore his dark blond hair cut *en brosse* and his moustache untrimmed. His chin and cheeks were clean-shaven, and rather sore from it. He carried his head a little on one side, and the gaze of his grey eyes told of shrewdness and practical goodness. His nose, which came down quite flat on his moustache, pointed to his origin.[13]

Whether it is called a heritage from the mother or a sign pointing to "origins," some "typical" facial traits were developed in order to denote "Semitic origins." Although Dr. Überbein is not an explicitly Jewish character, he is an outsider par excellence, and he is endowed with several physical traits that by now seem mandatory for this type:

> Raoul Überbein was not a handsome man. He had a red beard and a greenish-white complexion with watery blue eyes, thin red hair, and unusually ugly, protruding, sharp-pointed ears. But his hands were small and delicate. He wore white ties exclusively, which gave him rather a distinguished appearance. ...[14]

Apart from the "small and delicate hands," in all of these characters there are elements that found their way into the later construct of Naphta.

Several members of the Aarenhold family in the novella "The Blood of the Walsungs" were endowed with similar physical traits. Frau Aarenhold is "impossible, small and ugly"; her daughter Märit has "ashblond hair and grey eyes," a dominant "hooked nose," and a "bitter" or "pursed" mouth. It is true, the twins are exceptionally beautiful; still, Siegmund is described as having a "thin" and "white" face kept "closely shaven," and his feet are "small"; moreover, they both have "long slim hands" and "the same slightly drooping nose."[15] Should we try to make a composite of these fictional characters, we would come up (give or take one trait) with the physical description of Leo Naphta.

As Thomas Mann noted in his essay, "Goethe and Tolstoy," he considers certain "external facts" to be fundamental to certain characters and as such symbolic. The fact that he endowed certain types with a "characteristic" physiognomy has nothing to do with naturalistic description but everything to do with symbolism. The characters as types represent ideas, attitudes, situations, implied or formulated values, and *Weltanschauungen*. Clearly, Mann's declared artistic method is responsible for the strange character of the monk Girolamo (after Savonarola) in the play *Fiorenza*.[16] The monk's "poisonous fanaticism" stems from and at the same time is reinforced by his inability to partake in life's offering, be it beauty, women, or art. His outward appearance is accordingly constructed: he enters the scene as a man marked by "irredeemable ugliness"; his face is "sallow, woebegone, fanatical"; his profile is "bony" and "savage"; and in "startling contrast" he sports a "small and sickly figure." He has, moreover, a "great hooked nose" and a narrow, "peaked" forehead;

the "thin lips are compressed with a sort of finality."[17] One gains the impression from the cluster of extreme features that a "fanatic" has to look this way as he goes out in the world on a "mission" despising the "base, cautious, homely folk."[18] We are reminded of Mann's letter about Naphta's having a mission in *The Magic Mountain.* The fanatic monk who calls himself a prophet[19] and the almost-monk Naphta not only share certain "savage" notions and physical traits but are linked by their being "exceptional cases," albeit at different stages of conceptual development.[20]

Almost as an echo of these earlier outsiders, the figure surfaces again in *Doctor Faustus,* in the person of Privatdocent Eberhard Schleppfuss. Again, we have before us a "creature of hardly average height, puny in figure," who wore a "sort of soft hat like a Jesuit's."[21] Dr. Schleppfuss was given to lecturing "half-sitting on the balustrade," and his parted "little beard moving up and down. Between it and the twisted moustaches one saw his pointed teeth like tiny splinters." And his talk about God, Freedom, the Evil One, and the Middle Ages was "also pointed"; indeed, this irregular lecturer "spoke as a theologian."[22] The echo not only of Naphta's figure and social status but of many of the ideas of the intellectual debates in *The Magic Mountain* are to be found in Dr. Schleppfuss's story and lectures. The suggestion has been made that the figure of Eberhard Schleppfuss was modeled after Theodor W. Adorno, but the radicalism of Schleppfuss's theoretical positions renders this assumption unlikely.[23] Only the esoteric and elitist nature of Schleppfuss's lectures could make the connection to Adorno.

In the following chapter, I will investigate how physiognomy was regarded by Mann and others as part of the personality. Just as the association of disease with genius was part and parcel of Mann's conceptual construct (think of his "Goethe and Tolstoy" essay, where poor health and certain physical traits are fundamental and characteristic attributes of the "saints of the idea").[24] Mann once remarked that such a "striking phenomenon" as the Jewish element in the cultural life of his time deserved to be emphasized and paid attention to.[25] The outer appearance was perceived as equally striking and thus worth being emphasized and given form to. Thomas Mann's personal references to Jewish intellectuals in general and to some of his friends and acquaintances in particular are sprinkled with the same adjectives with which he endowed his fictional characters; for example, in his letters he was wont to call Samuel Lublinski, the Berlin literary critic whom he greatly respected, the "poor little," the "poor sick" or the "ugly little" Lublinski.[26]

Georg Lukács did not fail to recognize the nature and place of this very motif in Mann's oeuvre. In his essay "Das Spielerische und seine Hintergründe" (The Playful Style and Its Background) Lukács discusses how "the supremacy of the real over the subjectively imagined" asserts itself in Mann's exploration of the world and its problems, meaning simply that the *echte Wirklichkeit* (objective reality) underlies the *dichterische Wirklichkeit* (poetic reality). The motif of "biological reality" is only one of many. Lukács picks out that one motif and deals with it in the larger framework of Mann's artistic principles:

Thomas Mann begins…to *allot a decisive role to the purely physical basis of life and consciousness,* to make biological reality a *potent factor of personality.* Of course, ever since *Little Herr Friedemann,* the physical makeup of his characters had been important for what happened to them. But there is a qualitative difference between what is the point of departure, the outward form of a catastrophe and the process which determines the heart of a collision as in the later works.[27]

Chapter 6.
THE PERSONALITY OF LEO NAPHTA:
DER FREMDLING PAR EXCELLENCE

After a seven-month stay on the "magic mountain" in a "Walpurgis night of intoxication," Hans Castorp calls Settembrini, the man of letters, simply "thou" and takes leave of him as a teacher. It is confirmed for Settembrini that he is not "just any man, with a name" but rather a "representative" here and at Hans Castorp's side, someone who "explains things as *homo humanus*."[1] The "thou" is meant to indicate that Hans Castorp has learned everything that this enlightened scholar par excellence had to offer him; from now on he is Settembrini's equal. It further signifies that this "problem child of life" *(Sorgenkind des Lebens)* is mature enough and ready for further, deeper, or more complicated experiences and for a new type of educator. A short while later, Hans Castorp encounters him on the main street of town; the cousins see Lodovico Settembrini at the side of a "stranger" (372); then, after the encounter and the first discussion, Hans Castorp asks his cousin, the good Joachim, "How did you like him?" Joachim answers:

Who? The little man? Not very much. Though he said some things I liked. ... But I did not care much for the man himself—a person may say as many good things as he likes, it doesn't matter to me, if he himself is *a questionable character*. And questionable he is, you can't deny that. That stuff about the "place of intercourse" was distinctly shady, not to mention anything else. And did you see *the big Jewish nose he had?* Nobody but Jews have such puny figures. Are you really thinking of visiting the man? (385)

Hans Castorp answers the last question in the affirmative and disposes of the "puniness" issue by saying that Joachim views everything from a military standpoint. Concerning the rest, he is of a totally different opinion:

The Chaldeans had such noses too, and yet they were always in damn good form, not just in the occult sciences. Naphta has something of the mystagogue about him, he interests me a good deal. And I am not saying that I make him out altogether, yet, but if we meet him often perhaps we shall; and I don't think it at all unlikely that we may learn something from the acquaintance with him. (385)

The discussion about Naphta continues, touching upon disease, freedom, dignity, and personal courage. Finally, Hans Castorp claims that Settembrini is certainly afraid of quite a few things which the "little Naphta [does] not fear," and Settembrini's sense of freedom and his bravery are more or less "folderol"; a "prophetic" question follows: "Do you think he would have enough courage '*de se perdre ou même de se laisser dépérir?*'" (386).

This exchange of impressions of the new "acquaintance" is enlightening in more than one way. It makes clear that Naphta's personality does not fail to make an impression on the cousins. Indeed, they recognize the force of Naphta's personality.[2] Immediately, Hans Castorp chooses him as a new educator, because he has something of the "mystagogue" about him. Naphta's intellectual rank is thus determined: it is higher than Settembrini's.

Beyond this—and above all—Leo Naphta is a "stranger" and as such a "questionable character." His foreignness is felt by both men, with one essential difference: Joachim's misgivings are based more on appearance and essentially correspond to the usual, customary prejudice. Hans Castorp thinks in a much more differentiated way: he has progressed so far in his education that Naphta's strangeness does not alienate him. On the contrary, the beginnings of a critical appraisal of the possibilities inherent in this "type" are present in him.

Before Naphta's personality and its Lukács components can be discussed, we must concern ourselves with the question of personality. There are two reasons for this. First, Thomas Mann himself frequently discusses, applies, and even more often creates the phenomenon of personality.[3] The fact that the author is inclined to view the phenomenon itself from various points of view, to define it or to explain it in manifold ways, does not facilitate our task. His frequently mentioned irony does its share to heighten the confusion. Second, the secondary literature states that we are dealing here with a very well-known concept which is hard to define.[4] The word "personality" is used indiscriminately, but few people using it mean the same thing by it. Within the various special fields (psychology, sociology, antropology, philosophy) there are as many theories and characteristics as there are specialists, precisely because the issue is a central one and the object is elusive. At issue is the essence of being human (Menschsein). One rather imprecise term for personality is "individuality," meant as the distinguishing feature, that is, the quintessence of qualities and characteristics by which the unique individual announces himself.[5]

Thus the question concerning Naphta's personality is not as simple as Thomas Mann thought when he wrote to Wolff, "The role of Naphta's character and his 'mission' is made perfectly clear in the novel. ... I have given this character a careful biographical foundation, and the trick of combining the Communistic with the Jesuit–Catholic in him (with a Jewish background) was not bad."[6] Yes, it was quite good, even if it was not so self-evident or clear. It therefore seems necessary for us to acquaint ourselves with Thomas Mann's own conception of the idea of personality and to consult his essays and polemical writings as well as his creative works for this purpose.

Thomas Mann stressed over and over again that he was concerned "first and foremost... with the portrayal of man"; thus he creates "human characters" which arise "from their respective dispositions" (Gesinnung)—and vice versa.[7] Explaining his own "intellectual formation" he accords a lot of space to the description of his father's personality; it is supposed to provide connective clues to his entire life's work. Some of his father's characteristics were "inherited" not only by Thomas Mann, but by some of his literary characters as well. The father, the author writes, was "no longer a simple man, was not robust, but rather nervous and prone to suffering"; however, "he remained a self-disciplined and successful man." He "made something of himself in the world"; he was possessed of a sense of "ethics," which is actually "a deep sense of duty without which the entire drive for achievement, for a productive contribution to life...is missing."[8] Mann's interest in the human personality is a part of everything he undertakes and is the reason why he is constantly observing and collecting personal impressions (sometimes even with an opera glass—as in the notorious Holitscher case).

Mann's report of an evening of Karl Kraus readings is typical. He attended the readings "from beginning to end because it was... interesting and important to gain personal impressions from the editor of *Die Fackel*."[9] The author was spellbound by Kraus's "ecclesiastical manner" of reading; he was equally fascinated with the "witty passion" with which he approached his own writings. According to Mann, this passion had something "religious about it—and whoever has at some time grasped the contrast between intellect and art, between *Zivilisation* and *Kultur*, will feel himself carried away in sympathy... with the satirical pathos." Thomas Mann concludes his description of the evening by declaring that a narrator can always profit from hearing and reading such a "polemicist."[10]

The reason for his abiding interest is briefly summarized in Mann's short "Dante" essay, showing his awareness that the humanistic epoch is drawing to an end, and that "freedom," "individuality," and "personality" may soon cease to be "the greatest happiness of mankind." But "eminent personalities" will survive eternally—personalities such as Dante, "in whose breast the transformations and transitions of the spirit of the age [Zeitgeist] take place...in a uniquely dignified as well as uniquely decisive manner."[11] For Thomas Mann, Dante stood at the threshold of an epoch and embodied the "prototype" of visionary artistry; thus Mann demonstrated how he himself successfully attempted to transform the individual, the personality, into a historical prototype.

The important essay "Goethe and Tolstoy" represents one great debate on the phenomenon of personality (and its effect) and is equal in importance, as a polemical preparatory study for *The Magic Mountain*, to *Reflections of a Non-Political Man*. The essay is subtitled "Fragments on the Problem of Humanity."[12] Humanity *(Humanität)* in this context means humanness, its major goal being the greatest expansion and development of those valuable characteristics of the heart and of reason which are uniquely human. Thomas Mann was of the opinion that Goethe and Tolstoy, in spite of their differences, were of equal stature; therefore, the "aristocratic" question, the question of "rank" *(Vornehmheit)* is not a valid one. How is this to be understood? An earlier comment of Mann provides an answer. He states that there is no hierarchy in the question of personality. "Hierarchy *[Rangordnung]* is a good thing, but I believe that the realm of the personality constitutes a democracy of kings. If one is anything at all, then one is, I believe, beyond compare. ... Personality enjoys absolute rank..."[13]

We cannot here explicate the essay in all its complexity. Yet we can state by way of summary that the question of personality is played out here in many variations, whereby not only so called great personalities—writers, historical figures—are investigated as "final products" of certain periods but also as individuals *per se,* whose development is then sketched. We find out, for example, what contributed to Rousseau's personality and in what way his "appearance" interacted with his mental attitude and therefore with his thinking. Mann calls the "father of the French Revolution" an "unhappy wretch," at least "half or three-quarters mad" and quite suicidal. In short, he was a "stepchild" of Mother Nature, an "accident of birth."[14] Essentially the same situation is present in the cases of Schiller and Dostoevsky: disease and physical imperfections are "essential and typical traits of the kind of men they were," that is, they were "deeply founded in their very being" as types.[15] Neither is it a coincidence that certain types are of a certain origin: "heroes and saints of the idea" like Schiller and Dostoevsky were of humble parentage and spent all their lives "in pinched... and undignified circumstances." And it is just as natural that the "two great realists and creative artists," Goethe and Tolstoy (and Mann doubtless included himself too), were of patrician descent.[16] Physiognomy is one of the external facts that Mann assigns a significant role in the development of the personality. "The sons of spirit" are supposed to "make a spiritual impression" because they have experienced things that "shattered the soul" and the traces of their fate are written in their faces for us to perceive them. This is how Mann explains the "lofty, pale, suffering-saint and criminal face" of Dostoevsky and the visionary and "equally ailing physiognomy" of Schiller.[17]

Enculturation is also assigned its own function in the creative process: it brings together two such disparate types as Tolstoy and Dostoevsky. Both possess a "tremendous Easternness" which explains their reactionary stance; their fundamental Easterness finds intellectual expression in the "mockery at and denial of European progress." The other "great realist," Goethe, is put into an altogether different realm: this "humanistic deity" had nothing but "hatred" and "scorn" for that region where Tolstoy found himself at home, according to Mann. Goethe despised many peoples because of their "Easternness"—including the Magyars. We are told that Goethe made a journey into Poland and, having made a first contact "with the Slav," felt quite "remote from cultured men." All he observed was "ignorance,... low standards of living, stupidity."[18] Let it be simply noted here that the spirit of Goethean humanism does not reign supreme in this prejudiced assessment; rather, there are traces of the "maliciousness" and of the "unenlightened Godliness" which is attributed to Tolstoy's character.

All in all, we find in this essay the beginnings of a clarification and determination of Thomas Mann's idea of personality but no absolute definition of the phenomenon. The beginnings do help us, however, in ascertaining the poetic determination that takes place, for example, in *The Magic Mountain*. The author is himself aware of the difficulty of definition: " 'Personality,' for a lack of better term, stands for something which at bottom escapes being defined and named. Personality does not have anything to do directly with mind *[Geist]* or with culture, either. ..." It belongs "in the sphere of the mystical and the elemental, in the *natural* sphere."[19] This "definition" is a variation of an earlier attempt at definition in *Reflections of a Non-Political Man,* where the following is said about the personality:

> It is true: what characterizes the human being as a social being is not what is actually admirable in him. The human being is not only a social but also a metaphysical being; in other words, he is not only an individual but also a personality. It is therefore wrong to confuse the supra-individual element with the social one... for the personality, not the mass, is the actual bearer of the general.[20]

The fact that Thomas Mann regarded the realm of the personality as being above and beyond the political realm can be explained by his apolitical (or better: his anti-political) stance. Philosophically, this notion is derived from Kant's philosophy of reason, which as a variation of the Platonic idea of the two worlds, sharply divides the world of the sensuous and the world of the supersensuous. It is alone the nature of man that belongs in equal measure to both worlds: to the world of the sensuous (world of knowledge, of necessity) and to that of the supersensuous (world of freedom and of faith). As a member of the world of the supersensuous, man decides in free self-determination; in this world he is an intelligible character. But man is also a member of the natural order of things and as such he is a necessary product of the causal connection of phenomena; that is his empirical character.[21]

This is not to say that the philosophical grounding of the concept of personality is to be derived directly from Mann's experience of Kant. It is rather his "Goethe experience" which forms the basis for these views. In *Wilhelm Meister,* namely, Goethe brought to life in fiction the educational ideal of neohumanism—the realization of the harmonious, well-rounded personality in the spirit of *humanitas.* In the poem *"Urworte, Orphisch"* he described and defined the two "characters": the intelligible character appears as the "perfected form" and the empirical character is passed through lightly in life. The highest moral law is given in the poetic formulation of the categorical imperative: "Bedingung und Gesetz; und aller Wille / Ist nur ein Wollen, weil wir eben sollten" (Condition and Law; and all Will is merely wanting to do what we ought).[22]

Thomas Mann knew the poem and used to quote it. It is no coincidence that this humanistic educational ideal is put into Settembrini's mouth in the course of the great debate about personality and about the freedom and dignity of man (399–400).

But in the "Goethe and Tolstoy" essay, the personality is transported to the "sphere of the mystical and the elemental" and no longer moves in the neohumanistic, ethical (Kantian) realm. We may be allowed to conclude that Thomas Mann is approaching the position of philosophical anthropology, which at the beginning of the twentieth century stepped into the foreground as *the* new philosophy of man; it received its decisive impetus through Nietzsche's championing the significance of the "body" and the "physiological driving forces" in human attitudes and creation. Based on the conception of the "unity of life and soul" *(Leibseele-Einheit)* it was possible to stress and to explain the vital origins *(Urgründe)* of man's mental and spiritual life. Over against the one-sided, naturalistic models on the one hand, and the abstract and faded *humanitas* idea of idealism on the other, human existence was supposed to be grasped in its unity and totality.[23] One approach to philosophical anthropology was defined by the question of the meaning of human existence, a question which in that period of great change in the awareness of being and the world was most timely. Another approach, inspired mainly by Max Scheler's studies, led to the investigation of the "person" as the "center of the intellectual act" *(geistiges Aktzentrum)*: in this approach the philosophical problems relating to individuality, freedom, and personality were of the utmost importance. Henri Bergson and Nicolai Hartmann in particular concerned themselves with the essence and the ontological possibility of personal freedom; their efforts resulted in the positing of the concept of "antinomy of ought" *(Sollenantinomie)*. Such problems undeniably crop up time and again in the *disputations* on the "magic mountain."

Certain research trends within philosophical anthropology inaugurated the notion of *Leibseele-Einheit;* the medical science of man's physical makeup *(Konstitutionslehre)* had worked out the psychophysical types of personalities based on characteristics which were derived as much from the spiritual as from the physical, from the character as much as from the physical build. Psychology and characterology took up these questions, and the insights into the biology and pathology of man were worked into the philosophical view of man. This period displayed great interest "in the phenomena of the expression of the spiritual *[seelisch]* and of the spiritual–mental elements in physical form and manifestations."[24]

Ludwig Klages gained particular eminence in this field. His *Vitalpsychologie* was widely known and influential. Among other things, Klages invented the methods of a science of expression *(Ausdruckskunde);* it constitutes a science of the entire visible appearance and activity of man in gestures, walk, speech, and so forth. The underlying idea was that the material and perceivable expressions—as well as language— belong to the spiritual realm. In order to gauge and appreciate Klages's influence and that of his contemporaries, we merely have to think of the "personality of Mynheer

Peeperkorn" with his culture-laden gestures that command overall attention (620). In a similar vein, the ever recurring physical descriptions in Mann's work of the outsider point to a biological and pathological view of man. It cannot be denied that Mann was familiar with Klages's writings and that they had an impact on him.[25] Whether Mann accepted Klages's theoretical premises or not is not the question here; as with so many other things, they were "in the air" and were incorporated into the novel.

What Thomas Mann specifically thought about Klages and his biocentric metaphysics is best expressed in a letter written in 1934:

Permit me the confession that I am no friend of the anti-spiritual and anti-intellectual movement represented in Germany by Klages. Very early on I feared and fought it because I saw through it in all its brutally anti-human consequence before they became apparent. ... I contend that the "irrational" *fad* brings with it the sacrificing of achievements and principles that... make the human being human. That sort of thing is a "back to nature" movement of a far more ignoble sort... than the movement that prepared the way for the French Revolution.[26]

This statement should be accepted *cum grano salis*. Indeed, the figure of Mynheer Peeperkorn is in its "vitality" and majestic greatness just *one* of the possibilities of being human and with all its grandeur is just as doomed to failure as Naphta's; death by self-destruction has been "prescribed" for both. But this personality contains the mystical and the elemental and has been placed in the sphere of the "natural" as the definition of personality in the "Goethe and Tolstoy" essay required. Just as Klages and the "fad" of the period were called by Mann "irrational," Peeperkorn's person and his effect on others is "irrational." Mme. Chauchat says as much when she declares thet Peeperkorn's "feeling" forced her "to follow him and to serve him" (597). Anti-spirituality and anti-intellectuality are main features of this character, Peeperkorn expresses no thoughts; he merely possesses "gestures." One is inclined to agree with Hans Wolff when he assesses Peeperkorn's charismatic personality as a "caricature of a man wanting to live an absolutely vital life" and sees depicted in it the most extreme form of decadence.[27] It is of secondary importance here whether the author—like his character, Hans Castorp—believed in the "mystery" of personality or not. What is important is to see how Mann's poetic acuity and sensitivity toward trends of the times benefited his *Zeitroman* and secured the realness of his poetic world (as Lukács expressed it). In so doing he once again succeeded "better than the sociologists," as proudly boasted: Max Weber's sociological determination of the "charismatic personality" is expanded poetically in the figure of Mynheer Peeperkorn. But that could occur only because Thomas Mann was intent upon staying on the trail of the *Zeitgeist* and was willing to "capture" it, to build it in. ("The air was full of it" was one of his favorite replies when he was asked about the genesis of this or that element in his work.) He also grasped the extent of disorganization in the period during which he was working on *The Magic Mountain*, and in which the ability of man to orient himself was destroyed. He perceived with a great sense of loss the elimination of the last remnants of the nineteenth century. Thus, the period became receptive for the (false) "prophetic *Führer*" who announced *the* solution—or any solution.[28] The Klages quote registers this fact quite clearly. The positive approach of certain trends or "fads" did not escape Mann's attention, and he summed up their value as well as usefulness (for him) in a letter written in 1932:

> The sufferings and adventures [of Europe]... in recent times have stirred up a new and peculiarly intense interest in the problem of man himself—in his nature, his position in the cosmos, his past, his future. ... [It] inspired a new anthropology, perhaps especially here in Germany. ... In those efforts speculation has been passionately mingled with exact science in a way somewhat like the psychoanalytic investigation of primitive life. Physiognomy, characterology, linguistics have undergone revivals.
>
> Works such as those of Max Scheler... are especially characteristic of this new, humane interest which seems to me to constitute our period's chief intellectual tendency. ...such researches contain the germs of a new humanism in the sense of the Goethean *[sic]* maxim: "The proper study of mankind is man." [It] is bound to have artistic consequences. ... Once more I find that man, and especially the artist, is much less of an individual than he hoped or feared to be.[29]

Mann's demonstrated familiarity with the newly initiated "scientific" approaches to man, however, is not the sole or even the main basis of his preoccupation with the problem of personality. That preoccupation was grounded for the most part in his "Nietzsche experience." Nietzsche's critical cultural philosophy, particularly during the period of *Human, All Too Human,* demonstrated the anthropological orientation of his concept of morality. What mattered to him here was a philosophical attitude toward life, that is, a philosophical anthropology and psychology. Still, in *Zarathustra* the "attitude of the world and of science is derived from the biological and social preconditions of the species man."[30] Mann frequently points out that his great teachers were Schopenhauer and Nietzsche: Nietzsche's teachings on culture and on man were definitely of great significance. Not only opinions, but also figures of speech, concepts, and literal descriptions are appropriated from Nietzsche, as the large-scale essay "Goethe and Tolstoy" proves. From here they found their way into *The Magic Mountain*—although they are not totally absent from earlier works. One chapter heading of Nietzsche's *Zarathustra* is "On the Pale Criminal" *(Vom bleichen Verbrecher);* in Mann's essay this becomes Dostoevsky's *bleiche Verbrechermiene* (pale face of a criminal). Nietzsche equates asceticism with the physical form "thin, ugly, starved" as a way of suggesting the body's wish to "escape the body and the earth." Thomas Mann uses the very same adjectives in describing the physiognomy of many of life's "exceptional cases," thereby symbolizing the process of spiritualization or intellectualization. Repeatedly we hear from Nietzsche and then in connection with Naphta that "cruelty is the ecstasy of the [ascetic] soul." One could string the examples together infinitely, culminating in Nietzsche's conclusion with regard to contemporary reality: "Everything deserves to perish [*Alles ist wert, dass es zugrunde geht*]."[31] This statement constitutes the foundation of Naphta's ideology, which announces the "transvaluation of all values."

Thomas Mann is said to favor a style of realism which is painfully exact and almost too detailed. The author cheerfully owed up to the fact. In his letter to Hilde Diestel, for example, he was begging to be told about a sordidly fascinating story "precisely, carefully, in great detail"; "May I observe," wrote Mann, "that the details are what matter most to me. They are so stimulating."[32] What is characteristic of his artistry in general is also applicable to his fictional characters in particular. The "characters and personalities" of *The Magic Mountain* are depicted in an astonishingly varied manner and are by no means fixed as mere "final result" (that is, without being developed), as Herman Stresau and other critics of Mann thought. To be sure, they do appear as fully developed personalities and do not undergo a change within the novel's story (with the exception of Hans Castorp, of course). But the development *up to* their appearance in the course of the story is given in the form of the genesis of a personality. As Mann says in his study of Nietzsche, "We must look at the origins of this mind in order *to follow up on the influence operating in the formation of [his] personality*."[33] The following considerations come into play: Where Nietzsche was *born and raised*, his *education*, his *fate* (disease), his *innate gifts* (high intellectual endowment, his genius), the *time* into which he was born and which formed him (the "psychic possibilities of our feeble, rational epoch"), *tradition* (the "scholarly discipline and restraint of the humanistic German tradition" to be critiqued), and, finally, his *physical state* (his acquired "disease... which derives its meaning... from whom it belongs to"). The points of view just mentioned and those depicted in the "Goethe and Tolstoy" essay correspond by and large to present-day thinking about the traits and the constituting factors of that elusive concept, "personality."[34]

Leo Naphta's biography and his physiognomy have been discussed extensively; they were conceived and fixed in the novel as constituting factors of his personality, that is, in the case of Naphta's physiognomy as an important element of his personality. The cousins—and the reader—are not aware of Leo Naphta's prehistory when they first meet him. And yet Naphta's individuality and behavior leave a deep and decisive impression. To be sure, in Joachim's case it is merely the physical features—the "Jewish nose" and the "puny figure"—which catch his attention and put him off. Hans Castorp immediately *knows* that in Naphta he has found the right person to fulfil the role of the educator for him. With his "strangeness" and his "drawling accent," Naphta is predestined, so to speak, to be a teacher. This constellation is neither the first nor is it a unique occurrence in Mann's *oeuvre*; rather, it is an early feature and remains an important aspect of Mann's artistic enterprise. As Thomas Mann expounded in his study of Dostoevsky, this constellation, too, is grounded in his Nietzsche experience. Nietzsche had chosen Dostoevsky as his "great teacher," in Mann's opinion, because he came from the "Eastern sphere" and therefore lacked some "of the humanistic inhibitions which conditioned Nietzsche." Simply because he *"was not German"* (Mann's emphasis), Dostoevsky was eminently qualified as an educator.[35] It is worth pointing out that Hans Castorp's mentors all come from the "non-German" sphere: Settembrini from Italy, Naphta from the Eastern Jewish sphere, and Mynheer Peeperkorn from Holland (via the Asiatic region).[36]

As the cousins remark after the first encounter with Naphta, they do not succeed in "making him out altogether" (385). Nevertheless, some significant aspects of his personality can be ascertained already on this occasion; further meetings serve to strengthen and complement the picture they gain in the beginning. Settembrini's warning merely rounded off that picture. The characterization of Naphta occurs in a masterful way: the most typical traits of his personality, such as expression and style, temperament, intellect and ability, interests, and values are established by means of allusions, recurring designations and word combinations, and by a few fixed adectives and adverbial phrases.

"Everything about him was sharp," is what we hear first about Naphta—even the silence which he maintains and from which it could be inferred that his speech will be sharp and logical (372). Naphta is wont to scoff at the liberal views of the others, and he is in the habit of giving "a short laugh" at some of their naive ideas. Unlike his counterpart, Herr Settembrini, Naphta is anything but "gallant and human" following their heated exchanges; he is more inclined to "shrug his shoulders" and to disdain to reply when he feels *contemptuous* of a statement. Naphta is given to "smile maliciously" whenever he succeeds in "unmasking" the untenability of some of the arguments of his opponent (382).

The cousins gain further impressions when they visit Naphta in his apartment; his method of argumentation confirms their previous experiences. Whenever Naphta seems to suffer a "crushing rebuff," he just sits there "silent and sharp." But as the matter of "terror" comes up during one of the *disputationes,* Naphta's "sharp and apodictic" tone surfaces in full force: he utters the word "lower than the rest" and, while remaining motionless, is "flashing like a drawn blade" (400). At the conclusion of this intellectual duel, the author remarks: "Thus Naphta's sharp talk" (404). Not even at Joachim's deathbed does Naphta's sharpness subside: as Herr Settembrini has to recognize Naphta's temporary superiority over him, brought about by death, he remains silent, but Naphta cannot refrain from instructing him in a "sharply sententious manner" on the serious dignity of death (539). Finally, in the period of "great irritability" *(Hysterica Passio),* Naphta's snappishness reaches its height: he takes his physical deterioration with a mocking "expansiveness and aggressiveness" and manages to irritate Settembrini to extremes. Even Hans Castorp has to admit that Naphta's maliciousness surpasses the limits of what is mentally healthy (689). The intellectual quarrels appropriately intensify because Naphta's "malicious wit lay in ambush" to spy out the other's weaknesses (692). And this brings about the "prescribed" end: first, Naphta's last extensive monologue, "conducted in a manner singularly offensive, from a social point of view" and directed entirely toward Hans Castorp, followed by a short quarrel with Settembrini. Settembrini condemns Naphta's "scurrilities," and Naphta reacts in a way that provides Hans Castorp with an uncanny experience and "unmasks" Naphta's true character:

There was a stillness in which could be heard the gnashing of Naphta's teeth. To Hans Castorp this was an experience. ... He had supposed it to be a figure of speech, something which did not actually occur. Yet here was Naphta, and in the silence his teeth could be heard to grate; *a horribly unpleasant, a wild, incredible sound,* which *yet evinced a self-control equally fearsome,* for he did not scream but rather said quietly and merely with a sort of gasping half-laugh: 'Infamy?' (697; Emphasis added and translation slightly changed for accuracy and completeness.)

Naphta's death occurs in an atmosphere of chilly distance and arrogance; even Hans Castorp's humane words elicit no response. Only in the final moment does Naphta cry out ("coward") before he shoots himself in the head (705). Hans Castorp's prophetic words about courage echo in the author's remark that Naphta's last shriek is a confession to the fact that "it takes more courage to fire than to be fired upon."

Enough has been said to allow the conclusion that Naphta's temperament, expression and style are set almost completely in a way that let us discern their mutual dependence. Naphta's originally "wild" and "adventurous" temperament is kept under control by terrible discipline and mastery and pressed into the service of achievement. This in turn is the root cause of his absolute sharpness, snappishness, maliciousness, and the abruptness of his argumentation.

Naphta's motivation, intellect, ability, interest, and value judgments fully complement the other aspects of his personality. Although they unfold in the course of the encounters and disputations, they are founded in the biographical chapter "Operationes Spirituales" and extensively fixed there. The reasons for this are to be found in the ethnological–anthropological grounding of the Naphta portrayal. As we learn in the description of his prehistory, Naphta inherited "besides his small stature, an exceptional mind" from his father. From his mother, he had received "the seeds of the lung disease" (441). Both his talent and the disease—which makes for progressive spiritualization in Mann's opinion—are inherited features. Another inherited feature is equally important: we are told that Naphta's father, Elia Naphta, was not only a kosher butcher but was considered to be "something unusual" even by his brothers of the faith because he was a man "of more than common knowledge" and, in addition, of "matters that might be somewhat uncanny." There was something of a "sectarian irregularity" about him. He is placed in the company of "a Baal–Shem or Zaddik," and the suggestion is made that he had belonged to the Hasidic (mystical) sect.[37] In this regard, Elia Naphta was irregular as a Jew. His son, Leo Naphta, receives as his paternal inheritance this "sectarian irregularity"; indeed, this trait is given yet a further dimension in Naphta inasmuch as he is not only improper as a Jew but also as a Jesuit. Hans Castorp immediately grasps this side of Naphta's being: "I mean, is he a real, actual Jesuit?... What I mean is, is he *proper as a Jesuit?*... He said certain things... about communism, and about the religious zeal of the proletariat, and not withholding its hand from bloodshed. ... Is that allowed? ... Isn't it—what is the word?—heretical, abnormal, incorrect?" (410). At a later point, Naphta is described as a man of "assorted qualities,"[38] of combinatory power, a highly "unorthodox personage," a *"joli jésuite à la petite tache humide"* (466). Hans Castorp also calls him a "problem child of life" and thus underscores his inner affinity with Leo Naphta.

This notion is further strengthened by the "primeval imagining" in which both Hans Castorp and Leo Naphta indulged in childhood.[39] Naphta's father "gave" his son the images of "solemn mercilessness," the concept of piety coupled with cruelty, and the association of the idea with the sight of blood which was perceived to be holy and spiritual because of the allusion to the father's eyes: they sent out "gleams like starts" and "had held in their depth a wealth of silent spiritual fervour" (340). The child's imagination places the figure of the father in primeval (pre-Christian) times; this suggestion is meant undoubtedly to evoke the dignified, great and noble period of ancient Judaism. In the case of Hans Castorp, this recall of primeval times occurs under a very different sign: he looks at the "baptismal bowl" with eyes that are "transfixed" and he listens to the *"Ur–Ur–Ur–Ur"* sounds denoting origins and a primeval state, whereby spiritual feelings are mixed "with feelings of death," and a "sense of history" (22). As we are told subsequently, the little Hans Castorp awakens to all sorts of "Spanish, Dutch, late Middle Ages associations" (25) which without doubt have something in common with the spiritual sphere of the adult Naphta. The primeval sensibilities of both children point to something essential that they share: it is the realization that death is surrounded by a "pious, contemplative and mournfully beautiful, that is to say, spiritual aura "(27). Such common elements are not shared by Herr Settembrini: his grandfather, the prosaic Milanese attorney, is merely referred to as a historical figure, but there is absolutely no possibility of a "primeval" connection between the German "burgherly" sphere of Hans Castorp and the purely political-rational, enlightened one of Settembrini. It is different with the *Jewish* Naphta. A summary explanation of Thomas Mann in 1937 put it this way: "So much can be said jointly about the Germans and the Jews!"[40] Their task and their fate in the world as well as their "role as mediators" constitute this commonality. In the opinion of Thomas Mann, Judaism "represents the connection... between present and most distant past, between Europeanism and its Near Eastern origins."[41]

It is beyond the limits of this work to discuss in detail Thomas Mann's presentation of Judaism and his coming to terms with it in his life and work. But insofar as we made mention of certain "affinities" and "common elements" between Hans Castorp and Leo Naphta, that is, their respective realms, this entire problem area should not go completely unmentioned. It would definitely be somewhat daring to maintain that the inner relationship between these two fictional characters is as close as that of Joseph and Hanno Buddenbrook, for example. Thomas Mann had this to say about his *Joseph* novel:

> The biblical Joseph as I see and comprehend him, is completely determined and is filled in his own consciousness... by the blessing from above and the one from below... by a doubling of the blessing which gives to his character—despite all that is objectionable about it—its fascinating, highly charming, blinding and blind qualities, and by virtue of which he often leads his fellowman astray. ...[42]

Joseph is a "typical artist" and "all that is lovable and disagreeable, winning and dubious, enchanting and annoying about him," says Mann, "comes from this very fundamental makeup of his character."[43] Given that Joseph is this type of artistically inclined person, "he is the mythic brother of that little latecomer [*Spätbürger*], Hanno Buddenbrook."[44] Thus, each of them is in a sense a "latecomer," a grandchild, a descendant (in the latter case, of burghers), and as such "a complicated case, a borderline case at that point of development where refinement and degeneration mix disquietingly."[45] Apart from the fact that several aspects of Naphta's personality can be best described as disagreeable, dubious, and annoying, he is a kin of a sort to Joseph, Hanno and Hans Castorp, that is, he is also "the proper descendant of his fathers" who then "transforms their qualities and realizes them on a more precarious cultural level."[46] As Mann conceived the character, Joseph's "politically clever" hustling of God corrupted and transformed "the piety of the patriarchs." Much the same way, Naphta is portrayed as having transformed his father's quiet spirituality and piety into a "politically clever" hustling of God—although Naphta's God turned out to be of a completely different nature.

At the very beginning of the novel, some of the undeniably common elements are alluded to. We learn that Hans Castorp is a "still unwritten page" (36) and is thus open to possibilities. He could take after his grandfather, for example, "and be a drag, a conservative element." He "might turn out to be a radical," a "profane destroyer of old buildings," meaning traditional values; in this case, he would act "as unfettered as a Jew" (35). Leo Naphta, the "unfettered Jew," represents this latter, "radical" way in the novel. He is—as a Jew—highly qualified for this role because, according to Mann, "a significant share in the construction of the new, developing social world is reserved for worldly Jewish energy."[47]

Thus, Naphta had received as his "inheritance" in the broadest sense of the word his abilities and aspirations, and along with that, he was accorded a specific type of intellectuality. Early perceptions of "solemn mercilessness" and pious cruelty combined with the tendency to "brood," to think in a "sectarian manner,"—these are the traits handed down to him. The motivation is derived from Naphta's "ardent yearning" for more noble forms of existence, from lofty ambitions and "aristocratic instincts." Passionately, he reaches out "beyond the sphere of his origin." This instinctive aspect is usually stressed by the author and is presented as "typically Jewish." We are told:

> Like many gifted Jews, Naphta was by instinct both aristocrat and revolutionary. A socialist, yet possessed by the dream of taking part in the proudest, finest, most exclusive and conventional sphere of life. [His] first utterance... was in substance a declaration of affection for the Roman Church, as a power at once spiritual and aristocratic (in other words anti-material), at once superior and inimical to wordly things (in other words, revolutionary). And the homage he thus paid was genuine, and profound [stammte aus seines Wesens Mitte]; for, as he himself explained, Judaism, by virtue of its secular and materialistic leanings, its socialism, its political adroitness, had actually more in common with Catholicism than the latter had with the mystic subjectivity and self-immolation of Protestantism; the conversion of a Jew to the Roman Catholic faith was accordingly a distinctly less violent spiritual rupture than was that of a Protestant (443–444).[48]

Naphta's character and his inclination lead him almost necessarily to the Jesuit paedagogium, whose "scholarly and socially charming atmosphere" make him "exaggeratedly happy." The monastic-manorial life, with its discipline and elegance as well as its intellectuality and cultivated atmosphere, is flattering to "Leo's deepest instincts" (444). And young Leo Naphta finds most congenial the prevailing "cosmopolitanism" of the establishment, because it prevents his "race from being perceptible." What alone matters there is talent, the eagerness to learn, and a satisfactory "social bearing," not race (445). There are other "young exotics" there, so we hear, and some of them look "even more 'Jewish' than he" does. (This, of course, implies that elsewhere, in the normal world, people who look Jewish do not have such an easy time of it.)

The educational practices of the Jesuit establishment easily accommodate Leo's "personal abilities" and challenge them. What are these abilities? From early on, Naphta trains his mind "in an unsystematic and impatient" manner because he recognizes that education (here, self-education) can secure the possibilities of a "higher and nobler" form of existence. Young Leo's relationship with the district rabbi, from whom he learns the basics such as Hebrew, mathematics, classics and logic, comes to an abrupt and early end: just as was the case with his father, Leo's "sectarian" ways are the underlying cause (442). The young man's "craftiness" and his "intellectual burrowing" combine with a revolutionary tendency: the logical passion of Leo Naphta is developed in a "socially critical direction." No wonder, then, that his second mentor, the cultivated Jesuit, immediately notices Leo's tremendous talent; the "malicious elegance of his thinking" is found equally impressive. No less characteristic and noticeable is Leo's "sharp and tortured intellectuality," the unavoidable final outcome of such an educational process.

Naphta's zeal and desire make possible his acceptance in a novitiate of the order; his illness ensures that he can never fully belong to it. The disease which comes "from within" is in its worsening merely the result of Naphta's deep insight into the limits of his "assimilation." He finds it in the last analysis unimaginable that a life can be spent in "serving humility and silent subservience" in the *intellectual realm*. Thus, he engages in contradictions, quarrels and controversies with his tutors (445). "Brother Naphta" is admonished to pray for a more "tranquil spirit," but he has already made the decision that the "veritable 'graveyard peace'" which inevitably results in the "atrophy of the personality" is not for him. Seemingly, "fate" has intervened: his "hereditary complaint" takes him away from the flatlands and the possibility of full ordination. Naphta's path leads just as fatefully to the "magic mountain" and for not "so much a cure as [for] a fixed condition of existence" (47). Naphta, the improper *Jew,* now becomes improper as a Jesuit.

Such are the forming principles and the genesis of Naphta's personality which Hans Castorp finds extremely stimulating and which Herr Settembrini warns against. In answer to Hans Castorp's question, "Against what?" there comes Herr Settembrini's summary explanation: "Against the personage...[whose] form is logic but [whose] essence is confusion" (407). Settembrini complements the warning with a description of the nature of Naphta's intellectuality:

> Herr Naphta is *a person of most unusual mental powers.* He is by nature discoursive, and so am I. ... I avail myself of the opportunity to cross words with him with an antagonist who is after all my equal. We dispute. We quarrel... till we draw blood; but I confess *the contrariness and mischievousness of his ideas* but *render* our *acquaintance the more attractive.* I need the friction. ... You are defenceless against intellectual sophistry, you are exposed to danger from the influence of this *half fanatical,* half *pernicious* quackery—danger to the intellect and to the soul. (408)

Herr Settembrini recommends that his young friend counter Naphta with plenty of critical resistance. The reason: Naphta is a "voluntary" in a "broader, more intellectual sense." Naphta's thoughts are of the "voluptuous" type, for they stand "under the aegis of death," which is the "most dissolute of powers" (412).

These, then, are the facts concerning Naphta's personality which, according to Thomas Mann, are "carefully founded" biographically and which supposedly unite

Jesuit and Communist elements. The formulation was without a doubt carefully thought out. Naphta is neither Communist nor Jesuit—nor unequivocally Jewish. The character is "merely" a combination of "typical traits" with which Mann no doubt was personally familiar in many variations. This figure represents *one* of the possibilities *within* the novel; and it symbolizes *one* possibility *within* the character. This is the reason why various interpreters could see in Naphta a communist, a fascist, and more. In my opinion, there are—or were—*ascetic communists* with a shot of the religious (e.g., Lukács and Levine) but *no fascists* with such a combination. Naphta's personality contains a trait shared by both types: *asceticism*, one of the most outstanding features of Naphta's character about which, interestingly enough, Herr Settembrini does not speak. But it is noticed early by the "innocent" young man, Hans Castorp, who discovers Naphta's understanding of and sympathy for the "military," with its love of obedience and "service" and with its "serious side to it, sort of ascetic..." (378). At the same time, Leo Naphta embraces the idea of labor and its blessings, not because it is in the service of "progress" but because it is pursued at the cost of life ("wiles of the flesh") and thus becomes asceticism pure and simple in that it functions as "penitential discipline" and a means of salvation (377). Accordingly, Naphta here represents *Trotzdem* (defiance) as a formula for life; what was considered pure artistic egoism in the case of Tonio Kröger and Gustav von Aschenbach is given the character of religious egoism in the case of Naphta. But here as well as in the earlier works, the ascetic ideal is derived "from the protective and curative instincts of a life that is degenerating and yet fighting tooth and nail for its preservation."[49] Nietzsche calls this sort of man (the "sick animal") a "master of destruction, of self-destruction."[50] But destruction and self-destruction are violent acts; thus, the concept of violence and asceticism are correlated to each other.

The question of finding a living model for a character such as Naphta's is extremely difficult, as the figure resists any clear-cut identification. As is often the case with Thomas Mann, not only the ideas and statements but also the characters are ambivalent because of the "richness of interconnections."[51] And the figure of Naphta is unquestionably one of the most subtle ones. The "business of appropriation," as Mann called it, was particularly brisk at the time *The Magic Mountain* was being written. Literary tradition, personal experiences, and the taking up of earlier motifs all made their contribution to this character.

Still, it seems to me that the Lukács component can be traced precisely in the depiction of the personality of Leo Naphta—including the spiritual–intellectual aspect of his personality—more clearly and decisively than was the case with his life story or physiognomy. For reasons already discussed we shall separate the non-Lukács components before getting to the discussion of the Lukács traits in Naphta's personality.

As has already been stated, there are only vague indications of an ideal–typical treatment of Jewishness in the Hagenström figures of *Buddenbrooks*. They are simply presented as the upcoming, competing elite of the industrializing nineteenth century; they are the parvenus, the bourgeois upstarts. The portrayal becomes much more differentiated in the novella "The Blood of the Walsungs" and in the novel *Royal Highness;* here for the first time certain characteristics become visible which are retained and are influential up to *Doctor Faustus.*

In "The Blood of the Walsungs," it is the children of Herr Aarenhold who, far removed from the mere parvenu existence of their father, embody refinement, decadence, spiritualization, and the conscious ambivalence of their class. They show themselves contemptuous of their forefathers, that is, of their origins; they despise their parents for the inherited "blood." The parallel to Naphta's contempt of his family is evident. From this heightened awareness of their precarious status follows their behavior: they always speak with a "sharp tongue," seemingly on the attack, hurtful "perhaps...due to the sheer pleasure of turning a phrase."[52] In style and temperament, the debates at the Aarenhold table resemble Naphta's: matters are "dissected" with sharp wit, attacks are carried out "with steely and abstract dialectic," and the right to one's own terminology is insisted upon in "irritated words." They all speak well, and their "gestures [are] nervous and self-assured"; they all "march in the van of taste" and the best is hardly enough for them. What unites them, however, is that they "ruthlessly" insist "upon power and achievement" and want "success in the cruel trial of strength."[53] Important motifs such as a radical disposition, the steely and abstract intellectuality, the cruel ethics of achievement *(Leistungsethik)* and the irritated, arrogant, and "sharp" manner of expression were already present in this early work as attributes of certain "exceptional" or "special" cases of life.

Everything that first existed in the stories at the level of description received its philosophical grounding as early as 1909 in *Royal Highness.* It is enough to recall one single episode in the novel, when the Grand Duke asks Dr. Sammet whether he has ever felt his origins to be a hindrance, a disadvantage. Dr. Sammet's impassioned words summarize the nature and duties of an exceptional existence:

> No principle of equalization... will ever prevent the incidence... of exceptional and abnormal men who are distinguished from the bourgeois norm. ... It is the duty of the individual... to see what is essential in that distinction and to recognize that it imposes on him an exceptional obligation. ... A man is at an advantage... if he has one motive more than [the complacent majority] to extraordinary exertions.[54]

Motivation and its effect, extraordinary achievement, are thus presented as important aspects of personality. In Dr. Überbein's "biographical confession," this statement is dramatically heightened and expanded. It is in this regard that we perceive the prefiguration here of many aspects of the Naphta figure. Dr. Überbein tells of his preference—indeed, his love—for the "extraordinary in every form and in every sense," and declares: "I love those who are conscious of the dignity of their exceptional station, the marked men," all "those who are *visibly strangers*," and "all those whose sight causes people to make stupid faces."[55] (The emphasis is added and the translation slightly changed.) As a gypsy by birth, "a hard-working one," Dr. Überbein no doubt considers himself also an exceptional case to some degree; he, therefore, speaks of his "predestination to the role" of the tutor of the young prince.

Dr. Überbein elaborates on the problem by giving expression to his conviction—and at the same time teaching Klaus Heinrich a lesson—that this higher form of existence consisting of "reserve, etiquette, obligation, duty, demeanour, formality" has a special right to arrogance and that it does not include "humanity and good nature," meaning easy sociability. The "select and sadly isolated forms of life" Überbein refers to include other than merely princely existences. Rather, it takes into account all special and exceptional cases which transform unfavorable conditions, such as "miserable youth, loneliness, and exclusion from happiness," into "attractive qualifications." All those exceptional cases, those strangers, become stringy and tough on the inside (*innerlich sehnig*) without comfort; life for them is a "never-ceasing, imperious call to be up and doing."[56]

This personal "confession" is multilayered, rich in connections, and loaded with interpretive possibilities. At first it reads like a self-analysis of the writer, who in the notes to *Death in Venice* calls Gustav von Aschenbach a "libertine" and a "gypsy" and then in a letter to his future wife speaks of himself "as a kind of prince," and as such "something extraordinary."[57] That is to say, he emphasizes the aristocratic aspect of both existences. At the same time, the private tutor is being equated with the artist by means of the designation "hard working gypsy" and is being placed in the realm of higher forms of existence. Indeed, in the novel mention is made between their two different kinds of existence." Dr. Überbein, in turn, has certain characteristics in common with Dr. Sammet, the physician with the "unsympathetic name."[58] Dr. Sammet, who as a Jew is also found to have an "annoying and irritating" presence, represents here another exceptional case: he is the stranger and is also destined for a higher form of existence.

Dr. Überbein's physical appearance, temperament and style of expression are described in such a manner that we cannot help seeing in him a forebear of Leo Naphta. He appears different and thus alienates people (the "common herd") through his "demeanour, his loud, blustering mode of speaking [*scharf schwadronierende Redeweise*]." In Dr. Überbein's "immoderate and reckless striving" are concealed his "lack of modesty and his arrogance"; all this makes him a rather unpopular man with both his fellow citizens and the press. Since he is of the opinion that life consists solely of work and achievement, Dr. Überbein avoids "rest," "contentment," and "social intercourse."[59] As a fellow citizen he is "not pleasant," as a civil servant "not irreproachable," and as a colleague "not amiable." Thus, in every social category he is "improper," an "oddity" with a determined and uncomfortably reckless disposition who is unable to attain peace and satisfaction. All in all, Dr. Überbein is not a "harmonious personality," but in spite of that (or because of it), he is still capable of exerting "great magic" on his charge, the prince. "That attraction," we are told, is "very composite" and binds him forever to his pupil, who regards and treats him "as a comrade in fate and destiny."[60]

The determining factor, we hear further, is that Dr. Überbein's personality greatly supports his teachings and expectations. Thus, Mann correlates life (fate), style, temperament, values and manner of thinking. Here and in *The Magic Mountain,* the relationship between teacher and pupil is evoked by the same means. As Dr. Über-bein develops his ideas on the nature of exceptionality and related topics, the young prince is not quite able to comprehend and absorb everything, but he has already reached the stage when he is able to "imbibe the essence of ideas of that sort"; in this way, the teacher succeeds in influencing "Klaus Heinrich's mind and suscepti-bilities more...than was desirable." The overall effect of the private tutor's exposi-tions is to awaken "an echo deep down in the prince's soul."[61] As a result, the young man ignores the warning of the schoolmaster. (Cf. Herr Settembrini's warning against Naphta's "personality" and ideas.) Hans Castorp's experience is not much different: he associates the ascetic ideal of Naphta with "Spanish honor," with the discipline of death, with service and obedience. But we should not forget that this association and combination of "stand-up collar" and "Spanish ruff" has been brought up out of the depths of childhood memories and experiences of Hans Castorp (448).

Still, it seems significant that it was another "oddity," a stranger, another one of life's "exceptional cases," the "sharp-tongued" half-Jew Imma Spoelmann, who predicted that the "wretched" and unhappy Dr. Überbein would come to a bad end.[62] When we recall Hans Castorp's "prophetic question" to Joachim regarding Naphta, we discover the same motif being played out in different configurations. The grasp on two levels of the nature of exceptionality is already hinted at in *Royal Highness.* The citizens of the residential city exhibit the same unthinking surprise and unease at the sight of an "oddity" as does Joachim: the "unsympathetic name," the "Jewish nose," and the "puny figure" belong in this category of the "simple," uncon-scious, and "customary" prejudices of anti-Semitism, passed down from generation to generation. Imma Spoelmann, Klaus Heinrich, and Hans Castorp are capable of and ready to grasp instinctively the possibilities—and the limits—of this type. The reason for that lies in their being "comrades in fate and destiny": they are all special cases of life and as such are bound to each other for ever.

The obligation deriving from this extraordinary situation, the obligation to extra-ordinary achievements, that is, the *Leistungsethik,* the ascetic principle, made its appearance before *Royal Highness* in Mann's early "moralist of accomplishment" the figure of Thomas Buddenbrooks. Moreover, Mann reminds us, he has hardly written "anything that has not been symbolic of the heroism" of those who are "working at the edge of exhaustion"; this basic experience "worked formatively" from the main characters of *Fiorenza* through *Royal Highness* all the way to Gustav von Aschenbach, Mann says in the "Burgherly Nature" chapter of his *Reflections of a Non-Political Man*. To be sure, it had been thought and expressed differently at different stages of his artistic development; the development of the concept of exceptional existence, or more specifically its philosophical grounding, takes place in *Royal Highness* for the first time, in the "confessional" statements of Drs. Sammet and Überbein. The consequences are different, though. In the case of Dr. Sammet—and to a certain extent with Tonio Kröger—the possibility of a positive outcome is given. Dr. Überbein's unavoidable fate is the other path: it leads from him to Leo Naphta, with a detour over the artist's fate depicted in the figure of Gustav von Aschenbach. In *Death in Venice,* as with Dr. Überbein, the tragic outcome is the result of the *Leistugnsethik*. Without going into the relation of the figures and their destinies, the description of Dr. Überbein's end should support my claim. About the circumstances leading to his death by his own hand we learn that, for a man with Dr. Überbein's talents, it was a completely trivial occurrence that led to his ruin.[63] But he was predestined to end this way:

> The *quarrelsome and ungenial man,* who had never been a man amongst men at his club, who had haughtily resisted familiarity, and *ordered his life cold-bloodedly with a view exclusively to achievement*... there he lay now:... the first obstacle in the field of accomplishment, had brought him to a miserable end.[64]

Aschenbach's artistic egoism is subsequently transformed into Naphta's ascetic ideal with religious character. At the same time, the concept itself is expanded; the one-dimensional figure of Raoul Überbein evolves into the multifaceted one of Leo Naphta, which contains within it seemingly heterogeneous elements that are masterfully blended.[65]

As a final result, we can percieve in this figure *one* particular type and *one* extreme possibility which, as Thomas Mann said, has its role and its mission in *The Magic Mountain*. But the "trick" of combining the "communistic" with the "Jesuit-Catholic" (and the Jewish) elements was not as original as was first assumed; nor was it conceived like a flash of lightning out of the void. Readings, firsthand experiences, the social-political situation, and personal problems were all fused together here.

As was already pointed out in connection with Naphta's biography, we can safely assume that with regard to his personality, too, Ernst Bloch's book on Thomas Münzer proved inspirational. I am thinking in particular of the combination in one person of heretical theologian and revolutionary. Bloch describes Thomas Münzer as a "class conscious revolutionary and chiliastic communist" whose demands were of the "communistic-early Christian kind.[66] Being actively engaged, Thomas Münzer exercised the profession of the politician and the educator of the people rather than that of the preacher:

Indeed, *in the case of the active theologian* of the revolution, one element interlocks with the other, the deed with the distant goal, *the ideological with the religious idea;* and particularly in the pulsation... of an overflowing *feeling of mission,* they are interlocked to a degree that the concepts become almost directly interchangeable.[67]

Possessing this overwhelming feeling of mission is what distinguishes Münzer from Luther, whom he calls a preacher (of the establishment, the court) and a servile spirit.

From this view it is only one step to the claim that it is easy to recognize "in the Bolshevistic religion of Marxism the old, divinely inspired agressiveness, the Taborite–communist–Joash-like brand of radical Baptism.[68] Bloch's statement is from the year 1921, the "period of the last revolution on earth," as he and many others wanted to believe at the time. The intentions and the personal image of Thomas Münzer are "related in many ways to Liebknecht's," Bloch declares; moreover, the "inexorable organizer Münzer comes close to even a Lenin and his breed." For Bloch, such a combination is neither a daring nor a unique one for the "simple" reason that Münzer harbors within himself "the Russian, the most inwardly man" characteristic of "the Germanic 'Baptism' "; much "Slavic, Moravian, Silesian depth" lives in both.[69] Münzer's activities, after all, unfolded in the Saxon-Silesian region, where confessional and cultural tensions were not unknown. Silesia, "bastion and bridge between East and West," was the area where cultural currents flowed together and collided. Baptism—and Münzer—took a "left, radical direction" politically and were at the same time inwardly related to monarchism, specifically to the "anti-worldliness of lay mysticism."[70]

When it is claimed that Protestant mysticism also contains a "lot of the Middle Ages in it," Bloch has in mind the "other" Middle Ages in which took place "the radical attempt at the renewal of Catholicism" based on the spirit of Franciscan life and the Dominican mysticism of Eckhart."[71] In this respect, too, Münzer is a man between churches and spheres and at the same time a *Vermittler* (mediator). Bloch went even further and tried to establish an additional connection in the figure of Thomas Münzer: In contrast to Luther who was the ultimate source of the "legitimation of all governmental disdain of the *Geist* in Germany," Bloch's discerning eye sees in Münzer a kind of *Amtmann* (official) in the sense that Daniel (of the Old Testament) was one. In doing so, Bloch transfers to the modern revolutionary with a religious bent a quintessentially Jewish element, the idea of the *Amtmann,* as Naphta's father was called. (Bloch, by the way, was admittedly influenced strongly by Kautsky's treatment of Münzer's life and work in his 1895 book, *Vorläufer des neueren Sozialismus.*)[72] Bloch advances the argument that "all rebels (of history) displayed a chiliastic character," that is, the leadership was usually assumed by clairvoyant prophets. He reminds us that Luther called not only Thomas Münzer but also the Anabaptists a bunch of "Ultra-Mosaists"; he feared and fought them because of their social-revolutionary tendencies. From the time of Marx, Münzer's *Hoch verursachte Schutzrede* (1524) has been regarded as a crucial revolutionary statement, and he himself placed in line with the left-wing reformers.[73]

From this vantage point it can be argued by pointing to individual traits of the Naphta character that Bloch's portrayal of Thomas Münzer contributed substantially to the former. Münzer was a radical man, who was at his most effective in the Katharinenkirche (religious institution) supported by the working poor, Bloch writes. Münzer felt most at home in "religiously fanatic Zwickau" *(schwarmgeistige Zwickau)* because it was congenial to his own "fanatic disposition" *(schwarmgeistige Natur)*.[74] Münzer's most telling trait is his asceticism. Already in his early youth he was "an ascetic through and through." It was Münzer's stated belief that "by giving up all distractions and by deadening the desires of the flesh, and by the proper courage toward the absolute truth man becomes sensitive enough to be able to receive God's revelation."[75]

Naphta is also a "radical man" whose fanatic conceptions are transferred during his stay with the Jesuits to the religious—and political—realms. He, too, is an "ascetic through and through" and has high praise for "labour" for the sole reason that it helps to suppress "the wiles of the flesh" (377). The fanatic-visionary nature of Münzer and Naphta's "fanatic pettifogging" are just two different terms for the same phenomenon. What in Münzer is called "courage toward truth" is accorded without hesitation to Naphta by Hans Castorp: in contrast to Settembrini, whose "bravery is more or less folderol," Naphta's bravery is real. Hans Castorp's question of whether Naphta would muster enough courage to destroy himself is answered by Naphta in the affirmative.

In their attitude toward authority, Thomas Münzer and the Naphta figure have one more thing in common. After all, Münzer never joined the "establishment," not even the newly formed anti-establishment (i.e., Catholic) hierarchy; in his *disputationes* he never recognized the official (Lutheran) church as the supreme authority. In his religious duels with Luther, Melanchton and others, Münzer demanded a "hearing" *(Verhör)* before "all nationalities of all faith" with the justification that the "internationality of the spirit" should reign supreme—albeit under the leadership of the "chosen ones" *(Auserwählten)*. (This is an obvious example of the concept of elitism.)[76] Can it be a mere coincidence that the atmosphere of the Jesuitic institution is described as "cosmopolitan," where the "internationality of the spirit" is one of the principal characteristics? We hear that the institution "flattered" Naphta's deepest instincts because of the domination of the "principle of nobility," that is, the nobility of the spirit. Nationality and race are *not* determining factors in admission; what counts are "talent" and "ability." This fact constitutes the "elitist" character of the order. (It should be noted that "elitism" is not meant in the modern sense, that is, as a counterpart to democratism. The stress is on the state of being chosen, be it in a religious or intellectual–spiritual sense.)

But we should not go overboard with the comparison. Although Naphta clearly belongs to the "realm of the East," this certainly is not due solely to Mann's reading of Bloch. As was mentioned, Nietzsche's influence is certainly the most important here. Still, it is interesting to find some corresponding facts in the geographical grounding of Münzer and Naphta. Galicia, part of the Austro-Hungarian monarchy until 1918, was like Silesia, not a hermetically closed territory. Just as Silesia was bastion and bridge in an intellectual–spiritual sense, Galicia was in an ethnic one. Thus, Naphta is also a representative of a certain cultural realm and a mediator between different cultural currents. Indeed, with Bloch as well as with Thomas Mann, it is an absolute demand that this sort of revolutionary educator (of the people) and theologian possess the "Russian man" within himself.[77]

Thomas Mann's as well as Bloch's interest in and receptivity for these kinds of associations and connections are played out against a broad and general background and stand for all the tendencies, ideas, and peculiar people who populated Europe and Germany at that time. The way they reacted, Mann and Bloch were not unique among their contemporaries. Almost at the same time, Robert Musil, during his work *Der Mann ohne Eigenschaften* (The Man without Qualities), noted, "Irony is: to depict a cleric in such a way that the description would equally fit a Bolshevik. ... This type of irony... is but the context of things from which the naked truth emerges."[78] To be sure, Musil was extremely unfair in adding, "This sort of irony— the constructive irony—is virtually unknown in present-day Germany."[79] One has to assume that his notes were written before the publication of *The Magic Mountain;* otherwise, how can one explain his failure to discern that Thomas Mann displays precisely this constructive irony in the creation of the character of Naphta?

Musil, Bloch, Mann, and all the others who at that time and in view of the contemporary background were reflecting on the phenomenon of the "Russian man" were reacting to the general situation before, during, and after the Great War, which—according to Musil—was a "sordid period" *(niederträchtige Zeit).* Musil, the pessimist, saw only two possibilities: "to go along...to howl with the wolves...or to become neurotic."[80] Bloch, the eternal optimist, came up with the slogan: "Let's go East" because "following the collapse of the evil, hard, narrow, chillingly faithless life of the European [Western] world, the ethical–spiritual path of seeking help points once again towards the East."[81] (Thomas Mann's thoughts at that time also went "eastwards.")[82] For Bloch, needless to say, the "peak of the Oriental spirit" is to be found in the Bible. Together with "Russian warmth and expectations" it will result in an "apocalyptic consciousness."[83] These thoughts of Bloch's, published for the first time in 1918, were in all probability familiar to Mann. Bloch's reflections were directed against the wave of "the Romanticism of the more recent reaction" which, "out of the pathos of its 'old standing' ...was only able to lure into being the decline of the Occident."[84] They also wanted to become a "beginning," the search for "a salvation" (the idea of redemption). And in 1918 Thomas Mann asks just as despairingly, "What is to be?...What to believe?"[85] Mann was seriously thinking about Communism just emerging in Russia as a possibility (ironically, as one of depoliticalization). "Communism as I understand it," Mann writes, "contains much which is good and humane. Its goal is ultimately the dissolution of the state (which will always be dedicated to power), the humanization and purification of the world by depoliticalizing it. At bottom, who would be against that?"[86] Such considerations were neither unique nor isolated: intellectuals, writers, philosophers, artists and plain citizens of the times were all deeply concerned about their future chances. Their anxieties were engendered by the fundamental perception that the "decline and fall of the Western world" was imminent.[87]

In such a spiritual (and political) situation, all those people who "have partaken of the situation at one level or another" must find their way into a *Zeitroman* Musil believed. He made a list of the various types that belonged to this group as "representatives."[88] Next to the type of the religiously inspired revolutionary we find the type of the Jesuit. This is one combination that is missing from Bloch's work—or at least not present explicitly. (One could argue with a stretch of imagination that a Jesuit is also a theologian and thus establish a connection to Bloch that would not be too farfetched.) The catalyst for this combination must, however, be sought elsewhere, in my opinion. I give little credence to the suggestion that the political constellation prevalent at the time, that is, the collaboration of the Center (Catholic) Party, with the Social Democrats, served as inspiration.[89] It is more likely that two stimuli were responsible for this aspect of Naphta's personality. First, there was a prevailing interest at the time and a sudden wealth of literature about the Jesuits, the order itself and the personality of Ignatius of Loyola.[90] Second, the concept can also be explained by the "accumulation of all things" which at that time characterized Germany—and Europe; among the fashionable associations of the times one could often encounter the combination "Jew–Jesuit" and "Jesuit–Communist," to which later was added the combination "Jew–Communist," especially after the failed revolutionary experiments in Berlin, Munich and Budapest.[91] As was so often the case with Thomas Mann, he again merely captured and wove into his work what was in the air.[92] As his son, Golo Mann, once exclaimed, "the intimate contact with the past" was certainly one of the major obligations and a fundamental trait of Mann's work. Just as fundamental was his contact with what was contemporary, with the realities of the day: this trait supplies the realism of his work. Therefore, Scherrer's observation (not much different from that expressed by Lukács) is very fitting: Thomas Mann's writings "will always remain a mirror of the epoch where almost everything can be recognized that affected the times."[93]

The fact that the Jesuit order, banned since 1814 from Germany, was permitted to return and was eager to collect and increase its membership quickly clearly had something to do with public interest in the Jesuits. But the controversies, the reports, and the prejudicial sentiments revived noticeably beginning in the middle of the nineteenth century. The public debate reached its zenith in the 1920s and has not to this day disappeared from public view completely.[94] As early as 1834, Leopold von Ranke dedicated a substantial part of his history of the papacy to a determination of the historical role of the order and of Loyola. Ranke stressed the military character of the order, whose fundamental virtue is obedience. Whether Mann used Ranke is not certain, although it seems likely.

Certainly, Ranke's characterization of Loyola is suggestive: "From out of the fantastic dreams...and inner visions...there developed a clear, practical setting of goals, but worldly wisdom [Weltklugheit] somewhat curbed the ascetic demands."[95]

The emphasis on the "Spanish spirit" (via Loyola) in the Counter-Reformation was first given full-scale treatment in Eberhard Gothein's study *Ignatius von Loyola und die Gegenreformation* (1895). But a popular presentation of the history of the order by Heinrich Boehmer enjoyed the greatest success. The awakening of interest in the subject is generally attributed to this slim volume.[96] We can assume that Thomas Mann came across this book or Gothein's *Studien zur Geschichte der Gesellschaft Jesu* (1914). In his letter to Sagave, he pointed out that much in *The Magic Mountain* "had been studied"; among other things "the nature of Free Masonry and the education of a Jesuit." Heinrich Boehmer's portrayal of Loyola's personality is dominated by three characteristics which "very rarely come together in any one individual" and which were "the final cause and strongest motivating force" behind Loyola's activities:

> a *strength of will* heightened by means of methodical training to an almost superhuman level, a mind directed completely toward the practical but capable of the *most intense concentration* and penetration, and, finally, *the ability* acquired *by means of an iron self-discipline, to sacrifice* his own ego to the last breath on the altar of *the ideals* in which he believed.[97]

We hear further that Loyola learned much in the school of German mysticism, that he himself wanted to place contemplation in the service of action and knew how to accomplish this, and that he was an organizational genius. Boehmer devotes a lot of space to the question of the Jews in the Jesuit order. The first Jew was recruited by Loyola himself in Paris in 1533. The recruit, "at the time already a *magister*" was named Diego Lainez and is described as follows: "a small, delicate, indeed even frail man with an impressive Jewish nose and large, lively eyes." He was "untiring, quick and sharp" and held his own "as a teacher and disputator." His only "failing" was his origin, but Loyola had "no misgivings in this regard."[98] In the correspondence of traits lies the proof that Mann was familiar with Boehmer's study; this is only logical since this slim volume was about the only German contribution to the popular literature of the period dealing with the Jesuits which reported in detail on the personality, educational development, activities, and influences of Loyola. As I later demonstrate, Boehmer defines the spiritual character of the order as a "unique mixture" of spiritual–intellectual currents of the times, currents which really do not belong together. (As Naphta declared, "Opposites may be consistent with each other" [404].) In so doing, Boehmer emphasizes how in the Jesuits the reactionary, obscurantist elements are paired with modernity and progress. It would be impossible not to think in this connection of Naphta's combining the Middle Ages and proletarian dictatorship.

In summary, it should be pointed out that there are aspects of Boehmer's Loyola portrait which accommodated personality-creating factors that were already present and depicted by Thomas Mann only to be strengthened by the newly acquired knowledge. To begin with, Boehmer presents and partially explains Loyola's life course as being determined by his illness. Second, it is stressed by Boehmer that Loyola was not a genuine Spaniard but rather came from a Basque noble family which, to be sure, eagerly pursued the process of assimilation. In spite of his chivalric upbringing, Loyola deviated from the thinking of his contemporaries; he "tried hard" to overcome his "revulsion against everything Semitic" and consequently accepted Jews as members of his order. Indeed, he is said to have gone so far as to express the sentiment —a "perverse wish for a Spaniard of that time"—that he himself would prefer "to be a Jew by birth."[99] Loyola's need to affect people, to have them around him, and to transmit his experiences arises in part from his situation. Thus, we witness in Boehmer's study the broaching of the concept of the educator, of the *Vermittler* (mediator). It may not be too daring to call Loyola a stranger who is conscious of not-quite-belonging and who can develop his possibilities from precisely this vantage point: here too, "good conditions" are engendered by "bad situations." The interweaving of seemingly heterogenous elements and tendencies characterizes both Bloch's and Boehmer's *dramatis personae*—not only in their original way of combinig diverse elements, but also in their description of intrapersonal spheres. This fact may explain Thomas Mann's interest in and use of their writings; only that which was rich in connections was for Mann "the true," as well as the "only interesting" matter.

The opinions on what constitutes the "Jesuitic element" in a person, a deed, or an idea have been from the beginning very diverse, although in regards to certain aspects a surprising agreement prevailed. Dubiousness and a penchant for intrigue were generally considered characteristic traits of the Jesuits. Naphta is called a "dubious character" and a spirit who sows "confusion." The view that Jesuits possessed as people mainly negative traits and were even quite dangerous was widespread in Germany too. By means of Jansenist polemics the term "Jesuit morality" was introduced into public consciousness in the seventeenth century, and became a widespread catch-word. Laxism, probabilism, and the sanctioning of all means justified by the ends have been postulated as specific characteristics of Jesuit moral teachings. Although the Society was able to assemble anew and to develop in the course of the general ecclesiastic restoration in the nineteenth century, the liberal forces often regarded the Jesuits as a dangerous element in the state. The *Kulturkampf* between Bismarck and the national liberals led among other things to the *Jesuitengesetz* (Jesuit Law) of 1872, which was not repealed until 1904 and then 1917.

Strangely enough, it was Karl Marx who in his polemical writing "On the Jewish Question" introduced the direct connection between Jesuit and Jew. Marx wrote: "Jewish Jesuitism, the same practical Jesuitism which Bauer discovers in the Talmud, is the relationship of the world of self-interest to the laws which govern the world, laws which the world devotes its principal arts to circumventing."[100] Almost at the same time, a Catholic theologian, Jacob Marx (no relation to Karl but also from the city of Trier) published an essay with the title "The Jesuits as Teachers of Communism."[101] Jacob Marx offers a favorable view of Communism; only its atheism met with his disapproval. Thus, in the mid-nineteenth century there had already occurred the association of "Jewish–Jesuit" and "Jesuitic-communistic."

In the correspondence between Natalia Herzen and the Bakunin–Nechayev Circle (the Russian anarchists), the concept of the Jesuitic revolutionary is often alluded to. Bakunin's description of Nechayev's personality is the best example of what was meant by the concept at the end of the nineteenth century. In his letter to the so-called Committee of the Russian Revolutionary Party, intended as a "collective warning," Bakunin wrote:

He is a *fanatic* of the first order, and he has all the qualities as well as the failings of a fanatic. Such people frequently are capable of… dangerous errors. …With the fanatic…everything is on a large scale, and if he errs, then he errs on a large scale. …[Nechayev] is intelligent, *very intelligent.* …But everything in him—mind, heart and will…everything is *subordinated to a ruling passion for destroying* the existing order of things. Consequently his first thought was of necessity *to create an organization* or a collective power capable of carrying out this great work. …This organization [is] half-founded on coercion and deceit. … This is the first natural step towards the Jesuit system.[102]

Still, Bakunin confessed to being fascinated by such a personality and to love Nechayev dearly because among them all "he was the purest, or the most *saintly* person in the sense of his total dedication. …"[103] Thomas Mann obviously was unaware of this or any such personal evaluations; still, he managed to bring together in his Jesuit revolutionary all that was supposed to be characteristic of such a type. He even thought through and gave form to Bakunin's realization that this step toward the "Jesuit system" is a "desperate step" because it has to be carried out to "its ultimate, ugly extreme," with "characteristic passionate, pitiless impetuosity, sparing neither self nor others, sacrificing with savage passion both himself and other people. ..."[104]

After World War I, at the time of the Weimar Republic, several of those past combinations and associations became timely again. There were all those Jewish intellectuals, politicians and leading personalities whose role in the cultural and political life of Weimar as well as their character traits and style lent themselves to such typecasting. Harry Graf Kessler, a superb observer and commentator of the contemporary scene, noted in his diary after a visit with Hugo Haase, "More than anything, Haase gives an impression of great suppleness combined with a high degree of stubbornness, iron hand in rubber glove. *A small, dogged, somewhat Jesuitical Jew* with a clear, hard look"[105] Kessler's causal remarks underline my claim that the combination which in the end resulted in a type like Naphta was in no way so daring, unique, and unprecedented as was generally assumed and as the author wanted us to believe. It is another matter entirely how he mastered the existing material, models and inspirations, and how his narrative imagination absorbed and shaped the details and incorporated them into his fictional world.

For perceptive readers and interpreters alike, Mann's masterful blend of all existing and available details finally resulted in *the* type of the Jesuit. Thus, this figure and the concept itself not only entered public consciousness but helped in some instances —indeed, in some scholarly treatises—to elucidate the concept of the Jesuitic personality. What I have in mind is best illustrated by a 1927 review which I happened upon among Mann's notes to his *Joseph* tetralogy. The reviewer lists the following traits in addition to the evident characteristics of a Jesuit: "a daemonic ability to adapt," the "not quite admirable artfulness to ingratiate himself with aristocratic or powerful personages...by means of extraordinary exertions and achievements," the need for "absolute authority," for *Kadavergehorsam* (unthinking obedience) "twofacedness" and a "subservient humility coupled with unrestrained pride," and, finally, the appreciation of the "internationality of the institute."[106] We may consider this to be a case of absolute correspondence in characterization, a chance meeting of the minds, or, more likely, an appropriation of Thomas Mann's sketch of a Jesuitic personality by the reviewer. (The fact that Mann saved the review points to the latter assumption.)

In a study by Rene Fülöp-Miller still considered a standard work on the subject, we come upon Naphta quotes which illuminate the complex web of obligations and ideologies of the Jesuits.[107] Chances are that the Naphta image interjected itself into the depiction of the "Jesuitic personality," consciously or unconsciously. One is reminded immediately of Mann's creative assemblage of "necessary" traits when one reads in Fülöp-Miller's study that Loyola had to overcome his "lowly beginnings" by means of "diligent and untiring industry" which at the end made him successful in his quest. We are told of Loyola's "great mental power" combined with even greater ambition, of "superhuman perseverance" aided by "inhuman means of self-castigation."[108] We also hear that Loyola's illness was the source of his reflections, that he was "ascetic" but not so otherwordly that he would eschew good food and bodily comfort. His ambitions and his courage, his organizational talent and his "fanatical nature" made Loyola an ideal founder of an order. The statement that he "merged" himself completely in the Society of Jesus, that is, that he demanded anonymity for himself in the religious community, sounds very much like a passage from *The Magic Mountain* (Naphta's determination of "genuine individualism" as "anonymous and communal," [405, 467]. There is even mention of the originally adventurous nature of Loyola, which he tamed by "self-violation" and "self-discipline."

Fülöp-Miller's study, too, calls attention to the combination "Jesuit–Communist" by discussing the two "kindred historical personalities," Loyola and Lenin, and the secret of their effectiveness:

> No one else has ever understood to the same extent [as these two men] the importance of that power which alone can unite thousands of people in all parts of the world into a uniform and exactly functioning organization: the importance of absolute obedience. Both men, moreover, possessed an inflexible courage to carry into effect, even to its utmost consequences, a principle which they had once acknowledged as right. ...[They] compelled the complete subjugation and transformation...of the intellect, the beliefs, the perceptions and the desires of their followers.[109]

The juxtaposition of two seemingly different realms of action and belief is an idea whose time has not passed. It is alive, for example, in such pathbreaking sociological studies as Lewis Coser's discussion of certain "greedy collectives" which demand the kind of "real obedience" that involves an "internalized acceptance" of the collective's aims.[110] Since this was precisely the stage that Naphta could not bring himself to attain, because it resulted in "the atrophy of personality," he had become an "incorrect Jesuit" (446). The same idea informs Max Frisch's thinking when he writes in his diary after a meeting with Bertolt Brecht: "There exist also materialist Jesuits. ... The doctrine of 'the ends justifying the means' produces similar traits, even if the goal is completely opposite."[111] And Leszek Kolakowski examines in a large-scale essay how durable such a compromised moral slogan as the one just mentioned can be.[112] In his opinion, this moral slogan has been closely associated with the history of the Society of Jesus; now, it seems, it exists in the public consciousness as a moral slogan associated with communism—especially following the Stalinist era. It does not seem that the attraction and the timeliness of these mental connections become weaker over time; the reason for this may lie in the similarity of the historical situations. Whenever social and political upheavals bring with them an intensification of the arguments about alternatives, the discussion about "alternatives for the individual" as pitted against systems promising solutions (i.e., salvation) becomes ever more heated. But solutions—or salvations—are necessarily bound up with "the belief in their moral value,"[113] which originates in the theological sphere.

In this connection, Spengler's *Decline of the West* and its influence cannot be left out of consideration. The significance of this book for the intellectual content of the Naphta–Settembrini debates cannot be overestimated. This is not the place to go into the analysis of Spengler borrowings in *The Magic Mountain*. But insofar as Spengler also contributed to the complex Naphta personality, a close look at the passage in question from Spengler's book is warranted. In the section "Buddhism, Stoicisms, Socialism," Spengler combines seemingly disparate areas such as philosophy, religion, and political, social and economic development; what allows us to bring them together, states Spengler, is the "phenomenon of morality" and their relationship to it, which in its problematic nature is a "symptom…of the *Weltgefühl* of the Occident." Spengler defines the problematic as follows:

Everyone *demands* something of the rest. We say "thou shalt" in the conviction that so-and-so in fact will, can and must be changed or fashioned or arranged… to the order.

The belief in this and the right to do this is beyond question. Here, orders are issued and obedience is demanded. *That…is…morale.* In the ethics of the West everything is direction, claim to power, will to effect the distant. Here Luther is completely at one with Nietzsche, Popes with Darwinians, Socialists with Jesuits.[114]

Thomas Mann marked this passage, and on the next page he heavily underlined Spengler's remark that all those who wish to carry out their views "on behalf of all" are Socialists.[115] As in the previously cited works, the mutuality of supposedly disparate types and ideologies is stressed here. But Spengler went further in that he spoke of an absolute identity of the Socialists and Jesuits.

Besides Spengler's work, Georg Brandes's writings left a deep impression on Mann. As he noted in his diary on July 5, 1920, "These past days have read Brandes's 'The Romantic School in Germany' with keen interest. Staggered to discover ideas in Novalis that had come to me as I penetrated into the world of *The Magic Mountain*, unaware that they might [have] occurred earlier to others."[116] Accordingly, he marked the readings extensively, and even dated some of them (e.g., "read 1920") or suggested references by jotting down "Zbg." Mann must have experienced this meeting of the minds even more acutely when he read another book by Brandes, *Skandinavische Persönlichkeiten*. In the section devoted to Kierkegaard, Mann marked the passage referring to Kierkegaard's "Jesuitism":

Kierkegaard…believes in the *"acceptability of a teleological suspension of the ethical."* …One can sense a few sparks of such *a Jesuitic tendency* very early in Kierkegaard's life. He was…in his *inclination to let the religious break through the common ethical sphere* a born Jesuit, a Protestant one to be sure, who was his own pope but *who never* really *doubted that the ends justified the means* if it were a question of the highest possible goals.[117]

Just as assiduously, Mann put comments in the margin next to characterizations of Kierkegaard, such as "not a humane nature," "he is contemptuous of the world," and "he is immersed in Hegel up to his neck." The following passage is marked with an oversized exclamation point:

The highly dubious scientific nature [of theology], the genuine spiritual–intellectual interest it kindles without satisfying it, the perspective it opens, in many ways, on the *Humaniora,* are perhaps more stimulating and less of a hindrance for the independent and striving spirit *[Geist]* than this or that specialized discipline. Furthermore, Kierkegaard's talent, in spite of its penchant for respect, has the great advantage of being deeply and thoroughly combative.[118]

Should this reflection be considered as one contributing element to Naphta's choice of "calling"? It would seem so. It is quite plausible that this reading, Lukács's penetrating essay on Kierkegaard and then his "Von der Armut am Geiste" (On Poverty of Spirit), with its deep and thoroughly combative spirit, supplied Thomas Mann with some fundamental ideas for his curious "combination."

Not just readings, but also the author's immediate realm of experience, provided some interesting tidbits for the figure of Naphta. Lukács may have been the first or the sole socialist *Weltverbesserer* (utopian) whom Thomas Mann had met personally and with whom he had had a personal discussion. But if one is aware of the importance —and notoriety—of some of the revolutionaries during the period of the short-lived Soviet Republic in Bavaria, it is to be assumed that their appearances, ideas, behavior and personalities did not fail to have an effect on such a keen observer of reality as Mann. We have first and foremost Eugen Leviné in mind, a leader of the Communist Party who became the leader of the Soviet Republic after the assassination of Kurt Eisner. As the influential German Weekly *Die Zeit* reported, the *Nordbayrische Kurier* (a local daily newspaper) still "caused shudders" in the general populace in 1973 with Leviné's name.[119]

Leviné was a German-speaking, highly educated, self-confident Jewish emigrant from the upper middle class of St. Petersburg. He was said to have maintained a luxurious residence in Munich and to have led a double life in that he was a Spartacist orator in the industrial centers of the Ruhr; he took part in the Russian Revolution of 1905 and "survived the torture chambers of the Tsar." He had studied economics in Germany and turned down a "brilliant career as an academic" in Germany and as a "man of letters" in Heidelberg. As his widow reports in her memoirs, Leviné had no illusions whatsoever about the success of the Soviet Republic and took over the leadership purely out of duty and a sense of solidarity. As he himself admitted, with almost suicidal courage, he could promise himself as well as his comrades but "an honorable death" and a "demonstration lesson on the nature of the Soviet Republic."

His bearing at his court-martial was "memorable" and was generally much talked about, for he is supposed to have said, "We communists are all dead men on leave."[120] Thomas Mann reported on the goings-on in his diary and mentioned Leviné many times. Similarly, Marianne Weber, in her biography of Max Weber, describes the events and Leviné's role. (Both Mann and Weber had intervened on behalf of Ernst Toller, the German–Jewish poet, who was one of Leviné's comrades.)[121] When Leviné faced the firing squad without a blindfold, his last greetings were for the "world revolution." His fate was predestined: he had been warned beforehand that his striving "for the happiness of all mankind" was a highly dangerous undertaking.

Thus, Leviné was a socialist and a utopian par excellence, and a contemporary —indeed, almost a neighbor—of Thomas Mann. The writer was able to follow his career, influence and death from up close. Finally, when in 1922 Georg Lukács came to see him in Vienna and developed "his theories" (on art and revolution), the "symbolic physiognomy" was firmly set.

It seems that the personalities of Leviné and Lukács represent a very different kind of revolutionary than Lenin's and others; they are definitely closer to the type represented by Naphta. And it was Lukács who not only thought about this but explicitly mentioned it in a 1970 interview. Asked about his impressions of Lenin, he tried to convey some "idea of Lenin as a human type":

> Lenin was a new type of revolutionary. By saying this, I do not wish to cast doubt on the importance or contribution of the old revolutionaries: but they all had something aristocratic, with the worldview of wise men who were able to display the proper attitude as an answer to the false attitude of the masses. There was something ascetic about the great revolutionaries. This is clearly recognizable in Robespierre; it also holds true for some modern revolutionaries, such as Otto Korvin in Hungary or Max Lewin [sic] in Munich. Max Lewin said that communists are dead men on leave. This is *the highest degree of asceticism*. By contrast, Engels and especially Lenin have no ascetic traits at all.[122]

Lukács answered the question of whether there was a direct link between asceticism and Lenin's criticism of the "left" as follows: "Of course. Left radicals were usually revolutionary ascetics; among them, some were undoubtedly quite honorable and ready for sacrifice. ..."[123] In more than one respect, Lukács can also be placed in the ranks of the revolutionary ascetics. First of all, he was considered to be—and in fact was—a left radical; Lenin accused him of "left radicalism" as early as 1920. In a severely anti-parliamentarian essay, Lukács expressed himself in favor of the "flexibility" of communist tactics, and for this was called to account by Lenin: "The article of G. L. is a very *radical* and a very bad one." This was nothing new, to be sure: in the spring of 1919, at the time of the Hungarian Soviet Republic, Lukács had supported an extremely left course of the Communist Party.[124]

At this point, the question presents itself: at the time of his meeting with Georg

Lukács, how well informed was Thomas Mann about the man, that is, what did he know about Lukács's life and his fate? To what extent was it possible, in a meeting lasting one to two hours, to grasp the essence of a person in such a way that one could make sweeping, fundamentally correct, and very insightful comments about him? And finally, what impressions could Thomas Mann have gained from Lukács's writings which were confirmed or modified in the personal encounter? In asking these questions one must bear in mind that Thomas Mann—probably rightly—displayed no false modesty when describing his gift of "taking in" or "grasping" things with "both eyes," with eyes that had "learned to see more deeply" than those of others. Or, as he put it, "When I have observed someone...for twenty minutes, I have gained more intense, more essential impressions, that are more worth imparting, than... [someone else] does in twenty years."[125] It is to be assumed that in two hours, he was able to gain some intense essential and worthwhile impressions of Georg Lukács.

I have claimed that the Lukács component can be traced more clearly and in greater detail in the portrayal of the personality of Leo Naphta than in his biography and physical appearance, and I pointed in particular to one of the most prominent traits in Naphta's character: his *asceticism*. Asceticism, understood as (monkish) renunciation, harsh self-discipline, has many names in Mann's oeuvre. It is identified as "the fire of artistic egoism" in the essay on Schiller ("A Weary Hour"), and at another time as the absolute "commitment to achievement" that characterizes Gustav von Aschenbach in *Death in Venice;* it is one of the main characteristics of the artist in Mann's early work and is portrayed again in *Doctor Faustus,* with its ultimate consequences. In fact, this ascetic nature of the artist type who "cannot without suffering" create and raise himself (and his art) to ever greater heights is termed "truly ethical."[126] The creative labor, the work of art itself, is in this sense nothing other than service, and a "rigid, hard, passionate" service at that. Life, that is to say the "normal" everyday life (*Tonio Kröger*), is pushed aside: one can yearn for it a little bit and be contemptuous of it but one is not part of it, not "at home" in it. Whether Tonio Kröger truly represents this type of ascetic artist remains an open question: there is much yearning and bad conscience harbored within him, which in the Schiller essay is shown as the immoral aspect of the artist's fate. When we think of the demonstrable interplay of ideas and perceptions between the Venice story and Lukács's youthful work, *Soul and Form,* which proved inspirational and highly influential for *Death in Venice,* then we must recognize the fact that this Lukács work contains ideas that determined in a fundamental way Thomas Mann's perception of Lukács; in other words, this book gave Mann a very definite idea of the personality of its author.

In his reflections on the "really typical poet" and the "true Platonist" (i.e., the critic), Lukács comes to speak of the sort of men who are "determined to live their lives to the uttermost limits of their logic." They are the "true types" in whom "the work and the life coincide." Only that part of their lives which is related to work is considered valid. "The life is nothing, the work is all" for these "purest types." Lukács gives us *the credo of the ascetic type*—be it the artist or the Platonist (critic).[127] In the essay on Theodor Storm which Thomas Mann valued very highly and frequently praised as one of the most sensitive critical essays he had ever come across, Lukács investigates the problem of the modern artist who with the "hysterical nostalgia...of the sophisticated man" looks back at the time in which art was *not* the "consequence of a violent refusal of reality" but was there "for its own sake," as is true of every honest piece of work.[128] And then comes the passage which Thomas Mann marked with marginalia, where yearning and asceticism are placed in relation to each other:

> This nostalgia is...a longing for the thing most opposite to ourselves; a longing for the great, *holy simplicity,* the natural, *holy perfection* to be born out of the birthpangs of an ever-growing awareness, *to be forced into life by the* ultimate, *gasping energy of a sick nervous system.* The bourgeois way of life, which consists of *cutting down the conduct of one's life* to a strictly and narrowly bourgeois measure, *is simply a way* of coming closer to such perfection. *It is a form of asceticism, a renunciation of all brilliance in life* so that... all the splendour may be transferred elsewhere: into the work of art. Seen in these terms, the bourgeois way of life is a kind of forced labor, a hateful *servitude, a constraint against which every life instinct must rebel* and to which they can be made to bow only with the *most cruel* energy.[129]

In reading this passage, Mann probably realized that its author must have had much the same experience he did. The problematic situation of the modern artist and intellectual, indeed, of modern man in general to which this essay addressed itself was one of the *leitmotifs* of Thomas Mann's early work. And the realization contained in the Lukács essay that this modern asceticism, in which the order and severity of the bourgeois life manifest themselves, is but "the whip that drives the life-denying man to work without cease "—this realization finds its artistic depiction in many novellas and in some novels of Thomas Mann. To be sure, Lukács proceeds much more radically when he unmasks this asceticism as being "appearance" *(Schein)* only, arguing that it lacks the naivete of medieval knighthood's asceticism. He states, "This bourgeois way of life is merely a mask that hides the wild and fruitless pain of a failed and ruined life, the existential pain of the Romantic born too late."[130] Mann marked this passage also in the margin. This statement sounds like an outcry against the futility of such a model of behavior: renunciation and resignation, that is, self-discipline, reveal themselves in the end to be self-delusion. A comparison strongly suggests itself between these Lukácsian thoughts and Leo Naphta's bitter end: the "wild" and "adventurous" sounds he emits reveal what is behind the "fearsome self-control" (697), we are told, and at the moment of his self-destruction Naphta's outcry is a "confession" that his efforts (of self-negation and life-denial) had been in vain (705).

It is left to the Kierkegaard essay to discuss in greater breadth Lukács's own existential foundation, his own brand of asceticism, and the ensuing life possibilities. With the wisdom of hindsight, it is easy to see the confessional character of this essay; it is just as easy to discern certain positions of the young Lukács which prefigure his subsequent development. In this essay, there are numerous hints and indications which signal and in part help explain Lukács's "great transformation" from an upper-middle-class intellectual to a Marxist and communist. The reason lies in the genesis of the essay.[131] At the time, Lukács was called "the fanatic" by his friends because he sacrificed "Life," that is, his love for Irma Seidler, at the altar of "work." Lukács himself devoted considerable space in his diary to this problem. He noted, "Only a little inner productivity and I feel good and I need no one. That is the main thing, the most important point: I do not need anyone [keinen Menschen]."[132] He did not need the woman either; she never got over it and committed suicide in 1911. The inner truth of this gesture of separation that has been attributed to Kierkegaard in the essay also applies to Lukács. He writes that the main question was whether "the very thing, which, as [Kierkegaard] believed, made it necessary for them to part [was not] essential to his own life." Lukács is speaking here more about himself than about Kierkegaard.

He himself admits the self-referentiality of the essay, and calls not only the Kierkegaard essay but also some others (especially the essays on Stefan George, Charles-Louis Philippe, and Richard Beer-Hofmann) "the lyrical statement" of his own existential situation at that time because "the whole story is contained" in these essays.[133] In a letter, his best friend, Leo Popper, remarks very much to the point that these essays serve as camouflage for Lukács's self-portrait; he also tells Lukács that he didn't quite succeed in covering his tracks and might "give people reason to raise the question of whether a Kassner can serve as a symbol for Gy. L.?"[134] In view of the subjectivity of the statements contained in these essays, it is well for us to take a closer look at Lukács's train of thought. His reflections on Kierkegaard's asceticism are very enlightening in this regard. Kierkegaard's (and Lukács's) life is seen as "a gesture": the gesture of "turning away" from life. For Kierkegaard, this "turning away" meant breaking off the engagement to Regine Olsen; it had to be accomplished behind the mask of the "scoundrel and seducer." Since his penitence was to turn away from life, "that penitence had to be made the greater by the sinner's mask, chivalrously assumed, which disguised his real sin."[135] Under the mask of the seducer is revealed the "ascetic who, out of asceticism, voluntarily froze in his gesture." The gesture is thus felt to be "pure and all-expressive": behind the mask lies "the real face of the ascetic."[136]

Lukács believes to have found the underlying reason for Kierkegaard's (and for his own) attitude in his "forthrightness." A "man who wants to be 'honest'...must force life to yield up its single meaning, must grasp [it]...so firmly that...he can no longer move."[137] Why does it have to happen this way and not differently, Lukács asks, and he explains Kierkegaard's (and no doubt, his own) decision by asserting that one has to be *a certain type of person* in order to act in a specific manner and not in another way; thus, a certain type *has to choose* a certain path. The following passage is highly confessional and enlightening:

> The only essential difference between one life and another is the question *whether a life is absolute or* merely *relative*; whether *the mutually exclusive opposites* within the life are *separated* from one another sharply and definitely *or not*. The difference is whether the life-problems of a particular life arise in the form of an *either/or*, or whether *"as well as"* is the proper formula. ...Kierkegaard was always saying: I *want to be honest*, and this honesty could not mean anything less than *the duty—in the purest sense of the word—* ... *the duty to decide,* the duty *to go to the very end of every chosen road at every crossroad.*[138]

In Lukács's opinion, the most profound meaning of Kierkegaard's philosophy is that in life one sets "fixed points" and "draws absolute quality distinctions"; this means that one "must choose" one among the "things" one has found to be different and that one may not "seek 'middle ways'... which might resolve the 'merely apparent' contradictions." The honesty of this certain type of person entails the desire to see things sharply and *"to see the absolute in life, without any petty compromises."*[139] This view of honesty and the constant striving for absolute values represents not only Kierkegaard's but also Lukács's "life-necessity." It is their existential imperative. We are told by Lukács that he intends to describe the determination of purpose of such an ascetic life pattern in Kierkegaard's terminology. For all that, it is also a Lukácsian terminology: the gesture of an ascetic like Kierkegaard is that of someone who "does more than merely play with life" and whose soul executes the "leap by which it leaves the always relative facts of reality to reach the eternal certainty of forms." The gesture of a Kierkegaard (and Lukács) becomes the "leap (in the Schlegelian sense) by which "the absolute is transformed, in life, into the possible."[140] The "action" of such an ascetic personality is at the same time a "turning away" (from life) and "turning toward" (the absolute); with this formula Lukács defines the ascetic philosophy of life.

These elaborations make possible various interpretations and conclusions. The emphasis lies on the ascetic ideal and encloses within itself a yearning for the absolute, a heroic conduct of life, radical questions and solutions, the possibility of violence (including violation of self), and the religious element—though not "in a churchly-dogmatic sense" (443). Without examining in detail aspects of the asceticism depicted by Lukács, one can state summarily that all the aspects mentioned belong to Naphta's personality.

During the first debate that Hans Castorp witnesses, Naphta attacks Settembrini, in whom he senses a "general repugnance to the Absolute," to the broader application of categories. Naphta accuses the man of Enlightenment of rejecting the "absolute Spirit" in the name of democratic progress; contrary to Settembrini's belief, Spirit does *not* imply "frivolity," declares Naphta (374). In the name of the absolute, Naphta demands a new meaning of pedagogy, consisting of "absolute command, the iron bond, discipline, sacrifice, the renunciation of the self, the curbing of the personality"—in a word, absolute obedience in the service of the idea (400). Self-discipline, self-renunciation, and the curbing of the self are attributes of the "heroism" of the Kierkegaard essay. They may sound like the "whip" that drives the "life-denying man," Lukács believes, but they stem from the "most powerful life-necessity," the need to love that prevails absolutely. With Naphta, this erotic coloring of asceticism is defined as the "deepest desire" for "obedience" *(Ihre tiefste Lust ist der Gehorsam)*. Lukács concludes his essay with his definition of Kierkegard's heroism, which wanted to create forms from life and which determined his honest course of action. What constituted Kierkegaard's honesty? "His honesty was that *he saw crossroads and walked to the end of the road he had chosen."* And the tragedy of Kierkegaard's life was that "he wanted *to live what cannot be lived."*[141] Looking at the way Georg Lukács lived his life, many would say today that his insightful remarks on Kierkegaard point prophetically to his own life and could be its epitaph.

When Lukács wrote this essay, he was at the "aesthetic stage" of his life. But in life "there are some major, typical cycles of possibilities," declares Lukács. He defines them (using Kierkegaardian terminology) as *"the aesthetic, the ethical, the religious stage."* The distinction between these three stages can be bridged by a connecting "leap" which is a "miracle." What happens then is the "sudden metamorphosis of the entire being of a person."[142] In many respects, we can discern three stages in Lukács's life. We have the aesthetic stage until the middle of 1911. After 1911 (the year of Irma Seidler's suicide and his work on his confessional "Von der Armut am Geiste") there follows the ethical stage, and after 1918, the religious stage (in secularized form). The connection between them may seem—viewed from the outside—like a "miracle," like a "leap" in the wake of which we are confronted with the "metamorphosis of the entire being" of Lukács. At least with regard to his turning to Communism, it is still customary to speak of the inexplicable metamorphosis of the *haute bourgeois* intellectual Georg von Lukács. But all three stages have a common ground based on the sort of person Lukács was; there is a definitive interconnection between them, and one stage grows organically out of the other. As Lukács notes in his diary: "I develop less through [spiritual] struggles, more like a plant (morphologically). This is an observation and not a value judgment. *This is the way I am; therefore, this is the way I must live."*[143]

It is astonishing how Thomas Mann with his "sharp eyes" and his perceptiveness for such thought processes caught on, while reading these essays, to Lukács's tricks; he also knew how to assess the possibilities inherent in this type of person. The

Lukácsian formulation of the "frozen mask of the ascetic" is transformed into the rigidity that defines the essence of Naphta's character. The idea of violence is closely bound up with this sort of asceticism: the "heroic" act of turning away from life, of turning toward the absolute demand and commitment, is grounded in the capability of self-discipline and curbing of the self, the act of violation of the self. The main characteristic of this asceticism is that it does not evade the consequences of his "life's gesture": Lukács ultimately sees Kierkegaard's death as a "voluntary act" undertaken so that, "dying, he could be the blood-witness of his own struggle."[144] Naphta's "tortured intellectuality" is grounded in his profound grasp of the price one must be willing to pay for "terrible self-control." Naphta's self-discipline and self-control lend his character the heroic element that is described as his "courage": the ultimate act of courage is his self-destruction. Thus, Naphta, too, died "at the right time, just when he wanted it," that is, he, too, was destined to be a "blood-witness" of his own struggle. In stating that one should not keep ones's hands away from blood, Naphta gives evidence of his readiness to draw the ultimate consequences. Even Settembrini appreciates this position, when he makes the solemn announcement, "Whoever is unable to offer his person, his arm, his blood in the service of the ideal, is unworthy of it..." (609).

If one is ready and willing to sacrifice oneself for the sake of the absolute (be it the "work" or the "idea"), then the willingness to make sacrifices for one's fellow man may be only a logical next step. What Lukács's attitude was to this question and to what extent it contributed to Naphta's *Ideenwelt* (ideal world) we shall clearly see in the discussion of the dialogue, "Von der Armut am Geiste" (On Poverty of Spirit). But is it unquestionably true that the personality values which are embodied in Naphta and which define his own personality are reminiscent of the essays of *Soul and Form*.

It apparently did not escape Thomas Mann that in all these essays no "intellect," deeming itself "sovereign... is freely playing its games" with possibilities; rather, it seeks everything [forms of art] "in the name of order" and "with the utmost rigour of the law."[145] This way of thinking has come into existence because the "problematic of the situation" demands a new seriousness which is free of the "frivolity of thought and expression" that reigns supreme.[146] When we hear Naphta arguing passionately against "frivolity" in matters concerning *Geist,* we have the same train of thought slightly disguised. Lukács's prescription for the state of affairs when everything has become problematic is to seek *salvation (Heil),* which "can only come from accentuating the problems to the maximum degree, from going radically to [their] roots."[147] Naphta's attributes, such as "irritability, captiousness, scepticism and cutting dialectics" as well as his "turn for sophistry" are in fact symptoms for that accentuation of the problems "to a maximum degree" Lukács spoke of and from which salvation is to come. And Naphta's statement, "Any theoretical realization [*Erkenntnis*] which is without practical application to man's salvation [*Heilsidee des*

Menschen] is...without significance" (398), could have been formulated by the Lukács of the Kierkegaard essay. The notion that salvation can only come from going radically to the root of the problems indicates an extremely radical standpoint of the young Lukács—a standpoint one would hardly expect to find in a book like *Soul and Form,* the work of a bourgeois aesthete. One is reminded of Naphta's professed preference for the "pessimistic and ascetic" taste of the Gothic because it is the "most utter and radical declaration of submission to suffering and the weakness of the flesh" (394).

Quite a few things in Lukács—and of course a lot more in Naphta—suggest the lingering effect of Nietzsche's writings; we know that Lukács had avidly read Nietzsche in his youth, but it would be a most difficult undertaking to determine the Nietzsche influences in his early work. Not so in the case of Thomas Mann; his reading of Nietzsche played a role in his conception of the Naphta figure and was easy to coordinate with his Lukács experience. Especially important was the concept of modern asceticism in Nietzsche's *Genealogy of Morals.* Here Nietzsche compares the modern ascetic with the "Old Brahmans" who were impelled by "fundamental needs" to inspire "awe of themselves in their own hearts," and managed to "endow their existence with a solidity and depth of meaning *[ihrem Dasein und Erscheinen Sinn, einen Halt und Hintergrund zu geben].* This they did, Nietzsche wrote, "as men of a heroic age" by "heroic means." "Self-inflicted cruelty" and ingenious "self-castigation"—these were the main means of these "power-hungry anchorites and [intellectual] innovators."[148] In *The Magic Mountain,* this concept and similar ideas frequently crop up as, for example, in Naphta's excursion on the "monkish tradition" and asceticism: we hear that Hans Castorp and Joachim would listen "with avidity" to Naphta's stories of the "warlike monks" of the Middle Ages, who, "ascetic to the point of exhaustion" but filled "with a ghostly lust of power," had established the kingdom of God by being "unsparing in bloodshed" (448).

The problematic situation of modern man who seeks his "salvation" is treated extensively and intensively in Nietzsche as well as in Lukács. The *furchtbare Zeitalter* (frightful age) Nietzsche spoke of and Lukács's "problematic situation" refer to the same or similar experience of time and are as a state of mind "the most sinister symptom of our sinister European civilization."[149] In such times the demand arises for the "ascetic ideal" as an existential precondition (Nietzsche) or as a "most powerful life-necessity" (Lukács). In his essays, Lukács is engaged in all-out struggle against frivolity in thought and expression; not much differently, Nietzsche calls his "ascetic priest" (modern philosopher) the "representative of seriousness." According to Nietzsche, the ascetic ideal "arises from the protective and curative instincts of a life that is degenerating."[150] Lukács believes that salvation can only come "from going radically" to the roots of the problems. Naphta's concern is defined as the search for a menas to the "healing of the world, that man may finally achieve salvation and deliverance" (404). He finds and defines the means in "terror." At any rate, for the young Lukács, the main concern was his own salvation; later, in the dialogue "Von der Armut am Geiste" Lukács voices his regret that his "entire will and effort" to salvation existed solely with reference to himself, that is, it was an intrapersonal instead of an interpersonal aspiration. When Lukács is still thinking of himself as a "Platonist" and is speaking of the object of eternal longing, this all sounds like yearning motivated by "protective and curative instincts." His point of references is Kassner, but he has himself in mind when stating that *"the longing for certainty, for measure and dogma, is* unbelievably alive in him. ..."[151] This yearning is accompanied by the equally strong striving for "the heights," and to the heights, to the "unattainable ideal," everything is but "a step," states Lukács about Kierkegaard—and himself.[152]

Is it not written in Leo Naphta's life story that he was consumed by "ardent yearning"—be it for the "more refined side of life" or for the "proudest," "most exclusive," and "lawful forms of existence"? This longing—the longing for "dogma" or for a "lawful existence"—describes the same phenomenon and derives from a desire for security. Nietzsche depicts the same phenomenon against the background of a "sinister European civilization." In the case of Lukács—and in that of Leo Naphta, his fictional counterpart—this idea of the chosen elite is only part of the question; another aspect is its Jewish "inheritance" in that the longing arises from post-exile (Talmudic) Jewish Messianism.[153] Because of Naphta's renegade ways, the longing for "lawful existence" is externalized: he convinces himself that the structured way of life of a Jesuit institution could guarantee the desired security, the feeling o "being at home." Besides the intellectual atmosphere, we hear in *The Magic Mountain* it is the "discipline" which flatters Naphta's "deepest instincts." The demands o such a disciplined existence are the precision of its daily regimen, service, duty, and obedience. How Naphta reacted to this (and what were the limits of acquiescence) is described as follows: The "tranquil spirit... consisted of a complete atrophy of personality, a state of insensibility in which the individual became a lifeless tool" a state of a veritable "graveyard peace" (446).

This inability of Naphta's to become a lifeless tool is explained in the statement that "like many gifted people of his race," Naphta is by instinct both "aristocrat and revolutionary." Interestingly, not much attention has been paid so far to this modifying aspect of Naphta's personality. But this aspect constitutes an important part of Leo Naphta's "incorrectness" as Jesuit, Jew, and Communist. I am inclined to believe that with the help of this aspect, the author succeeded in capturing—at least partially—the complexity of Georg Lukács's personality. The Lukács picture which we gain from the early essays (and which Thomas Mann clearly gained) is that of a Platonist who in his various life stages followed one single path leading to ever new heights, seeking out the measures and dogmas as means and demanding radical decisions from life. Or, as one perceptive Lukács critic remarked: "The exemplary unity of his life and work founded on the intellectual love of man led him from the old Platonic stance of sacrificing life to forms to the more... hopeful view of making [the] self-made forms into vehicles. ...[154] Ultimately, a religious tinge is not missing from this Lukács image; in many respects, this corresponds to the quasi-religious world of Leo Naphta.

In reading the essays, particularly the one on Kierkegaard, one cannot help noticing that Lukács's concept of the ascetic is placed in a quasi-religious world of imagination. At first, it is the terminology that conveys this impression. Much is said here about sin and the mask of sin, of penitence and "isolation from the world," of the "revelation of the word" and of verdict and the "Day of Judgment." Lukács speaks of the travails of the modern essayist (that is, of himself and others of his calling) in an entirely Old Testament voice; he tells of the *"critic [who] has been sent into the world* in order...*to judge* every phenomenon by the scale of values glimpsed and grasped through... recognition."[155] In discussing the concept of love and in defining Kierkegaard's religiosity, the religious element forcefully moves into the foreground, but by no means in the "churchly–dogmatic sense" (Naphta). Interestingly, it occurs in conjunction with indications which can easily be transformed into the ideological–political. For Kierkegaard, "to love" meant "to try never to be proved right." Thus: love is a process of striving. This means that with this kind of love "the question of right and wrong...can never be posed, even as a question."[156] He calls this view of love a neo-Romantic version of the "ideal of love of the ascetic medieval knights," because naiveté has been lost to it (by Kierkegaard's, or modern man's, psychological insights). One must understand, Lukács continues, that a woman can never be the object of "absolute love," because she is not far enough removed from "reality."

How is this "absolute love" to be understood? Who stands so high as to be a worthy object of this kind of love? Lukács's answer: only "God can be loved thus, and no one else but God."[157] Just as *the absolute* has to reign supreme in life because it alone can accord us "security" to bear a wretched life full of troubles, so must love be absolute, that is, "unproblematic," because the object of love, namely God, is "enthroned so high above everything human."[158] This statement can be placed in connection with the "problematic situation": the uncertainty and the frightening aspect of his problematic situation could not bear further problematic elements, those of love. Lukács presents these conclusions as Kierkegaard's concept of love (and God) but sums up the situation in using the telltale first person: "My love is sure and unquestionable only if I am never in the right: and God alone can give me this assurance."[159]

It is a concept of love that does not in any way correspond to our everyday view of love, and its religious character should not be understood in an orthodox–dogmatic sense. Rather, it is in accord with a general religious sensitivity or movement of the beginning of the twentieth century. Lukács's friend at the time, the German poet and dramatist Paul Ernst, described this new sensitivity, "This movement... is completely formless,...so that one must assume... that a new feeling will express itself in an already existing form."[160] Ernst derives this definition of the religious from Schleiermacher, who sees religion as "the feeling of an absolute dependence on God." Accordingly, God is what one considers the "highest reality," above all human knowledge and the object of a "mystical" feeling; as such, God is something else for every person. Thus, God can be "that on which I feel dependent," declares Ernst; this new religiositiy is still "floating ...in the realm of feeling and in an unresolved will." Crystallization of the will—and of thought—shall possibly follow later. In short, this new world view is both unarticulated and vague.[161] It was a state of mind which Thomas Mann captured so well in the early, very short story, "At the Prophet's" (1904); the "proclamations" of Mann's prophet are, to be sure, an extremely shrill and eccentric variation of this "unarticulated feeling" presented "in a mingled style of psalter and revelation," but "all the conditions are present in the figure."[162]

The *Weltempfinden* of Ernst—and Lukács—was not only vague but also quite commodious: if instead of God we have a "higher unit," the "absolute truth," "absolute idea," or something that is "absolutely valid" *(absolut Geltendes),* then the possibility of "absolute love" will remain—albeit with a new content. And as Lukács states in the Kierkegaard essay, the "possibility of embracing the whole, without any reservation whatsoever" is inherent in this concept of love; moreover, this kind of love saves one from "tormenting doubts" and assures that one will "never have to try to be proved right."[163]

In the case of Lukács, the expansion—or transformation—of the concept of love has, indeed, taken place: his redirected "absolute love," his devotion to mankind, could spread out over all humanity. It is possible to interpret Lukács's musings in the early essays as an anticipatory stage of the existential–philosophical direction he later took, as Lucien Goldmann and others interpreted Lukács's early work.[164] Given the framework of this study, we cannot go into the extent to which the overwhelming problem of alienation and malaise of modern man was broached in these essays— a problem which culminated in Lukács's conviction that love between two people is impossible. This very theme, applied to the artist, is further developed in the Charles-Louis Philippe essay, "Longing and Form," and is given artistic form in Mann's *Death in Venice.*

If from love, as Lukács wanted it understood at that time, one expects "reassurance" and "firmness," then it becomes a question of a purely ascetic exercise, motivated by love: it is at the same time a "means of healing" (another term for "assurance" and "firmness') and in this sense synonymous with "unsullied religious egoism," as Naphta characterized the "labor of the religious" (377). Until now, this religious side of Lukács's character has hardly been noticed or analyzed: Lukács himself was silent on the subject—understandably so.[165] With his heightened sensitivity, Thomas Mann perceived this trait in Lukács's early work and was presumably able to discern it in their personal encounter and discussion; this was a great accomplishment and a testimony to Mann's sure poetic intuition. Mann's achievement is to be valued all the more because he did not personally know the young (pre-Marxist) Lukács, and only met the "later" Lukács once briefly. Also, he was not acquainted with Lukács's polemical and political writings. Nevertheless—particularly in the religious realm—Thomas Mann grasped the continuity, the thread through Lukács's different "life-stages": the aesthetic, the ethical and the political. Not until recently has it been possible—with the help of the newest publications and of the unpublished sources in the Lukács Archives in Budapest—to demonstrate that the religious element was there early and even characterized the thinking and expression of Lukács's Marxist period. In the following, a small sample of the material will be presented.

In 1918 Lukács, answering a questionnaire of a Budapest journal, listed all those books which had had a determining influence on his life thus far.[166] He was fifteen years old, Lukács said, when the intensive study of Genesis precipitated the first serious intellectual-spiritual crisis of his life. A friend of his, Béla Balázs, reports in his diary on countless conversations he had with Lukács in which they discussed God, Lucifer and religion in general, and salvation in particular.[167] We are told that in 1912, Lukács and Balázs spent some time in Florence. During this sojourn, Balázs made the following entry:

We have talked with Gyuri [Hungarian nickname for György] a lot about God... and his astute analyses have given me ideas, for instance that of Homo Dei,[168] that is, that only he is truly a person in a religious sense who rises up out of the chaos of life as "form" [something that is given form]. ... Anyway: religion is aristocratic.[169]

Balázs also comes to talk of Lukács's Weltbild, in which the latter established a "special principle of Evil" (Sonderprinzip des Bösen). Balázs remarks sceptically that "if there really is a principle of evil does that not mean that in the end we must arrive at the existence of two Gods?"[170] Hardly a year later Balázs is describing Ernst Bloch's undesirable influence on Lukács; as a consequence, Lukács's thought takes on a new, utopian direction. Balázs notes, "Gyuri is really a rational thinker and this utopian trait does not suit him well at all." He adds that Lukács himself is aware of this and "it seems to worry him. ...I cannot stand this tendency of Bloch at all that he has to proclaim a new religion whenever he is lighting up a new cigar."[171]

After a brief stay in Heidelberg (and an extremely close friendship with Bloch), a change took place in Lukács's thinking, according to Balázs and others. The utopian element in his thought acquired a stronger, more explicit religious coloring. This was the period of Lukács's friendship with Buber and the publication of his review of Buber's translation of the Hasidic tales entitled "Jewish Mysticism" (see Appendix).

We have the documentation of Lukács's state of mind at that time because Balázs made the significant entry in his diary sometime in 1914:

Gyuri's new philosophy: *Messianism. A homogeneous world* as the *redemptive goal.* Art as the possibility of a Luciferian "corrective" *(Besser-Machen),* that is, the *immorality of art.* ...*His big turn toward ethics.* It will be the center and the goal of his life and work. ...Gyuri *discovers* and *acknowledges his Jewishness! Search for his ancestors.* The sect of the Chassidism: Baal Shem. He too has now found his fore-fathers and his race. ... Gyuri's theory concerning a *new type of Jew* now develop-ing: it is that of the anti-rational ascetic and is the exact opposite of everything that we customarily call "Jewish."[172]

These entries of Balázs attest to a constant preoccupation with the nature of the religious, and they document the development and reshaping of the religious world view of Lukács and his friends. As late as 1915, Balázs reports on long theosophical discussions, in fact, even on a conversation about the "transmigration of the soul"; at the same time, they reflected on the relativity of all ethical values.[173] More and more, ethics moved to the foreground of Lukács's interest; the same was true of his left-oriented friends. In this context, they debated the possibility of an "adequate life" and closely examined "representative types" such as Don Quixote and the saints. The influence of Dostoevsky and of the Russian anarchists—one of whom Lukács had married—became more and more significant to Lukács's thought, according to Balázs.

These reports and diary entries of Balázs have been confirmed by several sources.[174] But it remains a fact that Thomas Mann built into the Naphta figure not only certain personality traits but also most of the topics, deliberations, and interests which captured Lukács's imagination at various times. Without knowing about this inti-mate side of Lukács, Thomas Mann succeeded in capturing the *young* Lukács, es-pecially the essential character of his Jewishness, when he portrayed in Naphta in an ironic way, so to speak "ideal-typically," the newly evolving, anti-rational, ascetic, and radically inclined Jewish intellectual of his time. In this regard it should be stressed that we are speaking here of only one side of the Naphta portrait, speci-fically of his intellectual-spiritual makeup.

Because he was schooled in Nietzsche, Thomas Mann was also aware of the "prob-lematic situation," as Lukács called it, and for this reason he spoke in favor of a con-stant spiritual-ethical effort on behalf of the problematic ego. (In *Reflections of a Non-Political Man,* he speaks of the times that had "drafted" him, so to speak, to do his "military" duty and engage in polemics with all the indescribable tendencies of the time.) The same efforts underlie his discussion *"Geist und Kunst,"* a never completed long essay, which intended to take a very critical look at art, contemporary trends, and artists but soon threatened to become a critique of modern civilization.[175] Like Lukács, he too believed that the man of letters (Lukács calls him the "Platonist," the essayist) has the overriding obligation to formulate the problems and questions of the times with "ascetic severity" and "critical passion" (like Nietzsche). Thomas Mann's much vaunted ability to pick up the trends of the times and of literature enabled him to track down the subjective elements in Lukács's utterances; the writer who admittedly always talked about himself, whatever his subject, no doubt soon caught on that Lukács too talked only about himself when he was discussing the problems of others; similarly, in the analysis of past times Lukács illuminated the problems of his own. About the Romantics and their time Lukács wrote:

> Each suffered all the torments of a man driven out into the wilderness, thirsting for culture and community, and the tragic, ecstatic pain of an idealism stretched to a breaking point. They felt that the way...led into nothingness; and ...simultaneously they saw the possibility of...freeing themselves from the anarchy of living as mere litterati ...and hastening towards fruitful, culture-creating new goals.

> They knew,... they felt that every conceivable experience had to be accepted and lived through in order that the "invisible church" which it was their mission to build should be all-embracing and full of riches. *It looked as though a new religion were about to be created*... it was *with a purely religious exclusivity and single-mindedness* that their...spirit *subordinated* every other aim to it. ... And *the apostles of this new religion* gathered...and *discussed in passionate paradoxes* the programme of *the new conquest of the world.* ...[176]

The quest of these "apostles" took an inward turn; they found a way to resolve life's contradictions in the "harmony of images of life" (meaning "abstractions"). Lukács asserts that this was the only "path open to their longing for the great synthesis of unity and universality." This synthesis was supposed to be "the order" that "comprised everything."[177] They were to the last man egoists on account of their seeking their own "salvation from loneliness and chaos."[178] To be sure, they had to pay a price: "a seemingly deliberate withdrawal from life," which is the essence of a certain kind of asceticism.[179] This egoism could not come to terms with the fact that action (praxis) demands great sacrifices. The final result and conclusion of this attitude is summarized by Lukács as follows:

> [Their] hope of the culture to come [dissolved]. Many became... worn out by the comfortless *search for a new religion* and the dismal sight of *increasing anarchy*... which merely *helped to intensify their desire for order;* some...returned with resignation into the quiet waters of the old religions. And so it happened that men who had ...*set out to remold and re-create the entire world* became *pious converts.*[180]

These insights contain a good portion of criticism, self-criticism, and discernment of the danger of such a search and longing; they may have heralded the beginning of a critical self-understanding for Lukács. What seems almost certain is the assumption that many recurring formulations in Lukács's early essays "unmasked" him, so to speak, in the eyes of the author of *The Magic Mountain*. The "longing for order" of the Romantics and Kassner's "yearning for the dogma, for measure" symbolized Lukács's own aspirations and feelings; the aspirations were given form and expressed in Naphta's *Lebensweg* (path in life) and in the statement that he displayed "an ardent yearning" for the "most exclusive and lawful sphere of life." It must have seemed almost uncanny to Thomas Mann that the "type" of litterati he had sketched in his unpublished draft to the essay *Geist und Kunst* now appeared before him in Lukács's *Soul and Form*. (Thomas Mann was working on his essay draft in the years 1908 to 1910; Lukács wrote his essays in exactly this period and they were published in 1911 in German. Mann bought the book that same year.) It was Mann's belief that this type should possess a moral sense next to his intellectuality: he should be a moralist "in a two-fold sense," as someone who knows the soul and is a judge of it *(Seelenkundiger* and *Seelenrichter)*, whose *ethical passion* is reflected in his style.[181] Also, this man of letters possesses both knowledge and a sense of justice; he is a "saint" and thus "pure," like the "prophets of the Old Testament."[182]

As Thomas Mann states in another context, this man of letters is an ascetic, a moralist, and a sage; besides "wisdom," he must possess "goodness." But, as he realizes, these are "priestly qualities: and who is going to chide me when I call this man of letters a priest?"[183] At the same time, Mann could come across in Lukács's book the statement that the "criteria of the essayist's judgment are...created within him"; he acts according to the highest command of the "great value-definer." This essayist, says Lukács, "is a John the Baptist *[Täufer]* who goes out to preach in the wilderness. ..."[184] The work of such an essayist does not culminate in pronouncing judgment, Lukács believes, "but in the process of judging." He also calls this essayist a "pure" type. A judge, a pure and saintly man, and a priest—these attributes come up time and again in Lukács's essays. The counterpart of Mann's *Seelenkundiger* (knower of the soul) is part and parcel of Lukács's concept of the essayist, albeit under a different name: we are told that "the Platonist [essayist] is a dissector of souls *[Seelenzergliederer]*."[185]

"Goodness" as a priestly quality and a necessary complement of the ideal type of the man of letters is, to be sure, not present in the essays of *Soul and Form*. It is, however, a crucial category in the next work of Lukács, the dialogue "Von der Armut am Geiste" (On Poverty of Spirit).[186] We do not have any documentary proof whether Thomas Mann had read this important transitional work of Lukács or not; striking similarities in concept and formulations in connection with Naphta let us assume that this work did not remain unknown to Mann, because the journal it appeared in, *Neue Blätter*, was widely read in Germany. (Besides Lukács, contributors to the same issue included Martin Buber, Rainer Maria Rilke, Rudolf Kassner, and Theodor Däubler.) This dialogue introduces the "ethical stage" of Lukács's life; at the same time it demonstrates both a transformation in his concept of the ethical and the peculiarity of his religiosity. The confessional quality of this work makes it even more important: it contains a pure, subjective statement and a barely concealed admission of guilt. One can discover significant passages in the dialogue which have been lifted verbatim from Lukács's diary, as for example the already quoted exclamation, "I am working. I do not need anyone."[187] In more than one sense, this dialogue is a continuation of the Kierkegaard essay and also represents a critical position on the opinions voiced there. The criticism culminates in the realization that in turning away from life (asceticism) one cannot lead a pure life, that is, possess "goodness" (Güte); as Lukács said of Kierkegaard, "His tragedy was that he wanted to live what cannot be lived."[188] It is also suggested that a "radical" solution is the only possible one: the protagonist puts a bullet through his head, whereby the absolute tribute is paid to humanity. (It echoes in the narrator's observation following Naphta's suicide that Naphta, with his last "shriek," made a confession to humanity.) Without going into an analysis of the philosophical premises and conclusions of this work, it is of considerable importance to take a look at those statements which help illuminate the personality of the protagonist—and of Lukács.

In the "hero" of the dialogue, we encounter the "modern intellectual" who is—in Thomas Mann's opinion—"an ascetic, a moralist and a saint" and furthermore someone who "knoweth" (ein Wissender); he possesses the "will to self-recognition" which can encourage "self-mastery."[189] What he does not possess is the priestly quality of "goodness." His longing for it is so intense that its lack leads him inevitably to self-destruction, as a sort of "self-mastery." The partner in the dialogue calls the hero an ascetic, specifically an ascetic of "frivolity" who thinks he can skip over stages on the path to grace (cf. the "leap" in the Kierkegaard essay) and still expect "absolution." Or, as stated elsewhere: "You wish to become a monk but one can no longer undo the Reformation."[190] The plea of the hero is a curious mixture fo Eckhart, Plotinus and Lao Tse (Lukács the Gnostic!) in which the concept of "poverty of spirit" is thus defined:

> Poverty of Spirit means freeing oneself from one's own psychological limitations in order to give oneself over to one's own deeper metaphysical necessity; it means giving oneself up in order, thereby, to realize the Work. ... Then *poverty becomes action, a fruitful and fearful raging of the obsession of the task* that hungers for realization.[191]

To be poor in spirit renders man "a vessel" but the only one that "contains the appearance of spirit." Only in such a man can "the wine of the [spirit's] manifestations be poured out. ... [therefore], we have no right to withdraw from it," states Lukács's protagonist.[192]

In concluding Lukács stresses that this is not to be confused with the "stupid modern individualism of duties toward oneself" and goes on to accuse the "hero" of wanting to "reinstitute the castes on a metaphysical foundation." The hero cannot and will not deny this; the caste is, after all, an aristocratic category (but not in a sociological sense). It cannot be denied that the concept of the elite *(Elitengedanke)* dominates this work. (The concept of caste itself reminds us of Nietzsche's concept of the Brahmans.) As Lukács understands it, only a *chosen* person, blessed with the virtue of goodness, can possess poverty of spirit. Goodness is *the* path to God. "An ordinary and unclear person is never poor in spirit," declares the dialogue's hero; in consequence, he can never become a "vessel" for the spirit and its "manifestation."[193]

It is not spurious to suggest that there is a direct connection between "longing for more noble forms of existence" and the fact that Lukács's protagonist longs for but never achieves the state of being chosen as the pinnacle of existence. Indeed, the "passionate" and "ardent yearning" for "higher forms of existence" is such an important attribute of Naphta's character that Mann found it necessary to dramatize and call attention to it: this is why this trait is reformulated and restated time and again. Whether we hear that young Leo inherited from his father the idea of a "starry eyed" spirituality and appreciation of the sacred that he left behind his family with "the callousness of the born aristocrat," or that the (Jesuit) institute flattered his deepest instinct with its manorial atmosphere and exceptional intellectuality (441–444), we are dealing with variations of the same concept: the aristocratic existence. The same idea is articulated by Lukács's protagonist when he denies the right to exist to all who are not endowed with that special "grace" (of God): "Just as in the philosophy of art only genius is permitted to exist, so it is only the person graced with Goodness who has the right to exist in life."[194]

At the same time as Lukács defines this aristocratic category, he also revolutionizes the concept of ethics: he regards the Kantian ethic as unsatisfactory and belonging to the "ordinary," the "everyday" sphere, because it is "general, binding and far removed from men." True ethics actually entails an "abandonment of ethic"; what is needed instead is "Goodness" which cannot be found in any ethical system. It is the "miracle, the grace and salvation."[195] What we have then is a "privatization of ethics" *(Verpersönlichung der Ethik)*. Lukács articulates an ethic which bursts the framework of accepted and generally held ethical categories. If we consider the definition of "Goodness" as a privilege of "caste," then we have in this case a new ethic, like Naphta's, which is both aristocratic and revolutionary.

But what is the meaning of this newly posited ethic? This new ethic, defined as "Goodness," is radically different from the "old" one in that it is not synonymous with having fulfiled all of one's duty. The new ethic means that "one is *not permitted to want to be good* to someone—or to oneself. *One must want to save someone,*" even if the act of saving includes sin. "One wants to save someone and behaves badly, cruelly, tyrannically…even sin itself in that case is not the opposite of Goodness," or "it is merely a necessary discordant note in the harmony."[196]

It is possible to call these statements paradoxical. How is it to be understood that sin does not constitute an opposite to "Goodness"? But as Naphta said, "Opposites may be consistent with each other" (404). Lukács's protagonist tries to bring harmony to that which does not rhyme. He who is blessed with "Goodness" knows of the impossibility of harmony, of the existence of this paradox, but nothing can shake his belief in the power of the "nevertheless." In sum: "Goodness is obsession; it is not mild, not artful and certainly not quietist; it is wild, cruel and adventurous."[197] Solely on the basis of this concept of ethics, the hero of the dialogue may be called a "fanatic," specifically a fanatic of the will to redeem, who is capable of believing that "remaining pure amid sin, betrayal and cruelty" is possible for him to whom the grace of Goodness has been granted.[198]

Lukács's peculiar religiosity becomes visible through the topics of discussion in the dialogue; we call it peculiar because this religiosity is a strange mixture (and adulteration) of Jewish and Catholic elements. In explaining goodness and grace, Lukács draws upon Francis of Assisi, whose knowledge lies beyond "sign and interpretation" *(Deutung)*, and to whom are revealed the "secret thoughts of others."[199] Today, there is little talk of how many of the young artists and intellectuals at the beginning of the twentieth century created an idealized picture of Francis of Assisi for themselves; based mainly on the work of Henry Thoda. They found a model in Saint Francis because of his emphasis on love instead of dogma, because of his monk's movement against the hierarchy of the Church, and—this affected Lukács most—because he saw ethics as the personal concern of every and each individual. Lukács's attitude was so well-known in Hungary that in a famous Hungarian collection of satirical portraits Lukács is depicted as a "neo-Franciscan."[200]

The hero of the Lukács dialogue is accused by his partner of wanting "mysticism as a form of life," that is, of expecting ecstasy as a gift, which Meister Eckhart had already combatted in his *Martha and Maria*. But what really turned the concept of goodness into a mystical one was the belief of the protagonist that one not only seeks God but that one is also sought by God; this is a characteristically mystical comprehension. The union of the "good" person with the "other" is a variation of the concept of *unio mystica*. (In connection with Francis of Assisi it is stated that "his knowledge went beyond signs and interpretation because he is good. In such moments, he is the other.") Those who possess "Goodness" are defined as "Gnostics of the deed," whose "knowledge has become deed," whose "thinking has left the purely discoursive realm of knowledge.")[201] This formulation harkens back to the pattern of Meister Eckhart's *Liebestat* (act of love).

But above all it is Meister Eckhart's concept of the soul which we see presented in this dialogue. And Lukács was by no means alone in this. Ernst Bloch, for instance, studied and appropriated Eckhart's mystical writings; indeed, for years mysticism was one of the main topics of discussion between Lukács and Bloch.[202] It is said of Georg Simmel, too, that he "experienced only one form of the religious within himself…which still had some validity: the mystical," and for days on end he would read Meister Eckhart.[203]

That Lukács might well have been inspired by Simmel to study mysticism is an assumption we cannot go into here. In his 1918 answer to a questionnaire, Lukács noted that "at a very opportune moment" in his development, he encountered mystical philosophy, which proved extremely inspirational; actually, he said, "it all started with Sebastian Franck's *Paradoxa*" and led to "Plotinus and Meister Eckhart, also Lao Tse, the Upanishads, the New Testament, Francis of Assisi, Valentin Weigel, etc., etc. Coinciding with this, I engaged in a fruitful study of Dostoevsky. …"[204]

Mysticism and Dostoevsky combined provided the background against which Lukács set up his reflections on the possibility or necessity of violent, cruel action. Interestingly, Thomas Mann alludes to the consequences of such an explosive combination when he lets *his* protagonist, Hans Castorp, remark, "Something pretty awful, terroristic might come to pass if the East went to Spain…" (505; by Spain, the author had in mind, among other things the "black…Inquisition, Loyola…") The exclusiveness with which mysticism "posits the absolute" permits tyrannical deeds and capricious opposites. Klaus Peter, in his treatment of the early phase of German Idealism, comes to discuss precisely this theme and cites Friedrich Schlegel's condemnation of the mystics. Schlegel called them *Rasende* (ravers, madmen) and "tyrants," and asserted that "the genuine mystic has a saintly mentality and yet there is no gruesomeness and no baseness of which he would not be capable."[205] In further developing the heritage of mystical thinking, Leszek Kolakowski states in "The Priest and the Jester," an essay devoted to the exploration of the problematic of "secular eschatology," that the mystics were masters of that manner of thinking "that expresses itself in the movement of thesis and antithesis." Kolakowski seems to see in the dialectic "the problem of mystic theology."[206]

Paradoxically—and Lukács was at that time full of paradoxes—he supports his conviction of the necessity of cruelty with words of Christ: "He who comes to me and hates not his father, mother, wife, child, brother, sister and not even his own life, he cannot be my disciple."[207] The protagonist comes to this conclusion after having alluded to an ancient legend about the building of a temple during which a worker's wife had to be sacrificed (immured) so that the edifice would stay standing. "The work grew out of life," writes Lukács, "but it outgrew life; it has its origin in things human, but is itself unhuman, indeed, anti-human. *The cement that binds the work to life…is…of human blood.*"[208] This assertion may be interpreted as the sign of "solemn mercilessness," a "cruel piety," and of "uncanny piety," which were the very attributes of Elie Naphta. Thus, the axiom that "one must not hold back one's hand from the shedding of blood" (448) has found its way into the Lukácsian argumentation. The idea of the necessity of human sacrifice (for the work—the end) is further grounded in the Abraham episode of the Old Testament. Like Kierkegaard,

Lukács expressed his admiration for Abraham and his deed. Abraham was greatly admired for being willing to sacrifice "human blood" and for his unconditional "obedience." Although God at the end did not accept the sacrifice, Abraham's *willingness* to sacrifice was as highly valued as the accomplished fact: "Now I know that thou fearest God, seeing thou hast not withheld thy son, thine only son from me" (Gen. 22:12).

When we claim that Lukács's religiosity was not without the Jewish element, we are thinking not only of the language, formulations and allusions that harken back to the Old Testament, but also—and primarily—of the inseparability of ethics and religion (God). As Hermann Cohen expressed it, "For the Jewish consciousness there is no separation between religion and morality."[209] And in his work, *The Essence of Judaism,* Leo Baeck notes that "what compels [the prophets of Judaism] to think is an *ethical urge*—they are overwhelmed by an irresistible truth"; thus, the prophet/thinker is "the vessel for the words of some higher power" (cf. Lukács's statement in the *Armut*).[210] Accordingly, Judaism's "predominant aspect from the beginning was its ethical character. ... *Ethics constitute its essence.*"[211] The Jewish religion has a practical orientation because it is placed in the dynamic experience of Jewish existence; consequently, it abstains from conceptions that attempt to visualize the beyond and focuses on "man in whom the world manifests itself." It does not perceive a division between the world and faith, between the "word" and the furthering of "moral commands" in the here and now. Even the contemplation of "the Lord's attributes lead[s] to ethical commands."[212]

The idea of responsibility is not to be separated from that of ethics. The "responsibility before God towards one's fellow man" is the postulate of the ethical attitude presented in Lukács's dialogue. This postulate has been violated by the hero; as he himself admits, his self-destruction is a "judgement of God" *(Gottesurteil)*. Even though we encounter here a highly secularized and aestheticized version, some of the characteristics of the Jewish religion as described by Leo Baeck are at work subliminally in the ruminations of Lukács's dialogue. There is, for example, the awareness of being chosen, a "peculiar position [of the Jewish people] by which it is distinguished from all other peoples."[213] The consequences of this awareness is the seemingly paradoxical existential duty: to live with the feeling of "humility, the feeling of standing before God as little and insignificant" ("poverty of spirit") and still carry within oneself the conviction that one is living an exalted, indeed, the most exalted history (aristocracy of the castes in the dialogue).[214]

Two important elements of Jewish faith, the commanding God and the just God, predominate in Lukács's references to God. Already in the Kierkegaard essay, in connection with the concept of love of God, Lukács presents the notion of the *absolute Recht* (that which is proved right against one): One can love "God alone... [because] before God [one is] always in the wrong." In the dialogue "On Poverty of Spirit," the "commanding God" also appears on the scene: "God's claim on us is absolute," declares the hero. There is a suggestion here of earlier positions of Lukács that were expressed, for example, in the notion of the absolute life as an either-or proposition in the Kierkegaard essay. The notion appears in similar form in Leo Baeck's treatise:

With this faith in the commanding God there has come into the world the opposition to any sort of ethical opportunism. ... This faith cannot compromise; it cannot be linked with anything but good. God gives commandments, not advice; he says "thou shalt" and "thou shalt not." Judaism was the first religion to establish this either–or. ...the absoluteness of God's command, which brings the unconditional and the real into man's life, makes impossible the mythological conception of fate.[215]

Let it be mentioned that Lukács also notes this basic divergence of Judaism from the thought of antiquity: "Abraham with his sacrifice," says the dialogue's hero, "has left the world of tragic conflicts and heroes, that of Agamemnon and his sacrifice."[216] The similarity of the formulation and of the conclusion is striking.

One can be of different opinions on how the seemingly grotesque blend of "goodness-grace-ethics-ecstasy-cruelty-justice" categories of the dialogue is to be interpreted. It may also seem daring to evoke the concept of *Zedakah*—which in its full meaning is untranslatable. The word includes the ideas of goodness and justice, which is the domain of absolute obligation: it implies the positive and emphatic insistence on "the right of our neighbour and his claim upon us"; the word connotes "justice and beneficence fused into a unity." As such, concludes Baeck, it is "positive religious and social justice in which is included the demanding messianic element."[217] In the final analysis *Zedakah* has nothing to do with mere general good will or with civic morality, not to speak of juristic equity. Aspects of this definition of *Zedakah* found their way into Lukács's dialogue. "One must not want to be good" for the sake of one's soul, declares the hero, "one must want to save someone"; that is "Goodness."[218] Lukács thus condemns that "fruitless sentimentality" Baeck was mentioning in negative terms; like Baeck, he has no use for the formal ethic, for bourgeois morality or "charity"; indeed, the hero insists on his being without guilt in the "normal" sense of ethical commands, since he "sincerely fulfiled" all his duties ("and he uttered the word, 'duty,' with utmost contempt"). The "Goodness" he has in mind cannot be found in any "consistent ethical system."[219] It is defined as "man's truly finding his way home," as the absolute fulfilment; in this we find the presence of that "messianic element" in Lukács's train of thought that Baeck was speaking of.[220] In Judaism, however, both the idea of *redemption* (the most frequently used word in Lukács's early work) and the yearning for "the return home," the *messianic* element, are central.

The messianic element can already be ascertained prior to 1914, the year in which Balázs reported on Lukács's "new philosophy: messianism." In this respect, too, Lukács as a thinker belongs to that generation of continental philosophers, aesthetes, and social scientists who assumed a position of Messianism. Important and influential in this respect were Hermann Cohen, Franz Rosenzweig, Walter Benjamin, Martin Buber, Max Horkheimer, Theodor W. Adorno, and, of course, Ernst Bloch, who at this time probably exercised the greatest influence on Lukács. There is no doubt in my mind that this tendency is related to Lukács's "new theory" of the "new, anti-rational type" of Jew, among whom he counts himself.[221]

Just how much of Lukács's "religiosity" and the complex blend of his personality were conveyed to Thomas Mann by the early writings of Lukács and how much their personal meeting contributed to it cannot be determined. When I asked him about this, Lukács answered that one can gauge the nature of impression from Mann's letter to Dr. Seipel.[222] Thus, he was in complete agreement with what had been said there. In this letter, Thomas Mann wrote that although he does *not* share Lukács's intellectual nature, *Weltanschauung,* and political beliefs, he nevertheless deeply respects his "austere, pure and proud mind." Mann emphasizes that in Vienna, Lukács was living in circumstances that could only be tolerated by his spiritually as well as intellectually ascetic nature. Mann also speaks of Lukács's "doctrinaire and unrelenting spiritual makeup." When Mann states that Lukács left behind the impression of "hair-raising abstractness," of "purity" and "intellectual nobility" which was compelling to the degree that "as long as he was talking, he was right," we are reminded of the impressionable hero of *The Magic Mountain* and the style of his "educator," Leo Naphta. Naphta's style of argumentation is characterized best in the short sentence: "He had spoken sharply and apodictically" (375). My own view is that the personal impression merely confirmed the one Mann had gained from the early essays and rounded off the picture. It is interesting to learn, then, that Lukács consciously strove to convey this impression. In a 1910 letter to Leo Popper, Lukács tried to "defend" his latest essay, "Esztétikai kultúra" (On Aesthetic Culture) as well as explain his stylistic aspirations:

> It undoubtedly contains something good—stylistically speaking. It is an attempt to overcome my "indecisive" style; it strives to develop an apodictic form, that is, that doubt should exist only during the thought process—*ante rem*—but the finished *work should have an apodictic character.* ...in this sense, the article is a sort of a beginning...the *prolegomenon to what is in the making...:* for the metaphysical justification of the concept of form. [I think] that form is a biological need (not in the "natural science" sense of the word)...but as a necessary element of life in its *totality.*[223]

Naphta's intellectual intensity and the calm, quiet manner of speech result in a contrastive combination which also could have originated in the Lukács model. A contemporary of Lukács and a fellow Party member in the years 1918–19, Ervin Sinkó, described "the astonishing phenomenon called Lukács": in the midst of the most heated theoretical and tactical debates and passionate controversies about his own person (in the wake of his article "Bolshevism as a Moral Problem"), Lukács sat there, "with his glasses on, a remarkable large forehead and large, extremely bright eyes, altogether calm, as if there were no hurry, as though on a desert island… and was silent. …"[224] We are told that even his most vocal opponents were "fascinated" and some of them succumbed to Lukács's arguments when he finally chose to speak ("As long as he was talking he was right"!). Thus, for instance, one of them said, exasperated: "Damn him, he is right almost about everything and that means that we must be wrong."[225] This exclamation again echoes Mann's own impression. In his novel, Sinkó gives ample illustration of the fact that Lukács was aware of both the manner and the dangers of his asceticism: "Ideas have a Mephisthophelean power," Lukács was to have said. "Every goal for which we must violate ourselves appears to us in the end as the good in and of itself."[226] At the same time, there lives on in Lukács the longing and the desire for "redemption," just as at the time of *Soul and Form* and "Poverty of the Spirit," but with one great difference: "*Today*, in the age of absolute sinfulness [Fichte's formulation], *salvation is only possible in the political realm*."[227] This sentence can be regarded as containing the explanation for Lukács's "transformation": it is less of a radical transformation than a new direction given to the old longing.

As has been shown, the view of life, the personal style, and the intellectual direction of the young Lukács is not too distant from the general impression which Leo Naphta makes on those with whom he comes into close contact, and which Lukács must have made on others beside Thomas Mann. The reminiscences of Paul Honigsheim from the Heidelberg period and those of Marianna Weber are often cited in this connection. Marianna Weber speaks of "some philosophers from Eastern Europe who were becoming known at that time, particularly the Hungarian, Georg von Lukács," with whom both Webers struck up a close friendship. Marianna adds:

> These young philosophers were *moved by eschatological hopes of a new emissary* of the transcendent God, and they saw *the basis of salvation* in a *socialist social order* created by brotherhood. For Lukács the splendor of inner-wordly culture, particularly its esthetic side, meant the Antichrist, the "Luciferian" competition against God's effectiveness. …The *final struggle* between God and Lucifer *is still to come* and depends on the decision of mankind. The ultimate goal is *salvation from the world,* not… fulfillment in it.[228]

The statements of former friends, like-minded companions, and other contemporaries who were acquainted with him are even more valuable; many of them were also members of the Sunday Circle which came into being around December 1915 in Budapest and from which later developed the Free School of Humanities. As Balázs, who was the organizing force and at whose apartment they regularly met, remarked, "Only those *serious* people who are metaphysically inclined are welcome." Among those Lukács, Karl Mannheim, Arnold Hauser, Frederick Antal and Emma Ritoók.

Arnold Hauser, one of the early members and a personal acquaintance of Lukács, characterized the young Lukács in the following way:

Georg Lukács was definitely one of the *most categorically thinking* persons I have ever met; he also *expressed himself in the most indomitable terms.* With his *fearlessness* and with his constant readiness to take his own measure, he *tended toward dogmatism* and *he sharpened the contrasts,* or opposites, he happened upon, *to alternatives.* Whenever it was a matter of decisions which were crucial morally or in terms of world view, *he adhered,* in keeping with his Kierkegaard heritage, *to inexorable principles.*[229]

Ernst Bloch expressed his identity with Lukács at the time of their intimate friendship during their Heidelberg sojourn: "At the beginning of our friendship, Lukács and I *put order above freedom,* put Marx above Bakunin for the same reason, *admired the Catholic hierarchy and transferred this too to the political sphere.*" Bloch was of the opinion that Lukács happened to cling to this "predilection for a system," and this played a significant role in their estrangement.[230] At the time of the October Revolution of 1917, however, they still had certain views in common: "We both, Lukács and I," said Bloch, "view the October Revolution as a fulfilment. Alexander Blok's poem of a Red Guard who marches at the head of a mob of rebelling workers and who is revealed to be Jesus Christ affected us tremendously and confirmed [the correctness of our views]."[231] Particularly with regard to the "religious" or the "prophetic" trait of Lukács, Karl Jaspers's recollections are highly illuminating. Jaspers, with whom Lukács struck up a somewhat superficial friendship in Heidelberg and with whom he often conferred about his wife's deteriorating mental state, remarked on the impression which Lukács (and Bloch) made in the early 1910s:

Many came to Heidelberg who were men of letters and potential candidates for *Habilitation.* Among them were Georg von Lukács from Budapest and Ernst Bloch from Mannheim. Both later made names for themselves as Marxists. At that time, they were Gnostics who shared their theosophical fantasies in their social circles. After a lecture by Lukácz [sic] Bloch stated ceremoniously: the world spirit *[Weltgeist]* had just gone through this room...and he let a pause ensue before he continued...with his announcements.

Lukács appeared to some to be a sort of saint, and he was, by the way, a very sensitive connoisseur of literature and a not uninteresting philosophical aesthetician. Bloch was rather a down-to-earth, quite open fellow who by his warmth and outgoing manner...aroused some sympathy. In Heidelberg people were talking about them. The philosopher Lask once made the humorous remark: "Do you know who are the four evangelists: Matthew, Marc, Lucacz [sic] and Bloch."[232]

It follows from this and similar comments that in the eyes of contemporary observers, Lukács and Bloch had much in common; but it is far from correct, as some people have thought, that the religious aspect in Lukács's thought and writings is to be ascribed solely to Bloch's influence. Nor is it true that it was entirely inconsistent with Lukács's "rational way of thinking."[233] One can, however, characterize Lukács's religiosity in the same way as Bloch's: it is religious atheism, that is to say, it is *incorrect* as a form of religiosity.

The question then arises: How does a quasi-religious man and thinker, imbued with a longing for absolute salvation and redemption, evolve, as one critic put it, into a "representative of the totalitarian idea"? Many critics of Lukács asked themselves this question and have spoken of his "seduction by politics" and called the metamorphosis of Lukács's philosophical and political thought an "enigma.'" This metamorphosis is relatively easy to explain, in my opinion, provided we play close attention to what Lukács had to say in the 1919 essay "Tactics and Ethics" and in the one immediately preceeding it, "Bolshevism as a Moral Problem." As Lukács sees it, the ethical considerations are what inspire a person to decide to participate actively in the realization of the utopia. This requires, of course, that one subscribe to that view of ethics which Lukács outlined in the 1912 dialogue, "Von der Armut am Geiste": the personalization of ethics, that is, that "ethics relate to the individual." As the "necessary consequence of this relationship," Lukács writes in the 1919 essay, "the individual's conscience and sense of responsibility confront[s]...the postulate that he must act as if on his action or inaction depended the changing of the world's destiny. ...." For, "in the realm of ethics there is no neutrality and no impartiality"; each individual has to defend his unwillingness to act before his own conscience.[234] Thus, there is in 1919 still the echo of the "Franciscan ethic" of "Von der Armut am Geiste," and it determines the action of the communist Lukács who has in the meantime "discovered" that the Marxist theory of society supplies the method and the means for the realization of utopia. Because socialism had presented the solution, Lukács was presented his salvation. It is not our concern here whether this was a "deliverance by Evil," as Thomas Mann said. Be that as it may, Naphta's ethic, which determined the manner of the realization of utopia, corresponds to the ethics developed by Lukács in his essay:

> The *only* valid yardstick is whether the *manner* of the action in a given case serves to realize this goal, which is the essence of the socialist movement. Hence...all means by which this historico-philosophical process is raised to the conscious and real level are to be considered valid.... [235]

The ultimate objective of socialism, the replacement of present reality by a "higher power" which corresponds to "the dignity of man," is thus a "moral question": therefore, all means should be regarded from an ethical standpoint as just as moral. This does not at all mean that in certain "tragic situations" one could not become guilty of committing a wrong. But we must choose, Lukács tells us in "Tactics and Ethics"—as Naphta does in the novel—between two different ways of incurring guilt according to "a standard attaching to correct and incorrect action." This very standard is called by Lukács "sacrifice." Thus, the individual, by making the "correct choice," might sacrifice "his inferior self on the altar of the higher idea." His sacrifice is assessed "in terms of the collective action."[236] (It is a "new elucidation" of the "ethical leap" from individual to collective action.) The idea appears as a command of the world-historical situation, as a calling. In the final analysis, fanaticism (called "obsession" in Naphta's case), ethical rigor, and a Jesuitic moral code (the end justifies the means) result in the ultimate conviction that regards *violence* as a necessity in certain "tragic situations." Combining the words of a Russian anarchist (Boris Savinkov) and Hebbel's tragic heroine Judith, Lukács sets up his thesis about the necessity of violence:

> In one of his novels, Ropshin [Boris Savinkov] formulated...the problem of individual terror in the following terms: murder is not allowed, it is an absolute and unpardonable sin; it "may" not, but yet it "must" be committed. Elsewhere in the same book he sees, not the justification (that is impossible) but *the ultimate moral basis of the terrorist's act as the sacrifice for his brethren,* not only of his life, but also of his purity, his morals, his very soul. In other words, only he who acknowledges unflinchingly and without any reservations that murder is under no circumstances to be sanctioned can commit the murderous deed that is truly—and tragically—moral. To express this sense of the most profound human tragedy in the incomparably beautiful words of Hebbel's Judith: "Even if God had placed sin between me and the deed enjoined upon me—who am I to be able to escape it?"[237]

Only if we realize that Thomas Mann had no knowledge of this essay and that he did not know *this* Lukács, only then can we appreciate with what visionary force he conjured up the possibilities inherent in this type. The religious bent is not missing at this stage either; this is not only expressed in the fact that the idea of a "higher power" is invoked in connection with guaranteeing the "dignity of man" and in Judith's calling, but first and foremost in the presence of the idea of redemption: in the essay after "Tactics and Ethics," Lukács's closing statement again harkens back to the language and sentiments of the 1912 dialogue—but is colored by Lukács's newly acquired Marxism:

> We Marxists not only believe that the development of society is directed by the so-often disparaged Spirit, but we also know that it was only in Marx's work that this spirit became consciousness and assumed the mission of leadership. The salvation of society is a mission which only the proletariat...can achieve.[238]

Not only the development of the ethical position but also the Lukácsian pronouncements in favor of "individual terror" for the sake of the salvation of mankind are presented in much the same manner in *The Magic Mountain*. After having determined and debated related matters such as asceticism, dogmatism, the Middle Ages and the spirit of militarism, Naphta finally comes to define and discuss ideas closer to the spirit of Lukács's essays from 1918 and 1919. To begin with, we have the linkup of individualism and collective goal and action (as Naphta would say, "opposites" that "rhyme"):

An individualism that springs from the cosmic, the...importance of the individual soul, *an individualism not social but religious,* that conceives of humanity not as a conflict between the ego and society, but as a conflict between the ego and God, between the flesh and the spirit—a genuine individualism like that *sorts very well with the most binding communism* (404–5; emphasis added).

This determination of individualism is identical with Lukács's individual who willingly "sacrifices" his ego "on the altar of the higher idea" in the name of collective interest. Or, as Hans Castorp perceives the concept, "anonymous and communal interest" (405). Almost as if following the argumentation of "Tactics and Ethics," Naphta terms not only the correctness of action but even that of theory as completely dependent on the measure of things: the welfare of man. "Any theoretical science which is without practical application to man's salvation is as such without significance," asserts Naphta (398). When pressed for elaboration of mankind's needs and its salvation, Leo Naphta first dismisses all "lofty sentiments" about liberalism, the cult of personality, and the principle of freedom, and declares that there is a way to reach the state where the conflict between the individual and the collective ceases, where the "Beyond is absorbed into the Here," and where "the absolute mandate, the iron bond, discipline, sacrifice, the renunciation of the ego" reigns. The key to everything and the demand of our age is Terror (400). In answer to Settembrini's demand that he name the agent of terror, Naphta says:

[It is] the world proletariat, which is today asserting the ideals of the *Civitas Dei.* ... The dictatorship of the proletariat, the politico-economic *means of salvation* demanded by our age, does not mean domination for its own sake...but rather in the sense of temporary abrogation, in the Sign of the Cross, of the contradiction between spirit and force;...in a transcendental, a transitional sense, in the sense of the Kingdom. ... *Its task is to strike terror* into the world *for the healing of the world, that man may finally achieve salvation and deliverance* (404; emphasis added).

Salvation as the mission of the proletariat was Lukács's ultimate (Marxist) demand, and "terror" was defined as the unsanctioned but "truly and tragically moral" act. The Lukácsian notions and Naphta's pronouncements at this point become identical.

We cannot but agree with Thomas Mann's own assessment of his Naphta conception: the "role and mission of the character" is carefully grounded and yet not removed from reality despite all of its "confusing" combinations. Indeed, it was possible for an old Party comrade and antagonist from the revolutionary (1919) period, József Lengyel to describe Lukács and his appearance among the cadres as follows:

This tourist from the West is quite a famous man. Before the war he lived in Switzerland, somewhere in Davos, I think, and in Germany, in Heidelberg, or so I heard. He is praised as a famous scholar. He himself spread the rumor that he, a baptized Jew, was a legitimate member of the Jesuit order—albeit sort of a layman, in some rank...and that he actually came from some very poor Jewish family.[239]

Lengyel published his autobiographical novel with the above passage in Budapest, but neither Lukács nor anyone else ever dignified it with a comment. Fiction and fact result in a peculiar mixture in the novel, and as such it represents a case where a fictional hero engendered another fictional character that was in part inspired by the same model.

Finally, we have to consider one more aspect of Naphta's personality which has much to do with how the others perceive him and which also has something to do with Thomas Mann's perception of Lukács. It is the question of the "stranger." Naphta is called that on the occasion of his first appearance at the side of Settembrini. He is given all the attributes which establish his outsider status: he is a "dubious" character, possesses the physical traits ascribed to the type (the "Jewish nose," the "puny figure"), and he comes from a region that supposedly lies beyond the boundaries of the "civilized" West. In a more subtle sense, he is a stranger because of his kinship with the ancient, mystical Chaldeans who had also "something of the mystagogue" about them (385). Last but not least, he is capable of making most intriguing pronouncements, such as "hurrahing for some universal unification he perceives on the far horizon" (386). Consequently, this stranger is capable of functioning as the educator of the "simple German burgher," Hans Castorp, and of undertaking the correction of Herr Settembrini's worldview. In this sense, the "stranger" is a double-layered concept: he has his charms and his magic, and at the same time his alien nature is found repulsive. In this respect, Dr. Sammet, the Aarenhold twins in the story "Blood of the Walsungs," and Leo Naphta are alike. It is safe to state that their depiction is based on Thomas Mann's personal and artistic relationship to the phenomenon of Judaism. In the aforementioned letter, "On the Jewish Question," the writer talks at some length about this: he readily admits that his "adventurous spirit" is proving itself in his relationship to Judaism: "My relationship to Judaism," he says, "was from the beginning a matter of adventurous–cosmopolitan attitude: I considered it a picturesque factum, well suited to heightening the colourfulness of the world." Well aware that this remark might sound "frivolous and irresponsibly aestheticizing," Thomas Mann was at pains to explain the positive in it: "I also saw in the phenomenon an ethical symbol,...one of the symbols of exceptionality and of great impediment which as a writer I could often be found in search of."[240] One must not forget that the writer often viewed his own existence as a symbol of exceptionality and of great impediment and that he repeatedly sought to come to terms with the predicament of the modern artist as an outsider in society by presenting the problematic in its greatest variations. The outsider theme, therefore, concerns his own existence as a writer as well as the Jewish question, for as Mann insisted, both have a similar status in the world. This view is admittedly "aristocratic and romantic but yet from early on in accordance with my thinking." The fact that he "does not overlook a striking phenomenon such as Judaism," but instead tries to accentuate it and in so doing emphasizes those attributes that make it different, has nothing to do with anti-Semitism, Thomas Mann believes.[241]

It would be of great interest to examine the variations, shadings and changing nature of this relationship in the life and work of Thomas Mann. To my great regret, this task cannot be undertaken here. But it is important to point out that on the one hand, Thomas Mann was not immune from the intellectual (or shall we say, ideological) influences of his time, and that on the other hand, he was intent to look at the "Jewish problem" from the very beginning in a more complicated way than his contemporaries. As noted at the beginning, it is possible to feel foreignness in different ways: while Joachim's misgivings correspond to the customary prejudice, Hans Castorp is not put off by Naphta's strangeness. Because of Naphta's higher intellectual rank, he is chosen as the new "educator"; Hans Castorp's readiness to accept him as such stems from his ability to perceive the possibilities inherent in this type. One has the sense that the seeds of critical appraisal of the possibilities of the phenomenon of Judaism were also present in Thomas Mann and were the foundation of the seriousness and the sustained element of attention he accorded the problem.

As to possible influences with regard to the phenomenon of Judaism, we should consider what Nietzsche had to say, as his influence on Mann was considerable, particularly his views in *The Genealogy of Morals*. Nietzsche in his discussion of the "priestly system of valuations" that has branched off from the "aristocratic" system, calls priests "the greatest haters in history—but also the most intelligent haters." And as to who best illustrated for Nietzsche the "brilliance of priestly vengeance" the following answer is given: it was "the Jews…, that priestly people who succeeded in avenging themselves on their enemies and oppressors by radically inverting all their values, that is, by an act of the most spiritual vengeance."[242] The inversion of the "aristocratic value equations" such as noble/beautiful/powerful/healthy, resulted in new equations, says Nietzsche; now, the new value equations are "poor/powerless/suffering/sick and ugly." Nietzsche terms this the "Jewish inversion of values." These value equations are in part borrowed by Thomas Mann for his artistic treatment of the "exceptional cases." And it is my opinion that Mann also followed in Nietzsche's footsteps when he ascribed certain "positive" traits and results to the "exceptional" phenomenon of Judaism. Nietzsche asserts in the following sub-chapter that "Jewish hatred and vengeance" was the "deepest and sublimest hatred in human history" because "it gave birth to ideals and a new set of values…that was equally unique:

a new love, the deepest and sublimest of loves... [in the figure of the] redeemer."[243] In one form or another, this line of thought crops up in the *disputationes* between Settembrini and Naphta; Settembrini imparts his "warning" to Joachim and Hans Castorp against Naphta because of his concept of "redemption" which is but an act of seduction by *Geist,* the Nietzschen "sublime" "vindictiveness" (411–12). Nietzsche's ambiguous position toward Judaism was only one of the influences; besides him, Treitschke, Lagarde and later Sombart influenced the intellectual molding of a large segment of an entire generation. As we know, Lagarde plays an important role in the intellectual shaping of *Reflections of a Non-Political Man,* but fortunately his views on Judaism did not exercise any lasting effect on Mann's own.[244]

Although we cannot document the fact that Thomas Mann had read and was influenced by Sombart's *The Jews and Modern Capitalism* (1911), there are many indications that he was acquainted with this work; another work by Sombart, *The Bourgeois,* is eminently mentioned in the *Reflections.* In all of these writings, the discussion—or clarification—of "the Race Problem" (Sombart) was the main goal; it is also a fact that they all had differing notions of what is "scientific" or "objective" (and in most cases proved to be pseudo-scientific and pseudo-objective). As Sombart remarked in *his* "scientific-objective" treatise, "it is almost as though at the point where the general Jewish Question intersects the race problem, a thousand devils had been let loose to confuse the mind of men."[245] The phenomemon of the "stranger" is an important element of the mental image and of the problem.[246] Georg Simmel approached this problem from the vantage point of the stranger in his 1908 essay "The Stranger." Simmel's sociological definition of the stranger "who is an element of the group itself" and whose "position...involves both being outside it and confronting it" has in due time become a classic. The history of European Jews provides the "classic example" for Simmel that a stranger is a person who is not—and cannot be—"the owner of soil" in both a physical and a figurative sense. There may develop more intimate relations between the "owner of soil" and the stranger who in this relationship may "develop all kinds of charm and significance." Nevertheless, the stranger will not become the (figurative) owner of soil until "he is considered a stranger in the eyes of the other."[247] This determination of the nature and position of the stranger corresponds exactly to the position of the Jews at that time within a German, or any other, group; it also describes correctly the manner in which "the others" and "the strangers" themselves perceived their respective positions. Naphta's situation is described in similar terms: he is an element of the group (the world of the diseased at Davos) and at the same time he stands "outside" and "opposite" this group. Moreover, Naphta's former life and career show the same constellation repeated time and again, starting with the village of his birth and ending with his position in the Jesuit institution.

As said before, the state of being a stranger has its positive side. It is the objectivity which can also be called "freedom": "he is freer, practically and theoretically; he surveys conditions with less prejudice; his criteria for them are more general and more objective ideals; he is not tied down in his actions by habit, piety and precedent."[248] Of course, this position "holds quite a few dangerous possibilities," in times of change, of upheavals, for example, and during uprisings. As is so often stated, "There was outside provocation,...by foreign agitators." The truth of Simmel's perceptive remarks was demonstrated by the events in Hungary, Bavaria, and elsewhere after 1919. Thomas Mann's appraisal of Judaism and the features common to Jews as a type contain these views: he expects the spirituality and the "ironic rationality" of the Jews to provide the needed "secret corrective" *(heimliches Korrektiv)*, and therefore he has "a very intense feeling of the importance, the indispensability of the Jewish spirit."[249] Just as strong is his belief in the inherent dangerousness of such a position, or more precisely in the "infamous" possibilities which the position may engender. There is a statement made by Thomas Mann in 1907 which up until now has been virtually unknown, which was not taken up in his collected works, and which deserves to be quoted at length in order to show to what extent the "complexity" of a Naphta character was fixed in Mann's mental image—psychologically speaking. Kurt Löwenstein not long ago published this essay in full in his article, "Thomas Mann on the Jewish Question." Among other things, Mann states:

Let the novelist be forgiven if in the Jewish question he first sees a personal, human conflict, a purely psychological problem—a highly stimulating one at that. *Known everywhere as a stranger,* carrying *in his heart the pathos of exceptionality,* he represents one of the extraordinary forms of existence, which survive in the midst of bourgeois life, standing out from the common norm *in a sublime or an offensive way,* despite all humanistic-democratic efforts at levelling. This is for the soul the decisive factor. Here is the source of everything: all *contrasts and complexities* of his being; on the one hand, free thinking and *revolutionary tendencies,* on the other, warped snobbism; a *longing to adapt* to the "normal people," and pride of the individual, a rugged *communal feeling* and *heretical individualism;* insolence and insecurity; cynicism and sentimentality, *sharpness* and melancholy and what all else—this all results from *his exceptionality,* not the least [of which] is his irritatingly frequent superiority in the competitive world of professions which are open to him. Voltaire once said: "By the way, it is not bad at all if one has to make good on a mistake. It commits one to great exertions for securing the respect and admiration of the public." That is perfectly clear. Whenever there is competition, one is not at a disadvantage against the correct and therefore unmotivated majority when one has one motive more for extraordinary achievements.[250]

It is not difficult to see that Thomas Mann's succinct summary of the assesment of Judaism contains certain trains of thought, phrases, and characterizations that can be found everywhere in his writings. The concluding sentence amounts to a quotation from his own novel *Royal Highness;* the phrase "humanistic-democratic levelling" represents Mann's own position in *Reflections of a Non-Political Man;* members of the German–Jewish literati, Maximilian Harden or Walter Kerr (essayist and theater critic), are accused in Mann's letters of "warped snobbism"; insolence, sentimentality, and extreme professional combativeness and drive characterize Fitelberg in *Doctor Faustus;* from the same novel, the characters Dr. Schleppfuss and Chaim Breisacher are included in the above characterization. It is the same with Naphta: as the embodiment of "incorrectness," he symbolizes all that stands in opposition to the correct and complacent majority.

Pride and longing, revolutionary tendencies, heretical individualism, commitment to extraordinary achievements, and the awareness that one represents an extraordinary form of existence—these are Leo Naphta's heritage as well. He is *the stranger par excellence,* who carries in his heart the pathos of exceptionality and who most decidedly opposes that effort for "humanistic–democratic levelling" which is represented by the figure of Ludovico Settembrini. (Once again we should recall that Thomas Mann himself represented this position in his *Reflections* and passed it on as an "inheritance" to his Royal Highness, Klaus Heinrich, as well as to the "politicized monk" in *Fiorenza* and the unfortunate private tutor, Dr. Überbein.)

In many respect, Georg Lukács conformed to the mental image that Thomas Mann made of the type; his intellectual personality could easily be worked into the complex and contradictory Naphta portrait. There can be little doubt that in Thomas Mann's eyes, Georg Lukács was a "stranger," though maybe in a "sublime" and not an "offensive" sense. In Lukács, Thomas Mann honored an "austere, pure and proud mind"; he did not hesitate to express his moral admiration for such a spirit in his letter to Dr. Seipel. Ironically, Thomas Mann succeeded in portraying in the figure of Naphta precisely *that* type of Jew (the Jewish intellectual) whom the young Lukács had outlined as a possible ideal: he is the "new type of Jew," the "anti-rational ascetic," who is the exact opposite of what is generally meant by a Jew. The interesting thing about it is that Thomas Mann appropriated quite a few traits for his Jewish characters from Werner Sombart's (often negative) characterization. At the same time (1911), Lukács developed his "new theory" of the new type of Jew as a reaction to Sombart's depicting the "typical Jew" as a totally rational being.

In summary we can say that while he was working on *The Magic Mountain* and even earlier, during the work on *Reflections* and the "Goethe and Tolstoy" essay, the question of personality and personality formation was a central one for Thomas Mann. This explains the grandiosely laid-out presentation of the character and its mission. It was not by chance, nor was it a matter of artistic caprice. The reason for Mann's serious and sustained attention to the problem of personality is to be found in the most confessional of Mann's writings, his *Reflections of a Non-Political Man:*

"In times of spiritual difficulty"—and at the beginning of the twentieth century such a spiritual crisis was apparent to all—"one searches for the answer to [the] question: Who am I, where do I come from, that I am as I am, and can neither make nor wish myself different?" Thomas Mann answered his own question the following way: "I am a city man, a burgher, a child and great-grandchild of the German burgherly culture."[251] Whatever the modifying effect of some "exotic blood," Mann adds, "it does not change the essence and the foundations, does not abrogate the main sprititual tradition."[252] Opposite the established burgher stands the "stranger" who can be assessed positively or negatively, but will never be the "owner of soil" and will remain an "intruder" into the group—and as such is perceived as a "questionable character."[253] He has his roles; the more noble one is that of a teacher. And as Werner J. Cahnman determined it, the main role of the stranger turns out to be the "intermediary." Others may have fulfilled this function but "none as exclusively as the Jew…who has lived always and everywhere on the periphery and consequently in mediation." Mediation, of course, has two sides: "on the one hand, the intermediary as an outsider is looked upon with suspicion; on the other hand, because he is an outsider, he is welcome as a…counsellor," or in Leo Naphta's case, as a teacher.[254]

In his *Reflections of a Non-Political Man*, Thomas Mann spoke of himself as one "who smilingly lets himself be taught by his learned son," and he meant the young Hungarian essayist, Georg von Lukács, who wrote a "beautiful, profound book" entitled *Soul and Form*. Regardless: one does not share certain inner experiences with a "stranger," and that creates distances which cannot be bridged. These relations provide the background for an understanding of the specificity of interaction between Thomas Mann and Georg Lukács.

APPENDIX

Bolshevism as a Moral Problem[1]

We chose not to consider here the possibilities for the realization of Bolshevism or to discuss its ensuing beneficial or harmful consequences. This author, for one thing, does not feel competent to come up with a decisive answer on these matters and, more important and for the sake of clarity, he deems a discussion of the practical consequences inopportune. The decision for or against Bolshevism—like a stand on any truly important matter—has to be an ethical one. For the sake of a truly honest choice, therefore, an immanent clarification of such a problematic decision has the highest priority.

The ethical formulation of this problem is partly justified by the fact that most discussion of Bolshevism center on the question of whether the economic and social conditions were "ripe" for an immediate Bolshevik revolution. Yet speculations of this kind will lead us nowhere because, in my opinion, this is never possible *to know in advance*. The *will* to realize Bolshevism, immediately and unconditionally, is just as integral a part of the "ripeness" of the circumstances as are the objective conditions. On the other hand, the thought that a victorious Bolshevik revolution could destroy great cultural and civilizational achievements would not influence those who, be it for ethical reasons or out of historico-philosophical considerations, opted for the Bolshevik revolution. These revolutionaries will take notice of that fact—with or without regret—and accept its inevitability. This insight will not change their objective and it should not. For they know only too well that a world-historical change of such magnitude is bound to destroy old values. Their determination for setting up new values makes them confident that they can compensate the coming generation for this loss.

It now seems to follow that a serious ethical problem has been solved for every true socialist, and that nothing should complicate his decision in favor of a Bolshevik revolution. What, after all, should stand in the way of achieving our goal, *immediately and unconditionally*, if one need not consider the "ripeness" of the circumstances and the annihilation of old values? Could anybody who opted for waiting and further deliberation, that is, for compromise, still be called a true socialist? If, however, a non-Bolshevik objects to the dictatorship of a minority in the name of democracy, he will encounter the response of Lenin's disciples who, following the directives of their leader, simply remove the designation "democratic" from the name and program of their party and call themselves "Communists."

The ethical formulation of the problem, therefore, depends on how one views the role of democracy, that is, whether democracy is believed to be a temporary tactic of the socialist movement, a useful tool to be employed in the fight against the legally sanctioned but lawless terror of the oppressive classes, or if democracy indeed is an integral part of Socialism. If the latter is true, democracy cannot be forsaken without considering the ensuing moral and ideological consequences. Therefore, every conscientious and responsible socialist is confronted with a grave moral problem when he considers the abandonment of the democratic principle.

In the past, Marx's philosophy of history has seldom been sufficiently separated from his sociology. As a result, it has often been overlooked that the two constitutive elements of his system, class struggle and socialism, that bring an end to the division of classes and thus oppression, are closely related but by no means the products of the same conceptual system. The former is a factual finding of Marxian sociology that has epochal significance. Class struggle has always been the moving force behind every existing social order; and class struggle is, at the same time, one of the main explanatory principles of the true interconnections of historical reality. Socialism, on the other hand, is the utopian postulate of the Marxian philosophy of history: it is the *ethical objective* of a coming world order. (By putting two different categories of reality on the same level, Marx's Hegelianism contributed somewhat to this confusion.) Although the class struggle of the proletariat is designed to produce a new world order, *qua* class struggle, it is not the embodiment of this new world order.

As the aftermath of the victorious class struggle of the bourgeoisie has demonstrated, the liberation of the proletariat will not necessarily mean the end of *all* class domination. Sociologically speaking, it will simply entail the reshuffling of classes: the previous oppressors will become the new oppressed class. Since the victory of the proletariat means the liberation of the last of the oppressed classes, this victory is an *irrevocable prerequisite* to the attainment of an era of true freedom when there will be no oppressors and oppressed. But it is only a stipulation—and as such a negative point. The *quest* for a world order that goes beyond mere sociological descriptions and laws governing social reality, that is, the quest for a democratic world order, is an absolute prerequisite for a truly free world.

The will,[2] therefore, that goes beyond the sociological stating of facts is an essential feature of the socialist *Weltanschauung,* which would collapse without it like a house of cards. It is precisely this will that enabled the proletariat to become the agent of the social salvation of mankind, the messianic class of world history. Without the fervor of this messianism, the victorious path of social democracy would have been impossible.

Engels was correct when he claimed that the proletariat is the sole legitimate heir to German classical philosophy; the no-longer-earthbound ethical idealism of the Kant–Fichtean thinking that wanted to change the world metaphysically was now being transformed into action. What had been theory turned into a revolutionary praxis when the proletariat proceeded on the straight path to the goal, while Schelling's aesthetics and Hegel's philosophy of right took a different, reactionary path.

Marx, no doubt, relied to a great extent on Hegel's *List der Idee* (Cunning of Idea) in the construction of his historico-philosphical process that claims the proletariat, while fighting for its immediate class interests, will also free the world of tyranny forever. In the moment of decision that has now arrived, one cannot overlook the dualistic separation of the soulless empirical reality and the human—that is, the utopian, the ethical—objective. Now we shall see whether socialism's redemptive role implies a voluntary and absolute willingness to bring about the salvation of humanity or was meant to be an ideological shell for mere class interests. In the latter case, it would differ only in content from any other class interests; no qualitative or ethical differences could be claimed. (Let us remember that in the eighteenth century all bourgeois theories of emancipation proclaimed the liberation of humanity, that is, the theory of *laissez-faire*. The purely ideological character of these theories was already revealed during the French Revolution when, ultimately, class interests alone prevailed.)

Were the ideal of true social democracy—that is, the attainment of a political system that knows of no class oppression—only ideology, we would not be confronted now with an ethical dilemma. Our ethical problem is the result of the fact that social democracy has only one ultimate aim that gives real meaning to its struggle: to bring an end to all future class struggles, to create a political system that will exclude class struggle even as a theoretical possibility.

Now the realization of this goal has become a distinct possibility. Consequently, we are faced with the following moral dilemma: If we take advantage of the given possibility for the realization of our goal, we have to accept dictatorship, terror, and the class oppression that goes with it. The existing class oppression will then have to be replaced by that of the proletariat—to drive out Satan with the help of Beelzebub, so to speak—in the hope that this last and therefore most open and cruel of all class oppressions will finally destroy itself and in so doing will put an end to class oppression forever. Should we, however, decide that we want to realize the new world order by truly democratic means (needless to say, true democracy remains a desideratum that has never been realized anywhere in the world, not even in the so-called democratic states), we run the risk of infinite delay, since most of the people might not yet want this new world order. If we refrain from forcing it upon this majority, our only option is to teach, enlighten, and wait, in the hope that one day humanity, through its conscious action, will achieve what has long been viewed by many as the only possible solution to the problems of the world.

Whatever the decision, inherent in both choices is the danger of committing unpardonable sins and innumerable errors. Everyone must face up to this fact, which, in turn, results in a real ethical dilemma. The ethical implications of the second choice are quite clear: it involves the necessity of a provisional alliance with parties and classes whose immediate interests coincide with those of a social democracy but who remain hostile and unreconciled to the ultimate objective. Thus it becomes imperative to find the correct tactical criteria that make cooperation possible but will neither endanger the purity of the ultimate objective nor weaken the fervor of the quest.

At this point, the dangers of deviation become apparent: it is difficult if not impossible to deviate from the *straight and narrow* path of action that leads to the attainment of an objective without letting detours become ends in themselves. And a *deliberate* slowdown of progress toward the ultimate aim would necessarily weaken the fervor of the quest. Thus we are confronted with a real dilemma that can be stated in the following terms: How can we adhere to the democratic principles in the realization of Socialism without letting the tactical compromises take root in our consciousness?

Bolshevism offers a fascinating way out in that it does not call for compromise. But all those who fall under the sway of its fascination might not be fully aware of the consequences of their decision. Their problem can be posed in these terms: Is it possible to achieve good by condemnable means? Can freedom be attained by means of oppression? Can a new world order emerge out of a struggle in which the tactics vary only technically from those of the old and despised world order?

Perhaps we could point to the assumptions of Marx's sociology in which history consists of a continuous sequence of class struggles between oppressors and oppressed. Consequently, the struggle of the proletariat cannot escape this "law" either. If this is true, socialism's ideal meaning, as we pointed out earlier, would be nothing beyond the material interests of the proletariat. It would be mere ideology. But this is not so. And because it is not so, this historical assumption cannot serve as the foundation of the quest for a new world order. We have to accept the wrong as wrong, oppression as oppression, and class oppression as class oppression. We have to believe— this being the true *credo quia absurdum est*—that no new class struggle will emerge out of this class struggle (resulting in the quest for a new oppression), which would provide continuance to the old sequence of meaningless and aimless struggles—but that oppression will effect the elements of its own destruction.

It is therefore, a question of belief—as it is in the case of any ethical question—of what the choice will be.* In the view of many otherwise critical but in this case

---

* In order to avoid any misunderstanding we must emphasize that only the most sharply typical purely ethical considerations are discussed and compared here. In both cases, frivolity, irresponsibility, and self-interest may dictate choices; their decision is beyond our concern. —G.L.

superficial observers, many old-time, tested socialists are reluctant to join the ranks of the Bolsheviks because their belief in socialism has been seriously weakened. I have to admit that I reject this interpretation because I reject the view that it takes a deeper conviction to choose the "instant heroism" of Bolshevism than to accept the democratic way, which does not seem heroic at all but does require a sense of deep responsibility and commitment to an uphill battle that entails a long, soul-wrenching process of teaching and waiting.

Those who opt for the former will seem at all cost to secure the purity of their conviction, which in the latter case has to be sacrificed. This self-sacrifice in turn helps to retain the central meaning of social democracy, that is, the realization of *social democracy in its totality* instead of in fragments. Let me emphasize again: Bolshevism rests on the metaphysical assumption that the bad can engender the good, or, as Razumikhin says in Dostoevsky's *Crime and Punishment,* that it is possible to lie our way through to the truth.

This author is unable to share this belief. Accordingly, he perceives the insoluble moral problem at the root of the Bolshevik standpoint. In the case of democracy, "only" superhuman efforts in the form of self-sacrifice and renouncement are required of those who made their choice consciously and are ready to follow it through honestly. However, although it might require superhuman strength, the democratic way does not confront us with an insoluble question as does the moral problem of Bolshevism.

Jewish Mysticism[3]

There is a widely held and seemingly justified prejudicial notion that the metaphysical well of Judaism has dried up in modern times and that, therefore it can only bring forth "sharpwitted" or "brilliant" thinkers but has not been able to produce creative geniuses. The chief merit of these books lies in their effective disposal of these notions.

With the great Baalschem at its beginning and Rabbi Nachtman at its end, the Hasidic "movement" stands before us as a primitively great mysticism. This is the first really significant mystical movement since the days of the German protestant and the Spanish counter-reformatorial mysticism—and it proves to be their equal and that of all the other preceding ones too. What seems to be most interesting about mysticism is that in spite of its inner religiosity, it is not bound to any specific religion: Baalschem's interpretation of the Old Testament is as refreshinghly free-handed as is Eckhart's of the New Testament.[4] Both of them make use of the Scriptures as a basic material for their newly created symbolism. Especially startling is the way in which just the very neglected aspects of the Jewish religion, the other-world and life-after-death concept, move to the center of Baalschem's mystical interpretation. Due to the lack of deeper insights and factual knowledge about this movement, one cannot judge how much of the frequent and varied theoreticizing about transmigration is a result of original insights or of the influence of Buddhism. Whatever the answer to that question turns out to be, the peculiar fact remains that the mystical way of thinking proves to be the most homogenous one in the history of mankind, notwithstanding the fact that it is the most individual, the least scientific, and therefore the least verifiable mode of thinking. Regarding the basics, the Vedas and Plotinus, Eckehart and Jacob Böhme said the same things over and over again.[5] Now we find in the case of Baalschem and his disciples a unison with all the preceding mystical movements. The texts provide ample proof that we are not witnessing a simple takeover of ideas or merely the result of an influence: among other things, Baalschem advances a highly original ethical exegesis of reincarnation. Another proof of the homogenous character of all mysticism is that we cannot in all truth speak of one great personality in any given mysticism but only of a movement; however, as in the case of all movements, the originator, the founder is the "classic" figure and the "master." After him comes the decadence, the baroque period of the movement. Baalschem and Rabbi Nachtman relate to each other in the same way that Eckehart and Suso did.[6]

We have no way of judging the authenticity of the translation. As far as the style of the text is concerned, however, the impression is that of a much modernized version of the old tales.

Thomas Mann
Letter to Dr. Ignaz Seipel, Chancellor of Austria[7]

May I be allowed to turn to you with deep human trust concerning a matter that no doubt others are just as apprehensive about as I am.

It concerns Dr. Georg Lukács, a man whose intellectual nature, *Weltanschauung,* and social credo I do not share at all, but whose austere, pure and proud mind I have learned to honor. His critical writings—*Soul and Form, The Theory of the Novel,* and others—belong unquestionably to the most significant works in the German language that have been produced in the last few decades on the subject.

You are familiar, I am sure, with his life story, his wealthy bourgeois origins, the advantages he sacrificed for the sake of his convictions with an idealism that you might think should have served better ends; it is nevertheless not the gesture of a small and indolent soul. You also know of the political role that this thoroughly theoretical man played—indeed, thought it his mission to play—in his homeland during the time when catastrophic conditions offered, for a short while, the possibility for woolly-minded social enthusiasts to experiment with their ideas on the living body of a nation. The situation was unique, a consequence of a lost war. The collapse of all order was an invitation for these believers—many of them undoubtedly less honorable men than Lukács—to try out their envisioned new order. I don't see any crime in that, only mistake and overthrowing. Austria, that is Vienna, offered asylum to this man who in his homeland had become an outlaw; he has been living here ever since in abject poverty, devoting himself entirely to his intellectual pursuits.[8] Without the unfortunate combination of his doctrinaire and unrelenting spritual makeup and the unfolding of a historical crisis situation, he could have gone on to lead the life of a young master of the house [Herrensöhnchen].

Now, there is the threat of banishment hanging over his head—that is, it has already been declared; it has been brought about by circumstances that have nothing to do with the propriety of his behavior. No indictment has been issued against Lukács, and it is therefore unlikely that his person would in any way present a real and practical threat to the order of the Austrian state. The banishment, if upheld, would be the end for him. He has a wife, has three children. He lives with them in Vienna in circumstances that are bearable, indeed even fitting, only to his ascetic stature, in the physical as well as spiritual sense. By the way, he is able to maintain this miserable existence for himself and his family only because he was granted rent-free housing by a relative of his wife, and has other advantages here which he could not have had in any other place. His helpless friends assure us that nobody could imagine what he and his family would do even on the first day, let alone on subsequent days, following his deportation.[9] Back to Hungary? Martyrdom and death await him there. To Munich? It would not accept him. To Berlin? He would have nothing to eat and no place to rest. It is no exaggeration when all those who worry about this unfortunate man say that banishment would mean a "death sentence in time."

I do not know, Esteemed Herr Chancellor, whether or not my name means anything to you, whether or not my words have any weight.[10] But let me ask a random question: Would it enhance the honor of the Republic at whose helm you stand if it would banish a scholar, an intellectual such as Lukács, as a "homeless vagabond"? For the expulsion could only be carried out under this designation, as he is not being accused of any criminal conduct nor of any acts against the security of the state. In the past I had often been a guest in his father's house, and I can't help thinking—while I am writing this letter to you—of the proud and blissful smile on the face of the recently deceased old gentleman when he heard one praise the great intellectual powers of his son. In due time, the son left him and his class behind. I have come to know Lukács himself in person. In Vienna, he once propounded his theories to me for a whole hour. As long as he was talking, he was right. Even if the impression he left behind was of an almost hair-raising abstractness, it was also one of purity and intellectual nobility. You might think of me as naive for wishing that you too had the opportunity to obtain your own personal impression by calling him to your office and having a talk with him, but I think it is possible that this would save him from the sword now hanging over his head.

I beg your forbearance, Herr Chancellor, for the great freedom I took upon myself in writing you this letter, and permit me to express my honest admiration and deep respect.

Georg Lukács: On the Occasion of His Seventieth Birthday[11]

My congratulatory letter on Georg Lukács's seventieth birthday has to be a short one; it is that of an overburdened old man. But I wish to say that I hold Lukács, the man, in the highest esteem because of the sacrifices he made for his convictions and for the self-imposed austerity of his life. I also wish to say that I have equally high esteem for his intellectual work, which I first came into contact with through his early essay collection, *Soul and Form,* a work of extraordinary aesthetic sensitivity. I have since followed his critical undertaking with due attention and respect and very much to my own advantage. What particularly aroused my sympathy is the sense of continuity and tradition that underlies all his work and to which it largely owes its existence. For, obviously by preference, his analysis is devoted to the older body of our literary heritage with which he is as familiar as a most conservative historian and which he endeavors to relate to the new world of his convictions; while doing so, he intends to awaken the interest of this new world for the knowledge and understanding of that cultural heritage. The fact that he wishes, first and foremost, to seek out and describe the sociocritical elements of bourgeois culture is only right and proper. It in no way diminishes my high esteem for his work that mediates between disparate spheres and epochs, and that seems to be inspired by an idea which nowadays is held in a lamentably low esteem, the idea of *Bildung*.[12]

NOTES

Introduction

[1] Harry Levin, "Toward a Sociology of the Novel" in *Refractions: Essays in Comparative Literature* (London: Oxford University Press, 1966), p. 248.

[2] For an account of the differences see Zoltán Tar and Judith Marcus, "The Weber–Lukács Encounter" in R. M. Glassman and V. Murvar, eds., *Max Weber's Political Sociology: A Pessimistic Vision of a Rationalized World* (Westport, Conn.: Greenwood Press, 1984), pp. 125–26. Both the Webers and George Simmel repeatedly discussed Lukács's inability to share their enthusiasm for what Weber called a "great and wonderful war." In response, Lukács had started to compose an essay on "The German Intellectuals and the War," which remained a fragment.

[3] Henry Hatfield, *Thomas Mann*, rev. ed. (New York: New Directions, 1962), pp. 1–2.

[4] Thomas Mann, Foreword to *The Magic Mountain*. Trans. H. T. Lowe-Porter (New York: Modern Library, 1955), p. x.

[5] Thomas Mann, *The Story of a Novel: The Genesis of Doctor Faustus*. Trans. Richard Winston and Clara Winston (New York: Alfred A. Knopf, 1961), p. 25.

[6] Mann's remarks conclude his reflections on the critical sensibilities of the "young Lukács." In *Reflections of a Non-Political Man*. Trans. W. D. Morris (New York: Frederick Ungar, 1983), p. 73.

[7] See the review by George Steiner of Lukács's *Gelebtes Denken*, entitled "Making a Homeland for the Mind," in *Times Literary Supplement*, January 22, 1982, p. 67.

[8] Ibid.

[9] References are made to a very few commentators as representative of well-informed and objective evaluation: Gyula Borbándi in *East Europe* (November 1962); Irving Howe, "A Word About Georg Lukács," as Preface to Lukács, *The Historical Novel*, trans. H. Mitchell and S. Mitchell (Boston: Beacon Press, 1963), pp. 7–10; Alfred Kazin, Introduction to Lukács, *Studies in European Realism* (New York: Grosset & Dunlap, Universal Library, 1964), pp. v–xiii.

[10] See Paul Honigsheim, *On Max Weber*, trans. J. Rytina (New York: Free Press, 1968), p. 28.

[11] Arnold Hauser, *Im Gespräch mit Georg Lukács* (Munich: C. H. Beck, 1978). The volume consists of interviews, radio reports, and an essay on Hauser's ambivalent relationship to Lukács. Hauser calls Lukács "the chosen of the chosen ones", whose genius was recognized by Simmel and others and who brought with him from Germany and introduced into the circle of the young Hungarian intelligentsia a "sociologically saturated atmosphere." For a brief version of Hauser's relationship to Lukács see Peter Ludz, "Hauser and Lukács", trans. Judith Marcus Tar in *Telos*, no 41 (Fall 1979), pp. 175–84.

[12] Levin, *Refractions*, p. 242.

[13] Lukács, *Record of a Life*. Trans. R. Livingstone (London: Verso Editions, 1983). This is a slightly different version of the German edition, *Gelebtes Denken*, and is inadequately rendered as "Record of a Life." Lukács's account of his youthful literary activities appear in the chapter "Childhood and Early Career," pp. 26–43.

[14] Ibid., p. 31. Lukács refers mainly to his plays and book reviews in Alfred Kerr's impressionistic style but leaves the other works unmentioned.

[15] For a concise and well-argued summary of this controversy see Stephen Eric Bronner, "Expressionism and Marxism: Towards an Aesthetic of Emancipation," in S. E. Bronner and D. Kellner, eds., *Passion and Rebellion: The Expressionist Heritage* (South Hadley, Mass.: Bergin 1983), pp. 411–53.

[16] Lukács, Foreword, to *Essays on Thomas Mann*, trans. Stanley Mitchell (London: Merlin Press, 1964), p. 10.

[17] Lukács, *Record of a Life*, p. 93.

[18] Such complaints were voiced in his private correspondence, especially in letters written to Hans Mayer, a noted Germanist, and to István Mészáros, his favorite student, former assistant, and friend, who now resides in England. He reacted sharply to Victor Zitta's 1964 book, *Georg Lukács' Marxism: Alienation, Dialectics, Revolution* (The Hague: Martinus Nijhoff), which conjured up a "keen and tortured" intellect given to "pathological" choices whose theoretical position is explained by quotations from *The Magic Mountain*. Cf. Zitta, p. 50 and 63.

[19] Lukács, *Record of a Life*, p. 95. Emphasis added.

[20] Ibid., p. 93.

[21] Lukács, *Essays on Thomas Mann*, p. 40. Translation slightly altered in order to convey the original phrasing and intention.

[22] Pierre-Paul Sagave (b. 1913), professor of German literature at Aix-en-Provence, was at that time working on *Réalité Sociale et ideologie religieuse dans les romans de Thomas Mann* (1954) and wrote a letter to Mann in California inquiring about the author's sources and models for *The Magic Mountain*. Mann asked Sagave not to bring Lukács into the picture in relation to Naphta. He also stated unequivocally that Carl Schmitt and his work never crossed his path. ("Ich wollte Sie recht sehr bitten, Lukács ja doch nicht in Verbindung mit dem Zauberberg und Naphta namhaft zu machen. Er hat sich über den Roman stets sehr ehrend geäussert und ist wohl nie auf den Gedanken gekommen, das man in ihm das Modell zu Naphta sehen könnte. Ich möchte wirklich nicht, dass er auf diesen Gedanken gebracht wird. Bild und Wirklichkeit sind ja auch so verschieden wie möglich und von Herkunft und Lebensumständen zu schweigen, hat die Kombination von Kommunismus und Jesuitismus, die ich da kreirt habe, und die geistig ganz gut sein mag, doch mit dem realen Lukács garnichts zu schaffen.") Sagave ignored Mann's request and named not only Lukács but also Carl Schmitt as possible models for Naphta. The unpublished letter of February 18, 1952, is at the Thomas Mann Archiv.

[23] Conversation with Lukács at his Budapest residence on May 7, 1971, shortly before his death. The interview was conducted in Hungarian, sprinkled with German sentences and phrases whenever Lukács was searching for the most expressive and/or concrete language. A copy of the taped talk is deposited at the Georg Lukács Archiv, Budapest.

1. Spiritual Closeness

[1] Georg von Lukács, "On the Nature and Form of the Essay. A Letter to Leo Popper," in *Soul and Form*. Trans. Anna Bostock (Cambridge: M.I.T., 1974), p. 3. The issue for Lukács was whether there is something in the essays that would make them "a new literary form of its own"; his main intention was not to "offer studies in literary history" (p. 1).

[2] Lukács, *Soul and Form*, p. 9.

[3] Ibid.

[4] Ibid., p. 21.

[5] Ibid., p. 26. Emphasis added.

[6] Georg Lukács, *Essays on Thomas Mann.* Trans. Stanley Mitchell (London: Merlin Press, 1964), p. 10.

[7] Thomas Mann, "Der Künstler und der Literat," in *Schriften und Reden zur Literatur, Kunst und Philosophie*, ed. Hans Bürgin, series number MK 113 (Frankfurt am Main: Fischer Bücherei, 1968), p. 75. Further references are to this series of Mann's collected works. See Bibliography.

[8] Lukács, *Soul and Form*, p. 15.

[9] See Hans Wysling, " 'Geist und Kunst': Thomas Mann's Notizen zu einem 'Literaturessay'," in *Quellenkritische Studien zum Werk Thomas Manns*, ed. Paul Scherrer and Hans Wysling, vol. 1 (Bern-Munich: Francke, 1967), p. 123.

[10] Ibid., p. 125. It should be pointed out in this connection that it is not possible to date every note to Mann's planned treatise "Geist und Kunst" (Intellect and Art), as Hans Wysling indicated in his scrupulously exact study of the sources for the project. Most notes date from the years 1909 and 1910; some of them are from 1916 or as late as 1924. The title of the project was first announced by the author in an interview he gave in the fall of 1909. The notes are preserved in the Thomas Mann Archiv, marked "Mp. ix. 168."

[11] See Lukács's Foreword in *Essays on Thomas Mann*, p. 10. Their spiritual closeness consisted, among other things, of an "irritability" with certain intellectual tendencies of the times and a propensity to react to them in a "critical polemic way," to extend the criticism of art into one of the age, and to hold the view that to criticize one's own time amounts to an intellectual and ethical probing of one's own problematic self—as Mann summarized *his* standpoint in *Reflections of a Non-Political Man*. Trans. Walter D. Morris (New York: Frederick Ungar, 1983).

[12] Wysling, p. 126. According to Wysling, the five main themes to be dealt with were: (1) the Wagner-Reinhardt controversy, that is, the question of artistic integrity, with regard to Wagner's tendency to clowning, theatricality and parody; (2) the concept of *Volkstümlichkeit*, the appeal to herd enthusiasm or artistic demagogy in pursuit of mass appeal; (3) the artist and artist-charlatan versus the writer who lives consciously and responsibly in his own time and thus fulfills a useful function; (4) the relationship between the pure creative writer and the critical writer; (5) "regeneration," that is, the discussion of a new generation beyond "modernity," which cultivates things considered "healthy" and "natural" with a "pure intensity of feeling."

[13] Ibid., p. 159.

[14] Ibid., p. 171.

[15] Ibid., p. 175.

[16] Ibid., p. 172.

[17] Quoted in Wysling, pp. 149–50. Original note in Mp. iii/33 at the Thomas Mann Archiv, Zurich.

[18] Lukács, *Soul and Form*, p. 1.

[19] Ibid.

[20] Ibid., p. 21. Emphasis added.

[21] Mann, *Tonio Kröger*, in *Stories of Three Decades*. Trans. H. T. Lowe-Porter (New York: Alfred A. Knopf, 1966), p. 106. Reference is to the conversation *(Kunstgespräch)* between the Russian painter and the German writer about art and its effect on "humanity" and about the "scorn and suspicion" of the ordinary people toward the artist. It is asserted by Tonio Kröger/ Thomas Mann that the Russian painter has every right to speak thus "because with reference to Russian literature and the words of [Russian] poets one can really worship them, they come close to being that elevated literature" she is talking about as having "redemptive power." Lukács harbored the same sentiment toward Russian literature (especially Tolstoy and Dostoevsky) on account of its ethical preoccupation.

[22] See note 19 at the Thomas Mann Archiv. Here, Mann echoes Nietzsche's conclusion about

the Wagner phenomenon and applies it to the cultural scene in Germany; by stating that Wagner —as well as the German "educated public"—was "lacking literature," Mann was alluding to a lack of critical insight *(Erkenntnis)*.

²³ Mann, "Der Künstler und der Literat", in MK 113, pp. 80–81.

²⁴ Ibid., p. 78. The German text is as follows: "Der Literat drückt aus, indem er erlebt, er erlebt, indem er ausdrückt und er erlebt, um auszudrücken." This line of thought makes a reappearance in Mann's *Reflections of a Non-Political Man,* in the chapter on "Burgherly Nature" in which the author describes his art as follows: "I did not just experience critically at first hand as a contemporary, but... I was born to contemplate directly and deeply. In a word: ...I experienced and formed—but I experienced it undoubtedly only by forming it. See p. 99.

²⁵ Lukács, *Soul and Form,* p. 7.

²⁶ Ibid., p. 8.

²⁷ Ibid., p. 10.

²⁸ Ibid., p. 15.

²⁹ Ibid., p. 16. Emphasis added. For futher discussion of the messianic and religious elements in Lukács's thought, see Chapter 6, "The Personality of Leo Naphta."

³⁰ Ibid., p. 18.

³¹ See Wysling, "Geist und Kunst," p. 211. The "Ibsen–*Erlebnis*" constitutes another link in the chain of shared intellectual experiences in the early period of Lukács and Mann, and it accounts for some of the similarities in posing problems.

³² Lukács, *Soul and Form,* p. 24.

³³ Ibid., p. 22.

³⁴ Wysling, "Geist und Kunst," p. 162.

³⁵ Lukács, *Soul and Form,* p. 15.

³⁶ Ibid., p. 18.

³⁷ Hans Joachim Maitre, *Thomas Mann: Aspekte der Kulturkritik in seiner Essayistik* (Bonn: H. Bouvier, 1970), p. 122.

³⁸ Lukács, *Soul and Form,* p. 55. Emphasis added. The intensity, sharpness of formulation, and radical tone of the original German passages are often lost, or at least tempered, in Bostock's translation. The difficulties of rendering not only the content but the style—and above all, the whole atmosphere—of literary texts in another language is well known. Even the title of the essay, "Bürgerlichkeit und l'art pour l'art," is inadequately rendered as "Bourgeois man..." It was precisely the difference between the "burgherly man" and "bourgeois" that both Mann and Lukács emphasized.

³⁹ See Arthur Eloesser "Zur Entstehungsgeschichte des 'Tod in Venedig' " in *Die Neue Rundschau* 36 (1925), p. 612. Eloesser, critic and literary historian, discusses at length possible sources for the atmosphere and experiences of *Death in Venice,* and describes in his essay the constitutive elements of the novella which make the relation of the Lukácsian essay to it even more obvious. See p. 616.

⁴⁰ Lukács, *Soul and Form,* p. 57.

⁴¹ Mann, *Reflections of a Non-Political Man,* p. 72.

⁴² Ibid.

⁴³ Ibid., p. 73.

⁴⁴ Ibid.

⁴⁵ Ibid., p. 72.

⁴⁶ Lukács, *Essays on Thomas Mann,* p. 10.

⁴⁷ Lukács, *Soul and Form,* p. 76.

⁴⁸ Mann, *Reflections,* p. 74. Mann confesses: "Perhaps I feel myself to be German because of my belonging to a burgherly ethical artistic community..." Although he states that "social and human

sympathy" pulls him to Conrad Ferdinand Meyer, his connection with Storm "is one of kindred origin." This is why he finds that Lukács said all this about Storm and himself so "very well."

[49] Mann, *The Story of a Novel: The Genesis of Doctor Faustus*. Trans. Richard Winston and Clara Winston (New York: Alfred A. Knopf, 1961), p. 37.

[50] The unique position of *Death in Venice* in Mann's oeuvre has often been pointed out. Indeed, the style, the technique of language, the use of myth, and, more important, the elaborate and tightly controlled symbol structure of the work make it a "very strange thing," as Mann said in his *Sketch of My Life*. It was also a departure from all earlier work, Eloesser says, in the choice of its locale: it was the first time that Mann used other than a Nordic (i.e., German) backdrop for his story. See Eloesser "Entstehungsgeschichte," p. 616. It could be argued that Lukács's contrasting a "typically" German and a "typically" Italian landscape—his description of the sad, nostalgic, and melancholy effects of German forests and the "hard" and "resisting," perfectly composed South, the home of "longing" that is "form-creating"—may have supplied another "element" in transposing the story into the "lovely Southern" locale, and the setting up of the conflict between the senses and the spirit through the symbolic Nordic-Southern atmosphere. Cf. the treatises on *Death in Venice* by Bruno Frank, Vernon Venable, and Ludwig Lewisohn in Charles Neider, ed., *The Stature of Thomas Mann* (New York: New Directions, 1947), pp. 119–41.

[51] For original note, see "Mappe XI, 13e, numbers 4 and 6" at the Thomas Mann Archiv, Zurich. Emphases here are Mann's. My findings were first published in an obituary essay on Georg Lukács, "Georg Lukács, Thomas Mann und 'Der Tod in Venedig' " in *Die Weltwoche* (Zurich), no. 26, July 2, 1971, p. 31.

[52] Lukács, *Soul and Form*, p. 93.

[53] Ibid., p. 94.

[54] Mann, *Sketch of My Life*. Trans. H. T. Lowe-Porter (New York: Alfred A. Knopf, 1960) p. 46.

[55] See Wolfgang F. Michael, "Stoff und Idee im 'Tod in Venedig'," in *Deutsche Vierteljahrschrift für Literaturwissenschaft und Geistesgeschichte* 33, no. 1 (1959), pp. 13–19.

[56] See Mann, *Briefe 1889–1936,* ed. Erika Mann (Frankfurt am Main: S. Fischer Verlag, 1962), p. 139. My translation. Cf. Lukács, *Soul and Form*, p. 9. Lukács writes, "The phrase perhaps expresses most clearly the twin aspects of the condition of poverty, its inner wealth and outward weakness." Mann was obviously thinking along the same line when his invalid existence (outward weakness) supplied him time for introspection (inner wealth).

[57] Lukács, *Soul and Form*, p. 102.

[58] See Gunilla Bergsten, *Thomas Mann's Doctor Faustus: The Sources and Structure of the Novel*. Trans. Krishna Winston (Chicago: University of Chicago Press, 1969), p. 58. This is an excellent study; it not only contains a highly reliable compilation of the sources for the novel, but is also highly instructive with regard to the novel's cultural background and Mann's literary techniques, such as the "montage" technique.

[59] See Mann, *Doctor Faustus*. Trans. H. T. Lowe-Porter (New York: Alfred A. Knopf, 1949), p. 155.

[60] Mann, *Briefe 1889–1936*, p. 175. My translation.

[61] My unpublished interview with Lukács, May 7, 1971.

[62] Lukács, Preface to *The Theory of the Novel*. Trans. Anna Bostock (Cambridge: M. I. T., 1971), p. 14. Emphasis added.

[63] Ibid., p. 15. As to the assertion that "Max Weber read this work with approval," Lukács's memory did not serve him well. Max Weber confessed in a letter to Lukács that he *"hated"* and "still hates" this work because this project—the planned treatise on Dostoyevsky—engaged Lukács's energies at a time when he should have been working on a systematic philosophical

work, the "Aesthetics." See *Georg Lukács: Selected Correspondence, 1902–1920.* Selected, edited, translated, and annotated by Judith Marcus and Zoltán Tar (New York: Columbia University Press, 1986), p. 1986.

[64] Lukács, *Theory of the Novel*, p. 122.

[65] Ibid., p. 124.

[66] Ibid., p. 129.

[67] Mann, "The Making of *The Magic Mountain*," in *The Magic Mountain*. Trans. H. T. Lowe-Porter (New York: Modern Library, n. d.), p. 723. The author's note, appended to the novel itself, first appeared in *Atlantic Monthly*, January 1952. In the Foreword to the novel (p. ix), Mann too makes references to the importance of the "passage of time"—in which statement the author intentionally touches upon the strange and questionable double nature of that riddling element.

[68] See Lukács, *Theory of the Novel*, p. 128.

[69] Mann, "Making", p. 723.

2. Respect and Distance

[1] Lukács wrote the Foreword in September 1956. See Lukács, *Thomas Mann* (Berlin/East: Aufbau Verlag, 1957), pp. 9–10. Another essay, "Franz Kafka oder Thomas Mann?" was not included; this treatise was first presented at a lecture tour in the fall of 1955 (in Berlin, Vienna, Poland, and Italy) and published in German in 1957. See Lukács, *The Meaning of Contemporary Realism* (London: Merlin Press, 1962), pp. 47–92. Kafka was for Lukács the "classic example of the modern writer at the mercy of... angst," whose originality lies "in the utterly convincing, and yet continually startling, presentation of his invented world, and of his characters' reaction to it." Lukács, however, came out against the "basically allegorical character" of Kafka's work. Mann was presented as Kafka's "counterpart" whose fictional world is "free from transcendental reference: place, time and detail are rooted firmly in a particular social and historical situation" (pp. 77–78). Thus, Lukács decides in favor of Thomas Mann and his "critical realism."

[2] See Hans Rudolf Vaget, "Georg Lukács, Thomas Mann, and the Modern Novel," in *Thomas Mann in Context: Papers of the Clark University Centennial Colloquium*. Ed. Kenneth Hughes (Worcester, Mass.: Clark University Press, 1978), p. 57.

[3] In the English-language selection of Lukács's essays, *Essays on Thomas Mann*. Trans. Stanley Mitchell (London: Merlin Press, 1964), pp. 152 and 158. Unfortunately, the volume offers a rather fragmentary picture of Lukács's writings on Mann. Originally published under the title "Thomas Mann über das literarische Erbe" in *Internationale Literatur* 6, no 5 (1936), pp. 56–66. Mann read the German-language journal faithfully in his American exile. As was his custom, he commented either negatively or positively on writings devoted to him or his work. An entry in his diaries on June 2, 1936, shows that he read Lukács's appraisal and found it "extremely interesting" *(äusserst interessant)*, without any objections. See Mann, *Tagebücher: 1935–1936*, ed. Peter de Mendelssohn (Frankfurt am Main: S. Fischer Verlag, 1978), p. 310. The entry is not included in the arbitrarily selected English-language edition. See *Thomas Mann: Diaries 1918–1939*, ed. Hermann Kesten. Trans. Richard Winston and Clara Winston (New York: Harry N. Abrams, 1982).

[4] Lukács, *Essays on Thomas Mann*, p. 11–12.

[5] Lukács, *Thomas Mann*, p. 10.

[6] Interview with Georg Lukács, May 7, 1971, in his home in Budapest. The taped interview is in my possession.

[7] Isaac Deutscher, "Georg Lukács and 'Critical Realism'," in *The Listener*, November 3, 1966, pp. 659–62.

[8] Vaget, "Lukács, Mann and the Modern Novel," p. 37.

[9] My translation. A copy of this typed and hitherto unpublished letter was given to me by Lukács's family in 1971. It is now deposited in the Georg Lukács Archives, Budapest.

[10] Original letter is in the Thomas Mann Archiv, Zurich. See letter no. 158 in Georg Lukács, *Selected Correspondence 1902–1920. Dialogues with Weber, Simmel, Buber, Mannheim and Others.* Selected, edited, translated, and annotated by Judith Marcus and Zoltán Tar (New York: Columbia University Press, 1986).

[11] My interview, May 7, 1971. According to Lukács, the correspondence was destroyed in order not to weaken the effectiveness of Thomas Mann's intervention by accidentally disclosing the fact that the appeal was made at the request of a communist functionary (Lukács). The reference is to Zoltán Szántó (1893–1977), politician and writer, one of the founding members of the Hungarian Communist Party who lived in exile in Vienna (1920–26) but returned to Hungary and was active in the underground. He subsequently received a prison term (1927–35), went to the Soviet Union, and returned to Hungary in 1945. Mann's trip to Warsaw took place March 8–15, 1927; he was the guest of the Polish section of PEN. Mann did not meet Marshall Pilsudski, only his aide, a Kaden-Bandrowski, according to Mann's recollections. See, "Im Warschauer Pen-Club" (Visit at the Warsaw PEN), in *Autobiographisches*, MK 119 (Frankfurt am Main: Fischer Bücherei, 1968), pp. 199. ff.

[12] See *Thomas Mann an Ernst Bertram: Briefe aus den Jahren 1910–1955.* Ed. Inge Jens (Pfullingen: Verlag Günther Neske, 1960). No correspondence existed between 1934 and 1949 on account of Bertram's Nazi sympathies. The 256 notes and letters are deposited at the Schiller National Museum, Marbach, Germany.

[13] Both have been published in English. See *Thomas Mann: Letters to Paul Amann. 1915–1952,* ed. Herbert Wegener, trans. Richard Winston and Clara Winston (London Secker & Warburg, 1961); *Mythology and Humanism: The Correspondence of Thomas Mann and Karl Kerényi,* trans. Alexander Gelley (Ithaca: Cornell University Press, 1975).

[14] Reference is to Goethe's *Faust,* Part I, line 3415 ("Martha's Garden"), where the worried Margarete asks her lover: "Nun sag: wie hast du's mit der Religion?"

[15] Vaget, "Lukács, Mann, and the Modern Novel," p. 37.

[16] Hermann J. Weigand, "Autobiography in Thomas Mann's *Königliche Hoheit,"* in PMLA 46 (1931), p. 878.

[17] Thomas Mann wrote this letter in February 1906 while on his honeymoon in Switzerland. See *Thomas Mann-Heinrich Mann: Briefwechsel, 1909–1949.* Ed. Hans Wysling (Frankfurt am Main: S. Fischer Verlag, 1969), p. 35.

[18] See Lukács, "The Foundering of Form Against Life: Søren Kierkegaard and Regine Olsen," in *Soul and Form,* p. 31.

[19] *Thomas Mann-Heinrich Mann Briefwechsel,* pp. 45–46. Emphasis added.

[20] Ibid., p. 60

[21] It must have been a painful experience for Lukács to have Mann answer his letter by addressing himself to Lukács's wife Gertrud—that is, that Mann used the fact that Lukács had to dictate his letter to Gertrud as a pretext not to establish direct contact with Lukács. This was not to deter him from approaching Mann again, however. The 1949 exchange of letters was only partially published in the "Thomas Mann — Gedenknummer," *Sinn und Form* 7, no. 5 (1955), pp. 669–76. The originals are in the Georg Lukács Archiv and the Thomas Mann Archiv respectively. The quotation is from Goethe's *Wilhelm Meister's Apprenticeship,* Book 4, chapter 9. Cf. Vaget, "Lukács Mann, and the Modern Novel" p. 40.

[22] Vaget, "Lukács, Mann and the Modern Novel," p. 40.

[23] Ibid., p. 41.

[24] Unpublished letter at the Thomas Mann Archiv, Zurich.

[25] Unpublished letter. Copy at the Georg Lukács Archiv, Budapest.

[26] Unpublished letter, ibid.

[27] Letter of March 22, 1949. See *Sinn und Form*, p. 669.

[28] Letter of March 25, 1949, printed in the context of a controversy about Lukács's *Faustus* essay, that was sharply attacked in *Der Monat* 6 (March, 1949). See "Thomas Mann und seine falschen Freunde" (Thomas Mann and his false friends), in *Der Aufbau* 5, no. 5 (1949), p. 473. Original at the Thomas Mann Archiv.

[29] Unpublished letter at the Thomas Mann Archiv. Emphasis added.

[30] Unpublished letter at the Georg Lukács Archiv.

[31] Mann, "Brief an Dr. Seipel," published in *Die Forderung des Tages* (Berlin: S. Fischer Verlag, 1930). Republished in *Miszellen*, MK 120. For English translation see Appendix.

[32] In *Miszellen*, MK 120, pp. 253–54. See Appendix.

[33] Mann, *The Story of a Novel: The Genesis of Doctor Faustus*. Trans. Richard Winston and Clara Winston (New York: Alfred A. Knopf, 1961), pp. 142–43.

[34] Ibid. Emphasis added.

[35] Mann, *Tagebücher: 1935–1936*, pp. 310 and 210.

[36] Mann, "Dr. Seipel." Cf. Foreword in Lukács, *Thomas Mann*, p. 10. It seemed to Lukács that Mann was "much too polite and gentle when he described our opposition in his letter to Dr. Seipel."

[37] Letter of February 17, 1915. In *Thomas Mann an Ernst Bertram*, p. 23.

[38] *Thomas Mann Diaries: 1918–1939*, September 11, 1918, p. 3.

[39] Ibid., p. 217.

[40] Ibid., p. 238.

[41] Ibid, p. 242.

[42] Letter of July 11, 1918. See *Thomas Mann: Letters to Paul Amann*, p. 101. Emphasis added except where indicated. Reference is made to Franz (Ferenc) Ferdinand Baumgarten, *Das Werk Conrad Fredinand Meyers: Renaissance Empfinden und Stilkunst* (Munich: Beck, 1917). Baumgarten was a close friend of Lukács who had tried to promote Lukács's work and advance his academic career in Germany in the 1910s. Part of their correspondence is to be found in Marcus and Tar, *Georg Lukács: Selected Correspondence*.

[43] Mann's reflections on Lukács's critical work is followed by the sentence: "I do not want to give the impression that good news and comfort came to me only from the non-German world." See Mann, *Story of a Novel*, p. 143.

[44] Mann writes, "I am, in what is intellectually essential, a genuine child of the century into which the first twenty-five years of my life fall: the nineteenth." See *Reflections of a Non-Political Man*, p. 10. Similar comments can be found in the "Lebensabriss" and other autobiographical writings of Mann. As for Georg Lukács, see "Lob des neunzehnten Jahrhunderts" (In Praise of the Nineteenth Century). *In Sachen Böll*, ed. Marcel Reich-Ranicki (Köln: Kiepenhauer & Witsch, 1968), pp. 325 ff.

3. Sources and Narrative Techniques in Mann's Work

[1] First publication in the original German, entitled "Einführung in den 'Zauberberg'. Für Studenten der Universität Princeton," as a foreword to *Der Zauberberg* (Stockholm: Bermann-

Fischer, 1939), pp. 326 ff. The passage cited was not included in the English-language version, "The Making of *The Magic Mountain*," (trans. H. T. Lowe-Porter), in *The Magic Mountain* (New York: Modern Library, n. d.), pp. 717–27. (A shorter version was also published in *Atlantic Monthly*, 1952). All further references to this essay or to the novel itself—including a brief Foreword by the author—will be based on this edition. The author's reflections on the novel as a *Zeitroman* are contained in several earlier essays of Mann, such as the "Lebensabriss" of 1930, and can be found scattered throughout his essays.

[2] Mann, "Making," p. 719.

[3] Ibid., p. 723.

[4] Mann, Foreword to *Magic Mountain*, p. ix.

[5] Mann, "Making," p. 722.

[6] Mann, Foreword, p. ix. H. T. Lowe-Porter rendered the German term as "exaggerated pastness," which is less satisfying than "extreme pastness," used by others.

[7] For a highly selective list of critical works, see Hermann J. Weigand, *The Magic Mountain: A Study of Thomas Mann's Novel 'Der Zauberberg'* (1933; reprint ed., Chapel Hill. University of North Carolina Press, 1964). Mann called Weigand's book the "most comprehensive and fundamental treatment" his novel ever received. Still the best documentation on its creation and sources is Heinz Saueressig, *Die Entstehung des Romans 'Der Zauberberg'* (Biberach a. d. Riss: "Wege und Gestalten" Series, 1965). Jürgen Schwarfschwedt's *Thomas Mann und der deutsche Bildungsroman* (Stuttgart: Kohlhammer Verlag, 1967) contains an elaborately detailed discussion of the philosophical themes and the contemporary historical background of the novel; the work is perceived as a continuation of the German tradition of *Bildungsroman*. The only positive outcome of Hans Castorp's educational process is seen in his rejection of all the (ideological) positions and solutions offered to him. Herbert Lehnert, in discussing the nature and conception of the educational process in Mann's novel, comes to the conclusion that its aim is the education of the readers and *not* of the fictional hero. See Herbert Lehnert, *Thomas Mann Forschung: Ein Bericht* (Stuttgart: J. B. Metzlersche Verlagsbuchhandlung, 1969), p. 117. This extremely useful survey of the critical literature on Mann's life work has only one drawback: it ends with 1968.

[8] Mann, "Making," p. 722.

[9] Louis Wirth, Preface to Karl Mannheim, *Ideology and Utopia* (New York: A Harvest Book, 1936), p. xxv.

[10] Mann, "Suffering and Greatness of Richard Wagner," in *Essays of Three Decades*, trans. H. T. Lowe-Porter (New York: Alfred A. Knopf, 1948), p. 347. This is a slightly altered version of Lowe-Porter's text, which often seems to miss the main thrust of the original.

[11] Lukács, "In Search of Bourgeois Man," in *Essays on Thomas Mann*, pp. 31–32. Entitled "Auf der Suche nach dem Bürger: Betrachtungen zum siebzigsten Geburtstag Thomas Manns," the essay was first published in German in *Internationale Literatur* nos. 6–7. (1945), pp. 58–75. Thomas Mann referred to this publication when stating that Lukács's essay contained "the best that had ever been said about my work." It was reprinted in *Thomas Mann* (Berlin/East: Aufbau Verlag, 1949) and in all five subsequent editions, the last in 1957. (The last is also the most comprehensive collection of Lukács's writings on Mann.)

[12] Mann, *Doctor Faustus*, p. 354. Who were these intellectuals, who practiced an "all-embracing critique of the bourgeois tradition?" Mann answers that they were "men of education, culture, science" (ibid.).

[13] Lukács, *Essays on Thomas Mann*, p. 32.

[14] Ibid., p. 36. We find in the critical literature similar views regarding the conception of the educational process and the idea of Mann's "mission" among the Germans of the Weimar Republic. See Hans Mayer, *Thomas Mann: Werk und Entwicklung* (Berlin) East: Verlag Volk un

Welt, 1950). Mayer's work contains some Lukácsian influences and reformulations of Lukács's thoughts.

[15] Mann, "Making," p. 724.

[16] See Mann, "Bilse und Ich," (Bilse and I) in "Autobiographisches," MK 119, p. 17. Reference is to Fritz Oswald Bilse, author of a scandalous *roman à clef, Aus einer kleinen Garnison* (1903), the target of a libel suit. During the proceedings, Thomas Mann's novel was mentioned as another *roman à clef*. Hence Mann's sharp retort. "Bilse und Ich" was first published in the *Münchener Neueste Nachrichten,* February 15 and 16, 1906.

[17] Ibid., p. 19, Thomas Mann goes on to say that "in each case, there is a certain poetic identification with one's created characters," meaning that "the figures of a work of art are emanations of the poetic 'I' [alle Gestalten einer Dichtung... sind Emanationen des dichtenden Ich]." Even if just for a fleeting moment, the author adds, the identification is there even though it may remain hidden for the reader. What is more, "It is there even if the reader thinks that the author feels nothing but disgust and mockery for his character." See pp. 18–19. Hans Mayer seems to have overlooked this statement—as did many other critics—when he declared that the author shows no sympathy whatsoever toward the sinister character of Naphta. See Mayer, *Thomas Mann.*

[18] Mann, "Bilse und Ich," p. 21. Emphasis added.

[19] Ibid., p. 18.

[20] Reference is made to Karl Kerényi, the eminent Hungarian classicist and theologist, who began his discussion of the "Naphta-problem" as follows: "Klaus Pringsheim's [Katia Mann's twin brother] recent report on the circumstances of the genesis and withdrawal of the short story, 'The Blood of the Walsungs', in the Munich of 1905 encourages us to explore other 'literary gossips.' ... It is a worthwhile task to hand down such past history to an appreciative posterity. This position of mine is more humane than that of a purely aesthetic one." In *Tessiner Schreibtisch* [At my Desk in Tessin] (Stuttgart: Steingrüben, 1963), p. 125. I may add that it is the more subjective and less reliable way to hand down "past history." This is especially true in Kerényi's case; his account of the "Naphta-Problem" is a highly biased one, as it reflects his immense personal dislike of Lukács. For him, Lukács and Naphta are devils incarnate.

[21] See *Thomas Mann an Ernst Bertram: Briefe aus den Jahren 1910–1955,* ed. Inge Jens (Pfullingen: Verlag Günther Neske, 1960), p. 18. Mann's letters to Bertram are an excellent guide for following the development and changes in the planned novel. As early as January 6, 1914, Mann decided on the title *Der Zauberberg,* and in early 1916, he promised Bertram a "second reading" from a chapter he had just finished. Then silence. In August 1918, shortly after finishing *Reflections of a Non-Political Man,* Mann reported on the continuation of work on the novel, describing the added chapter on "Snow." Ibid., p. 72.

[22] Mann, *Letters to Paul Amann 1915–1952,* ed. Herbert Wegener, trans. Richard Winston and Clara Winston (London: Secker & Warburg, 1961), p. 42. Emphasis added. About thirty years later, Thomas Mann himself called attention to the fact that Lukács's highly sensitive and intelligent remarks on *Death in Venice* point to this "premonition of reality" which was so "pertinent to the times." Lukács had observed that "Heinrich Mann's *Der Untertan* and Thomas Mann's *Tod in Venedig* can both be regarded as great forerunners of that trend toward signaling the danger of a barbarous underworld existing within modern German civilization as its necessary complement." Quoted in Mann, *The Story of a Novel: The Genesis of Doctor Faustus,* trans. Richard Winston and Clara Winston (New York: Alfred A. Knopf, 1961), p. 142. Thomas Mann's reference to Lukács's essay is incorrect, however, inasmuch as the cited passage comes not from the "birthday essay", "Auf der Suche nach dem Bürger," but from another work of Lukács, entitled *Die deutsche Literatur im Zeitalter des Imperialismus* (German Literature in the Age of

Imperialism), which was also published in *Internationale Literatur*, nos. 3–4. (1945). Hence Mann's mistake.

²³ Mann, *Letters to Paul Amann*, p. 44.

²⁴ *Thomas Mann an Ernst Bertram*, p. 33.

²⁵ Mann, "Making," p. 721. This essay is not only a work of "painful introspection" but it also approaches contemporary issues and problems with enormous intensity and honesty: it shows Mann, warts and all. Another of the large essays, entitled "Goethe and Tolstoy," in which the author similarly "unburdened" himself of a "quantity of material in the polemical and analytical" sense, weighs and discusses the nature and possibilities of the artist, of intellectuality, and of how life is lived, in an "ideal-typical" presentation.

²⁶ Mann, *Letters to Paul Amman*, p. 87.

²⁷ Mann, *Reflections*, p. 312. In this connection Mann evokes the words of Hans Pfitzner (1869–1949), German neoromantic composer and ardent nationalist, who compared his own opera, *Palestrina*, with Wagner's *Meistersinger* and saw the basic difference in the fact that "the *Meistersinger* is the apotheosis of the new, a praise of the future and of life; in *Palestrina* everything tends toward the past, it is dominated by *sympathy with death*." (His emphasis) Quoted in Mann, *Reflections*, p. 311. These words "shook and astounded" Mann, who recognized his "own expression" in them. The author added: "In order to characterize his elevated musical work properly, [he]... hit upon an expression of my ironical literary work. How much brotherhood comes readily from contemporaneousness itself! And how much similarity in terms of intellectual work there must be for two intellectuals, who, distant from one another, live in completely different... spheres, outwardly without connection, to agree upon the same literary symbol for whole spiritual complexes!" (ibid., p. 312). (I have altered the translation slightly.) One wonders whether Mann experienced similar astonishment when reading some of Lukács's musings in *Soul and Form*.

²⁸ Ibid., p. 312.

²⁹ Ibid., p. 313.

³⁰ As Mann stated in his introduction to *Reflections*, he is "in what is intellectually essential, a genuine child of the century into which the first twenty-five years of [his] life fall" (ibid., p. 10). The same statement can be found in several sketches of his life and elsewhere in his other writings. Things are not so straightforward or simple, however, and Mann was the first to admit that "modernity" did not pass him by. "To be sure," he writes, "I find in myself both artistic-formal and intellectual-moral elements, needs and instincts that... belong... to a more recent [period]." Regardless, such elements as "romanticism, nationalism, burgherly nature, music, pessimism, humor" from the "atmosphere of the past age in the main form the impersonal parts of my being as well." The nineteenth century differed from the previous one, Mann declared, in its "basic disposition and spiritual tendency, in a character trait." Mann referred to Nietzsche as the first to call attention to this difference and put it into "critical language." Ibid., pp. 10–11.

³¹ Hans Mayer, *Thomas Mann: Werk und Entwicklung* (Berlin: Verlag Volk und Welt, 1955), p. 13.

³² Ibid., p. 139. By "*Russland-Erlebnis*" Mayer first and foremost had in mind the 1917 revolution in Russia; the events preoccupied Mann for a while, as his letters and many of his statements attest. Prior to these events, Mann had already displayed an intense curiosity about Russian matters and discussed at length Tolstoy and Dostoyevsky. He exclaimed in a letter of October 4, 1917: "And how I love the Russian spirit. How its contrast to and contempt for Gallicism amuses me—one finds this throughout Russian literature. How much closer the Russian and German temperaments are! For years my heart's desire has been reconciliation and alliance with Russia." See *Letters of Thomas Mann*, trans. Richard Winston and Clara Winston (New York: Alfred

A. Knopf, 1971), p. 87. Cf. Mann, *Letters to Paul Amman*, pp. 31 and 52. (Mann's "Mereshkovsky experience" was of a different kind but no less intense.)

[33] Mayer, *Thomas Mann*, p. 141. It cannot be ascertained who Mayer had in mind; although he is inclined—as was Lukács—to see in Naphta the prototype of the prefascist intellectual instead of a communist one, he could hardly have had a specific individual in mind since he seemed to discover in Naphta's spiritual makeup the traces of Mann's "own youthful world."

[34] Arthur Eloesser, *Thomas Mann—Sein Leben und seine Werke* (Berlin: S. Fischer Verlag, 1925), p. 193. Eloesser's biography deals with Mann's life and work up to 1924, the year *The Magic Mountain* came out. Written for Thomas Mann's fiftieth birthday celebration, it is a very useful book as well as the only authorized biography of Mann. The cooperation of Mann and his family is evident throughout the book. Eloesser was granted the privilege of partaking in their everyday family life at their Munich residence in order to get the "feel" of their life style. It should be mentioned that it was Eloesser who first alluded to the so-called Holitscher case (and not Klaus Schroeter's RoRoRo monograph as generally assumed). Eloesser discusses at some length how and in what way Holitscher became the "living model" for the character of Spinell in Mann's short story "Tristan." Interestingly, Arthur Holitscher (1869–1941), author of novels and travel books, and a member of the Munich literati, was also from Budapest. As told by Mann "Holitscher had also become an ardent Bolshevik" and a "representative of this kind of ideological sentiment in the contemporary German literary life" (ibid., p. 124). This would mean that not one but two Hungarian-Jewish intellectuals served as "living models" for Mann's fictional characters.

[35] Ibid., pp. 193–94. Emphasis added.

[36] Ibid., p. 201.

[37] Ibid., p. 202.

[38] Ibid. Cf. Hans Mayer, *Thomas Mann*, p. 141.

[39] Eloesser, *Thomas Mann*, p. 202.

[40] Ibid., p. 196.

[41] See *Letters of Thomas Mann*, pp. 131–32. Emphasis added. In this letter of January 6, 1925, the author speaks of *one meeting* to which "the character owes a few living traits," and then asks plaintively: "Does that mean that I have profaned Germany's foremost writer by making a caricature of him?"

[42] Ibid., pp. 140–41. Emphasis added. Mann's letter of apology, dated April 11, 1925, shows that Eulenberg did make the matter public; and Hauptmann displayed a generosity of spirit and did not take offense. Indeed, his widow wrote to Mann upon Hauptmann's death (1946) and assured him that "the character of Mynheer Peeperkorn was the finest monument" that had been erected to the dramatist.

[43] Maurice Colleville, "Rezension," in *Études germaniques* 5, nos. 2–3 (Avril–Septembre 1950), p. 205.

[44] See Thomas Mann, *Briefe: 1889–1936,* ed. Erika Mann (Frankfurt am Main: S. Fischer Verlag, 1962), pp. 350–51. Letter is not included in the English language edition. My translation.

[45] Ibid., p. 382. My translation. The letter of January 18, 1935, is a thank-you note for Sagave's dissertation sent to Mann.

[46] Unpublished letter. Written in California on February 18, 1952. My translation. Original is at the Thomas Mann Archiv, Zurich.

[47] Pierre-Paul Sagave, *Réalité sociale et idéologie religieuse dans les romans de Thomas Mann*. Publications de la faculté des lettres de l'université de Strasbourg, Fasc. 124 (Paris: Société d'edition: Les Belles Lettres, 1954), pp. 43 ff.

[48] Henry Hatfield, "Drei Randglossen zu Thomas Manns *Zauberberg*," in *Euphorion* 56 (1962), pp. 365 ff. Responding to subsequent criticism charging plagiarism, Hatfield saw himself com-

pelled to defend what he called his "unconscious robbery of the thought of others," alluding to Sagave's work. See "Korrekturnote," in *Euphorion* 57 (1963), p. 226.

[49] Karl Kerényi, "Thomas Mann und der Marxist," in *Neue Zürcher Zeitung*, Juni 9, 1963, np. Cf. "Zauberberg-Figuren," in *Tessiner Schreibtisch* (Stuttgart: Steingrüber Verlag, 1963), pp. 125 ff. The first version appeared in Hungarian in the Munich emigré journal *Új látóhatár* 5, no. 1 (January February 1962), pp. 30 ff.

[50] *Neue Zürcher Zeitung*, column 5.

[51] Ibid., column 6. Kerényi's statement is basically correct in that it is grounded in the special Hungarian experience. Hungary's poets and writers were inclined to look toward France for inspiration, to take as examples French political movements, literature, and culture. This was even more so at the turn of the twentieth century, when they felt great affinity with the modernization and politicizing of literary life (e.g. surrealism) in France. All this had historical roots. In the course of Hungarian history, the often beleaguered country's best poets and intellectuals were not just eager participants but more often than not leaders in the vanguard of progressive and rebellious movements. This tradition made them more open to French influences than to German ones. However, in the light of what happened in Hungary in the last years of World War II, Kerényi's choice of contrast—true Hungarians on one side and the Jewish bourgeoisie on the other—was unfortunate, to say the least.

[52] See Mann, *Briefe 1937–1948*, ed. Erika Mann (Frankfurt am Main: S. Fischer Verlag, 1963), p. 579. My translation.

[53] Unpublished conversation with Georg Lukács at his Budapest residence on May 7, 1971, three weeks before he died of lung cancer. My translation of the interview, conducted partly in Hungarian, partly in German.

[54] See Ehrhard Bahr and Ruth Goldschmidt Kunzer, *Georg Lukács* (New York: Frederick Ungar Publishing Co., 1972), p. 3. This is a slightly enlarged and translated (by R. Goldschmidt Kunzer) version of the German-language original (1970). Bahr's slim volume is the best monograph of Lukács. My only disagreement is with the statement that "Lukács's physical portrait undoubtedly served as [Mann's] model for Naphta," unlike his "intellectual orientation." Lukács's physical portrait was undoubtedly *not* his main contribution to Naphta.

[55] Unpublished letter of May 18, 1965. Copy of the letter is at the Georg Lukács Archiv, Budapest. At almost the same time, Lukács complains in a letter written to István Mészáros, one of his most trusted students and a one-time assistant of the University of Budapest now living and teaching in England, that the "Naphta business is truly annoying." He mentions a "recent study" in which his whole life work is interpreted in light of Naphta's character. It seems almost certain that Lukács was alluding to Victor Zitta's work, *Georg Lukács' Marxism: Alienation, Dialectics, Revolution. A Study in Utopia and Ideology* (The Hague: Martinus Nijhoff, 1964). An extremely polemical and biased work, its best feature is its extensive bibliography. Whoever consults the work for reliable data should be forewarned: hardly any of the dates or biographical details are reliable. Only someone ignorant of early twentieth-century intellectual history (and Central European academic life) could state that Lukács took "his doctorate in sociology under Simmel in Berlin" in 1906. Another example of Zitta's "scholarship": "Lukács willingly relinquished his lectureship in aesthetic under Rickert at Heidelberg" in order to pursue his "mad dreams" (p. 86). The Lukács vita in the preface amounts to an approximation at best. Concerning the study, I must confess I am in agreement with Lukács.

[56] Saueressig, *Entstehung*.

[57] Max Rychner, "Gestalten und Bezüge in den Romanen," in *Die Neue Rundschau* 66, no. 3 (1955), p. 262.

[58] Ibid., p. 265.

[59] Lukács, *Essays on Thomas Mann*, p. 54. Cf. Mann's own references to the organic character of his development in *Reflections*.

[60] Mayer, *Thomas Mann*, p. 116.

[61] Max Weber, *The Methodology of the Social Sciences*, trans. and ed. E. A. Shils and H. A. Finch (New York: Free Press, 1949), p. 90.

[62] Ibid. Weber's "ideal-type" construct put the sociological imprint on the concept of type which was already present in the philosophy of antiquity (Plato, Aristotle) and was introduced through Greek philosophical thought into the scholastic system. In modern times, we find the typological approach dominant in Goethe's and Dilthey's work; the anthropological impulses coming from Nietzsche were deeply influential in the morphological and characterological approaches of Spengler and Ludwig Klages. The same *Typenlehre* (doctrine of type) was also the basis for the theory of constitution (Jaspers, Jung, Kretschmer). Thus, the typological thinking left its imprint on the social sciences as well as on the literature of the period.

[63] Ibid.

[64] See Herbert Lehnert, *Thomas Mann—Fiktion, Mythos, Religion* (Stuttgart: Kohlhammer Verlag, 1965), p. 138. At one point, Lehnert asserts that Lukács tends to "omit from his interpretative considerations the fictional world of Thomas Mann." On the contrary: just as Lehnert does, Lukács vehemently rejects the consideration of nonfictional texts and states that it is only appropriate "to concentrate on the work and to interpret Mann the thinker and political man starting from his writing and not, as is customary, the other way around." See Lukács, *Essays*, pp. 16 and 18.

[65] Mann, *Reflections*, p. 67. Emphasis added.

[66] Mann, *Briefe 1889–1936*, p. 76. My translation.

[67] In an unpublished letter of February 23, 1937, Mann wrote Sagave that there is a definite connection between his figures and certain sociological theories; he advised Sagave to take a look at his *Reflections*, especially in his allusions to Max Weber. Reflecting on "burgherly nature," Mann writes: "I place some value on the fact that I sensed and discovered the idea that the modern capitalist businessman, the bourgeois, with his *aesthetic* idea of duty to his career, was a creation of the Protestant ethic, of Puritanism and Calvinism, that I came to this idea completely on my own, without reading, by direct insight, and that I only discovered afterward, recently, that it had been thought and expressed at the same time by learned thinkers; Max Weber in Heidelberg, and after him, Ernst Troeltsch, have treated *The Protestant Ethic and the Spirit of Capitalism*, and the thought is also found in greatly exaggerated form in Werner Sombart's work of 1913, *The Bourgeois....*" pp. 103–4. The reference is, of course, to Mann's first novel, *Buddenbrooks*.

[68] Three main characters represent the *Sonderfälle des Lebens* in the novel: Klaus Heinrich, the prince; Dr. Überbein, the teacher; and Dr. Sammet, the Jewish physician who defines the "incidence" in the community of ordinary men as "exceptional or abnormal men who are distinguished from the bourgeois by their nobleness or infamy." He adds, "A man is at an advantage... if he has one motive more than [the herd] to extraordinary exertions." See Mann, *Royal Highness* (New York: Alfred A. Knopf, 1939), pp. 20–21.

[69] See Eloesser, *Thomas Mann*.

[70] See Mann, *Letters*, pp. 131–32.

[71] "Bei Thomas Mann in Budapest" (A Visit with Thomas Mann in Budapest), Report in *Pester Lloyd*, Thursday, January 12, 1922. "Upon our arrival," wrote the journalist, "we found Thomas Mann in the company of Béla Bartók and Dezső Kosztolányi. The Lukács residence, as is well-known, always has its door open to artists and friends." See Ida Herz Collection at the Thomas Mann Archiv, Zurich, reg. no. ZH 308. Cf. Elsa Ernst, "Aus den Erinnerungen" (From my Memories...), in *Paul Ernst und Georg Lukács: Dokumente einer Freundschaft*, ed. Karl-August Kutzbach (Emsdetten/West.: Lechte Verlag, 1974), p. 162. This is one of the best descriptions of the

milieu and life style of the Lukács family. She describes a mansion, luxuriously furnished and equipped and well tended by servants, visited by a never-ending flow of scholars and artists, journalists and diplomats, bankers and merchants, doctors and publishers, poets and musicians. "Our dear friend [Georg Lukács], the younger of the brothers, who now lives in Vienna, was the stellar offspring of the family. The two women, first the Tartare [Russian] Yelena, and then his second wife [Gertrud], have induced the man, who had become by then famous, to join the Bolsheviks. The relationship between father and son gradually evolved into a tragic drama [Trauerspiel]. Both of them had a steely aristocratic bearing—that had nothing to do with mannerism. These two men who at one time were so close are now torn in different directions by opposing forces." As Katia Mann told me, the Manns had rather similar impressions. Hence Mann's reference to the life that Lukács voluntarily left behind. (See Appendix.) Elsa Ernst's reminiscences also indicate whom the family blamed for Lukács's "conversion."

[72] See *Letters of Thomas Mann*, p. 114.

[73] Conversation with Lukács, May 7, 1971.

[74] The Hungarian Soviet Republic in which Lukács played a leading role followed Count Mihály Károlyi's democratic coalition government (October 1918–March 20, 1919). The Soviet Republic was proclaimed on March 21, 1919, under the leadership of Béla Kun and the Hungarian Communist Party. The CP, which formed a coalition government with the Social Democrats, was founded in October 1918 by Béla Kun and others who received their training in the Soviet Union along with other former prisoners of war, a number of anarcho-syndicalists of the Ervin Szabó group (mentor of Lukács in Marxism), and some left-wing Social Democrats. Lukács and other Budapest leftist intellectuals joined later, around the middle of December. Many factors contributed to the collapse of the bourgeois–democratic revolutionary government: the Entente's ill-timed *démarche*, economic problems, the slow enaction of social reforms, and so forth. Lukács had been named the Deputy People's Commissar for Public Education. As one Western journal, *The Liberator*, reported in August 1919 in the article "In Communist Hungary," while Lukács was "Commissar of Education on Sundays,"... he acted as "political commissar for one of the Red Guard companies [it was the Fifth Division] at the front on weekdays. He goes about in a leather uniform, an earnest little professor, very learned and intelligent, very kindly and humorous and awfully amused at his sudden transformation...." Participants, including Lukács, later recalled that their morale was greatly boosted by the proclamation of the Soviet Republic in Munich, Bavaria, on April 7, 1919. As Lukács said later, "We all believed that the *Weltrevolution* was coming." Soon after, opposition forces were forming both within and without; on July 30, 1919, "white" Rumanian troops surrounded Budapest. On August 1, 1919, the coalition government had its last meeting, in which the right wing of the Social Democratic Party formed a new government, and the "great experiment" was over. Béla Kun and other leaders—communist and socialist—and their families left for exile in Austria aboard a special train, thanks to diplomatic immunity. Some committed suicide, some stayed behind and were imprisoned or executed. In fact, at one stroke Hungary was emptied of most of her progressive intelligentsia (regardless of their attitude toward the Soviet Republic), including Karl Mannheim, Karl Polányi, Arnold Hauser, Charles de Tolnay, René Spitz, and many others. As told in his *Record of a Life*, Lukács— along with Ottó Korvin—was "ordered to stay" behind in Budapest and organize the illegal Communist Party. Lukács suspected that they were "prepared for martyrdom" because Béla Kun disliked them. Korvin was soon caught and executed; Lukács escaped detection for a while but then left for exile in Vienna in "late August or early September." His escape was "purely a business arrangement" between his father and an officer of Mankensen's army, which was occupying Budapest. See Lukács, *Record of a Life: An Autobiographical Sketch*, ed. István Eörsi, trans. Rodney Livingston (London: Verso Editions, 1983), pp. 66–69. Lukács summed up what led him to join

the revolutionary path in one sentence: "My interest in *ethics led me to the revolution*" (ibid., p. 53; my emphasis).

75 Lukács, *Theory of the Novel*, p. 18.

76 Ibid., p. 17.

77 Ibid., p. 20.

78 Conversation with Lukács, May 7, 1971.

79 *Thomas Mann an Ernst Bertram*, p. 109.

4. Leo Naphta – Jew, Jesuit, Communist

1 Unpublished letter to Pierre-Paul Sagave written February 18, 1952. My translation. Original at Thomas Mann Archiv, Zurich.

2 See Ehrhard Bahr and Ruth Goldschmidt Kunzer, *Georg Lukács* (New York: Frederick Ungar, 1972), p. 6.

3 Sagave, *Réalité sociale*, p. 44.

4 Thomas Mann, *The Magic Mountain*, trans. H. T. Lowe-Porter (New York: Modern Library, n.d.), p. 440. All subsequent page references in the chapter are to this edition.

5 See Mann, "The Blood of the Walsungs," in *Stories of Three Decades*, trans. H. T. Lowe-Porter (New York: Alfred A. Knopf, 1966), pp. 297 ff. The circumstances of "borrowing" were not as trivial as in the case of *Buddenbrooks* and Mann's subsequent self-defense in 1905 ("Bilse and I"). The story this time was intended to be a parody on Wagner worship juxtaposed with an incestuous relationship and assorted themes of "decadence." The resemblance between the twins, Siegmund and Sieglinde, and the Pringsheim twins (Klaus and Katia, later Mann's wife) unfortunately was too close for comfort. The description of the Aarenhold household was clearly based on Mann's experience in the palatial home of the Pringsheims. Beckenrath's feelings of inferiority amidst the wealth and pomp there have become part of Mann's own impressions. Be that as it may, the story was already set to appear in *Die Neue Rundschau*, the house organ of Mann's publisher, S. Fischer Verlag, when the family got word of the "anti-Semitic bent" of the story. A family crisis followed and the story was withdrawn by its author. It was a sign of Mann's stature that the whole issue of the *Rundschau* was pulped and reprinted without his contribution. The story was first published in 1921 in a "private edition," with the final paragraph (a Yiddish phrase considered highly derogatory) rewritten.

6 Ibid., p. 300.

7 Ibid., p. 297.

8 See Mann's letter to Alfred Knopf, which prefaces the novel. *Royal Highness*, trans. A. Cecil Curtis (New York: Alfred A. Knopf, 1939), pp. viii–x.

9 Ibid., p. x.

10 Ibid., p. xi. Not only the construction of the characters but many of the phrases Mann uses in describing his intentions point ahead to *The Magic Mountain*, including the world of the story as a "charmed circle" of existence; the question Mann poses, "Is literature a swan-song?" is answered later with a resounding "Yes" in the "The Making of *The Magic Mountain*."

11 Ibid., p. 69.

12 Ibid., p. 70.

13 Ibid., p. 71.

14 Ibid., p. 427.

15 Ibid., p. 102. Emphasis added.

16 Ibid., p. 72. Emphasis added.

[17] Ibid., pp. 20–21. Emphasis added. In the passage, the idea as well as the wording allude to Mann's Nietzsche experience.

[18] See Mann, *Doctor Faustus: The Life of the German Composer Adrian Leverkühn as Told by a Friend*, trans. H. T. Lowe-Porter (New York: Alfred A. Knopf, 1948), p. 8.

[19] Ibid., pp. 7–8.

[20] Ibid., p. 99.

[21] Ibid.

[22] Ibid.

[23] Ibid., p. 279. Lowe-Porter's translation — "he played the role of ferment and foreigner" — is strikingly inadequate, almost beside the point. The designation "foreigner" does not even come close to what Mann had in mind. To be a foreigner and to be "an alien body" in the society are clearly different things. Mann's *"fermentöser Fremdkörper"* is an allusion to a negative transformation of a culture by fermentation. One simple phrase can open up perspectives, as Mann was given to saying; and an inadequately translated passage can just as easily obscure those perspectives.

[24] Ibid., p. 284.

[25] See unpublished notes to *Doctor Faustus*, consisting of 216 sheets of handwritten papers, organized in files (marked "Mp."). On note no. 101 (Mp. 4), Mann jotted down the following: "The *Jewish scholar, Dr. Schalom (!) Breisacher* of Mainz or Rüdesheim or Mondstein or Karfunkelstein. *Mystic and Fascist."* [Emphasis added]. Cf. unpublished letter of February 20, 1949, to a Dr. Richard Pokorny, who presumably voiced some misgivings about Breisacher's portrayal. Mann declares, "I agree, Breisacher is dreadful, but this type of the Jewish fascist exists." Unpublished material is at the TMA, Zurich. There is evidence that Mann included in this characterization Paul Nikolaus Cossman (1869–1941), the editor of the journal *Süddeutsche Monatshefte* (1904–33) and a political commentator in the 1920s for the Munich daily *Münchner Neueste Nachrichten*. As Mann stated, for example, in a letter of August 5, 1928, to Stefan Grossman, he was again "attacked" by Cossman and Co., who "out of desperate nationalism" accused Mann of "betraying the German people." (A perusal of articles from that period indeed shows a "super German patriotic flair"; the irony is that Cossman died in the Theresienstadt concentration camp.) See *Letters of Thomas Mann*, pp. 166–67.

[26] Contemporaries of Goldberg learned of this claim from Goldberg himself. The late Professor Henry Pachter told me that he had met Goldberg in Berlin and had heard the story. However, he was not alone in giving the claim little credence. As to Goldberg's appearance, Henry Pachter said, "He was fat and cross-eyed with a huge ball-like head, in every respect the opposite of Georg Lukács — or Naphta."

[27] On July 12, 1934, Thomas Mann wrote in his diary: "The Jews who are now deprived of their rights and driven out of Germany are not only such dyed-in-the-wool and naïve German patriots that they are called in Paris *'les Bei-uns,'* but they also shared in the development of those intellectual currents which raise their ugly heads in the present political system — albeit in an extremely contorted way. They have helped to pave the way for antiliberalism not only as members of the *George-Kreis* — Wolfskehl, for example, who would, if only they would let him, easily adjust himself intellectually to the new order. How gladly and quite properly would these Jews offer their services to the Third Reich — and they could indeed be helpful to those blockheads who now expel them! How well, for example, Goldberg fits into this 'movement' with his *Wirklichkeit der Hebräer*: antihumanist, antiuniversalist, nationalistic and religiously prejudical. To him, David and Solomon represent liberal degeneration. The inner attitude of these Jewish writers to the new state must create a real conflict for them: the state rides roughshod over them and all the while they must theoretically approve what it does. The truly despicable

Th. Lessing wrote a book against the *Geist*—why was it necessary to kill him?" See Mann, MK 117, p. 297. First published in *Leiden an Deutschland: Tagebuchblätter aus den Jahren 1933 und 1934* (Los Angeles: Pazifische Presse, 1946) and edited by Ernst Gottlieb and Felix Guggenheim. A good illustration of Mann's "montage technique" is the figure of Goldberg, which shows how Mann's views were incorporated into the text of *Doctor Faustus*. We are told about Breisacher, for whom "biblical personages... King David and King Solomon and the prophets... were already debased representatives of an exploded late theology." Thus, even in his own personal sphere of origin, the Jewish race or people and its intellectual history, "he adhered to a double-faced, crass and malicious conservativism." See Mann, *Doctor Faustus*, p. 281.

[28] Mann, "Zur jüdischen Frage" (On the Jewish Question), in MK 119, p. 53. Emphasis added. Mann's autobiographical piece was written in response to a questionnaire—circulated among artists and intellectuals—sent out by Efraim Fischer, the editor of the Munich journal *Die Neue Merkur*, in 1921. Mann subsequently withdrew his contribution for "personal" and artistic reasons as explained in his October 18, 1921, letter to S. Fischer. First published in the *Frankfurter Allgemeine Zeitung* (January 15, 1966). My translation.

[29] Ibid., p. 54.

[30] Ibid. Emphasis added.

[31] See Ferdinand Lion, *Thomas Mann in seiner Zeit* (Zurich–Leipzig: Max Niehaus Verlag, 1935).

[32] Mann, *Diaries: 1918–1939*, p. 45. Emphasis added.

[33] Ibid., p. 47.

[34] Ernst Bloch, *Thomas Münzer als Theologe der Revolution* (München: Kurt Wolff Verlag, 1921), p. 17. My translation. Thomas Mann was certainly aware of the book's existence, as Siegfried Kracauer's review (severely criticizing the work, by the way) appeared in the *Frankfurter Zeitung*, August 27, 1922, which Mann regularly read and contributed to. In addition, Mann had paid regular visits to the publisher's offices and was usually alerted to interesting new books by Wolff himself, as Mann's correspondence demonstrates. Bloch's book remains untranslated.

[35] Ibid., p. 18.

[36] Bahr and Kunzer, *Georg Lukács*, p. 5.

[37] Marked "Curriculum Vitae," from dossier no. 224–27. Along with two other documents, "Bibliography" and "Topics for Colloquium," it constitutes part of Lukács's file pertaining to his attempt at *Habilitation* at the University of Heidelberg. The files are housed at the University Archives, Heidelberg, "File no. III, 5a, 186: *"Fakultätsakten Dekanat v. Domaszevski 1918/19*, fol. 223–253." First German language publication of the curriculum vitae in *Text + Kritik 39/40*, "Georg Lukács issue," (1973), p. 5. First reprints in my dissertation (1976) and the German edition of my book (1982). For an account of Lukács's ill-fated attempt at a German academic career see the Introduction and Appendix in *Georg Lukács: Selected Correspondence*, ed. and trans. Judith Marcus and Zoltán Tar (New York: Columbia University Press, 1986). The reference in Lukács's vita to his first Ph.D. at Kolozsvár is to the city now called Cluj; once the cultural and political center of Transylvania, it is still the center of Hungarian minority cultural life; the Versailles Treaty gave the former Hungarian territory to Rumania.

[38] See Mann's letter to Dezső Kosztolányi, dated January 1922. Cf. Judit Győri, *Thomas Mann Magyarországon* (Thomas Mann in Hungary) (Budapest: Akadémiai Kiadó, 1968), p. 46. Kosztolányi, a prominent Hungarian poet, knew Mann personally, translated some of his works, and corresponded with him. Mann reviewed his novel *Nero* in the *Frankfurter Zeitung* (March 7, 1924).

[39] See Lukács, *Record of a Life*, p. 28. For the most detailed account of the father-son relationship see *Georg Lukács: Selected Correspondence*, containing letters from Lukács's father, mother, and sister Maria (Mici).

[40] *Record*, p. 35.

[41] An interview with Lukács on his vacation, October 2, 1969. Aired by Hungarian television on May 30, 1972. First published in the journal *Kritika*, June 1973. Reprinted in the interview collection, *Sokszemközt tudósokkal* (Among Scientists and Scholars), ed. István Kardos (Budapest: MRT Minerva, 1974), p. 238. For more on his family life, see Lukács, "Methodischer Zweifel" in *Der Monat* 18, no. 211 (April 1966), p. 95.

[42] See Marcell Benedek, *Naplómat olvasom* (Reading my Diary) (Budapest: Szépirodalmi Kiadó, 1962), pp. 82 ff. Benedek, who calls himself the "honorary *goy*" of the Lukács house, supplies a lively and authentic account of the daily life of the family and the precocity of the boy Georg. Benedek confesses that only his love and respect for his friend and for the father enabled him to bear the rest of the family. Besides the mother, it was the elder brother, János, who aroused Benedek's ire: he calls János, the mother's favorite, a "snob," "extremely stupid," and a "shabby character." Lukács's own recollections of his brother are not much more favorable. See *Record of a Life*, pp. 26–36.

[43] Mann, "Goethe and Tolstoy," in *Three Essays*, trans. H. T. Lowe-Porter (New York: Alfred A. Knopf, 1929), p. 57. Emphasis added. Cf. p. 21. for the notion that Rousseau had a "one-sided" bond with nature insofar as he "was a stepchild of the All-Mother, ...an accident of birth," and "an unhappy wretch, half or three-quarters mad, and probably a suicide."

[44] Ibid., p. 21.

5. Physiognomy of Leo Naphta

[1] Reference is made to Karl Kerényi, "Thomas Mann und der Marxist," and to Henry Hatfield, "Drei Randglossen." Even Ehrhard Bahr and Ruth Kunzer's extremely insightful book starts out with Sagave's findings and concludes that Naphta's "outer appearance ...corresponds to the picture of Lukács in the 1920s" — meaning that "Lukács's physical portrait...undoubtedly served as... model for Naphta." See Bahr and Kunzer, *Georg Lukács*, p. 2.

[2] Notable exceptions are Bahr and Kunzer, who incisively point to the "underlying intellectual resemblance of [the two] disparate types," that is, Lukács and Naphta. Ibid., p. 5. Similarly, in the best book so far dealing with the "young Lukács," Michael Löwy points out that Thomas Mann "partly used Lukács" and stresses the young Lukács's romantic anticapitalist views as a component of Naphta's makeup. See Michael Löwy, *Georg Lukács: From Romanticism to Bolshevism* (London: NLB, 1979), pp. 56–65. Löwy's study contains an informative overview of French scholarship dealing with the "Naphta problem."

[3] See Mann, *The Magic Mountain*, trans. H. T. Lowe-Porter (New York: Modern Library, n.d.), pp. 372–73. Emphasis added. All further page references in the text are made to this edition.

[4] Fritz J. Raddatz, Lukács: *In Selbstzeugnissen und Bilddokumenten* (Reinbek bei Hamburg; Rowohlt, 1972), p. 62. See also "Georg Lukács zum 13. April 1970," *Ad Lectores 10* (Neuwied–Berlin: Luchterhand Verlag, 1970), p. 45.

[5] The picture is included in the highly interesting collection *György Lukács—His Life in Pictures and Documents*, ed. É. Fekete and É. Karádi (Budapest: Corvina Kiadó, 1981), p. 161.

[6] See Raddatz, *Lukács*, p. 23 and 36.

[7] See Fekete and Karádi, *György Lukács*, p. 127, 129, and 133.

[8] See Raddatz, *Lukács*, p. 31.

[9] In this case, we witness again the well-known tendency of Lukács to repress things from his pre-Marxist period. During my interview with Dr. Hans Staudinger, former friend and contemporary of Lukács and a high-ranking Weimar official who emigrated to the United States and became dean at the Graduate Faculty of the New School for Social Research in New York City,

Lukács was undeniably one of the best-dressed scholars around Heidelberg in the 1910s. "He looked like an aristocrat," said Staudinger, "and had the demeanor of one. I remember that he used to own a gracile, wonderfully carved ivory walking cane with a detachable handle that turned out to contain expensive perfume." Staudinger also mentioned that after 1919, Lukács presented him with several valuable Renaissance pieces, including a desk from Florence and a carved wood Madonna, which he used to own. " 'Now that I left behind my aesthetic period, I have no further use for them,' said Lukács and gave them to me." Staudinger's heirs still have the woodcarving but presented the desk to the Georg Lukács Archiv in Budapest, where it now stands. The unpublished interview, tape recorded, is in my possession. The interview was conducted in German. My translation.

[10] See Günther Specovius, "Gespräch mit Lukács," in *Ostbrief,* June 1960, pp. 249 ff.

[11] See Mann, *Buddenbrooks,* trans. H. T. Lowe-Porter (New York: Alfred A. Knopf, 1946), pp. 49, 50 and 96.

[12] Ibid., pp. 107 and 268.

[13] Mann, *Royal Highness,* p. 17. Lowe-Porter's rendering of the German text: "seine Nase, zu flach auf den Schnurrbart abfallend" as "his nose was too broad at the bottom" completely *disguises* — instead of illuminating — the similarity of expressions used by Mann in his descriptions. Hence the text appears in a slightly altered form. This is only one of the numerous instances when the English-language version does not appear to sufficiently back up the line of argumentation, which is fully supported by the German original. Thus, I have at times used my own translation.

[14] Ibid., pp. 68–69.

[15] Mann, "The Blood of the Walsungs," in *Stories of Three Decades,* p. 298. The Aarenhold children have, in addition, something else in common: they all feel the need to "assert [their] personality" (p. 300). They do it by a behavior and style that correspond to the sharpness of their appearance. They are, for example, "ruthlessly insisting on achievement, power," on the "cruel trial of strength," and their gestures are nervously "self-assured" (p. 303). It rounds off the picture that their intellectuality and style of argumentation are similarly attuned: their words "rang sharp," and they "contradicted everything." Their criticism is "deft and ruthless" (p. 303). This illustrates the way that physiognomy and intellectual makeup are part and parcel of a personality, of a *type.*

[16] Mann, "Fiorenza," in *Stories of Three Decades,* pp. 194 ff.

[17] Ibid., pp. 261–62.

[18] Ibid., p. 264. As Girolamo explains, "An inward fire burns in my limbs and urges me to the pulpit."

[19] In replying to Lorenzo de Medici's question "What is...a prophet?" the monk answers that he "is an artist who is at the same time a saint," whose "art is holy, for it is knowledge and a flaming denial" (p. 266). It should be mentioned that Lorenzo calls himself a "brother" of the monk because he is also "ugly...and weak" of body and has had to recognize (as do Mann's "outsiders" or "exceptional cases") that "hindrance is the will's best friend" (p. 268). And both of them thought themselves to be "heroes" of the spirit; according to Fiore, "He who is weak, but of glowing spirit...is a hero" (p. 235).

[20] On the occasion of a new production of *Fiorenza* at the Bremen Theatre in June 1955, Thomas Mann wrote an "Open Letter" to the *Weser Kurier* (July 1955). After fifty years, the author tried to explain to a new generation what made him write such a play in 1904. He said that it was "the dialectical, combatively contradictory, the basically discursive nature of things" that fascinated him. (Such an assessment is valid for *The Magic Mountain.*) Mann saw the monk Savonarola not as a religious or historic figure but in his "purely symbolic capacity," as the "ultimate ascetic–pessimistic critic of Life...as the morbidly fascinating prophet of the pure

spirit," and as such an "artist who is a saint of the idea." Naphta is thus a close kin of Savonarola/Girolamo. Mann further characterized his drama as "an anticipation" of the spiritual situation in 1919 or 1920; he thought it fitted the atmosphere of the later *(Magic Mountain)* period better than that of 1904, when it was created.

[21] See Mann, *Doctor Faustus*, p. 99.

[22] Ibid., pp. 100–101.

[23] Mann's real indebtedness to Theodor W. Adorno is exclusively for Adorno's musical theory and music history.

[24] The motif of physical inadequacy and the compensating (artistic) achievement or heightened sensitivity was guided by Nietzsche's views. For a more detailed discussion on the connection of Naphta and the Nietzschean idea, see Chapter 6. For one of the best discussions of Mann's views on disease as harking back not only to Nietzsche but also to Heine and the German Romantics—especially Novalis—see Hermann J. Weigand, *The Magic Mountain*, pp. 39–44.

[25] Mann, "Zur jüdischen Frage," in MK 119, p. 57.

[26] Ibid., p. 55. See also *Thomas Mann Briefe: 1889–1936*, p. 87. Mann writes to the critic Julius Bab: "The fact that Thomas Buddenbrook's life is the life of a hero [*Heldenleben*] as you suggest, has been recognized by only one critic before you: the ugly, little Lublinski." Cf. Mann, "Der Doktor Lessing," in MK 120, pp. 24 ff. Interestingly, a reproduction of a "Wanted" poster showing Ernst Toller, the German–Jewish poet, after the collapse of the Munich Soviet Republic strikes one as a passage from a Thomas Mann story: "The student whose picture is shown," says the poster, "is Ernst Toller, a student, who is of small stature,... has a thin, white face, is clean-shaven, has big brown eyes, and a very sharp look," and, concludes the "poetic" wanted poster, "when he is reflecting he is wont to close his eyes." See *Ernst Toller*, ed. Kurt Hiller (Reinbek bei Hamburg: Rowohlt Verlag, 1961), p. 135.

[27] Lukács, "The Playful Style," in *Essays on Thomas Mann*, p. 111. Emphasis added.

6. *The Personality of Leo Naphta*

[1] See Mann, *The Magic Mountain*, trans. H. T. Lowe-Porter (New York: Modern Library, n.d.), pp. 328–29. Further page references in the text are made to this edition.

[2] It was Hans Mayer who first called attention to the importance of the concept of personality for Thomas Mann; he devoted one whole chapter to the analysis of this theme but limited its scope by focusing on Mann's own perception of "nonpersonality" on the one hand and "charismatic personality" on the other—the latter represented by the figure of Mynheer Peeperkorn. See Mayer, *Thomas Mann: Werk und Entwicklung* (Berlin: Verlag Volk und Welt, 1955). Mayer did not consider Mann's essayistic treatment of the problem nor its analysis in the novel itself. As Mann pointed out in a short essay, all of Hans Castorp's "mentors" are personalities in one way or another. See "Die Schule des Zauberbergs," in MK 119, p. 317.

[3] Mann assigns a decisive role to the personality of his father in the formation of his own character and values. He speaks of it as "part of [his] inheritance." As he confesses in "Lübeck als geistige Lebensform," it is "the personality of my late father which—as a well-hidden ideal—determines my whole existence." See MK 119, p. 184. In the autobiographical writing "Lebensabriss," Mann explains why he cannot ignore the treatment of the problem of personality: "The problem of man, thanks to the advance of his experimentations upon himself, has attained a *peculiar actuality: the search for his essence, his origin, his goal*, evokes everywhere a new humane interest and sympathy—I am using the word *humane, in its most scientific, objective sense.* ..." See *A Sketch of My Life*, trans. H. T. Lowe-Porter (New York: Alfred A. Knopf, 1960), pp. 66–67.

The stating of the problem is similar to that of philosophical anthropology. Further discussions of the problem are to be found in the Goethe–Tolstoy essay and, of course, in *Reflections of a Non-Political Man*. See especially the chapter on "Politics," where Mann writes: "The human being is not only a social but also a metaphysical being: in other words, he is not only an individual but also a personality. ...for the personality...is the actual bearer of the general element" (p. 179).

[4] Some of the most pertinent discussions of the problem of personality are to be found in Erich Rothacker, *Die Schichten der Persönlichkeit* (1938); Ludwig Klages, *Persönlichkeit* (1928); and Windelband and Heimsoeth, *Lehrbuch der Geschichte der Philosophie*, 15th edition (Tübingen: J.C.B. Mohr [Paul Siebeck], 1957), pp. 577 ff. Unfortunately, the English edition of the volume does not contain the last chapter on twentieth-century philosophical currents. See also S. Calvin Hall and Gardner Linzey, *Theories of Personality* (New York: John Wiley and Sons, 1957), in which personality is defined as a behavioral complex. Gordon W. Allport, who along with most Western theorists holds "the integumented view of the personality system," emphasizes the need for finding the proper way to reconcile psychological and sociocultural sciences for a more appropriate definition of personality. He sees personality as an amalgam of "attitudes, abilities, traits, trends, motives, and pathology of the individual—his cognitive styles, his sentiments, his individual moral nature, and their interrelations." See "The Open System in Personality Theory," in Hendrik M. Ruitenbeek, ed., *Varieties of Personality Theory* (New York: E. P. Dutton, 1964), p. 159. With some exaggeration, one could trace the positing of the problem to Hippocrates, who differentiated between two types: the *habitus apoplecticus* (strong, broad, muscular) and the *habitus phthisicus* (weak, or more precisely, tubercular).

[5] See chapter on "Individualism" and "Personality" in *Philosophisches Wörterbuch* (Stuttgart: Alfred Kröner Verlag, 1965), especially pp. 271 and 449. This is the most concise statement of the German position, and it supplies the literature with which Mann himself was familiar.

[6] Letter to Hans M. Wolff, November 25, 1950. First published by Karl Guthke, "Thomas Mann on his 'Zauberberg', in *Neophilologus* 44, no. 2 (1960), pp. 120–22.

[7] Letter to Pierre-Paul Sagave in *Thomas Mann: Briefe 1889–1936*, pp. 350–51. Not included in the English-language edition. My translation.

[8] Mann, "Lübeck als geistige Lebensform," in MK 119, p. 185. Excerpts from the essay were printed as "A Way of Life and Thought" in the *New York Times*, December 30, 1971, p. 25. As might be expected, only some of the most general statements were included—and none of the more personal, more important ones.

[9] Mann, "Über Karl Kraus," in MK 120 *(Miszellen)*, p. 47. My translation.

[10] Ibid., pp. 47–48.

[11] Mann, "Über Dante," in MK 120, p. 74. My translation.

[12] Mann, "Goethe and Tolstoy," in *Three Essays*.

[13] Mann, "Zum Tode Eduard Keyserlings," in MK 113, p. 96.

[14] Mann, "Goethe and Tolstoy," p. 21. The phrase "accident of birth" *(Malheur vom Geburt)* also occurs in the fictional work *Royal Highness*, where it is applied to Dr. Überbein. This constitutes one more example of Mann's tendency to borrow—even from himself.

[15] Ibid., p. 28.

[16] Ibid., p. 57.

[17] Ibid., p. 62.

[18] Ibid., p. 90.

[19] Ibid., p. 25.

[20] Mann, *Reflections of a Non-Political Man*, p. 179.

[21] See Wilhelm Windelband, *A History of Philosophy*, 2 vols. (New York: Harper Torchbooks 1958), 2, p. 555.

[22] Johann Wolfgang Goethe, "Urworte, Orphisch," in *Gedichte* (Munich: W. Goldmann Verlag, 1958), pp. 279–80. My translation.

[23] See Windelband and Heimsoeth, *Lehrbuch,* pp. 605 ff; and Michael Landmann, *Philosophical Anthropology,* trans. David J. Parent (Philadelphia: Westminster Press, 1974). The German original of Landmann's book is the standard authority in the field and the textbook most widely used at German universities. Landmann gives an account of the reasons for the emergence of this field of investigation and delineates its place among the philosophical disciplines. For a highly informative discussion of Nietzsche as the founder of philosophical anthropology, see Theobald Ziegler, *Die geistigen und sozialen Strömungen des neunzehnten Jahrhunderts* (Berlin: Georg Bondi, 1899), pp. 586 ff. It is possible to call this new field "the newly awakened awareness of the theme: man," as Windelband and Heimsoeth's *Lehrbuch* states (p. 609). The truly interesting question is, however, why at that point the problem of man, of individuality, became a pressing one. Most cultural critical works point to the "crisis situation," meaning the problematic state of culture at the beginning of the twentieth century. As Hermann Noack's study states, there was indeed a crisis situation in which *all* the previous underlying assumptions—including those of the natural sciences, especially of physics—became unhinged. In this state of "disorientation," the interest for an assessment of the human condition was overwhelming and perceived as an urgent need. (Thomas Mann, too, felt the "need" for this assessment as "the order of the day.") The rise of "sciences of man" in diverse forms (from philosophical anthropology to psychoanalysis) is attributed by Noack to man's desire to "grasp his own situation," his own nature and essence, his position in the world as well as his chances and possible risks. See Noack, *Die Philosophie Westeuropas* (Darmstadt: Wissenschaftliche Buchgesellschaft, 1962), pp. 28–30.

[24] See Windelband and Heimsoeth, *Lehrbuch,* p. 609.

[25] Ludwig Klages (1872–1956) first attracted attention as cofounder (with Alfred Schuler, Stefan George, and Karl Wolfskehl) of the so-called Cosmic Circle in Munich around 1900. His relationship with George soured partly because of George's "many Jewish friends" and partly because both had aspired to a leadership role. Klages and his circle were part of the "antipositivistic" and antiprogressive trend, and opted for the primacy of mythology, anthropology, instinct, and intuition. He was described by contemporaries as "a personality." Although his most influential and best-known work is the 1929 monograph, *Der Geist als Widersacher der Seele* (Mind as Enemy of the Soul), based on the body-soul polarity, his biometaphysical studies were published before Mann's *The Magic Mountain.* Thomas Mann was acquainted with Klages's *Prinzipien der Charakterologie* (1910), *Mensch und Erde* (1920) and, especially, with *Die Grundlagen der Charakterkunde* (1923). It is a misunderstanding, in my opinion, to associate Klages with Binet's work, to stress the "utility in educational and vocational selection and guidance" of his ideas, and to assign a "quantitative character" to his efforts, as American psychological textbooks do. See, for example, G. Murphy and J. Kovach, *Historical Introduction to Modern Psychology,* 3d ed. (New York: Harcourt Brace Jovanovich, 1972), p. 423. Thomas Mann perceived the true nature of Klages's ideas, especially in his 1929 book, as a product of the "intellectual anti-intellectuality in which trend can be found the seeds of the Evil that was to come" (meaning: Nazism). In "Leiden an Deutschland," see MK 117, p. 262.

[26] See Mann, *Letters of Thomas Mann,* pp. 213–14.

[27] Hans M. Wolff, *Thomas Mann: Werk und Bekenntnis* (Bern: Francke Verlag, 1957), p. 73.

[28] For the exposition of "charismatic" personalities and types, see Max Weber, "Charismatic Authority," in *Economy and Society,* ed. Guenther Roth and Claus Wittich, 3 vols. (Berkeley: University of California Press, 1978), 1., pp. 241–45. Weber remarks on the relationship between a (genuine) charismatic leader and his followers that "psychologically [the recognition of genuineness] is a matter of complete devotion to the possessor of the quality, arising out of en-

thusiasm, or of despair and hope." Weber's elaboration includes not only heroes, prophets, saviors, and political leaders but also artistic types who may possess "charismatic quality"; among the latter types, the "demagoguery" of Kurt Eisner and Stefan George receive special mention. See pp. 242 and 245.

[29] See *Letters of Thomas Mann*, pp. 182–83.

[30] Hans-Heinz Holz, "Einleitung" in *Nietzsche: Studienausgabe* (Frankfurt am Main: Fischer Bucherei, 1968), 3, p. 9.

[31] Chapter 36, "The Land of Culture," of Part Two in *The Complete Works of Friedrich Nietzsche*, ed. Oscar Levi, trans. Thomas Common (New York: Russel and Russel, 1964), p. 144. This first "complete and authorized" English translation has two drawbacks: first, the unfortunate inclusion of Mrs. Förster-Nietzsche's introduction, "How Zarathustra Came into Being?"; and second, the archaic language chosen by the translator.

[32] See *Letters of Thomas Mann*, p. 28. Mann makes reference to a "sad story [that] went the rounds of the journals—an episode in Dresden between a young musician...and a society lady. It involved an unrequited love...on the part of the woman, and one evening after the theater, the affair came to a bad end in a streetcar." Mann adds that "it made a strong impression on me, and it is not impossible that *one of these days I shall use it as the factual and plot framework* for a wonderfully melancholic love story" (emphasis added). Mann saved the description of this story from 1902; forty-three years later he used it in *Doctor Faustus* for the love story between Rudi Schwerdtfeger and Inez Institoris.

[33] See Mann, "Nietzsche's Philosophy in the Light of Recent History," in *Last Essays*, trans. Richard Winston and Clara Winston (New York: Alfred A. Knopf, 1959), p. 142. First given as a lecture in Zurich in 1947.

[34] See note 4 above and the essay "Individuality and Personality," in E. Hilgard et al., *Introduction to Psychology* (New York: Harcourt Brace Jovanovich, 1971), pp. 356 ff. Special attention is paid to the personality theory formations of Allport and Guilford. While Allport lists ten aspects of the personality, Guilford's system consists of seven: "Physiology, Morphology, Aptitudes, Temperament, Attitudes, Interests and Needs" (p. 423).

[35] Mann, "Dostoevsky—mit Massen" in MK 115, p. 8. Mann let it be known that he was impressed by and learned much from those Dostoevsky heroes who displayed a "tortured spirituality"—this, of course, in addition to the "lessons" imparted to him by Nietzsche. The traits Man alluded to were religiosity, "Easternness" combined with *Enthemmung* (lack of restraint or inhibition), and illness endured with strength *(getragen mit Würde)*.

[36] In this case too, we find a perfectly coordinated cluster of elements such as personality, life spheres, ideology, and geography. Thus, Settembrini means Italy and humanism, i.e., the Renaissance; Naphta means the East, antiprogress, unrestrained spirit, mysticism, irrationality; Mynheer Peeperkorn means Holland, the land of seafarers and planters.

[37] Hasidism, a movement developed among Eastern European Jews in the middle of the eighteenth century. This mystical movement tried to bridge the dualism between nature and mind, world and God, historical present and eschatological past, by way of ecstatic devoutness. To interpret the meaning and thereby to master history is one of the main goals of Hasidism in its original form. For Central European Jewish intellectuals such as Martin Buber (and Georg Lukács), the discovery of this mystical movement became (for a while) a source of inspiration as they perceived the elementary and immediate quality of Jewish religion therein. It is safe to assume that Thomas Mann became aware of Martin Buber's translation of the Hasidic tales that appeared in 1908 and 1906 *(Die Legendes de Baalschem* and *Die Geschichte des Rabbi Nachman)*. Lukács's enthusiastic review of the two books appeared in the Hungarian little magazine, *Szellem* (Logos) in 1911. See Appendix. Lukács's interest was both deep and genuine, as Buber's work

coincided with his discovery of his "Jewishness." Since Thomas Mann could not have known of this fact, it is even more uncanny that this obscure mystical movement (obscure at least in Germany) was connected with Naphta. It is also an interesting coincidence that Lukács's characterization of Jews, mentioned in his review as the customary perception (sharp-witted, brilliant), is attributed by Mann to his outsider types. The impact of Buber's discovery is aptly illustrated by the fact that Georg Simmel, who was the embodiment of a completely assimilated Jewish-German intellectual, was deeply moved by the tales and supposedly exclaimed, "What a curious people we really are!" According to Martin Buber, this was the only time he heard Simmel use the pronoun "we." See "Martin Buber," in *Buch des Dankes an Georg Simmel,* ed. K. Gassen and M. Landmann (Berlin: Duncker and Humblot, 1958), p. 222.

[38] This very character trait of Naphta, together with others described in the chapter "Operationes Spirituales," which present the intellectual portrait of Naphta, allow us to assume that Thomas Mann was cognizant not only of the Sombart book, *Der Bourgeois,* but also of Sombart's next work, *Die Juden und das Wirtschaftsleben* (1911). Especially in the chapter "The Vicissitudes of the Jewish People," Sombart described the kind of "Jewish genius" that is echoed in the Naphta portrait: we hear of the "keen intellect," the "exceptional intellectuality" of the Jews, their "fondness of abstraction," their constant alertness "to new possibilities," "new combinations," and "new goals." We are also told that the sharp and keen intellectuality often enough leads to a tendency for "sophistry and hair-splitting [Rabulistik]." It is easy to see that all of these characteristics crop up in the passages relating to Naphta. See Werner Sombart, *The Jews and Modern Capitalism,* trans. M. Epstein (New York: Collier Books, 1962), pp. 299–323.

[39] In Mann's personal recollections, there is a reference to the very same interest: "the idea of assimilation, of continuation, continuity, of contributing to human tradition...[gained] a power attraction. ...The material belonged to an ancient, primeval realm of civilization and fancy...." In *A Sketch of My Life,* p. 68.

[40] See Mann, "Zum Problem des Antisemitismus," in *Sieben Manifeste zur jüdischen Frage, 1936–1948,* ed. Walter A. Berendsohn (Darmstadt: Joseph Melzer Verlag, 1966), p. 35.

[41] Ibid.

[42] Ibid., p. 39. Interestingly, in describing Joseph's essential nature, Mann uses some of the expressions he applied to Breisacher (and to Oskar Goldberg) in *Doctor Faustus.* The German text says, "Alles Liebenswürdige und Fatale, alles Gewinnende und *Bedenkliche,* alles Bezaubernde und *Ärgerliche* seines [Joseph's] Wesen ergibt sich aus dieser Grundverfassung" (emphasis added).

[43] Ibid., p. 40.

[44] Ibid., pp. 40–41.

[45] Ibid., p. 40.

[46] Ibid., p. 41.

[47] Ibid., p. 24.

[48] Emphasis added. We have here the case of two disparate things brought together to which Naphta's dictum, "Opposites...may be consistent with each other," may apply. In addition, however, there seems to be a break in logic in Mann's statement that Catholicism, being spiritual and antimaterial, is more accessible to the Jewish spirit because of its secular and materialistic bent. Such a gaffe in logic is a very rare occurrence in Mann's work.

[49] See Friedrich Nietzsche, *The Genealogy of Morals,* trans. Francis Golffing (New York: Doubleday Anchor, 1956), p. 256.

[50] Ibid., p. 57.

[51] See Helmut Koopmann, *Die Entwicklung des intellektuellen' Romans be Thomas Mann* (Bonn: H. Bouvier & Co., Verlag, 1962), p. 3.

[52] See Mann, "The Blood of the Walsungs," in *Stories of Three Decades,* p. 299. In depicting

the relationship between Herr Aarenhold and his children, the author touches upon a subject that has not received extensive literary treatment: the phenomenon of Jewish self-hatred. It has been noted in the lives and writings of many enlightened, assimilated Central European Jews, from the ladies of the Berlin salons (Rahel von Varnhagen, Dorothea Mendelssohn, Henrietta Herz, et al.) to Heinrich Heine, up to the twentieth century. Max Brod, Kafka's friend, discusses the phenomenon at some length in his book, *Prager Kreis* (Stuttgart, 1966), and cites Theodor Lessing as a prime example. Lessing devoted a whole book to this subject, *Der jüdische Selbsthass* (Berlin, 1930). Ernst Bloch declared in a conversation with Michael Landmann; "Jewish self-hatred...may be a form of anti-Semitism, claimed by Jews who want to pretend to be something else. But in the case of Marx, Karl Kraus, or Otto Weininger, it is not a hatred à la Lueger; rather, it reminds us of the laments of Isaiah, of the ancient outcry of the prophets against apostasy, usury, and the daughters of Zion. It may be just the sign that one is truly Jewish." (Unpublished conversations; manuscript is in my possession courtesy of Prof. Landmann.) My translation.

[53] Ibid., pp. 302–3.

[54] See Mann, *Royal Highness*, pp. 20–21. Cf. Herr Aarenhold's statement about his origins and motivations, suggesting that early misfortunes and deprivation necessarily result in a special awareness of the limitations set by fate, which has to be countered by "extraordinary efforts."

[55] Ibid., p. 75.

[56] Ibid., p. 71. Thomas Mann's understanding and depiction of the nature of being a "stranger," *(Fremdling)*, an "outsider," is akin to Georg Simmel's *positive conception* of the role of the stranger. In 1908, Simmel stated, "The stranger is... *the person who comes today and stays tomorrow*" (emphasis added). Simmel's perception is colored by his (and his kin's) existence within a "landlocked group." He elaborates: "To be a stranger is... *a very positive relation; it is a specific form of interaction.*" The stranger, as a newcomer (as Naphta was called), as a new element in the group life, has a position "as a full-fledged member [which] involves both being outside it and confronting it." This indicates "how *elements which increase distance and repel... produce* a pattern of *coordination* and consistent *interaction*" (emphasis added). This is precisely the sort of interaction that Dr. Über-bein, Dr. Sammet, and Naphta are thought to provoke. Simmel also touches upon the "objectivity" of the stranger, which is synonymous with "freedom" (from certain bonds and commitments). In certain circumstances, this very freedom may result in producing "emissaries and instigators" (Naphta!); this is one of the possibilities inherent in the position, says Simmel. It should be noted that Simmel's treatise was published at the same time (1908) that Mann was working on *Royal Highness*. It is also one of the most striking examples of sociological postulates to come alive in a work of literature. See Georg Simmel, "The Stranger," in *The Sociology of Georg Simmel,* ed. and trans. Kurt H. Wolff (New York: Free Press, 1950), pp. 402–5. Cf. the treatment of the problem of "Pariahvolk" by Hannah Arendt, in *The Origins of Totalitarianism* (New York: Meridian, 1971); and in Werner J. Cahnman "Pariahs, Strangers and Court Jews: A Conceptual Clarification," *Sociological Analysis* 35, no. 3 (Autumn 1974).

[57] See *Letters of Thomas Mann*, p. 45. While courting Katia Pringsheim, Mann wrote to her in 1904: "Do you know why we suit each other so well? Because you belong to neither the bourgeois nor to the Junker class; because you, in your way, are something extraordinary—because you are, as I understand the word, *a princess*. And I...have always seen myself as a kind of prince, and (in you) have found ... my predestined bride...." The parallels to Prince Klaus Heinrich and Irma Spoelmann, the Jewish outsider of the story, are apparent.

[58] See *Royal Highness*, pp. 101–2.

[59] Ibid., p. 102.

[60] Ibid., pp. 69 and 77. The narrative flow at one point is interrupted by the interpretative statement of the author, which is a crucial one for the understanding of the outsider types in Mann's

oeuvre. "The main point was," writes Mann, "that Doctor Überbein's *doctrines and aoptheoms were so exceptionally supported by his personality*" (emphasis added).

[61] Ibid., p. 78.

[62] Ibid., p. 241.

[63] Ibid., p. 323.

[64] Ibid., p. 327. Emphasis added.

[65] See Koopmann, *Die Entwicklung*, p. 13.

[66] See Bloch, *Thomas Münzer*, pp. 21–25.

[67] Ibid., p. 21. Emphasis added; my translation.

[68] Ibid., p. 94.

[69] Ibid., p. 110.

[70] Ibid., p. 102. There is more to this than connecting Münzer, the Protestant theologian, with Catholic monasticism. Other, diverse influences come into play, including the neoplatonic Plotinus; Meister Eckhart, the medieval mystic; the chiliastic prophecies (of the coming of the Third Reich) of Joachim of Fiore (also a heretic); and biblical allusions. All these themes are bandied about in the debates between Settembrini and Naphta.

[71] Bloch refers here to the "Franciscan spirit" which was supposed to contain the seeds of the revival of genuine Catholicism. We will discuss the importance of the "Franciscan idea" for a considerable segment of left-oriented intellectuals, artists, and philosophers, Jews and Christians alike, in the pre-World War I period. Lukács's interest in Catholicism harkens back to the religious piety and ethics of Saint Francis of Assisi. (See the treatment at a later point of Lukács's "religious period.") It was István Hermann who first pointed out the impact of the ideas and life of Francis of Assisi at the turn of the century, which today seems difficult to comprehend. What attracted these intellectuals and artists was the "critical position" of Saint Francis vis-à-vis an "alienated, formalistic and highly hierarchic, bureaucratic nature of the Church." Lukács and his friends (Ernst Bloch among them) venerated Saint Francis because of his ethics, which, for the first time, postulated ethical duty as intrapersonal. See István Hermann, *Die Gedankenwelt von Georg Lukács* (Budapest: Akadémiai Kiadó, 1978), pp. 35–36.

[72] See Bloch, *Thomas Münzer*, p. 32. Bloch refers in this connection to an earlier treatment of Thomas Münzer's revolutionary spirit and activities in Karl Kautsky's *Vorläufer des Sozialismus*, 2 vols. (Stuttgart: J. H. W. Dietz, 1895). According to Bloch, Kautsky's statement is "very much to the point" that all those religious rebels from the Taborites to the Puritans "chose the Old Testament as their supreme witness," buttressing their arguments with peasant-democratic principles and with one eye on the "final judgment of the apocalypse."

[73] See Benjamin Nelson, *The Idea of Usury* (Chicago: University of Chicago Press, 1969), p. 45. Not much different is the position Karl Marx had taken in his essay "On the Jewish Question." Marx argues by invoking Münzer's ideas and stand: "Thomas Münzer declares it intolerable 'that every creature should be transformed into property—the fishes in the water, the birds of the air, the plants of the earth: the creature too should become free.'" (Lukács takes up this notion again when he speaks of the salvation of not only man but all "creatures.") It is interesting here that Marx's essay connects three spheres that have attained symbolic character in Naphta: the Jewish, the Jesuitic, and the theological, that is, religious spheres. See Karl Marx, "On the Jewish Question," in Robert C. Tucker, ed., *The Marx–Engels Reader*, 2d ed. (New York: W. W. Norton 1978), pp. 50–51.

[74] Bloch, *Thomas Münzer*, pp. 18–19.

[75] Ibid., p. 31.

[76] Ibid., p. 28.

[77] Bloch, *Geist der Utopie* (Frankfurt am Main: Suhrkamp Verlag, 1973). This new edition is

the reproduction of the second edition of 1923. Bloch writes about the "spirit of the North... which has some kinship with the Asiatic spirit due to their shared tendency for internal arousals" (p. 215). The first edition, which we assume Thomas Mann read, appeared in 1918 and contains some fascinating passages on terror, religion, and violence, which were omitted from the second edition. The original (1918) publication was by the Munich–Leipzig firm of Duncker and Humblot. For Bloch, the Bible represents the "peak of the Orient;" thus the concept of the "Russian man" receives an extra dimension. Cf. Thomas Mann, "Russische Anthologie," in MK 113, p. 115.:

[78] See Robert Musil, *Der Mann ohne Eigenschaften* (The Man Without Qualities), (Hamburg: Rowohlt Verlag, 1965), p. 1603.

[79] Ibid.

[80] Ibid., p. 1594.

[81] Bloch, *Geist der Utopie*, p. 213.

[82] Mann, *Letters of Thomas Mann*, esp. pp. 87, 91, and 93.

[83] Ibid., p. 215.

[84] Bloch alludes here to Spengler's *Decline of the West;* the first volume appeared in 1918. Mann's evaluation of Spengler is much the same as Bloch's; in discussing Spengler's "historical pessimism," Mann exclaims that "he is dreadful" *(er ist fatal)*. See "Über die Lehre Spenglers," in MK 113, p. 225.

[85] *Letters of Thomas Mann*, pp. 90–91. Mann refers back to his feelings and considerations of that time in his late novel, *Doctor Faustus*. The narrator, Serenus Zeitblom, reports, "As a moderate man and son of culture I have indeed a natural horror of radical revolution and the dictatorship of the lower classes... [But] my notions about classes and masses take on another colour, and the dictatorship of the proletariat begins to seem to me, a German burgher, an ideal situation compared with the now possible one of the dictatorship of the scum of the earth [i.e., the Nazis]. Bolshevism to my knowledge has never destroyed any works of art." Serenus Zeitblom/Thomas Mann remarks that "twenty-six years ago... revulsion made me think... that my conquered country should turn toward its brother in tribulation, toward Russia." He concludes: "The Russian Revolution shook me. There was no doubt in my mind of the historical superiority of its principles over those of the powers [the Entente] which set their foot on our necks" *(Doctor Faustus*, pp. 339–40). Mann's reminiscences give some credence to Lukács's statement that, politically speaking, Thomas Mann was on his side when they discussed the situation in 1922.

[86] Mann, *Letters*, pp. 92–93.

[87] Mann, *Briefe 1889–1936*, p. 163. Not included in the English-language edition.

[88] See Robert Musil, *Der Mann ohne Eigenschaften*, p. 1592.

[89] See Ferdinand Lion, *Thomas Mann in seiner Zeit* (Zurich–Leipzig: Niehaus Verlag, 1935), p. 124.

[90] One of the most prominent scholars on Jesuitism was Eberhard Gothein, who wrote several studies on the subject. See *Ignatius von Loyola und die Gegenreformation* (Halle: M. Niemeyer Verlag, 1895); and *Reformation und Gegenreformation* (Munich–Leipzig: Duncker & Humblot, 1924). Gothein's work was widely read and discussed; he and his wife were among Lukács's closest friends during his Heidelberg sojourn and also belonged to the "Max Weber *Kreis*." Mann consulted the more popular works on Jesuitism, such as Heinrich Boehmer, *Die Jesuiten: Eine historische Skizze* (Leipzig–Berlin: B. G. Teubner, 1913); *Studien zur Geschichte der Gesellschaft Jesu* (Bonn: A. Falkenroth, 1914), vol. 1; and *Loyola und die deutsche Mystik* (Leipzig–Berlin: B. G. Teubner, 1921). Troeltsch also wrote several studies about the Jesuits and Ranke discussed the Society in his *Papstgeschichte*.

[91] Even such a prudent observer of the contemporary scene as Max Weber, "who despised anti-Semitism," as Marianne Weber notes, "regretted the fact that in those days there were so many

Jews among the revolutionary leaders," and although he thought it understandable that on the basis of the historical situation of the Jews "they particularly produced these revolutionary natures," it was "politically imprudent for Jews to be admitted to leadership." He termed the "foreign Jewish revolutionary leaders" as "*Stamm- und Landfremde*" (belonging to another racial and ethnic group). Marianne Weber concludes that the danger Weber perceived in the situation was that "the great outrage among the population at the revolutionaries and their foreign Jewish leaders" would "result [in] an increase in xenophobia, anti-Semitism, and Pan-Germanism." See Marianne Weber, *Max Weber: A Biography,* trans. and ed. Harry Zohn (New York: Wiley Interscience, 1975), pp. 648–49 and 660–61. Lukács concurred in the above judgment about Weber's integrity: when asked whether he thought Weber might have become reconciled to National Socialism he said emphatically: "No, never. You must understand that Weber was an absolutely honest person. ... he never made concessions to anti-semitism, for instance." Lukács also remarked that Weber "was a sworn enemy of the October and November Revolutions." See *Record of a Life,* pp. 175–76.

[92] In this connection, Robert Michels's important political theoretical work is a case in point. Although Thomas Mann did not know of Michels's work, striking similarities exist in the development of their thinking about what constitutes a "typical Jewish" socialist and revolutionary. Michels lists the following attributes ("specific racial qualities") which make "the Jew a born leader..., a born organizer and propagandist": (1) sectarian fanaticism; (2) invincible self-confidence; (3) oratorical and dialectical aptitudes; (4) a remarkable ambition; and (5) an almost unlimited power of adaptation. Michels calls special attention to "the Magyars," among whom "the most fanatical persons are of the Jewish race." Again, Mann's acute perception of trends, intellectual currents, and sentiments has been vindicated. See Robert Michels, *Political Parties: A Sociological Study of the Oligarchical Tendencies of Modern Democracy.* (1911; reprint ed., New York: Collier Books, 1962), pp. 245–46.

[93] Paul Scherrer, "Vornehmheit, Illusion und Wirklichkeit," in *Blätter der Thomas Mann Gesellschaft,* no. 1 (1958), p. 8.

[94] See "The Jesuits: Catholicism's Troubled Line," in *Time,* April 23, 1973, pp. 40 ff. Not long ago, a monograph appeared in Hungary on the subject of Jesuitism. See Zoltán Rácz, *Jezsuiták tegnap és ma* (Jesuits Yesterday and Today) (Budapest: Kossuth Kiadó, 1974).

[95] See Leopold von Ranke, *Die Geschichte der Päpste,* new ed. (Wiesbaden: Vollmer, 1957), vol. 2.

[96] The popularity of Boehmer's books is evident from the fact that they were so frequently reprinted: his *Geschichte des jesuitischen Ordens* (1904), for example, came out in 1921 in its fourth edition. For more on Boehmer, see note 90 above.

[97] Emphasis added. A new edition of Boehmer's *Ignatius von Loyola,* edited by Hans Leube (Leipzig: Köhler & Ameland, 1941), p. 50. Boehmer died in 1927, leaving his project unfinished. Parts of his studies were incorporated in the biography of Loyola by Richard Blunck, entitled *Der schwarze Papst* (1937). No doubt the fact that this volume was published in Nazi Germany played a role in including an extended discussion of the position of Loyola and the Society toward Jews and their possible acceptance in the order.

[98] Boehmer, *Ignatius von Loyola,* p. 109.

[99] Ibid., p. 48.

[100] See Marx, "On the Jewish Question," p. 51. It should be noted that Marx's treatise, a response to Bruno Bauer's discussion of the emancipation of Jewry in Europe, has been widely discussed and attacked on account of its supposed anti-Semitism. It serves as the basis of the controversial assertion that not only Marx but the socialist movement *in toto* contained a good portion of anti-Semitism from its earliest phase. Considering the indisputable fact that many of

the leaders—if not the majority—of the socialist and communist movements were Jews, this remains a highly contested thesis. See, for example, Edmund Silberner, "Was Marx an anti-Semite?" in *Historica Judaica* 9 (1949), pp. 3–52; and Arnold Künzli, *Karl Marx–Eine Psychographie* (Vienna–Frankfurt–Zurich: Europa Verlag, 1969). Both Silberner and Künzli speak of Marx's "Jewish self-hatred." Cf. Ernst Bloch's statement, note 52 above.

[101] Jacob Marx, "Die Jesuiten als Lehrer des Communismus," in *Jahrbuch für Katholiken auf das Jahr 1847* (Trier, 1846). Jacob Marx was a Catholic theologian from Trier.

[102] Michael Bakunin's "Collective Message to Ogarev, Tata, Ozerov and Serebrennikov, et al.," dated June 1870. In Michael Confino ed., *Daughter of a Revolutionary: Natalia Herzen and the Bakunin–Nechajev Circle* (La Salle, Ill.: Library Press, 1973), pp. 294–95. Emphasis added.

[103] Ibid., p. 292.

[104] Ibid., pp. 295–96.

[105] Harry (Count) Kessler, *In the Twenties: The Diaries of Harry Kessler,* trans. Charles Kessler (New York: Holt, Rinehart and Winston, 1971), p. 36. The date of the entry is December 17, 1918. Emphasis added. Hugo Haase, first chairman in the Reichstag of the Social Democratic Party, left the Party in 1916 for pacifist reasons, along with Karl Kautsky and Eduard Bernstein. W. H. Auden calls Count Kessler one of the "most cosmopolitan men who ever lived," and adds: "There is hardly anyone in political or artistic circles...whom he does not seem to have met." See Auden's review, "A Saint-Simon of Our Time," in the *New York Review of Books,* August 31, 1972, pp. 4 ff. Kessler is also the author of the standard biography of Walter Rathenau.

[106] Fritz Lienhard, "Aus Theologie und Kirche: Rezensionen verschiedener theologischer Neuerscheinungen," in *Neue Schweizer Rundschau* 20, no. 2 (February 1927), pp. 199 ff. Thomas Mann had saved the review and included it in his files, Mp. 4a/93. Notes for the *Joseph* tetralogy at the Thomas Mann Archiv, Zurich.

[107] See René Fülöp-Miller, *The Jesuits: A History of the Society of Jesus,* trans. F. S. Flint and D. F. Tait (New York: Capricorn Books, 1963). Originally published in German, *Macht und Geheimnis der Jesuiten: kulturhistorische Monographie* (Leipzig: Grethlein & Co., 1929). The Hungarian-born author lived in Vienna at that time. Fülöp-Miller selected a passage from Novalis's *Christenheit oder Europa* as the motto for his book; Thomas Mann studied and was influenced by Novalis's treatment during his work on *The Magic Mountain* and relied on it extensively for his 1922 speech, "Von deutscher Republik".

[108] Ibid., pp. 30–31.

[109] Ibid., p. 29.

[110] See Lewis Coser, *Greedy Institutions: Patterns of Undivided Commitment* (New York: Free Press, 1974), p. 123. In his interesting discussion, Coser takes a hard look at certain military collectives whose members are engaged in "an essentially *instrumental* activity." I was intrigued by his quoting a significant passage from the Jesuit *Constitutions* which evokes the injunction of Christ to forsake the world and family to follow him because he who "hates not his father and mother...and his own life...cannot be [his] disciple." This injunction is the same Lukács cites toward the end of his work, "Von der Armut am Geiste." Coser makes it clear that he considers the organizations and their members (Jesuits or communists) as ideal types. For contemporary treatises on the "revolutionary ascetic" which connect the religious and political realms, see Bruce Mazlish, *The Revolutionary Ascetic: Evolution of a Political Type* (New York: McGraw-Hill Paperbacks, 1977); and Michael Walzer, *The Revolution of the Saints: A Study in the Origins of Radical Politics* (New York: Atheneum, 1976).

[111] See Max Frisch, *Tagebücher 1946–1949* (Frankfurt am Main: Suhrkamp Verlag, 1950), p. 280.

[112] See Leszek Kolakowski, "Über die Richtigkeit der Maxime 'Der Zweck heiligt die Mit-

tel,'" in *Der Mensch ohne Alternative: Von der Möglichkeit und Unmöglichkeit, Marxist zu sein* (Munich: Piper & Co. Verlag, 1964), pp. 225 ff.

[113] Ibid., p. 229. The philosophical interpretation of this sort of argumentation has been developed further in another essay, "The Priest and the Jester," in which Kolakowski states that "philosophy has never freed itself from its theological heritage." Contemporary philosophy has taken over from this theological tradition the question "of the very possibility of eschatology." To put it apodictically: Should man rejoice because the ultimate moderator, moral law, will lead to a stage when things even out, and "abundant rewards await us in heaven"? Or: Should one believe that one day "human values will be fully realized" and actively seek the realization of redemption (or actively engage to bring it about, as Lukács's concept of ethical communism suggests)? Ibid., pp. 252 ff. Cf. Kolakowski, "The Priest and the Jester" in *Toward a Marxist Humanism: Essays on the Left Today,* trans. Jane Z. Peel (New York: Grove Press, 1969).

[114] Oswald Spengler, *The Decline of the West,* trans. C. F. Atkinson, 2 vols. (New York: Alfred A. Knopf, 1980). Quoted from vol. 1 p. 341.

[115] Ibid., p. 342.

[116] Mann, *Diaries, 1918–1939,* ed. Hermann Kesten, trans. Richard Winston and Clara Winston (New York: Alfred A. Knopf, 1959), p. 100. Reference is made to George Brandes, *The Romantic School in Germany,* vol. 2 of the series *Main Currents in Nineteenth Century Literature* (New York: Boni & Liveright, 1923). For Mann, the chapter "Novalis" was especially important, pp. 182 ff. For the statement on Novalis's praise "of the priesthood and of the Jesuits," see p. 204.

[117] See Georg Brandes, *Skandinavische Persönlichkeiten,* vol. 2 of the series *Dichterische Persönlichkeiten* (Munich: Albert Langen Verlag für Literatur und Kunst, 1902), p. 368. My translation, emphasis added.

[118] Ibid., p. 272.

[119] See Karl–Heinz Janssen, "Ein Toter auf Urlaub: Levine—das gefährliche Leben eines Weltrevolutionärs," in *Die Zeit,* September 14, 1973, p. 14. Review of the first edition of the memoirs of Leviné's widow, Rosa Meyer–Leviné (1972).

[120] See Rosa Meyer–Leviné, *Leviné: Leben und Tod eines Revolutionärs; Erinnerungen* (Frankfurt am Main: Fischer Taschenbuch Verlag, 1974). This is a remarkable document of the events leading up to and occurring during the 1919 revolution in Bavaria, and a highly interesting account of the fate, life style, and thinking of many of the Russian-Jewish emigrées—socialists, anarchists, or just plain intellectuals—in Germany during World War I and the early period of the Weimar Republic. Appended are some fascinating documents of the trial for high treason following the collapse of the Soviet Republic.

[121] See Marianna Weber, *Max Weber,* esp. p. 660. See also Thomas Mann, *Tagebücher 1918–1921* (Frankfurt am Main: S. Fischer Verlag, 1979), pp. 223 ff. and 236. How closely Mann followed the unfolding of events is illustrated by his jotting down on "Sunday, May 3, 1919, 11:30 a.m.": "Levine–Niessen was arrested today" (p. 224). At the same time, Mann reports a conversation about "the *type of the Russian Jew* as leader of world movement, this *explosive mixture* of intellectual-radical and eastern-Christian visionary elements" (emphasis added), and adds, "Immediately, I thought of incorporating these Russian (Eastern)-chiliastic-communistic things into my 'Zbg'" (p. 223). See also Mann's harsh words on the leadership of the Soviet Republic being composed" of the "Jewish literati" such as Wieland Herzog, Erich Mühsam, and Ernst Toller (pp. 63–64).

[122] Georg Lukács, "Erst Demokratie, dann Wirtschaftsreform." Interview with G. Klos, P. Petkovic, and J. Breuer, second session. In *Neues Forum* 17 (Mid–March 1970), p. 377. Emphasis added. See also Lukács, *Lenin: A Study on the Unity of His Thought,* trans. Nicholas Jacobs (Cambridge: M.I.T. Press, 1971). On Lenin's personality see "Postscript 1967," p. 93.

[123] Lukács, "Erst Demokratie," p. 377.

[124] For an account see Fritz J. Raddatz, *Lukács in Selbstzeugnissen und Bilddokumenten* (RoRoRo, 1972), p. 42.

[125] Mann, "Über Königliche Hoheit," in MK 119, pp. 32–33.

[126] Mann, "A Weary Hour," in *Last Essays*, p. 208.

[127] Lukács, "Platonism, Poetry and Form: Rudolf Kassner," in *Soul and Form*, trans. Anna Bostock (Cambridge: M.I.T. Press, 1974), pp. 21–22. Emphasis added.

[128] Lukács, "The Bourgeois Way of Life and Art for Art's Sake: Theodor Storm," ibid., p. 55.

[129] Ibid., pp. 55–56. Emphasis added. There are other, equally important passages marked by Mann, with added notes in the margin in some cases. One of the passages declares that "the bourgeois order...is only a mask that hides a most self-willed and anarchistic preoccupation with the self..." (p. 56). Mann no doubt recognized the special critical sensitivity that informed this statement, and also recognized himself in it.

[130] Ibid., p. 56.

[131] Lukács was twenty-two years old when he first met Irma Seidler (1883–1911). She was born into a middle-class Hungarian Jewish family of Budapest; among her cousins were Karl and Michael Polányi and Ervin Szabó, a syndicalist Marxist and one of Lukács's mentors in Marxism. Her brother, Ernö S., was a cofounder of the Hungarian Communist Party (November 1918) and perished in the Stalinist purges in the Soviet Union. Her sister, Emmy, married Emil Lederer, professor at Heidelberg, and after the Nazi takeover, at the New School for Social Research in New York City. Like her sister, she committed suicide (1933). Lukács made Irma's acquaintance at the salon of "Mama Cecile," mother of the Polányis and a famous Budapest hostess, on December 18, 1907. She studied to be a painter and when she traveled to Florence, Lukács and his best friend, Leo Popper, accompanied her. As Lukács noted in his diary, Irma meant "Life" and as such presented a challenge to Lukács's absolute commitment to "Work." Lukács was unable at that time to commit himself to marriage and life in the ordinary sense of the word (cf. Thomas Mann and Franz Kafka). Irma subsequently went to Nagybánya, a well-known artist colony (now Baia Mare, Romania), where she met and married Károly Réthy, a fellow painter. Before and during her marriage, she maintained a heavy correspondence with Lukács, which mirrors the doubts, Lukács's vacillation, and, finally, the realization of the "unbridgeable gap between man and woman, work and life, as the paradigm of the universal tragedy of human alienation" (Congdon). As Lukács summed up the situation in a letter to his friend Leo on December 10, 1910: "It...has been accomplished—the exclusion of 'life.' This doesn't have to mean asceticism in absolute terms. It merely means that the center of gravity has ultimately...shifted toward 'work.'...The Irma case had a decisive importance for my life: there was someone who was able to touch the inner core of my existence, who meant *life* to me, and who was woven into all of my thoughts and feelings. And then she left (and *how* she left!) and I am alive and moving around. One can die of something like this but once one survives, the case is finished" (my translation). Although Lukács did not die "of it," Irma Seidler did. Her marriage never became a meaningful relationship for her, and she had a brief affair with one of Lukács's friends, Béla Balázs, who, however, broke off with her on account of his friendship with Lukács. The same evening, on May 18, 1911, Irma Seidler jumped to her death from a bridge over the Danube. Lukács was consumed by feelings of guilt; as once before, he contemplated suicide. But on December 15, 1911, he jotted down in his diary: "The crisis appears to be at an end." Lukács's existential crisis found its expression in the essays of *Soul and Form* (the book is dedicated to Irma Seidler) and, above all, in two "artistic" products: the first is a so-called fairy tale, "The Legend of King Midas" (November 1908), and the second the dialogue "On Poverty of Spirit" (1912). This confessional work represents the beginnings of the second (Kierkegaardian) stage of Lukács's life. For the best account of the Lukács–Irma Seidler relationship see Lee Congdon

The Young Lukács (Chapel Hill: University of North Carolina Press, 1983). See also Judith Marcus and Zoltán Tar, eds., *Georg Lukács: Selected Correspondence. 1902–1920*, especially the exchange of letteres between Irma Seidler, Lukács, Leo Popper, and Paul Ernst.

[132] György Lukács, *Napló – Tagebuch: 1910–1911; Das Gericht (1913)*, ed. Ferenc L. Lendvai (Budapest: Akadémiai Kiadó, 1981), p. 26.

[133] Ibid., p. 23. Date of the entry is May 20, 1910. Lukács singles out four essays as reflecting most truly his state of mind: those on Stefan George, Kierkegaard, Richard Beer-Hoffman, and Charles–Louis Philippe. He calls the last one ("Longing and Form") "the Irma essay." Its first German-language publication was in *Die Neue Rundschau* (February 1911) where Thomas Mann first read it originally. Cf. n. 51, chapter one, above.

[134] Letter of Leo Popper to Lukács, June 7, 1909. See letter no. 33 in *Georg Lukács: Selected Correspondence*.

[135] Lukács, *Soul and Form*, p. 30.

[136] Ibid., p. 31. The strongly autobiographical nature of these reflections is illustrated by Lukács's letter of January 1909 to a young woman whom he was courting in Budapest: "I wanted desperately to resist the temptation to let go, and so *I held on to the mask* with both hands so tightly that the plaster-cast cut into my flesh. I was hoping it would adhere so that there would be no hours of weakness anymore....But the question remains: why *the fear...that somebody would glimpse what is behind the mask?*" See *Georg Lukács: Selected Correspondence*, letter no. 26.

[137] Lukács, *Soul and Form*, p. 29.

[138] Ibid., p. 31. Emphasis added.

[139] Ibid., pp. 31–32. Emphasis added.

[140] Ibid., p. 29.

[141] Ibid., p. 40. Emphasis added.

[142] Ibid., p. 32. Emphasis added.

[143] Lukács, *Napló*, p. 26. Date of entry is May 29, 1911.

[144] Lukács, *Soul and Form*, p. 41.

[145] Lukács, "On the Nature and Form of the Essay: A Letter to Leo Popper," ibid., p. 2. The content and language of the essay let us conclude that while he is ruminating about the essay as a form of art, Lukács reveals his own problematic self. It is helpful to approach the often complex, extremely abstract, and sometimes barely comprehensible statements on the art form with this in mind. There is, for example, the passage about the interweaving of experience, intellectuality, and world view: "There are experiences," writes Lukács, "which cannot be expressed by any gesture and which yet long for expression." It is the "*intellectuality,* conceptuality as *sensed experience [sentimentales Erlebnis],* as immediate reality, as spontaneous principle of existence; the *world view* in its undisguised purity *as an event of the soul [seelisches Ereignis]*" (p. 7; emphasis added). Here lies a partial explanation for Lukács's attitude toward "Life" (meaning: love, interpersonal relationship). Form is the "great event" of the soul, that which is really alive. This "form" as "experience" becomes "a world view," and as such, "a standpoint, an attitude vis-à-vis the life from which it sprang: a possibility of reshaping it, of creating it anew." It is therefore, the form which contains the ethical thrust. "Form...is the voice with which [to] address...questions to life" (p. 8).

[146] Ibid., p. 15.

[147] Ibid.

[148] See Friedrich Nietzsche, *The Genealogy of Morals*, trans. Francis Golffing (Garden City, NY: Doubleday Anchor Books, 1956), pp. 250–51.

[149] Ibid., p. 154.

[150] Ibid., p. 256. These statements of Nietzsche have provided the arguments for those inter-

preters who regard Naphta's ideological stand as an act of revenge on mankind corresponding to Nietzsche's concept of "ressentiment." See, for example, Hans M. Wolff, *Thomas Mann: Werk und Bekenntnis* (Bern: Francke, 1957).

[151] Lukács, *Soul and Form*, p. 24. Emphasis added. Dogma is not to be understood in a "churchly" sense, as Naphta would say. For Lukács, the "longing for dogma" and measure is an ardent yearning and search for "system." We may read it as a desire born out of the *Heil und Schutzinstinkt* which alone could provide a degree of "security" in a fragmented world. From this vantage point, it becomes clear what Lukács meant when he said in an 1968 interview: "When all is said and done, there are only three truly great thinkers in the West, incomparable with all others: Aristotle, Hegel and Marx." See *New Left Review* 68 (July-August 1971), p. 58. What these three truly great thinkers have in common is the construction of a philosophical system.

[152] Lukács, *Soul and Form*, p. 36.

[153] According to Kurt Hruby, Jewish Messianism is the result of a development in the history of ideas in which "political and religious elements have an equal role." See "Der talmudische Messianismus," in *Emuna* 9, no. 5 (November-December 1974), p. 324. Hermann Cohen also emphasizes the "this-wordly" aspect of Messianism when stating that "the ethical worth of Messianism lies in its political ramifications." In *Ethik des reinen Willens*, 2d edition (Berlin, 1907), p. 406. Martin Buber speaks of the messianic strain in Judaism in a similar vein when he exclaims, "The yearning is burning and the Absolute has to become reality." See *Die jüdische Mystik* (Munich-Heidelberg: Kösel Verlag KG, 1963), p. 12. This is the third volume of the collected works in German. Cf. Ernst Bloch's *Geist der Utopie*, and Lukács's and Naphta's statements. Martin Buber espoused this special kind of utopian socialism, which had its roots in both Messianism and Marxism and which had to respond to "society...with its present contradictions." What was akin in Bloch's, Lukács's, and Buber's "utopian socialism" was the "quest for a regenerated man" in a restructured society. And thus, writes Buber, "into these 'utopian' social systems there enters all the force of dispossessed Messianism. The social system of modern socialism or communism has, like eschatology, the character of an annunciation or of a proclamation." See *Paths in Utopia*, trans. R. F. C. Hull (Boston: Beacon Press, 1960), p. 9. Karl Löwith sees Marx as part of this tradition: "The real driving force *behind Marx's conception is* a transparent Messianism which has its unconscious root in *Marx's own being, even in his race.* ... It is *the old Jewish messianism and prophetism...and a Jewish insistence on absolute righteousness* which explains the idealistic basis of Marx's materialism" (emphasis added). In *Meaning in History* (Chicago: University of Chicago Press, 1962), p. 45. This messianic consciousness is demonstrably present in Lukács's early writings, from *Soul and Form* to "On Poverty of Spirit" up to his "Tactics and Ethics" of 1919. In stating that "the essayist's judgment" is based on criteria awakened by "the great value-definer of aesthetics, the one who is always about to arrive" (*Soul and Form*, p. 16), Lukács transports the messianic concept (and language) into an alien sphere: into the realm of aesthetic.

[154] See Elfie Stock Raymond, "The Future Comes by Itself. Progress Does Not." Unpublished paper, quoted by permission of the author.

[155] Lukács, *Soul and Form*, p. 16. Emphasis added.

[156] Ibid., p. 34.

[157] Ibid.

[158] Ibid.

[159] Ibid., p. 35.

[160] See Paul Ernst, "Gespräch mit Georg Lukács: Aus der Rahmengeschichte des Novellenbandes 'Die Taufe'," in *Paul Ernst und Georg Lukács: Dokumente einer Freundschaft*, ed. Karl-August Kutzbach (Emstetten]West.: Verlag Lechte, 1974), p. 88.

[161] Ibid., p. 89.

[162] See Mann, "At the Prophet's," in *Stories of Three Decades,* pp. 288–89. A closer look at the contemporary account reveals not only an increased interest in matters religious but also its divergent manifestations. Although Mann presented a hysterical variation of the type, he was not off the mark when he generalized thus: "Strange minds, strange realms of the spirit" wrestled here "with devastatingly ultimate ideals," and delivered their "proclamations" in which "fevered and frightfully irritated" egos expanded themselves (pp. 283–88). The German poet and revolutionary Ernst Toller's reflections on the *Zeitgeist* during the World War I show just how wide and diverse were these religious impulses which he calls *neue Stimmung* (the new mood). See "Eine Jugend in Deutschland," in *Ernst Toller,* ed. Kurt Hiller (Reinbek at Hamburg: Rowohlt Verlag, 1961), pp. 75–77. Paul Ernst's notes and brief essays from the period illustrate the intensity of the preoccupation and the shared experience with Lukács. And finally, there exists a little-known letter of Lukács from March 1913, composed as an answer to a questionnaire sent to him by Felix Bertaux, a French scholar. The questionnaire intended to address the problems that at that time preoccupied German artists and critics. Responding to a question about the "chances of contemporary German literature," Lukács wrote:

> It is fortunate that in Germany the dissatisfaction with today's disoriented state of affairs...grows steadily. The significance of the dissatisfaction, *the yearning for a real Gemeinschaft,* is in its accent on sentiment, which lies somewhere other than in the renewal of the arts; it lies rather in the hope *for a reawakening of German philosophy and religiosity.* Because here and only here lies the opportunity for a German *Kultur* (and as its necessary consequence, a German art). Germany has never possessed a culture in the sense of France or England; in its best periods her culture was but an "invisible church," the all-penetrating and *Weltanschauung-*creating power of philosophy and religion (emphasis added).

See letter no. 113; cf. letter no. 111. In *Georg Lukács: Selected Correspondence.* My translation.

[163] Lukács, *Soul and Form,* pp. 34–35.

[164] Lucien Goldmann, "The Early Writings of Georg Lukács," in *Tri-Quarterly,* Special Issue, no. 9 (Spring 1967), pp. 165 ff. This is a somewhat shortened version of the French-language essay in *Temps Modernes,* no. 195 (August 1962).

[165] Even in the last months of his life, when Lukács finally agreed to commit his autobiographical sketch *(Gelebtes Denken)* to paper and was submitting to questions about certain points of his brief text (fifty-seven typewritten pages), he was reluctant to elaborate on this question. Only this much was said: "Of pure Jewish family. For that very reason: the ideologies of Judaism had no influence whatever on my spiritual development." See *Record of a Life,* p. 26. When queried further, he said only that "the *Leopoldstadt* [Lipótváros] families were completely indifferent to all religious matters,...[They] interested us as a matter of family convention," as they played "a certain role at weddings and other ceremonies" (ibid.). But at the same time, Lukács jotted down notes about his evolution which he judged led him into a "theoretical cul-de-sac": "Kierkegaard: rejection of art as life-principle in the name of a...gradually emerging ethic. ...Now the 'Luciferian' nature of such a philosophical conception in the name of an *ethical revolution, which should lead* to a genuine 'redemption.'..." See *Record of a Life,* p. 153. Lukács's was an ethical religiosity.

[166] See Béla Kőhalmi, ed., *Könyvek könyve* (A book on books) (Budapest: Lantos Kiadása, 1918), pp. 166 ff. Cf. Lukács, *Record of a Life,* p. 28.

[167] See Béla Balázs, *Napló: 1903–1914* (Diaries), ed. Anna Fábri (Budapest: Magvető, 1982), vol. 1, pp. 518–20. Excerpts appeared in English, "Notes from a Diary," ed. É. Fekete, in *New Hungarian Quarterly* 13, no. 47 (Autumn 1972), pp. 123 ff.

[168] Ibid., p. 519. Emphasis added.

[169] Ibid., p. 520. Emphasis added.

[170] Ibid.

[171] Ibid., pp. 506–7. Emphasis added. Emma Ritoók, Hungarian philosopher and participant in the Sunday Circle, had much the same reaction to the spiritual "symbiosis" between Bloch and Lukács. She wrote to Lukács that in spite of her mediation between the two, she was displeased by the obvious influence of Bloch on Lukács's way of thinking. "By influence I do not mean that you are in the process of adopting Bloch's philosophical system. ... But, at our last meeting, you discussed the relationship between form and matter in terms of such comparisons as: pure form is Christ and pure matter is Anti-Christ (and there was mention of a possible synthesis on the basis of *coincidentia oppositorum*). This way of thinking, the theological wording of ideas and concept, I heard the first time from Bloch—and I believe, it is unworthy of the high quality of your thinking..." (my translation), letter of January 17, 1913. See *Lukács György levelezése: 1902–1917*, ed. Éva Fekete and Éva Karádi (Budapest: Magvető Kiadó, 1981), pp. 516–19. First German translation is in my dissertation, *Thomas Mann und Georg Lukács*, 1976, published in 1982. In my opinion, Emma Ritoók's criticism of Bloch and his influence is too harsh; after all, we can find this "theological wording" already in Lukács's essay period, that is, before he had made the acquaintance of Bloch in the winter of 1910.

[172] Béla Balázs, *Napló*, pp. 613–14. Emphasis added. See also Werner Sombart, *The Jews and Modern Capitalism*, trans. M. Epstein (New York: Collier Books, 1962). Sombart writes, for example, that "the conception of the universe in the mind of such an intellectual people must perforce have been that of a structure well-ordered in accordance with reason. By the aid of reason, therefore, they sought to understand the world; they were rationalists, both in theory and practice" (p. 248). Sombart makes the categorical statement that "we can scarcely think of a Jewish mystic like Jacob Böhme" (p. 246). Lukács's reaction was swift and negative.

[173] Balázs, *Napló*, pp. 613–14.

[174] Lukács's review of Martin Buber's translation of Hasidic tales contains some of the formulations and topics mentioned in Balázs's diary, such as transmigration of souls and Hasidism. See Lukács, "Jewish Mysticism," in Appendix.

[175] See Hans Wysling, "'Geist und Kunst': Thomas Mann's Notizen zu einem Literaturessay," in *Quellenkritische Studien zum Werk Thomas Manns*, ed. Paul Scherrer and Hans Wysling (Bern-Munich: Francke, 1967), vol. 1.

[176] Lukács, "On the Romantic Philosophy of Life: Novalis," in *Soul and Form*, pp. 45–56. Emphasis added.

[177] Ibid., p. 48.

[178] Ibid., p. 49.

[179] Ibid., p. 50.

[180] Ibid., pp. 50–51. Emphasis added.

[181] See Wysling, "Geist und Kunst," p. 136.

[182] Mann, "Der Künstler und der Literat," in MK 113, p. 80.

[183] Wysling, "Geist und Kunst," p. 148.

[184] Lukács, *Soul and Form*, p. 16.

[185] Ibid., p. 24.

[186] Lukács, "Von der Armut am Geiste: Ein Brief und ein Gespräch," in *Neue Blätter*, nos. 5–6, second part (1912), pp. 67 ff. In the following, referred to as "Poverty of Spirit." My translation. As of today, there exists no *authorized* English-language translation of this work. For information on the events which inspired this confessional "dialogue," see note 131 above Cf. Lukács's *Napló–Tagebuch, Record of a Life*, and *Georg Lukács: Selected Correspondence*. The "plot" of this writing can be summed up in a few sentences: A man learns of the tragic suicide of a friend

[Irma Seidler]. He sends a note to the sister of the dead woman [Emmy Seidler–Lederer]. She looks him up because she senses the desperation behind his declaration that he wants to be alone, that he "doesn't need anyone." During their long-winded discussion, he accepts the blame for the friend's death because his attitude and actions were governed by the (Kantian) ethics of duty instead of the "ultimate goodness," meaning the identification with the other person. Much of the dialogue is an indictment of the formal ethic in the name of the individual ethic. Goodness is defined as "miracle, grace and redemption." Informed by Kierkegaard, the mystics, Old Testament deeds, and the ethical world of Agamemnon, Lukács's concept of ethics amounts to "the teleological suspension of the "ethical" (Kierkegaard). Abraham of the Old Testament possessed "goodness" because he was willing to sin and kill his innocent son at the behest of the absolute command. Goodness is beyond morality. At the end of the dialogue, the protagonist puts a bullet through his head (just like Naphta!), leaving an open Bible on his desk as the only clue to his action, in which he has marked the following passage: "I know thy works, that thou art neither cold nor hot: I would thou wert cold or hot. So then because thou art lukewarm and neither hot nor cold, I will spue thee out of my mouth" (Revelation: 3:15 and 16). It should be noted that two contemporary writings had also influenced Lukács's thinking and some of the arguments of the dialogue: First was Thomas Mann's *Tonio Kröger*, especially the conversation between Lisaweta and Tonio during which the dangers of a purely aesthetic existence were broached. Second was Georg Simmel's 1908 essay, "Der Arme," especially Simmel's statement that there is a fundamental opposition between the sociological and ethical categories and the "rights of the poor." Simmel's conception of goodness and love underlies Lukács's reflections, as the following excerpts illustrate: "*Mit einem Radikalismus...im Sinne ethischidealer Konstruktion...könnten alle Leistungen der Liebe und des Mitleids...als Rechte des Empfangenen aufgefasst werden. Der ethische Rigorismus [Kant]...hat behauptet, das Äusserste, was ein Mensch...leisten könne, sei die Erfüllung der Pflicht*" (emphasis added). See "Der Arme," in *Soziologie* (1908; reprint ed., Berlin: Duncker & Humblot, 1968), p. 345. Unfortunately, the English-language edition omitted a lengthy passage from the essay, which contained the above statement. See *Georg Simmel on Individuality and Social Forms*, ed. Donald N. Levine (Chicago: University of Chicago Press, 1971), pp. 150 ff.

188 Lukács, *Soul and Form*, p. 40.

189 See Wysling, "Geist und Kunst," pp. 162 and 184.

190 Lukács, "Von der Armut," p. 83.

191 Ibid., pp. 85 and 89. Emphasis added.

192 Ibid., p. 88.

193 Ibid., p. 85.

194 Ibid., p. 80.

195 Ibid., p. 75.

196 Ibid., p. 79. Emphasis added.

197 Ibid., p. 78.

198 Ibid., p. 80.

199 Ibid., p. 70.

200 Frigyes Karinthy, *Így írtok ti!* (This is How You All Write!) (Budapest: Szépirodalmi Kiadó, 1959), vol. 1, pp. 145–48. Cf. István Hermann, *Die Gedankenwelt von Georg Lukács* (Budapest: Akadémiai Kiadó, 1978), p. 36.

201 Lukács, "Von der Armut," p. 74.

202 See "Ernst Bloch und Georg Lukács im Gespräch mit Iring Fetscher, Johannes B. Metz und Jürgen Moltmann." in *Neues Forum* 14, nos. 167–168 (November-December 1967), pp. 837 ff. It is important to know in this respect that both Lukács and Bloch had been influenced

at a certain stage of their development by Simmel, at whose "house-seminar" they often heard his discourse on Eckhart. As Bloch put it, "Our symbiosis, how shall I say: it went from Eckhart to Hegel." Ibid., p. 839.

[203] See Margarete Susman, "Erinnerungen an Georg Simmel," in *Buch des Dankes an Georg Simmel,* ed. Kurt Gassen and Michael Landmann (Munich: Duncker & Humblot, 1958), pp. 283–84.

[204] Lukács's response to a questionnaire about the books that influenced his development. As Balázs's diary entries indicated, Sebastian Franck's (1500–45) view of human existence as one great battleground of opposite forces colored Lukács's concept of God (and evil). Valentin Weigel (1533–88) was first a recipient and later a transmitter of Franck's *Gotteslehre* to the Protestant mystic, dialectician, and sectarian Jakob Böhme (1575–1624). Of Böhme too it was said that "there was something irregular, schismatic, about him" and his theosophy had a "gnostic–world–negating" strain to it. Böhme's thought contained some of Plotinus's themes and this must have appealed to Lukács, who around 1910 was preoccupied with Plotinus's aesthetics, especially his concept of the "intellectual beauty," that is, that which is beyond the empirical world. Moreover, Böhme's view of the world process as a struggling of the will between good and evil, extending the *coincidentia oppositorum* to an extreme limit, meaning, that God's goodness is revealed in his anger (punishment), finds its echo in Lukács and Balázs's discussions (the Luciferian principle) and in "On Poverty of Spirit." See Balázs, *Napló;* and *Georg Lukács: Selected Correspondence,* especially letter no. 58.

[205] For a discussion see Klaus Peter, *Idealismus als Kritik: Friedrich Schlegels Philosophie der unvollendeten Welt* (Stuttgart–Berlin: W. Kohlhammer Verlag, 1973), p. 9. See also fn. 4 and p. 10.

[206] Leszek Kolakowski, "The Priest and the Jester," in *Toward a Marxist Humanism: Essays on the Left Today,* trans. Jane Zielonko Peel (New York: Grove Press, 1969), pp. 9 ff.

[207] Lukács, "Von der Armut," p. 82.

[208] Ibid., pp. 82–83. Emphasis added.

[209] See Hermann Cohen, *Religion der Vernunft aus den Quellen des Judentums* (Leipzig: G. Fock GmbH, 1919), p. 381.

[210] See Leo Baeck, *The Essence of Judaism* (New York: Schocken Books, 1970), pp. 31–32 (The German original, *Das Wesen des Judentums,* appeared in 1905). Baeck's work, considered the classic presentation of Judaism in his time, was engendered by his argument with Adolf Harnack's 1900 publication, *Das Wesen des Christentums.* For the best exposition on Baeck's life and work, see Albert H. Friedlander, *Leo Baeck. Teacher of Theresienstadt* (New York: Holt, Rinehart and Winston, 1968), esp. Chapter Four, "The Essence of Judaism," pp. 61 ff.

[211] Baeck, *Essence,* p. 59. Emphasis added.

[212] Ibid., p. 41. For a recent excellent discussion on the emergence of ethical monotheism, see Irving M. Zeitlin, *Ancient Judaism: From Max Weber to the Present* (Cambridge: Polity Press, 1984), pp. 70 ff. On the ethical aspect of Judaism, see also J. Marcus and Z. Tar, "The Judaic Element in the Teachings of the Frankfurt School," in *Leo Baeck Year–Book XXXI* (London: 1986) pp. 339–53.

[213] Baeck, *Essence,* p. 61.

[214] Quoted in Friedlander, *Leo Baeck,* p. 64. Friedlander's references are to the first (1905) German-language edition of Baeck's *Essence of Judaism.* (Some of the passages are left out of the English-language edition). For further elaboration see Baeck, *Essence,* pp. 61–62. Cf. Lukács, "Von der Armut," pp. 90–91.

[215] See Baeck, *Essence,* p. 129.

[216] Lukács, "Von der Armut," p. 74.

[217] See Baeck, *Essence,* p. 195. Contrary to St. Augustine's saying that "God and the soul, and

nothing else" matter, the whole and true content of Judaism is not the self-centered faith, but our relation to our fellow man which is thereby "lifted out of the sphere of good will, affection, or even love; it is exalted into the sphere of the established relationship with God..." (p. 194). This exaltation is described in the hero's definition of "Goodness" of the Lukácsian dialogue. Cf. Kurt Hruby, "Der talmudische Messianism," pp. 342 ff.

[218] Lukács, "Von der Armut," p. 79.

[219] Ibid., p. 75.

[220] Ibid. "Güte ist...das wahre Heimfinden des Menschen."

[221] Lukács, of course, also alludes to Sombart's notion that the "rationalizing tendency" is the most striking attribute not only of the Jews but of Judaism itself. Little wonder that the book's index does not contain the word "messianism." See Sombart, *Jews and Modern Capitalism.* As to the historical background against which the messianic movement and its aspirations should be judged, we find a most apt description in Johann Maier's magnificent study, *Das Judentum* (Munich: Kindler Verlag. Reihe 'Kindlers Kulturgeschichte', 1973); see also Kurt Hruby's and Henning Günther's essays. The well-known scholar of German literature Walter Muschg gives a somewhat exalted account from another perspective. He calls this modern type of "messianic fanatic" the "mystic of politics." See, *Tragische Literaturgeschichte* (Bern: Francke Verlag, 1953), pp. 110 ff.; one of the most insightful studies from a social scientific perspective is Julius I. Löwenstein, *Marx Contra Marxism,* trans. Harry Drost (London: Routledge & Kegan Paul, 1980). The German title is more appropriate to the content: *Vision und Wirklichkeit* (1970). Löwenstein's treatment of the messianic element is also relevant to Lukács's later development and the continuance of the messianic strain in his thought as one more point of linkage between the pre-Marxist and Marxist thought of Lukács. In the sub-chapter "The religious element in communism," Löwenstein discusses the "messianic or millennarian element" which gave "a special dynamic" to continental socialism: he illustrates this with Lessing's exclamation in his *Education of the Human Race* that "it will come, it will certainly come, the time of consummation," when human reason will "attain its full enlightenment." Similarly, in the nineteenth century, Wilhelm Weitling, the first German socialist, "accepted communism as 'the Gospel'," But "the Jews, who had been expecting the Messiah for more than two millennia, were especially predestined to become the prophets of socialism. Above all, *those Jews who had renounced Judaism endeavoured to give a new contemporary* meaning *to* the traditional content of *messianic expectations*," concludes Löwenstein; Ernst Bloch came to a similar assessment. See pp. 26–29. In that Löwenstein compares this first generation of assimilated Jewish intellectuals in central Europe to the situation of the Westernized liberals in Russia, he finds Dostoevsky's psychological analysis particularly adept: the fanaticism for ideas is an unconscious protest against an alien world and a yearning for "the motherland," the state of redemption, at the same time (see p. 28). Löwenstein regards Kierkegaard's concept of the "demonic" as a symbol for the striving for the absolute in a relative world, engendered by experience of the world. It is possible to interpret the complexity of Lukács's spiritual makeup from this perspective. This short discussion of the concept and the contemporary view of messianism would not be complete without mentioning some of the most important treatises on the subject. From the Jewish perspective, the classic work of the twentieth century is Gershom Scholem's book, *The Messianic Idea in Judaism and Other Essays on Jewish Spirituality* (New York: Schocken Books, 1971), for an insightful treatment of central European messianic thought, see Michael Löwy, "Jewish Messianism and Libertarian Utopia in Central Europe (1900–1933)," in *New German Critique,* no. 20 (Spring/Summer 1980), pp. 105–15; on the German–Jewish constellation, see Joseph B. Maier, "Jüdisches Erbe aus deutschem Geist," a lecture delivered on the International Conference: Critique of Instrumental Reason: On the Occasion of Max Horkheimer's Ninetieth Birthday (Frankfurt am Main, September 1985); from the Christian

perspective, see Arnold Künzli, "Zur Befreiung der Emanzipation von der Hypothek der Erlösung," in *L'80: Zeitschrift für Literatur und Politik* 35 (September 1985); and Hans Küng, *Christ Sein* (Munich, 1974); Karl Löwith's work has been mentioned before: he was the teacher of Jürgen Habermas and decisively contributed to Habermas's sensitivity toward those subterranean impulses that German idealism received from the Kabbalah and Jewish messianism, from Jakob Böhme through Schelling to Marx. Habermas devoted a series of essays to the critical assessment of other thinkers and the German-Jewish philosophical constellation. The essays have been published under the title *Philosophical–Political Profiles*, trans. Frederick G. Lawrence (Cambridge: M.I.T. Press, 1983). See especially the essays on Bloch, Scholem, and on "The German Idealism of the Jewish Philosophers," pp. 21 ff., 61 ff. and 199 ff.

²²² My unpublished interview with Georg Lukács. Cf. Thomas Mann's letter to Dr. Seipel, in Appendix. For an account of Lukács's activities in the years of exile, see Julius (Gyula) Háy, *Geboren 1900* (Reinbek bei Hamburg: Christian Wegner Verlag, 1971), pp. 106 ff.

²²³ Except for *totality*, emphasis added. Lukács wrote the letter on June 15, 1910 to Leo Popper, his most intimate friend about whom he felt "with the old vehemence and intensity" that he was his "only reader, the only one who counts." See letter no. 50 in *Georg Lukács: Selected Correspondence.*

²²⁴ See Ervin Sinkó, *Optimisták: Történelmi regény 1918/19-ből* (Optimists: A Historical Novel from the Years 1918–19), (Novi Sad: Fórum Könyvkiadó, 1965), vol. 1, p. 256. In this *roman à clef*, Sinkó introduces many of the principal players in the drama of the revolutionary events. Two of the chief protagonists—and antagonists—are Vértes (Lukács) and Lányi (József Révai).

²²⁵ Reference is to József Révai (1898–1959) who was among the younger members of the Sunday Circle, and later of the Free School of Humanities in Budapest. He started as a literary critic, became the chief ideologue of the Hungarian Communist Party, and attacked Lukács after the publication of Lukács's essay, "Bolshevism as a Moral Problem" (See Appendix). Although Révai at first protested against Lukács's joining the editorial board of the Party organ, *Vörös Újság* (Red Gazette), he later was won over by Lukács and supported his position during the short-lived Soviet Republic. In their Vienna exile, Révai again joined the reconstructed Sunday Circle (in January 1921), but soon opposed Lukács and was one of his sharpest critics in their Moscow exile (1933–45). After their return to Hungary in 1945, Révai became the editor-in-chief of the Party organ, *Szabad Nép,* and belonged to the inner circle of the Party leadership under Rákosi. During the years of Stalinism in Hungary, Révai played the role of "cultural commissar" (the Hungarian Zhdanov); he was instrumental in removing Lukács from his university post, led the attacks against him in the daily press, branded him a "revisionist," and demanded "self-criticism." Révai's influence came to an end in 1956. Ibid., p. 270.

²²⁶ Ibid., p. 272.

²²⁷ Ibid., p. 307. Emphasis added. Here, Sinkó reports that one evening he visited Vértes/Lukács and during the ensuing conversation the reasons for Lukács's embracing communism came to the fore. Vértes/Lukács declared that "the statement of the problem and the solution has been provided by Hebbel who puts into the mouth of his heroine [Judith] the following words: 'If God had placed sin between me and the deed enjoined upon me—who am I to be able to escape it?'" Indeed, Lukács argues with the same quote from Hebbel's tragedy, *Judith,* in his 1919 treatise "Tactics and Ethics." Lukács/Vértes further concluded that "today, with the help of the Marxist method, it is possible for us, Marxists, to do the good deed enjoined upon us by the historical necessity. And still: in order to do what is right, we need more than theoretical insight. We need ethics" (ibid., pp. 317–18).

²²⁸ Marianna Weber, *Max Weber,* p. 466. Emphasis added. We are also told that "the intellectual atmosphere provided by these intellectuals stimulated Weber's already strong interest in the

Russians," especially Dostoevsky. Paul Honigsheim tells much the same story and emphasizes the significant role that "Lukács played in Weber's thinking," but he regards the influence as mutual. It was Weber's empathy, declares Honigsheim, that enabled him "to understand Lukács's position...his turning from modern occidental individualism to a notion of collectivism." See Paul Honigsheim, *On Max Weber*, trans. Joan Rytina (New York: Free Press, 1968), pp. 24–28. In tune with Marianna Weber, Honigsheim characterizes Bloch and *his* relations to the Heidelberg circle as quite negative: "It wasn't so much the content of Bloch's philosophy as the prophetic manner of its presentation that irritated Weber so much," who was supposed to have exclaimed that Bloch "cannot be taken seriously" (ibid., pp. 28–29).

[229] See Arnold Hauser, "Variationen über das *tertium datur* bei Georg Lukács," in *Im Gespräch mit Georg Lukács* (Munich: C. H. Beck, 1978), p. 82. Emphasis added. Hauser spoke here and on other occasions of the immense and lasting influence of Lukács on his life and work, which came into play in Hauser's consideration of the importance of ethics "for everything we do, we create or plan to accomplish." As he described it, Lukács put his stamp on the intellectual and spiritual atmosphere of the Sunday Circle gatherings. Strangely, he said, *the main interest lay in religion and mystics*—albeit on an ethical foundation: "our 'house-saints' were: the German mystics, Kierkegaard, and Dostoevsky" (ibid., p. 31). The epilogue to this slim volume was written by Peter Ludz, and translated by me. See "Hauser and Lukács" in *Telos* (Fall 1979), pp. 175–84. As Ludz correctly points out, the members of this group as well as the Free School of Humanities criticized "the mechanistic materialism and the often empty positivism of their time"; all their discussions were characterized by "a strong moral impetus." They held that "art and philosophy were to form a harmonious whole; life and spirit were thought to be reconciled." They opted for "neither the passivity of the melancholic attitude nor for the expressionistic-activist demand for radical reassessments," although almost without exception they held progressive or left-liberal views. Ibid., p. 176.

[230] "Ernst Bloch im Gespräch mit Michael Landmann." Unpublished manuscript. Emphasis added. Landmann had taped his conversations and discussions with Bloch over the years; the transcribed material amounts to over 600 typewritten pages. The passage is on page 196 of the manuscript, and is quoted with the permission of Professor Landmann.

[231] Ibid., p. 217.

[232] See Karl Jaspers, "Heidelberger Erinnerungen," in *Heidelberger Jahrbücher* 5 (1961), pp. 1–10. Cf. Karl Löwenstein, "Erinnerungen," in *Max Weber Gedenkausgabe der Universität zu München* (Berlin, 1966); and Helmut Plessner, "Heidelberg in 1913," in *Kölner Zeitschrift für Soziologie* 7 (1963). For more on the Heidelberg period, Lukács's ethical position, and his turn to "collectivistic values," see Zoltán Tar and Judith Marcus, "The Weber–Lukács Encounter," in Ronald M. Glassman and Vatro Murvar, eds., *Max Weber's Political Sociology: A Pessimistic Vision of a Rationalized World* (Westport, Conn.: Greenwood Press, 1984), pp. 109 ff.

[233] See Sinkó, *Optimisták*, pp. 338 ff. As mentioned before, some members of the Sunday Circle, especially Balázs and Emma Ritoók, viewed with alarm Lukács's friendship and intellectual-spiritual "symbiosis" with Ernst Bloch. According to Sinkó and other contemporary observers, Lukács was very much his own man in "consciously cultivating" the irrationality of belief." Lukács, for example, mentioned as *the* most important aspect of the proletariat's readiness for sacrifice its *belief* in its historical mission. In the novel, Vértes/Lukács states: "Belief means to take up consciously an irrational position against one's individual life. It has to be clear to us that there is no rational tragedy—*all heroism is irrational*." Sinkó countered that, although Marxism is a rational and scientific theory, it is capable of inspiring heroic acts. To which Lukács/Vértes replied: "One may acquire all the theories of Marxism and still not be a hero. Action does not follow from knowledge. One acts *in spite of* knowledge—which produces only sceptics. Purely

on the basis of theoretical knowledge we would never even dream of becoming a leader of people or a revolution. In order to do this, one has to subscribe to what *I believe in*: in the power of belief." As Sinkó describes it, his "educator" ended his "lesson" with the pronouncement: "In the knowledge about the existence of Good and Evil in the human heart, *man needs to believe in order to be able to live and to do battle*" (ibid., p. 338). It helps to comprehend the complexity of Lukács's ideas if we know that in addition to the aforementioned studies in the 1910s, Lukács also was preoccupied with another earlier strain of medieval thought, the doctrine of *realism*, brought forward by Anselm of Canterbury (1033–1109), who developed the ontological argument for the existence of God as "the highest unit." Lukács may have received the impetus from Kierkegaard to go back to Anselm's attempt at establishing the rational foundation for dogmas. We thus find in Lukács's reflections the echo of the principle *credo ut intelligam*. The mystical and scholastic strains together produce the strange mixture in the Lukácsian thought and formulations. Lukács's diary entries, in fact, demonstrate that he simultaneously studied the writings of Meister Eckhart and Anselm of Canterbury, juxtaposed with his ongoing wrestling with the problem of ethics. And what does Naphta think about these things? Without possibly knowing Lukács's innermost feelings and train of thought, Thomas Mann puts the following words into Naphta's mouth: "A vindication…of scholasticism is on the way," and "science will see itself philosophically enforced.… there is no such thing as pure knowledge. The validity of the Church's teaching on the subject of science, which can be summed up in the phrase of Saint Augustine: *Credo, ut intelligam*: I believe, in order that I may understand, is absolutely incontrovertible." Naphta concludes his statement much the way Lukács's ruminations run in the 1918 essay, "Bolshevism as a Moral Problem": Since "pure science is a myth," it follows that "*a belief,…an idea,…a will*, is always in existence." It is "the task of intellect to expound and to demonstrate it" (397). Cf. Lukács's essay "Bolshevism as a Moral Problem" in Appendix. A recent, extremely perceptive essay by Marshall Berman alluded to this aspect of Lukács's intellectual makeup. Berman writes that by reading of and about Lukács, he was "confirmed" in his "sense of Lukács as a religious figure. His capacity for abjection and repentance, his drive to punish and mortify himself for the sake of sanctity, had more in common with the inner world of Augustine's *Confessions* than with the sensibility of Karl Marx. But this was a very modern Augustine, as he might have been imagined by Dostoevski or Freud: endlessly reinventing himself, hoping to obliterate his past once and for all, only to trip over it—or maybe dig it up—again and again…" See "George Lukács's Cosmic Chutzpah," in the *Village Voice*, Voice Literary Supplement, no. 37 (July 1985), p. 8.

[234] Lukács, "Tactics and Ethics," in Georg Lukács: *Political Writings, 1919–1929*, ed. Rodney Livingstone, trans. Michael McColgan (London: NLB, 1972), p. 8. This is a translation of a translation and there is some variance with the Hungarian original, "Taktika és etika," written in February 1919 and published in a collection of essays entitled *Taktika és etika* (Budapest: Közoktatásügyi Népbiztosság, 1919). It is a follow-up to the first "ethical essay," which appeared in December 1918, "Bolshevism as a Moral Problem." See Appendix. For its genesis and place in Lukács's development, see Judith Marcus Tar, " 'Introduction' to Georg Lukács: Bolshevism as a Moral Problem," in *Social Research* 44, no. 3 (Autumn 1977), pp. 416 ff.

[235] Lukács, "Tactics and Ethics," pp. 5–6. Lukács's ruminations on the problem of ethics had impressed as well as inspired Max Weber's thinking on the subject. Already in 1913, he saw the possibilities of Lukács's approach and when he wanted to help a jailed anarchist clarify his thinking on a moral problem, he wrote to his wife from Ascona at the Lago Maggiore: [He] has *depth*. But he lacks the power to express even simple thoughts. Jail has affected him in such a way that he cannot stop meditating on the meaning of goodness. The facts that the *result* of good actions is so often wholly irrational and that 'good' behavior has bad consequences have made him doubt

that he *ought* to act well—an evaluation of moral action on the basis of *results* rather than intrinsic value. I shall try to obtain *The Brothers Karamazov* for him and at some later time Lukács's dialogue about the poor in spirit [sic], which deals with the problem..." (see Marianne Weber, *Max Weber*, p. 490).

[236] Lukács, "Tactics and Ethics," p. 10.

[237] Ibid., pp. 10–11. Ropshin was the pseudonym of Boris V. Savinkov (1879–1925), son of a Tsarist judge in Russia who joined the party of Socialist-Revolutionarists in 1899, to which Lukács's first wife (Yelena Grabenko) also belonged. He was a poet, novelist, revolutionary, and terrorist, and he participated in the assassination of von Plehve, the minister of interor (July 15, 1904) and that of the Grand Duke Sergius (February 4, 1905). He became assistant minister of war in the 1917 Provisional Government and after November 17, 1917, he organized rebellions against the Bolsheviks. Several times he lived in exile in Paris but returned finally to the Soviet Union in 1924 and was captured. His death sentence was later commuted into a ten years' sentence. On May 7, 1925, he committed suicide by jumping from a window into the prison courtyard. His books were widely read and highly influential in Europe at that time. Lukács's reference is to his novel *The Pale Horse*, trans. Z. Vengerova (New York: Alfred A. Knopf, 1919). This book is correctly called one of the most characteristic and enlightening products of a "tragically un-balanced generation" that faced by "heroic will and mystic tendencies" the problems of a period just before World War I. It contains "the tragedy of every individual conscience...possessed by the necessity of violent political action and the equally strong religious objections to it." See "Introduction," pp. v-vi. As Lukács wrote to Paul Ernst during World War I, he happened to "believe that we are now faced with a new type of man that we should become familiar with." Shortly after he again wrote to Ernst about his preoccupation with Ropshin's work: "I...see in Ropshin...a new manifestation of an old conflict between the first ethic (duties toward social structure) and the second (imperatives of the soul)." See letters 133 and 134 in *Georg Lukács: Selected Correspondence*, and Boris Savinkov, *Memoirs of a Terrorist*, trans. Joseph Shaplen (New York: Albert & Charles Boni, 1931). For an account of the then almost "fashionable" discussions about the concept of violence, of action, and of the permissibility of certain deeds regarded as "means" see Zoltán Tar, *The Frankfurt School: The Critical Theories of Max Horkheimer and Theodor W. Adorno* (New York: Wiley Interscience, 1977; new paperback edition: New York: Schocken, 1985), pp. 43 ff.

[238] Lukács, "'Intellectual Workers' and the Problem of Intellectual Leadership," second essay in "Tactics and Ethics," in *Political Writings*, p. 18. Cf. Lukács's statement in "Bolshevism as a Moral Problem": "Socialism...is the utopian postulate of the Marxian philosophy of history: it is the *ethical objective* of a coming world order." The *quest* itself is thus an "absolute prerequisite of a truly free world," and the *will* is "an essential feature of the socialist Weltanschauung.... [It] enabled *the proletariat* to become *an agent of the social salvation of mankind*, the *messianic class* of world history." Nothing could have been accomplished without the "fervor of this messianism," concludes Lukács. Emphasis added. See Appendix. In my introduction to the English translation of "Bolshevism," I have sketched the story of Lukács's "conversion" to communism one week after he had stated unequivocally that he was "unable to share the belief" of the Bolsheviks. But, he announced at a Sunday Circle get-together, "I just met somebody who possesses the truth... whose thought and conviction do not exist in a vacuum but are transformed into action. We try to compress our convictions within bourgeois forms. For the first time, I have met someone in whom Hegel's dialectic has become flesh and blood. He experiences what we converse about. He has proven it to me that until now I was unable to accept the consequences for my thoughts. I will see to it that this will change." The description of the events was given by Anna Lesznai, a Hungarian poet and artist of left-liberal persuasion, at one time the wife of Oszkár Jászi, poli-

tician and political scientist. Both Lesznai and her later husband, Tibor Gergely, were members of the Sunday Circle in Budapest and later in the Vienna exile. Tibor Gergely made the now famous caricatures of many of the Sunday Circle members, including Lukács, Karl Mannheim, Béla Balázs, József Révai, and René Spitz. Lesznai and Gergely escaped Europe in 1938 and settled in New York City. Gergely became a well-known illustrator of children's books (*The Little Engine that Could,* for example, is one of his books), and an invaluable source of information about the preoccupations, feelings, and life style of that group of Budapest (mostly) Jewish intellectuals that is today called, in Hungary, "The Great Generation." During our numerous conversations he confirmed many of the stories and descriptions of Sinkó's and Lesznai's books. As he was a close friend (and/or schoolmate) of Karl Mannheim, Charles de Tolnay, Arnold Hauser, André Kertész and others, I gathered a treasure trove of data as well as a good understanding of what these people were about. I greatly regret that I have never met his wife, Anna Lesznai, who was a true representative of a "Great Generation of Women" in Hungary of that time—women whose lives and contributions also await their chronicler. Her autobiographical-historical novel, *Kezdetben volt a kert* (At the Beginning was the Garden), 2 vols. (Budapest: Szépirodalmi Kiadó, 1966), is one book that cannot be ignored if a story of that period is to be written. For the account of Lukács's "confession," see vol. 2, pp. 472 ff. Cf. Lee Congdon, *The Young Lukács,* esp. Chapter 5; and Michael Löwy, *Georg Lukács: From Romanticism to Bolshevism,* esp. "How an Intellectual Becomes a Revolutionary?"

[239] See József Lengyel, *Prenn Drifting,* trans. Ilona Duczynska (London: Peter Owen, 1966), p. 155. (Original Hungarian edition: *Prenn Ferenc hányatott élete* [Budapest: Magvető Kiadó, 1959; 1969]). For a more reliable source on some of the same episodes see Julius (Gyula) Háy, *Geboren 1900,* p. 61. Háy reports, among other things, that in 1919 Lukács had already used some of the formulas and concepts that can be found in his "Armut" and *Soul and Form.*

[240] See Thomas Mann, "Zur jüdischen Frage," p. 56.

[241] Ibid., p. 57.

[242] See Friedrich Nietzsche, *Genealogy of Morals,* pp. 166–67.

[243] Ibid., p. 168.

[244] The famous (or infamous) work of Heinrich Treitschke appeared in the *Preussischen Jahrbüchern 1879]80,* entitled "Ein Wort über unser Judentum." Paul de Lagarde's work, which Thomas Mann read in 1913 (according to his notes in the margin), contains the following statement: "Take away all these Jews who claim to have a right to exist in Germany *as Jews*... [and] give the German people a magnificient goal for which we all work together. ..." (in *Deutscher Glaube. Deutsches Vaterland, Deutsche Bildung,* ed. Friedrich Daab [Jena: Eigen Diederich, 1913], p. 14). Mann had underlined the passage in which Lagarde says about the so-called literati "this water-weed has to be...exterminated." Lagarde's language and formulations are the most repugnant examples of intolerance and rabid nationalism to have appeared before 1933 in Germany. For a general treatment of Judaism in Germany, see Hans Liebeschütz, *Das Judentum im deutschen Geschichtsbild von Hegel bis Marx* (Tübingen: J. C. B. Morh [Paul Siebeck], 1967).

[245] See Werner Sombart, *The Jews and Modern Capitalism,* p. 264.

[246] Thomas Mann, "Zur jüdischen Frage," p. 59. Cf. Hannah Arendt, *The Origins of Totalitarianism,* pp. 31 ff.

[247] Georg Simmel, "The Stranger," in *The Sociology of George Simmel,* ed. Kurt Wolff (New York: Free Press, 1950), pp. 402–3. Martin Buber, explaining his motivation for joining Zionism, said that to him it meant the restoration of a link to *Gemeinschaft,* the reestablishment of "connection." There is nobody so in need of connecting up to a community as a very young man, states Buber, and "no young man as much as a young Jew" because the others are linked to the soil

and the tradition of a people." See *Werke* (Munich: Heidelberg: Kösel Verlag Kg., 1963), vol. 3, pp. 966–67.

[248] Simmel, "Stranger," pp. 402–3.

[249] Mann, *Sieben Manifeste zur jüdischen Frage,* ed. Walter Berendsohn (Darmstadt: Joseph Melzer Verlag, 1966). pp. 34–35.

[250] Thomas Mann, "Zur Lösung der Judenfrage," in *Die Lösung der Judenfrage,* Eine Rundfrage, veranstaltet von Dr. Julius Moses (Berlin: Modernes Verlagsbureau Curt Wiegand, 1907). Cited by Julius Löwenstein in his essay, "Thomas Mann zur jüdischen Frage," in *Bulletin des Leo Baeck Instituts* 10, no. 37 (1967), p. 27. Löwenstein remarks that he had obtained the rare book containing the responses of contemporaries to a questionnaire collected by J. Moses from Erich Gottgetreu, now living in Jerusalem.

[251] Mann, *Reflections of a Non-Political Man,* p. 81.

[252] Ibid.

[253] Robert Musil in his novel, *The Man Without Qualities* (New York: Capricorn Books, 1965), describes a "great man," Dr. Paul Arnheim, much the same way. The model for Dr. Arnheim was Walther Rathenau, an industrial magnate and minister in the Weimar Republic. Dr. Arnheim represents here the "union of soul and economics" and was said "to be of Jewish descent." Although he was destined to attain a high government position and was immensely rich, he remained an "extremely brilliant outsider" who wanted to partake in the "age-old culture of the Habsburg capital" (pp. 118–25).

[254] See Werner J. Cahnman, "Pariahs, Strangers and Court Jews: A Conceptual Clarification," in *Sociological Analysis* 35, no. 3 (Autumn 1974), pp. 158–59.

Appendix

[1] The Hungarian article, "A bolsevizmus mint erkölcsi probléma," first appeared in *Szabadgondolat* (Free Thought), in December 1918, pp. 228–32. *Szabadgondolat* was the official journal of the so-called Galileo Circle, an organization of radical intellectuals at the University of Budapest. Lukács wrote the essay for a special issue devoted to a then raging controversy about Bolshevism, presumably at the request of its editor, Karl Polányi. English-language Lukács scholars have often referred to this article without having read it; indeed, it has been considered lost by many, an excusable assumption since the Hungarian-language material has been inaccessible to them. The essay was first translated into German by me and appended to my doctoral dissertation of 1976. For the English-language publication with my Introduction, see *Social Research* 44, no. 3 (Autumn 1977) pp. 416–24.

[2] The term is meant here as a concept of ethical idealism.

[3] Lukács's review of Martin Buber's translations of Hasidic tales (*Die Legends des Baalschem* in 1908 and *Die Geschichte des Rabbi Nachman* in 1906), entitled "Zsidó miszticizmus," was published in a Hungarian philosophical journal of which Lukács was a cofounder. See *Szellem,* no. 2 (1911), pp. 256 ff; signed L. Gy. Lukács received the books from Martin Buber, with whom he struck up a friendship in 1911. Lukács's interest in mystical thought was at its peak at that time; he was genuinely and deeply interested in Jewish mysticism and urged Buber to give "more." Lukács's newly won knowledge about things Hasidic coincided with his discovery of his "Jewishness" and was further enhanced by his yearning for *Gemeinschaft* in an alienated world. For further information, see the exchange of letters between Lukács and Buber, in the *Georg Lukács Correspondence.*

[4] Meister Eckhart (1260?–1327), Dominician monk, father of German mysticism, and creator

of the German language of mysticism. A younger contemporary of Thomas Aquinas, he became professor of philosophy in Paris in 1311, in Strassbourg in 1313, and in Cologne in 1320. At the time of his death he was embroiled in a church dispute on orthodoxy *versus* heresy. Four of his sermons were published in Hungarian translation in the second issue of the little magazine *Szellem*, most likely at Lukács's behest.

⁵ The Vedas are Hindu sacred writings. Plotinus (204–269), founder of the Alexandrian neoplatonic school, attempted to construct a new religion by means of a system of science. His work deeply engaged Lukács's interest and influenced his thinking, as his letters to his friends show. See letter no. 58 (December 20, 1910) in the Georg Lukács Correspondence. Jakob Böhme (1575–1624), the best-known representative of German Protestant mysticism and dialectician, exerted great influence not only on German romantic mysticism, but also on Schelling, Baader, Hegel, Goethe, and Novalis. Among his works were *Drei Prinzipien* (1619), *Signatura Rerum* (1622), and *Mysterium Magnum* (1623).

⁶ Heinrich Suso or Seuse (1296?–1366), was a Dominican monk, German mystic, and pupil of Meister Eckhart. In the development of German mysticism, he represented one branch, that of the heresies of the Berghards. The author of mystical, poetic songs, he also wrote *Büchlein der ewigen Weisheit* (Pamphlet on Eternal Wisdom) and *Leben*, an autobiography. His *German Theology* was edited by Luther and published in 1516.

⁷ First published in Mann, *Forderung des Tages* (Berlin: S. Fischer Verlag, 1930); reprinted in MK 120 *(Miszellen)*, pp. 172 ff. The Austrian government served an expulsion order on Lukács and at the request of Lukács's friends, Thomas Mann interceded on his behalf with the then Chancellor of Austria, Dr. Ignaz Seipel (1926–29). The expulsion order was subsequently revoked, but Lukács left Vienna nevertheless and went to Moscow, where from 1930 to 1931 he did research in the Marx–Engels Institute under the direction of D. Riazanov.

⁸ As is well known, Lukács continued his activities and took part in the Hungarian Communist Party and Comintern political debates; moreover, he spent three months in Budapest in 1929 at the behest of Béla Kun directing underground party work. Thus, Mann's reference to Lukács's purely intellectual pursuit is somewhat ironical.

⁹ Lukács's own recollections differ a bit from his friends' appraisal of the situation. He "wrote, sold [his] possessions," and "for three years, [he] edited the Russian Embassy trade journal for a hundred dollars a month." At last, states Lukács, "in 1928, my father died and, after all sorts of complicated manoeuvres, I finally managed to get hold of the inheritance. We lived on that until my departure for Russia" *(Record of a Life, p. 70)*. It should be noted that the "inheritance" was not substantial due to several factors. First, Lukács's father lost his high position because of his son's political activities. Second, Lukács had a sister and a brother who shared the inheritance. Third, Lukács's father sacrificed a substantial part of his fortune when in 1919 he paid an exorbitant sum to a member of the Western military commission that smuggled Lukács out of the country after the collapse of the Hungarian Soviet Republic in August 1919. See Lukács's account of those events in *Record*, pp. 68–69.

¹⁰ Mann is unduly modest here (or ironically hints that a politician could not be expected to be well versed in literary matters) because on November 12, 1929, he received the Nobel Prize for literature.

¹¹ First published in the Lukács Festschrift entitled *Georg Lukács zum siebzigsten Geburtstag* (Berlin-East: Aufbau Verlag, 1955). Reprinted in MK 120 *(Miszellen)*, pp. 253–54. As to the question of why Mann merely composed a brief note instead of a personal letter to Lukács, it should be kept in mind that Mann was then in his eightieth year (he died on August 12 of the same year), and although often unwell, he still had to endure celebrations from Zurich to Amsterdam and Lübeck (his home town); he also went to East Germany in May on the occasion of the

Schiller festivities (celebrating the 150th anniversary of Schiller's death). Interestingly, it was during the festivities that Mann and Lukács met the second—and last time. (The cover photo was taken on that occasion, with Johannes R. Becher, German poet and minister of culture at the time). In Lukács's recollection, Thomas Mann was again "diplomatic" and behaved "very typically." "In the course of the celebrations in Jena [sic] we were staying in the same hotel," said Lukács, and "the meals were organized in such a way that the bigwigs, the top bureaucrats, Ulbricht and the rest, all ate together in a separate room together with Becher and the bourgeois writer Thomas Mann, whereas I dined together with the middle classes in the hotel. It did not occur to Thomas Mann once to say to Becher, 'Surely we could invite Lukács to join us.'" (*Record*, p. 95).

[12] This elusive German term may be rendered into English as "development of the mind"; it is more than that, though, as education means the unfolding of individual personality, including moral growth and character formation as well as cultural refinement. In its true meaning, *Bildung* transcends purely practical aims; Hermann J. Weigand correctly defines it as "the approach to a totality of integrated human experience." See Weigand, *Magic Mountain*, p. 4.

BIBLIOGRAPHY

The bibliography has been revised for the present translation. English translations of the writings of both Thomas Mann and Georg Lukács have been listed whenever available. The German-language quotations from Thomas Mann's collected works are based on the twelve-volume paperback edition, "Moderne Klassiker," MK 101–12, and the eight-volume essayistic writings, MK 113–20, edited by Hans Bürgin (Frankfurt am Main: Fischer Bücherei, 1967 and 1968). Unpublished material of Mann is housed at the Thomas Mann Archiv (TMA) of the Eidgenössische Technische Hochschule, Zurich. Unpublished material of Lukács is housed at the Georg Lukács Archiv of the Hungarian Academy of Sciences, Budapest.

Primary sources: Thomas Mann

WORKS

"At the Prophet's". *Stories of Three Decades.*
"Die Betrogene." MK 112.
"Bilse und Ich." MK 119.
"The Blood of the Walsungs." *Stories of Three Decades.*
Buddenbrooks. Translated by H. T. Lowe-Porter. New York: Alfred A. Knopf, 1946.
Death in Venice and Seven Other Stories. Translated by H. T. Lowe-Porter. New York: Vintage Books, 1954.
"Der Doktor Lessing." MK 120.
Doctor Faustus: The Life of the German Composer Adrian Leverkühn as Told by a Friend. Translated by H. T. Lowe-Porter. New York: Alfred A. Knopf, 1948.
"Dostojewski—mit Massen." MK 115.
"Einführung in den 'Zauberberg.' Für Studenten der Universität Princeton." MK 114.
Essays of Three Decades. Translated by H. T. Lowe-Porter. New York: Alfred A. Knopf, 1965.
"Fiorenza." *Stories of Three Decades.*
Die Forderung des Tages. Berlin: S. Fischer Verlag, 1930.
"Geist und Kunst." In Wysling, Hans *Secondary Sources.*
"Die geistige Situation des Schriftstellers in unserer Zeit." MK 117.

"Goethe and Tolstoy." *Three Essays*. Translated by H. T. Lowe-Porter. New York: Alfred A. Knopf, 1929.

"Im Warschauer PEN–Club." MK 119.

"Der Künstler und der Literat." MK 113.

Last Essays. Translated by Richard Winston and Clara Winston. New York: Alfred A. Knopf, 1959.

"Lebensabriss." MK 119.

Leiden an Deutschland. Tagebuchblätter aus den Jahren 1933 und 1934. MK 114.

"Leiden und Grösse Richard Wagners." MK 114.

"Lübeck als geistige Lebensform." MK 119.

"Georg Lukács." MK 120. (See Appendix).

The Magic Mountain. Translated by H. T. Lowe-Porter. New York: The Modern Library, n. d.

Thomas Mann Diaries: 1918–1939. Edited by Hermann Kesten. Translated by Richard Winston and Clara Winston. New York: Harry N. Abrams Publishers, 1982.

"Nietzsche's Philosophy in the Light of Recent History." *Last Essays*.

Order of the Day: Political Essays and Speeches of Two Decades. Translated by H. T. Lowe-Porter et al. New York: Alfred A. Knopf, 1942.

Reflections of a Non-Political Man. Translated by Walter D. Morris. New York: Frederick Ungar Publishing Co., 1983.

Royal Highness. Translated by A. Cecil Curtis. New York: Alfred A. Knopf, 1939.

"Die Schule des Zauberbergs." MK 119.

Sieben Manifeste zur jüdischen Frage: 1936–1948. Edited by Walter A. Berendsohn. Darmstadt: Joseph Melzer Verlag, 1966.

Sketch of My Life. Translated by H. T. Lowe-Porter. New York: Alfred A. Knopf, 1960.

Stories of Three Decades. Translated by H. T. Lowe-Porter. New York: Alfred A. Knopf, 1966.

The Story of a Novel: The Genesis of Doctor Faustus. Translated by Richard Winston and Clara Winston. New York.: Alfred A. Knopf, 1961.

"Suffering and Greatness of Richard Wagner." *Essays of Three Decades*.

Tonio Kröger. Death in Venice and Seven Other Stories.

Tagebücher 1935–1936. Edited by Peter de Mendelssohn. Frankfurt am Main: S. Fischer Verlag, 1979.

Tagebücher 1918–1921. Edited by Peter de Mendelssohn. Frankfurt am Main: S. Fischer Verlag, 1979.

"Über die Lehre Spenglers." MK 113.

"Über Dante." MK 120.

"Über Karl Kraus." MK 120.

"Über 'Königliche Hoheit'." MK 119.

"Wälsungenblut." MK 111.
"A Weary Hour." *Last Essays* and *Stories of Three Decades*.
"Zum Tode Eduard Keyserlings," MK 113.
"Zur jüdischen Frage." MK 119.
"Zur Lösung der Judenfrage." *Die Lösung der Judenfrage. Eine Rundfrage. Veranstaltet von Dr. Julius Moses. Berlin–Leipzig. Modernes Verlagsbureau Curt Wiegand, 1907.

CORRESPONDENCE

Briefe 1889–1936 and *Briefe 1937–1948*. Edited by Erika Mann. Frankfurt am Main: S. Fischer Verlag, 1952 and 1963.
Thomas Mann: Letters to Paul Amann. 1915–1952. Edited by Herbert Wegener. Translated by Richard Winston and Clara Winston. London: Secker and Warburg, 1961.
Thomas Mann an Ernst Bertram: Briefe aus den Jahren 1910–1955. Edited by Inge Jens. Pfullingen: Verlag Günther Neske, 1960.
Thomas Mann–Heinrich Mann: Briefwechsel 1900–1949. Edited by Hans Wysling. Frankfurt am Main: S. Fischer Verlag, 1969.
Letters of Thomas Mann: 1889–1955. Selected and translated by Richard Winston and Clara Winston. New York: Alfred A. Knopf, 1971.
Mythology and Humanism: The Correspondence of Thomas Mann and Karl Kerényi. Translated by Alexander Gelley. Ithaca: Cornell University Press, 1975.
Letter to Desider Kosztolányi. In Réz, Pál (see *Secondary Sources*).
Letter to Gertrud Lukács. "Briefwechsel mit Thomas Mann." *Sinn und Form* 7, no. 5 (1955), p. 669.
Letter to Dr. Seipel. See Appendix. For the German text, see MK 120.
Letter to Hans M. Wolff. "Thomas Mann on his *Zauberberg*: An Unpublished Letter to Hans M. Wolff." Edited by Karl S. Guthke. Neophilologus 2 (1960), pp. 120–22.
"Offener Brief an den Weserkurier." MK 120.

UNPUBLISHED MATERIAL (TMA)

Mp XI, 13^e, Notes to "Der Tod in Venedig."
MS 33. Notes to *Doktor Faustus*.
Letter of Georg Lukács to Thomas Mann, February 18, 1918.
Letters of Thomas Mann to:
    Dr. Kerpely (January 11, 1940)

Hans Mayer (October 11, 1948)
Dr. Richard Pokorny (February 20, 1949)
Pierre-Paul Sagave (February 23, 1937; February 18, 1952)
Bodo Uhse (March 25, 1949)

Primary Sources: Georg Lukács

WORKS

Lukács, György. "An Answer." *Könyvek könyve*, edited by Béla Kőhalmi. Budapest: Lantos Kiadása, 1918.

Lukács, Georg. "Auf der Suche nach dem Bürger. Betrachtungen zum siebzigsten Geburtstag Thomas Manns." *Internationale Literatur*, nos 6–7 (1945), pp. 58–75.

Lukács, György. "A bolsevizmus mint erkölcsi probléma." *Szabadgondolat* 8, no. 10 (December 1918), pp. 228–32.

Lukács, Georg. "Bolshevism as a Moral Problem." Translated by Judith Marcus-Tar. *Social Research* 44, no. 3 (Autumn 1977), pp. 416–24.

Lukács, Georg von. "Curriculum Vitae." First published in *Text+Kritik*. 39/40 (October 1973), pp. 5–7. Special Lukács issue.

"Curriculum Vitae." Translated by Judith Marcus. Appendix to *Georg Lukács: Selected Correspondence 1902–1920*.

Lukács, Georg. *The Destruction of Reason*. Translated by Peter Palmer. London: Merlin Press, 1980.

"Die deutsche Literatur im Zeitaler des Imperialismus." *Internationale Literatur* (1945), no. 3. pp. 53–65; no. 4, pp. 62–68. Also in *Skizze einer Geschichte der neuen deutschen Literatur*. Berlin/East: Aufbau Verlag, 1953.

Lukács, Georg von. "Die deutschen Intellektuellen und der Krieg." *Text+Kritik* 39/40 (October 1973), pp. 65–69. Special Lukács issue.

Lukács, Georg. *Essays on Thomas Mann*. Translated by Stanley Mitchell. London: Merlin Press, 1964.

"Franz Kafka or Thomas Mann?" *The Meaning of Contemporary Realism*. Translated by John Mander and Necke Mander. London: Merlin Press, 1962.

"Gelebtes Denken". *See unpublished material (GLA)*.

History and Class Consciousness: Studies in Marxist Dialectics. Translated by Rodney Livingstone. Cambridge: M. I. T. Press, 1971.

"In Search of Bourgeois Mann." *Essays on Thomas Mann*.

" 'Intellectual Workers' and the Problem of Intellectual Leadership." *Georg Lukács: Political Writings. The Question of Parliamentarism and Other Essays.*

Edited by Rodney Livingstone. Translated by Michel McColgan. London: NLB, 1972

Lukács, Georg von. "Jewish Mysticism." See Appendix.

Lenin: A Study on the Unity of his Thought. Translated by Nicholas Jacobs. Cambridge: M. I. T. Press, 1971.

"Lob des neunzehnten Jahrhunderts." In *Sachen Böll: Ansichten und Einsichten.* Edited by Marcell Reich-Ranicki. Köln, Kiephenhauer & Witsch, 1968.

"Methodischer Zweifel." *Der Monat* 18, No. 211/April 1966, p. 95.

Lukács, Georg von. *Napló–Tagebuch 1910–11: Das Gericht (1913).* Edited by L. Ferenc Lendvai. Budapest: Akadémiai Kiadó, 1981.

Lukács, Georg. "The Playful Style." *Essays on Thomas Mann.*

Record of a Life: An Autobiographical Sketch. Edited by István Eörsi. Translated by Rodney Livingstone. London: Verso Editions, 1983.

Lukács, Georg von. *Die Seele und die Formen.* Berlin: Egon Fleischel & Co., 1911.

Lukács, Georg. *Soul and Form.* Translated by Anna Bostock. Cambridge, Mass.: M. I. T. Press, 1974

"Tactics and Ethics." *Georg Lukács: Political Writings, 1919–1929.*

"Taktik und Ethik." In *Schriften zur Ideologie und Politik.* Edited by Peter Ludz. Neuwied–Berlin: Hermann Luchterhand Verlag, 1967, pp. 1–40.

Lukács, Georg von. *Die Theorie des Romans: Ein geschichtsphilosophischer Versuch über die Formen der grossen Epik.* Berlin: Cassier, 1920.

Lukács, Georg. *The Theory of the Novel.* Translated by Anna Bostock. Cambridge: M. I. T. Press, 1971.

Thomas Mann. Berlin/East: Aufbau Verlag, 1949.

Thomas Mann: Essays. Fifth enlarged and revised edition. Berlin: Aufbau Verlag, 1957.

"Thomas Manns Gegensatz zur Dekadenz der Gegenwart." *Heute und Morgen* 6 (1955), pp. 331–39. See under new title, "Das Spielerische und seine, Hintergründe." *Thomas Mann: Essays.*

Lukács, Georg von. "Über Sehnsucht und Form." *Die Neue Rundschau* 22, no. 1 issue 1 of 2 issues (February 1911), pp. 192–98. Enlarged version in *Die Seele und die Formen.*

"Von der Armut am Geiste: Ein Gespräch und ein Brief" (On Poverty of Spirit). Neue Blätter 2, nos. 5-6 (1912), pp. 67–92.

L.[ukács] Gy.[örgy] "Zsidó miszticism." (Jewish Mysticism) *Szellem* (1911), p. 256. English translation in Appendix.

"Ernst Bloch und Georg Lukács im Gespräch." With Irving Fetscher, J. B. Metz und Jürgen Moltmann. *Neues Forum* 14, nos. 167 and 168 (November–December 1967), pp. 837 ff.

"Erst Demokratie, dann Wirtschaftsreform." With G. Klos, K. Petkovic and J. Breuer. Part Two. *Neues Forum* 17 (March 1970), pp. 377 ff.

"György Lukács on Stalinism and Art. "With Antonin Liehm. *East Europe* 13, no. 5 (May 1964), pp. 22–26. Original publication: *Literarni Noviny* (Prague), January 18, 1964.

"Gespräch mit Lukács." With Günther Specovius. *Ostbrief* (Luneburg), June 1960, pp. 249 ff.

"Lukács György: Beszélgetés." (Interview with Lukács) October 2, 1969, on Hungarian television. Printed in *Kritika* (June 1973). Reprinted in *Sokszemközt tudósokkal*. Edited by István Kardos. Budapest: Minerva MRT, 1974, pp. 238 ff. English translation in *Scientists Face to Face*. Budapest: Corvina, 1978.

"On his Life and Work." An Unofficial Interview. *New Left Review* 68 (July–August 1971), pp. 48–58.

CORRESPONDENCE

"Brief an M. Jean Richard Bloch." Editor of *L'Effort Libre* (Paris). Dated Heidelberg, March 1913. Reprinted in English translation in *Georg Lukács: Selected Correspondence, 1902–1920*. Original at the GLA.

"Briefwechsel: Georg Lukács–Thomas Mann." *Sinn und Form* 7, no. 5 (1955), pp. 669–71.

Georg Lukács: Selected Correspondence. 1902–1920. Selected, edited, translated, and annotated by Judith Marcus and Zoltán Tar. With an introduction by Zoltán Tar. New York: Columbia University Press, 1986.

Lukács György levelezése (1902–1917). (Correspondence of Georg Lukács). Edited by É. Fekete and É. Karádi. Budapest: Magvető Kiadó, 1981.

Paul Ernst und Georg Lukács: Dokumente einer Freundschaft. Edited by Karl-August Kutzbach. Emsdtetten/West: Verlag Lechte, 1974.

Letters of Georg Lukács to:
  Thomas Mann (January 4, 1955)
  Erika Mann (October 17, 1961)
  István Mészáros (April 26, 1965)
  Hans Mayer (May 18, 1965)
"Midász király legendája" (The Legend of King Midas).
"Gelebtes Denken" (Lived Thought) Original text.
Tape of interview by Judith Marcus, May 7, Transcript of the talk in the possession of J. M.

Secondary Sources

Adorno, Theodor Wiesengrund. "Glosse über Persönlichkeit." *Neue Deutsche Hefte* 109–13, no. 1 (1966), pp. 47 ff.

Allport, Gordon W. "The open system in personality theory." *Varieties in Personalities.* Edited by Henrik M. Ruitenbek. New York: E. P. Dutton & Co, 1964.

Altmann, Alexander. "Moses Mendelssohns Kindheit in Dessau." *Bulletin des Leo Baeck Instituts* 10, no. 40 (1967), pp. 237 ff.

Arendt, Hannah. *The Jew as Pariah: Jewish Identity and Politics in the Modern Age.* Edited by Ron H. Feldman. New York: Grove Press, 1978.
  The Origins of Totalitarianism. New York: Meridian, 1971.

Auden, W. H. "A Saint Simon of Our Time." *New York Review of Books,* August 31, 1972, pp. 4 ff.

Baeck, Leo. *The Essence of Judaism.* New York: Schocken Books, 1970.
  Das Wesen des Judentums. Fourth edition. Frankfurt am Main: J. Kauffmann, 1926. First published 1905.

Bahr, Ehrhard. *Georg Lukács.* Berlin: Colloquium Verlag Otto H. Hess, 1970.

Bahr, Ehrhard, and Kunzer, Ruth Goldschmidt. *Georg Lukács.* New York: Frederick Ungar Publishing Co., 1972.

Bahr, Hans-Dieter. "Zuversicht statt Hoffnung." *Der Monat* 18 (February 1966), pp. 72 ff.

Balázs Béla. *Napló: 1903–1914* and *Napló 1914–1922.* 2 vols. Edited by Anna Fábri. Budapest: Magvető Kiadó, 1982.
  "Notes From a Diary." *New Hungarian Quarterly* 13, no. 47 (Autumn 1972), pp. 123–28.

Baumgarten, Franz Ferdinand. *Das Werk Conrad Ferdinand Meyers: Renaissance Empfinden und Stilkunst.* Munich: Beck, 1917.

"Bei Thomas Mann in Budapest." *Pester Loyd,* Thursday, January 12, 1922. Ida Herz Collection of the TMA.

Benedek, Marcell. *Naplómat olvasom.* (Reading My Diary) Budapest: Szépirodalmi Könyvkiadó, 1962.

Benjamin, Walter. *Briefe.* Vol. 2. Edited by Theodor W. Adorno and G. Scholem. Frankfurt am Main: Suhrkamp Verlag, 1966.

Bergsten, Gunilla. *Thomas Mann's Doctor Faustus: The Sources and Structure of the Novel.* Translated by Krishna Winston. Chicago: University of Chicago Press, 1969.

Berman, Marshall. "Georg Lukács's Cosmic Chutzpah." *The Village Voice.* Voice Literary Supplement (VLS) 37 (July 1985), pp. 1–11.

Bloch, Ernst. *Geist der Utopie.* Munich–Leipzig: Duncker & Humbolt, 1918. Second revised reprint, Frankfurt am Main: Suhrkamp Verlag, 1973.
  Thomas Münzer als Theologe der Revolution. Munich: Kurt Wolff Verlag, 1922. Reprint, Frankfurt am Main: Suhrkamp Verlag, 1969.

Blunck, Richard. *Der schwarze Papst.* 1937. Reprinted as *Ignatius von Loyola: Leben und Werk.* Hamburg: Hammerich & Lesser, 1947.

Boehmer, Heinrich. *Geschichte des jesuitischen Ordens.* Series "Aus Natur- und Geisteswelt." Leipzig–Berlin: B. G. Teubner Verlag, 1904. Reprint, 1921.
  Ignatius von Loyola. Edited by Hans Leube. Leipzig: Köhler und Amelang, 1941.
  Die Jesuiten: eine historische Skizze. Third, revised and enlarged edition. Leipzig–Berlin: B. G. Teubner Verlag, 1913.
  Loyola und die deutsche Mystik. Leipzig–Berlin: B. G. Teubner Verlag, 1921.
  Studien zur Geschichte der Gesselschaft Jesu. Vol. 1. Bonn am Rhein: A. Falkenroth, 1914.

Brandes, Georg. *The Romantic School in Germany.* Vol. 2. of "Main Currents in Nineteenth Century Literature." New York: Boni & Liveright, 1923.
  Skandinavische Persönlichkeiten. Part 2 of the series "Dichterische Persönlichkeiten." Vol. 3, Munich: Albert Langen Verlag für Literatur und Kunst, 1902.

Brod, Max. *Der Prager Kreis.* Stuttgart: W. Kohlhammer Verlag, 1966.

Bronner, Eric Stephen. "Expressionism and Marxism." *Passion and Rebellion: The Expressionist Heritage.* Edited by Stephen Eric Bronner and Douglas Kellner. South Hadley, Mass.: J. F. Bergin, 1983. Pp. 411–53.

Buber, Martin. "Erinnerungen an Simmel." *Buch des Dankes an Georg Simmel.* Edited by Kurt Gassen and Michael Landmann. Berlin: Duncker & Humbolt, 1958. P. 222.
  Paths in Utopia. Translated by R. F. C. Hull. Boston: Beacon Press, 1960.

Werke, Vol. 3, *Schriften zum Chassidismus*. Munich–Heidelberg: Kösel Verlag Kg., Verlag Lambert & Schneider GmbH., 1963.

Cahnman, Werner J. "Pariahs, Strangers and Court Jews: A Conceptual Clarification." *Sociological Analysis* 35, no. 3 (Autumn 1974), pp. 158–59.

Cohen, Hermann. *Ethik des reinen Willens*. Berlin: 1907.

Religion of Reason out of the Sources of Judaism. Translated by Simon Kaplan. New York: Frederick Ungar Publishing, 1972.

Colleville, Maurice. "Georges Lukács; Breve historie de la litterature allemande. (Revue)." *Etudes Germaniques*. 5e année, nos. 2–3 (April–September 1950), pp. 205–7.

Confino, Michael, ed. *Daughter of a Revolutionary: Natalia Herzen and the Bakunin–Nechayev Circle*. Translated by Hilary Sternberg and Lydia Bott. LaSalle, Ill.: Library Press, 1974.

Congdon, Lee. *The Young Lukács*. Chapel Hill: University of North Carolina Press, 1983.

Coser, Lewis. *Greedy Institutions: Patterns of Undivided Commitment*. New York: Free Press, 1974.

Deák, István. "Budapest and the Hungarian Revolutions of 1918–19." *Slavonic and East European Review* (January 1958), pp. 129–40.

Deutscher, Isaac. "Georg Lukács and 'Critical Realism'." *Listener* (November 3, 1965), pp. 559–62.

Dostoyevsky, Fyodor. *The Idiot*. Translated by Eva M. Martin. London: Dent. Everyman's Library, 1970.

Eloesser, Arthur. *Thomas Mann: Sein Leben und seine Werke*. Berlin: S. Fischer Verlag, 1925.

"Thomas Mann's 'Zauberberg'." *Die Neue Rundschau* 35, no. 1 (1925), pp. 59–64.

"Zur Entstehungsgeschichte des 'Tod in Venedig'." *Die Neue Rundschau* 36, no. 2 (1925), pp. 511–15.

"Ernst Bloch im Gespräch mit Michael Landmann." Unpublished MS. Courtesy of Michael Landmann.

Ernst, Else. "Aus den Erinnerungen." *Paul Ernst und Georg Lukács: Dokumente einer Freundschaft*. Edited by Karl-August Kutzbach.

Ernst, Paul. "Ein russisches Buch." In *Paul Ernst und Georg Lukács*. Edited by Karl-August Kutzbach.

"Gespräch mit Georg Lukács. Aus der Rahmengesichte des Novellenbandes 'Die Taufe'." In *Paul Ernst und Georg Lukács*. Edited by Karl-August Kutzbach.

Fekete, Éva and Karádi, Éva. *Georg Lukács—His Life in Pictures and Documents*. Budapest: Corvina, 1981.

Friedlander, Albert H. *Leo Baeck: Teacher of Theresienstadt*. New York: Holt, Rinehart and Winston, 1968.

Frisch, Max. *Tagebücher 1946–1949*. Frankfurt am Main: Suhrkamp Verlag, 1950.

Fülöp–Miller, René. *The Jesuits: A History of the Society of Jesus*. Translated by F. S. Flint and D. F. Tait. New York: Capricorn Books, 1963.

Georg Lukács zum siebzigsten Geburtstag. Berlin/East: Aufbau Verlag, 1955.

Georg Lukács zum 13. April 1970. Goethepreis '70. *Ad Lectores 10*. Neuwied–Berlin: Hermann Luchterhand Verlag, 1970.

Goethe, Johann Wolfgang von. *Faust*. Edited by Cyrus Hamlin. Translated by Walter Arndt. New York: W. W. Norton & Co., 1976.

"Urworte. Orphisch." (1817) *Gedichte*. Munich: Wilhelm Goldmann Verlag, 1958.

Goldberg, Oskar. *Die Wirklichkeit der Hebräer: Einleitung in das System des Pentateuch*. Berlin: David, 1925.

Goldmann, Lucien. "The Early Writings of Georg Lukács." Translated by Joy N. Humes. *Tri-Quarterly*. 9 (Spring 1967), pp. 165 ff. Special issue.

Gothein, Eberhard. *Ignatius von Loyola und die Gegenreformation*. Halle: M. Niemeyer Verlag, 1895.

Günther, Henning. "Der Messianismus von Hermann Cohen und Walter Benjamin." *Emuna* 9, nos. 5–6 (November–December 1974), pp. 352 ff.

Györi, Judit. *Thomas Mann Magyarországon* (Thomas Mann in Hungary). Budapest: Akadémiai Kiadó, 1968.

Habermas, Jürgen. *Philosophical–Political Profiles*. Translated by Frederick G. Lawrence. Cambridge: M. I. T. Press, 1983.

Hall, Calvin and Linzey, Gardner. *Theories of Personality*. New York: John Wiley & Sons, 1957.

Hatfield, Henry. "Der Schneider Lukacek. Drei Randglossen zu Thomas Manns Zauberberg." *Euphorion* 56 (1952), pp. 365–72.

"Korrekturnote." *Euphorion* 57 (1963), p. 226.

Thomas Mann. Revised edition. New York: New Directions, 1962.

Hauser, Arnold. *Im Gespräch mit Georg Lukács*. Munich: Verlag C. H. Beck, 1978.

Háy, Gyula. *Geboren 1900*. Reinbek bei Hamburg: Christian Wegner Verlag, 1971.

Hermann, István. *Die Gedankenwelt von Georg Lukács*. Budapest: Akadémiai Kiadó 1978.

Lukács György élete (Biography). Budapest: Corvina Kiadó, 1985.

Hilgard, E. et al. *Introduction to Psychology*. New York: Harcourt Brace Jovanovich, 1971.

Hiller, Kurt, ed. *Ernst Toller*. Reinbek bei Hamburg: Rowohlt, 1961.

Holz, Hans-Heinz. "Einleitung." *Nietzsche Studienausgabe*. Vol. 3. Frankfurt am Main: Fischer Bücherei, 1968.

Honigsheim, Paul. *On Max Weber*. Translated by J. Rytina. New York: Free Press, 1968.

Howe, Irving. "A Word about Georg Lukács." In Georg Lukács, *The Historical Novel*. Translated by H. Mitchell and S. Mitchell. Boston: Beacon Press, 1963, pp. 7–10.

Hruby, Kurt. "Der talmudische Messianismus." *Emuna* 9, nos. 5–6 (November–December 1974), pp. 324 ff.

Janssen, Karl-Heinz. "Ein Toter auf Urlaub: Levine—das gefährliche Leben eines Weltrevolutionärs." *Die Zeit* (September 14, 1973), p. 14.

Jaspers, Karl. "Heidelberger Erinnerungen." *Heidelberger Jahrbücher* 5 (1961), pp. 1–10.

"The Jesuits: Catholicism's Troubled Front Line." *Time*, April 23 1973, pp. 40 ff.

Kardos, István, ed. *Sokszemközt tudósokkal* (Among Scientists). Budapest: MRT Minerva, 1974.

Karinthy, Frigyes. *Így írtok Ti!* (This Is How You All Write). Budapest: Szépirodalmi Könyvkiadó, 1959.

Kautsky, Karl. *Vorlaufär des neueren Sozialismus*. 2 vols. Stuttgart: J. H. W. Dietz, 1895.

Kazin, Alfred. "Introduction." In G. Lukács, *Studies in European Realism*. New York: Grosset & Dunlap, Universal Library, 1964.

Kerényi, Károly. "Thomas Mann–Naphta–Lukács György." *Új Látóhatár* (New Horizon) 5, no. 1 (January–February 1962), pp. 30–38.

Kerényi, Karl. "Thomas Mann und der Marxist." *Neue Zürcher Zeitung* June 9, 1963, n. p.

"Zauberberg Figuren. Ein biographischer Versuch." *Tessiner Schreibtisch. Mythologisches. Unmythologisches*. Stuttgart: Steinbrüber Verlag, 1963.

Kessler, Harry (Count). *In the Twenties: The Diaries of Harry Kessler*. Translated by Charles Kessler. New York: Holt, Rinehart and Winston, 1971.

Kettler, David. *Marxismus und Kultur*. Mannheim und Lukács in den ungarischen Revolutionen 1918-19. Neuwied-Berlin: Hermann Luchterhand Verlag, 1967.

Kierkegaard, Søren. *Entweder–Oder: Ein Lebensfragment*. Translated by O. Gleiss. Fifth edition. Dresden: Verlag von C. Ludwig Ungelenk, Justus Wallmanns Buchhandlung, 1909.

Either/Or. Translated by David F. Swenson and Lillian Marvin Swenson. 2 vols. Garden City, N. Y.: Anchor Books, 1959.

Klages, Ludwig. *Der Geist als Widersacher der Seele*. 3 vols. Leipzig: J. A. Barth, 1929.

Persönlichkeit. Einführung in die Charakterkunde. Potsdam: Miller & Kiepenheuer, 1928.

Köhalmi, Béla, ed. *Könyvek könyve* (Book about Books). Budapest: Lantos kiadása, 1918.

Kolakowski, Leszek. "The Priest and the Jester." *Toward a Marxist Humanism: Essays on the Left Today*. Translated from the Polish by Jane Zielonko Peel. New York: Grove Press, 1969.

"Über die Richtigkeit der Maxime 'Der Zweck Heiligt die Mittel'." *Der Mensch ohne Alternative: Von der Möglichkeit und Unmöglichkeit, Marxist zu sein*. Munich: R. Piper & Co. Verlag, 1960.

Koopmann, Helmut: *Die Entstehung des 'intellektualen' Romans bei Thomas Mann: Untersuchungen zur Struktur von 'Buddenbrooks,' 'Königliche Hoheit' und 'Der Zauberberg'*. Bonn: H. Bouvier & Co. Verlag, 1962.

Kracauer, Siegfried. "Thomas Münzer als Theologe der Revolution: Rezension." *Frankfurter Zeitung* (August 27, 1922).

Küng, Hans. *On Being a Christian*. Garden City, N. Y: Doubleday, 1984.

Künzli, Arnold. *Karl Marx—Eine Psychographie*. Vienna–Frankfurt am Main–Zurich: Europa Verlag, 1966.

"Zur Befreiung der Emanzipation von der Hypothek der Erlösung." *L'80. Zeitschrift für Literatur und Politik* 35 (September 1985).

Kutzbach, Karl-August, ed. *Paul Ernst und Georg Lukács: Dokumente einer Freundschaft*. Emsdetten/West: Lecte Verlag, 1974.

Lagarde, Paul de. *Deutscher Glaube. Deutsches Vaterland. Deutsche Bildung*. Edited by Friedrich Daab. Jena: Eugen Diederich, 1913.

Lamm, Hans. "Karl Marx und das Judentum." *Karl Marx. 1818–1968. Neue Studien zur Person und Lehre*. Mainz: von Haase & Koehler Verlag, 1968.

Landmann, Michael. *Philosophical Anthropology*. Translated by David J. Parent. Philadelphia: The Westminster Press, 1974.

Lehnert, Herbert. "Leo Naphta und sein Author." *Orbis Litteratum* 37 (1982), pp. 47–69

Thomas Mann—Fiktion, Mythos, Religion. Stuttgart–Berlin–Cologne–Mainz: W. Kohlhammer Verlag, 1965.

Thomas Mann-Forschung: Ein Bericht. Stuttgart: J. B. Metzlersche Verlagsbuchhandlung, 1969.

"Thomas Mann's Interpretations of 'Der Tod in Venedig' and their reliability." *Rice University Studies: Studies in German Literature* 50, no. 4 (1964), pp. 41–60.

Lengyel, József. *Penn Drifting*. Translated by Ilona Duczynska. London: Peter Owen, 1966.

Lessing, Theodor. *Der jüdische Selbsthass*. Berlin: Jüdischer Verlag, 1930.

Der Untergang der Erde am Geist. Hannover: W. Adam Verlag, 1924.

Lesznai, Anna. *Kezdetben volt a kert* (At the Beginning was the Garden). 2 vols. Budapest: Szépirodalmi Könyvkiadó, 1966.

Levin, Harry. "Toward a Sociology of the Novel." *Refractions: Essays in Comparative Literature.* London–Oxford–New York: Oxford University Press, 1968.

Liebeschütz, Hans. *Das Judentum im deutschen Geschichtsbild von Hegel bis Max Weber.* Tübingen: J. C. B. Mohr [Paul Siebeck], 1967.

Lienhard, Fritz. "Aus Theologie und Kirche: Rezensionen." *Neue Schweizer Rundschau* 20, no. 2 (February 1927), pp. 199–204.

Löwenstein, Julius I. *Marx Contra Marxism.* Translated by Harry Drost. London–Boston–Henley: Routledge & Kegan Paul, 1980.

Löwenstein, Karl. "Erinnerungen." *Max Weber Gedenkausgabe der Universität zu München.* Edited by K. Engisch et al. Berlin; Duncker & Humbolt, 1966.

Löwenstein, Kurt. "Thomas Mann zur jüdischen Frage." *Bulletin des Leo Baeck Instituts* 10, no. 37 (1967), pp. 1 ff.

Löwith, Karl. *Meaning in History.* Chicago: University of Chicago Press, 1962.

Löwy, Michael. *Georg Lukács: From Romanticism to Bolshevism.* Translated by Patrick Camiller. London: NLB, 1979.

"Jewish Messianism and Libertarian Utopia in Central European Messianic Thought." *New German Critique* 20 (Spring–Summer 1980), pp. 105–15.

Lublinski, Samuel. *Die Bilanz der Moderne.* Berlin: Verlag Siegfried Cornbach, 1904.

Der Ausgang der Moderne: Ein Buch der Opposition. Dresden: Verlag von Carl Reissner, 1909.

Ludz, Peter. "Hauser and Lukács." Translated by Judith Marcus-Tar. *Telos,* no. 41 (Fall 1979), pp. 175–84.

"Marxismus und Literatur–eine kritische Einführung in das Werk von Georg Lukács." *Literatursoziologie.* Edited by Peter Ludz. Neuwied–Berlin: Hermann Luchterhand Verlag, 1963.

Maier, Johann. *Das Judentum.* Reihe "Kindlers Kulturgeschichte." Munich: Kindler Verlag, 1973.

Maier, Joseph B. "Jüdisches Erbe aus deutschem Geist." Unpublished ms. Courtesy of J. Maier.

Maitre, Hans Joachim. *Thomas Mann: Aspekte der Kulturkritik in seiner Essayistik.* Bonn: H. Bouvier & Co. Verlag, 1970.

Mann, Golo. "Ein Stück Erinnerung." *Du* 20, no. 12 (1960), pp. 72–76.

Mann, Katja. *Unwritten Memories.* New York: Alfred A. Knopf, 1975.

"Der Mann mit dem Koffer." *Der Spiegel* 35 (1973), pp. 100 ff.

"Thomas Mann und seine falschen Freunde." *Der Aufbau* 5, no. 5 (1949), p. 473.

Marcus, Judith. "Toward a Sociological Understanding of the Revolutionary Intelligentsia." *Contemporary Sociology* 11, No. 6 (November 1982), pp. 645–47.

Marcus, Judith and Tar, Zoltán. "The Judaic Element in the Teachings of the Frank-furt School." *Leo Baeck Year Book XXXI*. Jerusalem–London–New York: Leo Baeck Institute, 1986

Marcus-Tar, Judith. "Introductory Essay: Georg Lukács, 'Bolshevism as a Moral Problem'." *Social Research* 44, no. 3 (Autumn 1977), pp. 416–18.

    Thomas Mann und Georg Lukács. Beziehung, Einfluss und repräsentative Gegen-sätzlichkeit. Cologne: Böhlau Verlag, 1982; and Budapest: Corvina, 1982.

Marx, Jacob. "Die Jesuiten als Lehrer des Communismus." *Jahrbuch für Katholiken auf das Jahr 1847*. Trier, 1846.

Marx, Karl. "On the Jewish Question." *The Marx–Engels Reader*. Edited by Robert C. Tucker. Second edition. New York: W. W. Norton & Co., 1978.

Mayer, Hans. *Thomas Mann: Werk und Entwicklung.* Berlin/East: Verlag Volk und Welt, 1950.

Mazlish, Bruce. *The Revolutionary Ascetic: Evolution of a Political Type.* New York: McGraw-Hill Book Company, 1977.

Meyer-Leviné, Rosa. *Leviné: Leben und Tod eines Revolutionärs.* Erinnerungen. Mit einem dokumentarischen Anhang. Frankfurt am Main: Fischer Taschenbuch Verlag, 1974

Michael, Wolfgang. "Stoff und Idee in 'Tod in Venedig'." *Deutsche Vierteljahrsschrift für Literaturwissenschaft und Geistesgeschichte* 33, no. 1 (1959), pp. 13–19.

Michels, Robert. *Political Parties: A Sociological Study of the Oligarchical Tendencies of Modern Democracy.* New York: Collier Books, 1962.

Moser, Dr. Julius, ed. *Die Lösung der Judenfrage.* Eine Rundfrage. Berlin–Leipzig: Modernes Verlagsbureau Curt Wiegand, 1907.

Murphy G. and Kovach, J. *Historical Introduction to Modern Psychology.* Third edition. New York: Harcour, Brace Jovanovich, Inc., 1972.

Muschg, Walter. *Tragische Literaturgeschichte.* Bern: Francke Verlag, 1953.

Musil, Robert. *Der Mann ohne Eigenschaften.* Hamburg: Rowohlt Verlag, 1965.

    The Man without Qualities. Translated by Eithne Wilkins and Ernst Kaiser. New York: Capricorn Books, 1965.

    Evangelische Akademie, no. 14 (1973), pp. 2 ff.

Neider, Charles, ed. *The Stature of Thomas Mann.* New York: New Directions Books, 1947.

Nelson, Benjamin. *The Idea of Usury.* Chicago: University of Chicago Press, 1969.

Niekisch, Ernst. *Gewagtes Leben: Begegnungen und Begebnisse.* Cologne-Berlin: Kiepen-heuer & Witsch, 1958.

Nietzsche, Friedrich. *Complete Works of Friedrich Nietzsche.* Edited by Oscar Levi. Translated by Thomas Common. New York: Russel and Russel, Inc., 1964.

    The Genealogy of Morals. Translated by Francis Golffing. New York: A Doubleday Anchor Book, 1956.

Noack, Hermann. *Die Philosophie Westeuropas*. Darmstadt: Wissenschaftliche Buch-gesellschaft, 1962.

Peter, Klaus. *Idealismus als Kritik: Friedrich Schlegels Philosophie der unvollendeten Welt*. Stuttgart-Berlin: .W. Kohlhammer Verlag, 1973.

Plessner, Helmut. "Heidelberg in 1913." *Kölner Zeitschrift für Soziologie* 7 (1963), pp. 30–34. Max Weber issue.

Rácz, Zoltán. *Jezsuiták tegnap és ma* (Jesuits: Yesterday and Today). Budapest: Kossuth Kiadó, 1974.

Raddatz, Fritz J.. *Lukács in Selbstzeugnissen und Bilddokumenten*. RoRoRo Monograph Reinbek bei Hamburg: Rowohlt Taschenbuchverlag, 1972.

Ranke, Leopold von. *Die Geschichte der Päpste*. 2 vols. New edition. Wiesbaden: W. Vollmer, 1957.

Raymond, Elfie Stock. "The Future Comes by Itself. Progress Does Not." Unpublished paper. Courtesy of author.

Reich-Ranicki, Marcel, ed. *In Sachen Böll: Ansichten und Einsichten*. Cologne: Kiepenheuer & Witsch, 1968.

Réz, Pál. "Thomas Mann and Hungary: His Correspondence with Hungarian Friends." *The New Hungarian Quarterly* 2, no. 3 (July – September 1961), pp. 84–99.

Ritoók, Emma von. *A szellem kalandorai* (The Adventurers of the Spirit). Budapest: Athenaeum, 1922.

"Georg Lukács: Die Seele und die Formen." *Zeitschrift für Ästhetik und allgemeine Kunstwissenschaft* (1912), pp. 324–26.

Ropshin, See Savinkov, Boris.

Rothacker, Emil. *Die Schichten der Persönlichkeit*. Leipzig: Verlag von Johann Ambrosius Barth, 1938.

Ruitenbek, Hendrik M. ed. *Varieties of Personalities*. New York: E. P. Dutton & Co., Inc., 1964.

Rychner, Max. "Gestalten und Bezüge in den Romanen." *Die Neue Rundschau* 66, no. 3 (1955), pp. 261–77.

Sagave, Pierre-Paul. *Réalité sociale et idéologie religieuse dans les romans de Thomas Mann*. Publications de la Faculté des lettres de l'Universite de Strasbourg. Fasc. 124. Paris: 1954.

Saueressig, Heinz. Die Entstehung des Romans 'der Zauberberg'. Zwei Essays und eine Dokumentation. Biberach an der Riss: Series "Wege und Gestaltung," 1965.

Savinkov, Boris. *Als war' es nie gewesen*. Frankfurt am Main: 1913.

Memoirs of a Terrorist. Translated by Joseph Shaplen. New York: Albert & Charles Boni, 1931.

The Pale Horse. Translated by Z. Vengerova. New York: Alfred A. Knopf, 1919.

Scharfschwerdt, Jürgen. *Thomas Mann und der deutsche Bildungsroman: Eine Untersuchung zu den Problemen einer literarischen Tradition.* Stuttgart–Berlin–Cologne–Mainz: W. Kohlhamm Verlag, 1967.

Scherrer, Paul. "Vornehmheit, Illusion und Wirklichkeit." *Blätter der Thomas Mann Gesellschaft* 1 (1958).

Scholem, Gershom. *The Messianic Idea in Judaism and Other Essays in Jewish Spirituality.* New York: Schocken Books, 1971.

Silberner, Edmund. "Was Marx an Anti-Semite?" *Historica Judaica* 11 (1949), pp. 3–52.

Simmel, Georg. *Georg Simmel on Individuality and Social Forms.* Edited by Donald N. Levine. Chicago: University of Chicago Press.

    Gesammelte Werke. Vol. 2: *Soziologie.* Fifth edition. Berlin: Duncker, & Humblot, 1968

    The Sociology of Georg Simmel. Edited by Kurt H. Wolff. New York: Free Press, 1950.

Sinkó, Ervin. *Optimisták. Történelmi regény 1918–19-ből. (The Optimists.* A Historical Novel from 1918–19). 2 vols. Újvidék/Yugoslavia: Fórum könyvkiadó, n. d. (First edition: 1953–55).

Sombart, Werner. *Der Bourgeois: zur Geistesgeschichte des modernen Wirtschaftsmenschen.* Munich–Leipzig: Duncker & Humbolt, 1913.

    Händler und Helden: patriotische Besinnungen. Munich–Leipzig: Duncker & Humblot, 1915.

    The Jews and Modern Capitalism. Translated by M. Epstein. New York: Collier Books, 1962.

    The Quintessence of Capitalism (Originally: *Der Bourgeois*). Translated by M. Epstein. Glencoe, Ill.: Free Press, 1951.

Specovius, Günther. "Gespräch mit Lukács." *Ostbrief* (Lüneburg, June 1960), pp. 249–53.

Spengler, Oswald. *The Decline of the West.* 2 vols. Translated by C. F. Stkinson. New York: Alfred A. Knopf, 1980.

Steiner, George. *Language and Silence: Essays on Language, Literature and the Inhuman.* New York, Atheneum, 1972.

    "Making a Homeland for the Mind." *Times Literary Supplement,* January 22, 1982, pp. 67–68.

Stern, Guy. "A Case for Oral History: Conversations with or about Morgenstern, Lehmann, Reinacher and Thomas Mann." *German Quarterly* 37 (November 1964), pp. 490 ff.

Susman, Margarete. "Erinnerungen an Georg Simmel." *Buch des Dankes an Georg*

Simmel. Edited by Kurt Gassen and Michael Landmann. Munich: Duncker & Humblot, 1958.

Tar, Judith. "Georg Lukács, Thomas Mann und 'Der Tod in Venedig'." *Die Weltwoche* (July 2, 1971), p. 31.

Tar, Zoltán. *The Frankfurt School: The Critical Theories of Max Horkheimer and Theodor W. Adorno.* New York: Schocken, 1985.

Tar, Zoltán, and Marcus, Judith. "The Weber-Lukács Encounter." *Max Weber's Political Sociology: A Pessimistic Vision of a Rationalized World.* Edited by R. M. Glassman and V. Murvar. Westport, Conn.: Greenwood Press, 1984.

Thoda, Henry. *Franz von Assisi und die Anfänge der Kunst der Reniassance in Italien* Berlin: G. Grote, 1885.

Toller, Ernst. "Eine Jugend in Deutschland." *Ernst Toller.* Edited by Kurt Hiller. Reinbek bei Hamburg: Rowohlt Verlag, 1961.

Treitschke, Heinrich von. "Ein Wort über unser Judentum." *Preussische Jahrbücher 1879–80.* Vols. 44–48. Berlin: G. Reimer, 1880.

Tröltsch, Ernst. *Die Soziallehren der christlichen Kirchen und Gruppen.* 1912. New edition: Tübingen: J. C. B. Mohr. 1919.

Vaget, Hans. "Georg Lukács und Thomas Mann." *Die Neue Rundschau* 88, no. 4 (1977), pp. 656–63.

"Georg Lukács, Thomas Mann and the Modern Novel." *Thomas Mann in Context: Papers of the Clark University Centennial Colloquium.* Edited by Kenneth Hughes. Worcester, Mass.: Clark University Press, 1978.

Weber, Marianne. *Max Weber: A Biography.* Edited and translated by Harry Zohn. New York: Wiley Interscience, 1975.

Weber, Max. "Christmatic Authority." *Economy and Society.* Vol. 1. Edited by Guenther Roth and Claus Wittich. Berkeley: University of California Press, 1978.

The Methodology of the Social Sciences. Translated and edited by E. A. Shils and H. A. Finch. New York: Free Press, 1949.

The Protestant Ethic and the Spirit of Capitalism. Translated by Talcott Parsons. New York: Charles Scribner's Sons, 1958.

Walzer, Michael. *The Revolution of the Saints: A Study in the Origin of Radical Politics.* New York: Atheneum College Edition, 1976.

Weigand, Hermann J. "Autobiographie in Thomas Manns 'Königliche Hoheit'." PMLA (1931), p. 878.

The Magic Mountain: A Study of Thomas Mann's Novel 'Der Zauberberg'. 1933. New edition, Chapel Hill: University of North Carolina Press, 1964.

Windelband, Wilhelm. *A History of Philosophy,* 2 vols. New York: Harper Torchbooks, 1958.

Windelband, Wilhelm and Heimsoeth, Heinz. *Lehrbuch der Geschichte der Philosophie.* Fifteenth edition. Tübingen: J. C. B. [Paul Siebeck] Mohr Verlag, 1957.

Wirth, Louis. Preface to Karl Mannheim, *Ideology and Utopia*. New York: A Harvest Book, 1936.

Wolff, Hans M. *Thomas Mann: Werk und Bekenntnis*. Bern: Francke, 1957.

Wysling, Hans. " 'Geist und Kunst': Thomas Manns Notizen zu einem Literatur-essay." Paul Scherrer and Hans Wysling. *Quellenkritische Studien zum Werk Thomas Manns*. Vol. 1. Bern–Munich: Francke Verlag, 1967.

"Zu Thomas Manns 'Maja'-Projekt." *Quellenkritische Studien zum Werk Thomas Manns*.

Zeitlin, Irving M. *Ancient Judaism: From Max Weber to the Present*. Cambridge: Polity Press, 1984.

Ziegler, Theobald. *Die geistigen und sozialen Strömungen des neunzehnten Jahrhunderts*. Berlin: Georg Bondi, 1899.

Zitta, Victor. *Georg Lukács's Marxism: Alienation, Dialectics, Revolution*. The Hague: Martinus Nijhoff, 1964.

INDEX